The Political Economy of Poverty, Vulnerability and Disaster Risk Management:

Building Bridges of Resilience, Entrepreneurship and Development in Africa's 21ˢᵗ Century

Edited by

Munyaradzi Mawere

Langaa Research & Publishing CIG
Mankon, Bamenda

Publisher:
Langaa RPCIG
Langaa Research & Publishing Common Initiative Group
P.O. Box 902 Mankon
Bamenda
North West Region
Cameroon
Langaagrp@gmail.com
www.langaa-rpcig.net

Distributed in and outside N. America by African Books Collective
orders@africanbookscollective.com
www.africanbookscollective.com

ISBN-10: 9956-763-11-X

ISBN-13: 978-9956-763-11-5

About the Contributors

Munyaradzi Mawere is a Professor in the Simon Muzenda School of Arts, Culture and Heritage Studies at Great Zimbabwe University in Zimbabwe. He holds a PhD in Social Anthropology, three Masters Degrees – Social Anthropology, Development Studies, and Philosophy –and a BA (Hons) Degree in Philosophy. Before joining this university, Professor Mawere was a lecturer at the University of Zimbabwe and at Universidade Pedagogica, Mozambique, where he has also worked in different capacities as a senior lecturer, assistant research director, postgraduate co-ordinator, and professor. He is an author of more than 50 books and over 200 academic publications with a focus on Africa straddling the following areas: poverty and development, African philosophy, society and culture, democracy, politics of food production, humanitarianism and civil society organisations, urban anthropology, existential anthropology, cultural philosophy, environmental anthropology, society and politics, decoloniality and African studies. Some of his best selling books are: *Humans, Other Beings and the Environment: Harurwa (Edible stinkbugs) and Environmental Conservation in South-eastern Zimbabwe* (2015); *Theory, Knowledge, Development and Politics: What Role for the Academy in the Sustainability of Africa?* (2016); *Democracy, Good Governance and Development in Africa: A Search for Sustainable Democracy and Development*, (2015); *Culture, Indigenous Knowledge and Development in Africa: Reviving Interconnections for Sustainable Development* (2014); *Myths of Peace and Democracy? Towards Building Pillars of Hope, Unity and Transformation in Africa* (2016); *Harnessing Cultural Capital for Sustainability: A Pan Africanist Perspective* (2015); *Divining the Future of Africa: Healing the Wounds, Restoring Dignity and Fostering Development*, (2014); *African Cultures, Memory and Space: Living the Past Presence in Zimbabwean Heritage* (2014); *Violence, Politics and Conflict Management in Africa: Envisioning Transformation, Peace and Unity in the Twenty-First Century* (2016); *African Philosophy and Thought Systems: A Search for a Culture and Philosophy of Belonging* (2016); *Africa at the Crossroads:*

Theorising Fundamentalisms in the 21st Century (2017); *Colonial Heritage, Memory and Sustainability in Africa: Challenges, Opportunities and Prospects* (2016); *Underdevelopment, Development and the Future of Africa* (2017), and *Theorising Development in Africa: Towards Building an African Framework of Development* (2017); *African Studies in the Academy: The Cornucopia of Theory, Praxis and Transformation in Africa?* (2017); *GMOs, Consumerism and the Global Politics of Biotechnology: Rethinking Food, Bodies and Identies in Africa's 21st Century* (2017); and *Human Trafficking and Trauma in the Digital Era: The Ongoing Tragedy of the Trade in Refugees from Eritrea* (2017).

Sjaak Kroon is a Professor of Multilingualism in the multicultural society. He is a member of the Department of Culture Studies and Babylon, Center for the Study of Superdiversity at Tilburg University, the Netherlands. His main focus in research and teaching is in the field of linguistic and cultural diversity, language policy and education in the context of globalization and superdiversity. He has been involved in a number of research projects dealing with linguistic diversity, language policy and literacy in countries in the Global South such as Eritrea, Suriname and Timor-Leste.

Fidelis Peter Thomas Duri is a Senior Lecturer of History in the Department of Archaeology, Culture and Heritage, History and Development Studies at Great Zimbabwe University. He is a holder of a PhD in History from the University of the Witwatersrand in Johannesburg, South Africa. He has published a number of books and articles which focus on environmental history, socio-cultural dynamics, subaltern struggles, African border studies, and Zimbabwe's socio-political landscape during the colonial and post-colonial periods. In addition to reviewing a number of scholarly articles, he has also edited books such as *Resilience Amid Adversity: Informal Coping Mechanisms to the Zimbabwean Crisis during the New Millennium* (2016) and *Contested Spaces, Restrictive Mechanisms and Corridors of Opportunity: A Social History of Zimbabwean Borderlands and Beyond since the Colonial Period* (2017). He is also a member of the editorial boards of international journals which include the *Zimbabwe*

Journal of Historical Studies and the *International Journal of Developing Societies*.

Veerle Draulans took her PhD in 1994 at KU Leuven (Belgium) in Ethics. Till 2015, she combined an appointment at Tilburg University, the Netherlands with an appointment at KU Leuven. Currently, she is an associate professor in Gender Studies at KU Leuven, Faculty of Social Sciences, and teaches in an interuniversity master program Gender and diversity. Her research focuses on diversity and care, gender and leadership, gender and STEM, and values and religion in Europe. She is member of the Belgian Governmental Advisory Committee on Bio-ethics, the Board of Governors of Emmaus healthcare and welfare organisations and co-chair of the taskforce Services of the COST-program ROSE, Reducing Old-Age Exclusion in Europe: Collaborations in Research and Policy.She is also involved in various VLIR UOS research and development programs in Ethiopia and South Africa.

Mohammed Abubakar Yinusa is an Associate Professor and Lecturer in the Department of Sociology, University of Ilorin, Nigeria. His area of specialization is in Sociology of Development and Social Problems. He has several publications and has attended various conferences both locally and internationally.

Artwell Nhemachena holds a Ph.D in Social Anthropology; MSc in Sociology and Social Anthropology and BSc Honours Degree in Sociology. He has lectured at a number of universities in Zimbabwe before pursuing his Ph.D studies in South Africa. Currently he lectures in Sociology at the University of Namibia. His current areas of research interest are Knowledge Studies; Development Studies; Environment; Resilience; Food Security and Food Sovereignty; Industrial Sociology; Conflict and Peace; Transformation; Science and Technology Studies, Democracy and Governance; Relational Ontologies; Decoloniality and Anthropological jurisprudence. He has published in the areas of social theory, research methods, democracy and governance; conflict and peace; relational ontologies; industrial sociology; development; anthropological jurisprudence, environment, mining, biotechnology and knowledge studies; transformation and decoloniality. He has been a CODESRIA Laureate since 2010 and has been participating in the CODESRIA Democratic Governance Institute.

Peter Ateh-Afac Fossungu holds a PhD in Law from the Universite de Montreal, two Master's degrees in Law from McGill University and University of Alberta. He has taught law at the Université de Yaounde and University of Buea in Cameroon. Dr Fossungu has published extensively on various aspects of society and life in Cameroon, Africa and Canada. He is currently a researcher in Montreal, Canada.

Ephraim Taurai Gwaravanda holds a Doctor of Literature and Philosophy in Philosophy from the University of South Africa (UNISA). He also holds a Master of Arts Degree in Philosophy (University of Zimbabwe) and a Bachelor of Arts Honours Degree in Philosophy (University of Zimbabwe). He is a Senior Lecturer in Philosophy in the Department of Philosophy and Religious Studies at Great Zimbabwe University where he teaches Logic, Metaphysics and Philosophy of Law. His research interests are in the areas of Philosophy of Development, Indigenous Knowledge Systems, Globalisation, Epistemic Justice, Governance and Philosophy of Law. He has published several articles with international peer reviewed journals.

Clementia Murembe Neema in a senior Lecturer at Mbarara University of Science and Technology (MUST). She obtained her PhD at Tilburg University, the Netherlands in 2015 dealing with Women's empowerment and decision-making in Ankore families. She has a Master of Ethics and development studies from Uganda Martyrs University Nkozi (1998), in addition to being a professional trained secondary school teacher (1987). Since 2016, she heads the department of Human development and relational sciences in the Faculty of Interdisciplinary Studies. Her research focuses on family relations, cultural studies, gender and power relations, and development at the micro level in the African context. She does a Saturday-family development discussion radio program as a form of community engagement and ethnographic monitoring. She teaches

Anthropology of gender and Gender mainstreaming. She had the lead in drafting the 2017 MUST gender and anti-sexual harassment policies. Currently she is a member of the Uganda Episcopal social communication commission representing the ecclesiastical province of Mbarara Arch-diocese.

Jenny-Louise Van der Aa is a postdoctoral researcher and Lecturer at the Department of Culture Studies at Tilburg University, the Netherlands where she is affiliated to Babylon, Center for the Study of Superdiversity. In 2012 she obtained her PhD at Tilburg University dealing with ethnographic monitoring in a Caribbean classroom. She was the 2011-2012 Daytal L. Kendall Library Fellow at the American Philosophical Society, researching the oeuvre of Dell Hymes. She is currently active in linguistic and psychological anthropology and develops strategies to involve participants more actively in the ethnographic research process.

Eusebiah Chikonyora is a Zimbabwean Primary School Senior Teacher. She graduated with a Diploma in Education from Seke Teachers' College, Zimbabwe, in 1992. She is currently teaching at Sheni Primary School in Zimbabwe's eastern border city of Mutare. Previously, she taught at various primary schools in the country such as Matanda, Munyarari, Chitakatira and Mutanda. She is also a renowned human rights defender who has articulated the socio-economic and political plight of Zimbabwe's marginalised communities through research, conference presentations and political activism, among other initiatives. She has a passion for research on issues concerning governance, human rights, environmentalism, uneven development and subaltern livelihood dynamics in post-colonial Zimbabwe.

Nkwazi Mhango is author of *Saa ya Ukombozi, Nyuma ya Pazia, Souls on Sale, Born with Voice, Africa Reunite or Perish, Africa's Best and Worst Presidents: How Imperialism Maintained Venal Regimes in Africa, Psalm of the Oppressed, Perpetual Search, Dependency: Can Africa Still Turn Things Around for the Better?* and *'Is It Global War on Terrorism' or Global War over Terra Africana?: The Ruse Imperial Powers Use to Occupy Africa Militarily for Economic Gains;* member of Writers' Association of

Newfoundland and Labrador (WANL) St. John's NL Canada and is an alumnus of Universities of Dar es Salaam (Tanzania) Winnipeg and Manitoba (Canada) majoring in Conflict Resolution and Peace and Conflict Studies and Law. Also, Mhango has contributed many chapters in various academic books.

Joseph Adesoji Oluyemi is a PhD student in the Department of Sociology, University of Ilorin, Nigeria. His areas of specialisation include Medical Sociology and Sociology of Development with special interests in Adolescent Health, Occupational health, Infectious diseases, Emerging diseases, Sexualities and issues in development.

Davidson Mabweazara Mugodzwa is currently a lecturer in Economic History and Development Studies at the Great Zimbabwe University in Mashava. He has been lecturing for over three decades at Government and private tertiary institutions in the United Kingdom, Botswana, Namibia and Zimbabwe. He has published several textbooks currently in use in Namibian and South African Secondary Schools under the auspices of Zebra Publishing House and has also published several articles in refereed international journals. He is interested in carrying out research in Historical and environmental issues..

Simeon Maravanyika is a holder of a PhD in African Environmental History from the University of Pretoria in South Africa. He is currently a lecturer in the Department of History, Archaeology and Development Studies, Simon Muzenda School of Arts, Culture and Heritage Studies, Great Zimbabwe University. His main research focus is commodity history, aspects natural resources management praxis, climate change and adaptation in Africa and soil conservation on white farms in the colonial period.

RAJI Abdulateef is a PhD student and lecturer II in the Department of Sociology, University of Ilorin, Nigeria. His areas of specialization include Sociology of Development, Rural Sociology and Social issues.

Harro Maat holds a PhD in the History of Agricultural Science from Wageningen University. He is currently a Sociologist and Historian of Agricultural Science and Technology at the Knowledge, Technology and Innovation Group of Wageningen University, the Netherlands. His main focus is on crop improvement in the colonial period and current [bio-] technologies for international development in India, South-East Asia and Africa.

Costain Tandi is a Graduate teacher for Advanced level History and Sociology as well as Head of Department (Humanities) at Rufaro High School in Chatsworth, Zimbabwe. He holds a Master of Arts Degree in Development Studies from Midlands State University; Bachelor of Arts 4th year Honours Degree in History from Great Zimbabwe University; Bachelor of Arts General Degree from the University of Zimbabwe; Graduate Certificate in Education from Great Zimbabwe University; An Executive Certificate in Project and Program Monitoring and Evaluation from the University of Zimbabwe; and An Executive Certificate in Project Management from the University of Zimbabwe. Tandi has six publications and his research interests include but not limited to Indigenous Knowledge Systems, Climate Change and Variability, Rural Poverty, Agriculture and Community Development.

Aluko Opeyemi Idowu is a lecturer in the Department of Political Science University of Ilorin. He is currently on his PhD Studies in Kwara State University Malete Kwara State Nigeria. His research interests include Comparative Politics; Urban Violence, Judicial Studies, Political Economy, Security Management, Democracy and Election, Police and Informal Security provisions. He has published a number of works on his research interest area and other areas.

Golden Maunganidze is a holds a Master of Arts Degree in Media and Society Studies from the Midlands State University (MSU) and several midcareer journalism courses from Germany. He is Edward R. Murrow fellow (2011) as well as 2016 Mandela Washington fellow and has won several awards in the past, which include The child reporter of the year from National Journalistic and Media Awards (NJAMA) in 2009 and National Integrity Award from

Transparency International Zimbabwe (TIZ). He has over ten years experience working in the Zimbabwean media industry. He currently lectures in the Department of English and Media Studies at Great Zimbabwe University (GZU), where he teaches practical journalism courses. Before joining GZU, Maunganidze worked as a journalist and editor for various community newspapers in Masvingo, Zimbabwe.

Romeo Mudimu is a holder of an Honours Degree in Sociology and Industrial Psychology from the University of Namibia (UNAM). His research interests include but not limited to comparative politics, urban violence, democracy, governance in Africa and political economy.

Table of Contents

Chapter 1
Poverty and Vulnerability in Africa:
Reversing the Losses and
Capitulating on the Gains.....................................1
Munyaradzi Mawere

Chapter 2
The Political Economy of Poverty
and Vulnerability: How Africa can
break the Cycle of Poverty to unlock its
Underdevelopment Jam? 11
Munyaradzi Mawere

Chapter 3
Poverty and the Discourses about
the Global North's Playing of the Global South.............39
Nkwazi Mhango

Chapter 4
Breaking the Cycle of Poverty:
Rethinking Africa's Socio-political Economy............... 63
Aluko Idowu Opeyemi & Munyaradzi Mawere

Chapter 5
Resorting to Illegality:
The Illicit Shangwe Cannabis
Trade as an Anti-cotton Response
to Agrarian Policy in Colonial
Zimbabwe, c. 1962-1979.......................................93
Simeon Maravanyika & Harro Maat

Chapter 6
Political Naivety, Corruption, and
Poverty Promotion in Africa:
Riding the 'Poorest-ugliest French'
Bijuralism Horse from Cameroon
to Canada via Britain...123
Peter Ateh-Afac Fossungu

Chapter 7
Poverty and Environmental Degradation
on a Large Scale: The History of the
Establishment, Operation and
Management of a Multinational
Mining Enterprise at Mashava, 1903-2015....................175
Davidson Mabweazara Mugodzwa

Chapter 8
Ethnographic Monitoring Through
Phone-in Radio Programs:
An Example from Ankore, Uganda.......................... 205
*Clementia Murembe Neema, Jenny-Louise Van der Aa,
Sjaak Kroon & Veerle Draulans*

Chapter 9
Fighting Fellow Comrades in the
Trenches of Poverty in Africa?
Interrogating the Fees Must Fall
Movement at the University of
Namibia and Universities in South Africa................... 277
Artwell Nhemachena & Romeo Mudimu

Chapter 10
The Impoverished African and
the Poverty of Colonially Inherited
Education in Africa..255
Ephraim Taurai Gwaravanda

Chapter 11
Children, Women, Development
and Fundamental Human Rights
in Some African Societies..................................... 279
Muhammed A. Yinusa; Joseph A. Oluyemi &
Raji Abdullateef

Chapter 12
Community Engagement for
Development and Poverty Alleviation
in Rural Zimbabwe:
A Case Study of Chikunguwo Community
Gardening in Bikita.....................................309
Costain Tandi & Munyaradzi Mawere

Chapter 13
Seeing Beyond National Borders:
Impoverished Visually-impaired
Zimbabwean Beggars in
Johannesburg, South Africa..................................333
Fidelis Peter Thomas Duri & Eusebiah Chikonyora

Chapter 14
Disasters, the Marginalised and
Media Preparedness in Zimbabwe:
Reflections on the Masvingo-based
Community Media Organisations'
Coverage of the 2017 Cyclone
Dineo Victims.......................................361
Golden Maunganidze & Munyaradzi Mawere

Chapter 1

Poverty and Vulnerability in Africa: Reversing the Losses and Capitulating on the Gains

Munyaradzi Mawere

Introduction

The discourse on poverty in Africa is fraught with a multiplicity of exogenously generated theories, models and ideas, all with the purported goal of either alleviating or eradicating poverty and instilling development in the continent. Within the poverty discourse, which like fashion goes round in circles, connections are often forged between poverty and vulnerability [whether naturally inflicted or anthropogenically influenced], with poverty found at the core of the matrix. Poverty like development is both dynamic and multidimensional besides being relative. It has platitudinous elements, affecting humanity in many different ways. However, its real cause remains an enigma yet to be solved. In fact, the actual reason why some societies [and even people] are 'poor' in relation to others remains a mystery mired with controversies of epic proportions. It becomes even more complex when related to societies of the Global South such as Africa, where the blame game for poverty and vulnerability is normally pitted against history and geopolitics more than poor governance and corruption.

Even more worrying is the fact that the approach to poverty and vulnerability in the Global South often takes a top-down dimension neglecting the experiences, links and on-the-ground realities of the affected people. Yet, vulnerability and risk drivers such as "increasing urbanisation, poor urban governance, vulnerable rural livelihoods and the decline of ecosystems" (UNISDR 2009: iii) are often described and stated as leading to high hazard exposure, extreme poverty and massive human misery. With this reality on the ground, it is likely that extreme poverty will continue to haunt the global world until "governments come to terms with the increased risk of [natural] disasters in some of the poorest *and most vulnerable people* of the world" (DeCapua 2013; emphasis mine).

Furthermore, the approach to poverty and vulnerability – especially those to understand poverty and vulnerability drivers – in the Global South often downplays the historical and political realities surrounding these communities. The past abuses of political and commercial power receive no full direct and explicit mention as critical drivers of poverty and vulnerability which create disaster risks, foment and perpetuate different faces of poverty among African communities. Neither does "greedy and unjust behaviour of concessionaries, politicians, and law enforcement officers" (Harwell 2000: 330) are articulated in its depth as cornerstones of extreme poverty and vulnerability. Critical questions arise: "if poverty and disaster management agencies and governments choose to ignore the historical and political origin of poverty and vulnerability as well as the idiosyncratic egocentrism of some people of the government [national or international], how can poverty and vulnerability reduction ever happen? Besides, why there seem to be more production than there is eradication of poverty in Africa than elsewhere in the Global North?"

The poverty and vulnerability problem that the Global South especially Africa faces is reportedly aggravated by gross gender inequalities in some societies therein, which in no doubt erodes societal resilience and development bridges. It, in fact, shatters the boundless efforts to undo the deep and wide river of poverty which stifle the pregnant and eternal prospects of global hope.

The broad theme of this book seeks to interrogate the politics, controversies, and events, which stymie and constrain poverty and vulnerability reduction efforts by poverty and vulnerability professionals. Most crucially, the book seeks to forge ways to reduce poverty and vulnerability among the [poor] African communities, particularly in those places with high hazard exposure and extreme poverty levels.

It is in view of the above standing observation that the present volume comprises chapters that range from the historical and political causes and implications of poverty and vulnerability to Africa's social, cultural, political, economic and natural milieu. On this note, the book explores the linkages, relationships and effects of poverty and vulnerability to socio-economic development as well as African environments, resources and the attendant politics of food production. The key issue here is that poverty is not merely a natural phenomenon, but it is also anthropogenic as it is political, economic and socio-cultural.

The book asks critical questions such as those around the role and impact of trans-Atlantic slave trade, colonialism, capitalism, neo-colonialism, corruption, poor governance, culture and technology on Africa's poverty and vulnerability.

Organisation of the book

Munyaradzi Mawere's Chapter 2 critically examines why the talk about Africa's poverty continue looming large day-by-day. Mawere further interrogates the political-economy surrounding the whole question of poverty and underdevelopment in Africa. He does so as part of an attempt to unravel the root cause(s) of the resilience of poverty (and vulnerability) in Africa. In this whole attempt, Mawere advances the argument that "poverty in Africa is a human creation by some buffoons: it is neither a natural nor a biologically inherent phenomenon". Thus, for Mawere, poverty in Africa can be totally eliminated if governments and people of Africa and the world at large fully commit themselves and live up to the task.

In Chapter 3, Nkwazi Mhango takes a deconstructionist slant to interrogate the failure to deconstruct and reconstruct certain terms, injustices, hoaxes, and exploitation hidden behind the terms. In his quest to decolonise and terms related to development and poverty, Mhango highlights experiential and historical realities which he believes play a fundamental role in formulating fair and feasible solutions to the problems that emanate from the asymmetrical relationship between the Global South and the Global North. Noting that the highlighted exploitative and asymmetrical relationship between the Global North and the Global South is a social construction, Mhango is convinced that such a relationship is reversible. He, thus, concludes that "subjectively and objectively", the relationship between the Global North and the Global South "needs deconstruction and general overhaul in order to serve both parties equally and equitably".

Aluko Opeyemi and Munyaradzi Mawere's Chapter 4 examines cycles of poverty, its components, manifestations and regeneration strategies in Africa. The cycles of poverty that Opeyemi and Mawere examine include the Social Cycle of Poverty (SCP), Political Cycle of Poverty (PCP), and the Economic Cycle of Poverty (ECP), which they believe though prevalent and seem inherently natural in Africa, can possibly be broken. Armed with such fervent hope, Opeyemi and Mawere explore strategies that can possibly be deployed to break the cycle of poverty in Africa and other developing countries across the globe. For Opeyemi and Mawere, breaking the cycle of poverty in Africa is critical as it reverses the catastrophes and losses that poverty has inflicted on humanity, especially the vulnerable groups.

In Chapter 5, Simon Maravanyika and Harro Maat examine interventions that were instituted by the colonial regime in peasant agriculture in Zimbabwe in general, and in particular areas such as Gokwe. They argue that agricultural transformations by the colonial government faced resistance from indigenous communities. To demonstrate resistance by indigenous populations such as the Shangwe in areas were agricultural transformations were made, Maravanyika and Maat focus on two of the responses – gambling and illegal production and marketing of cannabis. The duo is apt to argue that "illegal activities, apart from negating colonial agrarian design, provided Shangwe families with alternative sources of livelihood" which made it feasible to resist 'modernity' and avoid cotton production, which for them was not only foreign but contrary to their 'traditional' way of life.

Peter Ateh-Afac Fossungu's Chapter 6 argues essentially that political naivety and corruption in Africa have served as [exceptionally efficient] vectors for the implantation of poverty and underdevelopment in the continent. For Fossungu, it is in fact this culture of political naivety and corruption by Africa's 'elite' group, especially politicians, which have reversed the continent's development fortunes resulting in what Fossungu himself describes as *Quagmatickism* – "which is actually a cloaked means of continuing the trans-Atlantic slave trade and colonialism in Africa under innocuously new names like 'brain-drain' or *'voluntary* slavery'''. Fossungu's argument just like that of Mawere expressed in Chapter 2 of this book is that poverty is a human creation, and as such it can possibly be eradicated so long people of the world fully commit themselves to cast it into the abyss of oblivions.

Davidson M. Mugodzwa's Chapter 7 demonstrates how the establishment, operation and management of a multinational mining enterprise at Mashava since 1908 has created underdevelopment, poverty and environmental degradation. On this note, Mugodzwa argues that both the local Karanga people and Malawian migrant labourers working for the European multinational mining enterprise at Mashava were systematically underpaid and overworked before they were later on abandoned. In his chapter, Mugodzwa clearly demonstrates how both working and living conditions amongst labourers in Mashava dismally deteriorated to sub-human levels as a result of both overexploitation and struggles over the ownership of the Mashava Mines, prompting acute poverty and environmental degradation, among other problems, in the Mashava area.

In Clementia Murembe Neema, Jenny-Louise Van der Aa, Sjaak Kroon & Veerle Draulans' Chapter 8, the deployment of radio shows as a novel approach to ethnographic monitoring is discussed. The authors note that the approach, which stems from a study on women's empowerment and decision-making at the household level in Ankore families in Uganda, helps establishing power dynamics in view of family resource use in an African place. The chapter reveals that Ugandan married women's decision-making power regarding family resources' use, control and ownership is relatively low as compared to that of their husbands. For the authors, the need for a reverse of such a scenario is long overdue as has already been realised by the Ugandan government itself, which has since instituted a range of empowerment measures and strategies to undo asymmetrical relationships between men and women. The authors, though believe that a lot still needs to be done in Uganda as elsewhere in the developing world, successfully demonstrate that empowerment measures and strategies in Uganda have contributed significantly to the empowerment of women at both family and national levels. It has had a positive effect on poverty eradication and power relations between men and women in developing countries of Africa.

Artwell Nhemachena and Romeo Mudimu's Chapter 9 relates issues of poverty to the 'Fees Must Fall' protests against the university and the government of Namibia. Nhemachena and Mudimu meticulously show how students at the University of Namibia felt short-changed and impoverished by the university which continue to raise fees almost every semester. On the other hand, the duo reveals how the University of Namibia has considered the fee increases as necessary to keep operations of the financially embattled institution on the show. It is on the basis of such a scenario that Nhemachena and Mudimu argue that both the students and the university were pleading impoverishment and incapacitation, yet they [the university and the students] seem to have failed to realise that the scuffles between them was in fact a result of neo-colonialism. Thus, Nhemachena and Mudimu audaciously argue that the struggle between the university and the students should be understood as a battle between the [impoverished] tussling for survival. They conclude that "both the students and the university were impoverished by the invisible global structural and systemic forces yet, the impoverished in Africa often do not notice that global structural and systemic impoverishment sets one African against the other such that comrades in trenches of poverty paradoxically resort to fighting one another instead of fighting the global (neo-)imperial root causes of their impoverishment".

Ephraim Taurai Gwaravanda's Chapter 10 is manifold in its argumentation. Firstly, it argues that Western education imposed on Africa by the colonial regimes during colonialism created a dependency syndrome and epistemological docility among Africans. For Gwaravanda, such a Eurocentric education also created epistemological hegemony which paved way for European capitalism in Africa and poverty among African populations. Taking it from this understanding, Gwaravanda further argue that "the bottle-necking approach to education which has been inherited by the postcolonial African governments justifies and maintains a cycle of poverty among Africans" for the major reason that such education privileges the few elite group. Worse still, Gwaravanda feels that the education

6

curricula inherited from the colonial governments in Africa is useless for Africans as it creates a society of job seekers rather than employment creators, hence it perpetuates instead of eradicating poverty in Africa. Thus, for Gwaravanda, to ensure innovation, creativity and eradication of poverty in Africa, there is need to decolonise and reconstruct education in many countries across the continent.

In their Chapter 11, Muhammed A. Yinusa; Joseph A. Oluyemi and Raji Abdullateef explore the fundamental human rights of African children and women in view of development. The authors argue that the fundamental human rights of the child and women in many African countries such as Nigeria are often violated and compromised in a manner that limit opportunities to both groups – children and women. Such lack of opportunity, for the authors, translates to impoverishment, hence such constraints should be eliminated to ensure poverty eradication and holistic development in Africa.

Costain Tandi and Munyaradzi Mawere's Chapter 12 critically examines the link between politicking and human-induced violence, and how both defy the logic of democracy and socio-economic development as well as the fight against poverty in many rural communities of Africa such as Zimbabwe. Tandi and Mawere compare and contrast grassroots politics with politicking at national level, and show how these betray development efforts by both government and non-governmental development agencies. Thus for Tandi and Mawere, to foster development and eradicate poverty in Africa, there is need to separate politics from the economy and development issues.

In their Chapter 13, Fidelis Peter Thomas Duri and Eusebiah Chikonyora employ a qualitative research methodology to corroborate data on livelihoods for many vulnerable Zimbabweans living in the country or abroad. Basing on their findings, Duri and Chikonyora argue that begging for livelihoods across national borders remains "a high-risk coping mechanism employed by downtrodden Zimbabweans, mostly the visually-impaired, who exhibit competence to negotiate the world in times of crises". While Duri and Chikonyora believe that insecurities and uncertainties often invoke innovativeness, there is need for Zimbabwe as a country to protect its vulnerable groups such as the visually-impaired to ensure that their needs are well met. Duri and Chikonyora, thus, contribute significantly to poverty discourse in Africa as their chapter illuminates how physically-challenged people, particularly the visually-impaired in many African countries such as Zimbabwe, continue to languish on the wheel of poverty as they desperately try to forge livelihood initiatives in adverse dispensations where they are constantly pushed to the margins by their governments.

Golden Maunganidze and Munyaradzi Mawere's Chapter 14 focuses on media and the role it plays in view of natural disasters. More precisely, Maunganidze and Mawere examine the state of preparedness by media organisations in Zimbabwe, particularly community newspapers based in Masvingo Province as they tried to cover the naturally striking Cyclone Dineo which wreaked havoc affecting the southern part of Zimbabwe, southeastern part of Mozambique and western part of Botswana during the first three months of 2017. They argue that while media play a very critical role in helping members of the public with current information that can assist them to make informed decisions before, during and after disaster strikes, many countries of Africa remain legging behind media-wise. This, for Maunganidze and Mawere, exposes the vulnerable and the poor continue struggling to access information pertaining to impending natural disasters such as cyclones. Thus, basing on their findings in view of Zimbabwe's failure to cover the 2017's Cyclone Dineo, Maunganidze and Mawere, call for the Zimbabwean government to come to the fore in ensuring that all its citizens especially the poor and the vulnerable are protected from natural hazards.

On note, the book reflects on the resilience of poverty and vulnerability in Africa and explore ways by which bridges of resilience, entrepreneurship and development can be erected and in a way that eradicate poverty from the face of the earth.

References

DeCapua, J. 2013. Natural disasters worsen poverty, *Voice of Africa News*, 16 October 2013.

Harwell, E. E. 2000. Remote sensibilities: Discourses of technology and the making of Indonesia's natural disaster, *Development and Change* 31: 307334.

UNISDR. 2009. *Global Assessment Report on Disaster Risk Reduction*, United Nations International Strategy for Disaster Reduction (UNISDR): Geneva.

Chapter 2

The Political Economy of Poverty and Vulnerability: How Africa Can Break the Cycle of Poverty to Unlock its Underdevelopment Jam?

Munyaradzi Mawere

> *"Poverty will forever remain a nemesis for the larger portion of the world population as long as we live in an unequal society where incompleteness and conviviality are neither recognised nor practised" (Mawere, 2017a).*

Introduction

Africa is on record as a poor and underdeveloped continent. It is widely known as a continent plagued with a litany of problems – both natural and anthropogenic – such as diseases of all kinds, natural disasters, poverty and civil unrest of all sorts, including wars. But why is it that the talk and manifestations of poverty continue zooming large on Africa? What causes poverty in Africa? Why does it seem that there is more manifestation of poverty than is its eradication from the face of Africa? Is poverty a natural or biologically inherent phenomenon at the core of the physiological make-up of the African race? Or is it something inherent in the culture of the African people? Might poverty be exogenously imposed on Africa? And, is it possible for Africa to be extricated from decades of poverty and underdevelopment either on its own or by the help of the international community? These are legitimate questions that should be understood as warranting rigorous stock-taking and soul searching, and no one can be faulted for asking them. A close look at all these questions, however, makes one realise that the actual cause(s) of poverty in Africa remain an enigma yet to be unearthed and dealt with accordingly if at all poverty is to be eradicated from the face of the continent.

Some scholars and researchers believe that Africa's poverty is something "natural", while others believe it is biologically and inherently planted in the people of Africa's physiological and cultural fabric. Those who believe that poverty is "natural" in Africa argue that it is impossible to separate poverty from Africa and Africa from poverty because for them poverty is part of the whole chemistry that constitute "Africanness". However, the truth of this claim is yet to be proved. Drawing on the quote above and my empirical research findings, this chapter advances the argument that while poverty in Africa has no single cause, inequality at both local and global scales can be singled out as one of the major reasons why poverty remains a towering ghost on the continent. It is inequality which remains at the centre of all forms of poverty – whether material, moral, economic or mental –; and poverty badly affects us all in one way or another. It spares no one. As the activist-cum-scholar, Martin Luther King (1963: n.p) noted: "injustice anywhere is a threat to justice everywhere. We are caught in an inescapable network of mutuality, tied in a single garment of destiny. Whatever affects one directly affects all indirectly." This is the same with the seed of inequality which I think breeds abject poverty. It catches all of us in an inescapable matrix of asymmetricism.

The task of this chapter is to critically examine why the talk about Africa's poverty continue looming large day-by-day. The chapter further interrogates the political-economy surrounding the whole question of poverty and underdevelopment in Africa. This is done as part of an attempt to unravel the possible causes of the resilience of poverty (and vulnerability) in Africa. The chapter advances the argument that poverty in Africa is a human creation by some buffoons: it is neither a natural nor a biologically inherent phenomenon. Granted as a true observation, the chapter further argues that poverty in Africa can be totally eliminated if governments and people of Africa and the world at large fully commit themselves and live up to the task.

Why too much talk about Africa's poverty?

Many reasons can be suggested as to why Africa deserves special focus as far as poverty (and its twin-sister, underdevelopment) are concerned. As the British Prime Minister declared in 2001, Africa's poverty is "a scar on the conscience of the world" (see www.poverties.org). Yet, the poverty situation of Africa remains a mystery that escapes the logic of many development experts on Africa and beyond. Since the scramble and partition of Africa from November 1884 to February 1885 at Berlin and even before – e.g. during trans-Atlantic slave trade –, the global news on the global economy have largely focused on Africa and the African people. There has been, in fact, too much talk about Africa's poverty, let alone the continent's underdevelopment. A number of reasons can be suggested for this obtaining reality.

First, many have always been wondering why the number of poor people in Africa keeps on increasing day-by-day when Africa's economies are reportedly said to be growing. There is a dissonance between Africa's growth performance and its poverty numbers. We can note, for example, that the year 2017 marks the 22nd year since sub-Saharan Africa started following a path of fast economic growth. Since the mid-1990s, Africa's annual economic growth has been averaging 5.2 % (Chandy 2015). The million dollar question remains: 'Why then do the numbers of poor people in Africa keep on increasing when Africa's economies are growing at that rate?' For instance, the number of people in Africa living under $1.25 a day has soared up from 358 million in 1996 to 415 million in 2011 (Ibid); a trend that is very disturbing and indeed difficult to explain, at least in the economic sense. Using data from Mozambique, I explain elsewhere (Mawere 2011) that this trend is a result of historical legacies (particularly, trans-Atlantic slave trade, colonialism and neo-liberal policies of the 1990s) and soaring levels of corruption in Africa which allow the few rich people at the top echelons of society to enjoy more than their share of the spoils of economic growth. Unfortunately, data on this "top" class is always missing in statistics of many African countries as this rarified class tends not to participate in household surveys from which distributions are derived (Chandy 2015). So, is the data on the amount of resources that Africa has lost to slave trade and colonialism, which is hard to come across. I argue that such realities have the net effect of dampening the genuine developmentalists' spirit and the momentum of the pathway to poverty eradication in Africa.

Second, the talk on poverty keeps on zooming large on Africa given that the continent has the most rapid population growth of 2.6% per year. This means that even though Africa is generating a lot of income, this is shared among an ever-increasing number of people. The rate at which poverty is falling thus, remains far less as compared to the rate at which the population in Africa is rising. This means that not only the number of people living in poverty continues to grow, but also the talk about Africa's poverty sounds louder by day.

Third, while inequality in Africa is not rising in most countries, it is already so entrenched and at unusually high levels (Ibid). The same applies to the level (and depth) of poverty (and underdevelopment) which is unusually far behind the poverty line. What this entails is that where the initial level of inequality and poverty is very high, it is always expected that economic growth will impact less to reduce poverty since the absolute increase in average income will be much smaller for the poor as compared to the rich.

Fourth, in many African countries the Gross Domestic Product (GDP) per capita has been consistently falling since the past century or so. In 1820, for example, the average European worker earned about three times what the average African did, but today the average European earns twenty times what the average African does (Sachs 1998). This means that the people who should develop Africa are continually deprived of the means to do so to allow the achievement of sustained economic growth and the reversal of the continent's losses over the years.

Fifth, Africa is a continent with unique circumstances and events – such as trans-Atlantic slavery and colonialism – which have impacted variably on the continent's development trajectory and poverty woes. The indelible psychological damage, physical battering, institutional distortions and economic pillaging that ensued cannot be overcome in a short space of time, but may as well need the same number of years (or even more) that the African people were subdued under oppression for them to shake off the legacies. Without compensation from the perpetrators (or their descendants) of slave trade and the whole chagrin of colonialism or at least global efforts to reverse the effects of these circumstances and events, the talk on Africa's poverty and underdevelopment will remain zooming large on the continent.

Sixth, in terms of natural resources – here I mean the under- and aboveground resources – Africa is the richest continent in the world yet it is the poorest continent in terms of wealth of its citizens. This is worrying! And if anything, all this reveals that as long as the majority of Africans live in poverty in a continent of plenty the talk on poverty will remain printed in bold on the face of Africa.

Yet, the talk on Africa's poverty (and vulnerability) can never be complete without a discussion on the root cause(s) of poverty on the continent: the talk is intricately linked to the cause(s) of poverty in Africa. In the next section, I focus on the latter.

The [alleged] cause(s) of poverty in Africa

The "why talk" on Africa's poverty (and underdevelopment) I have just discussed links up with the question on the cause(s) and perpetuation of poverty in Africa. The richness of Africa in natural, human and supernatural resources astounds every average mind when reminded that Africa remains one of the poorest continents in the world to date. This, however, is a question which though critical to Africa and the world at large, has not received serious attention from scholars, non-governmental organisations and governments of African countries. It is the very question that this section and indeed the larger part of this chapter focuses on.

Admittedly, Africa's poverty situation is a complex one, entangled and enmeshed in historical and contextual mirage. It is complex in the sense that there is a "hard-to-understand" interplay of a plethora of factors which contribute to the resilience and perpetuation of poverty in Africa, including historical, political, cultural and institutional factors. Worse still, there is no simple answer to Africa's quandary of poverty. On the other hand, Africa's poverty is paradoxical. While the richness of Africa especially in natural resources cannot be summarily dismissed, its poverty cannot be lightly denied. The million dollar question, however, is reiterated: "Why Africa remains poor in the midst of plenty?" Africa, for instance, has 8 % of the world's natural gas reserves, 45 countries

15

with oil reserves, 57 % of the world's cobalt, 47 % of the world's diamonds, 49 % of the world's manganese, 31 % of the world's phosphate, and 21 % of the world's gold, not to talk of wildlife and marine resources (cf. Didia 2015). In addition, the continent has a very high potential for solar energy, geothermal power and hydro-electric power. Besides being the richest resource-wise, in terms of size and population, Africa is the second largest continent in the world after Asia and followed by North America, South America, Antarctica, Europe and Australia in that order. Moreover, Africa has abundant arable lands, some of which are being grabbed by transnational corporations. By virtue of this reality about the plethora of resources it has, Africa should be the richest continent and with the richest people in the world, by whatever scale. Sadly, the opposite is true. Africa is the least developed continent in the world with 34 of the 49 poorest countries of the world and 40 % of its population living on less than a $1 a day (Oktar 2006). I reiterate the question, 'why is Africa this poor?' In response, I acknowledge that the causes of poverty in Africa are multifaceted. However, for purposes of this chapter, I will only focus on five of these for I cannot exhaust all of them in a chapter.

To begin with, Africa's poverty is a result of the legacies of the most regrettable and extremely unfortunate events of trans-Atlantic slave trade and colonialism, which today have transfigured themselves into what has come to be generally known as "neo-colonialism". In any case, it is difficult to fully understand and appreciate the present poverty condition of any given country (African countries included) without examining its past events – good or bad – that shaped the present condition the country in question finds itself in. It is in this sense that trans-Atlantic slave trade and colonialism are implicated in the poverty mantra of Africa. As Didia (2015: 20) rightly notes "for about three hundred years, Africa was plundered of human and natural resources where the brightest and strongest were captured and forced into captivity to farm distant lands in the Americas and Europe". Slave trade in which nearly all the maritime countries of Western Europe were major players, for example, resulted in the exportation of between 12 and 20 million enslaved Africans (excluding casualties and fatalities), between the

16th and 19th centuries (Ibid). With this magnitude of enslavement and later the dramatic effects of colonialism with its attendant heinous and callous acts of wanton violence, thuggery, pillaging and other such dastardly acts, it is beyond doubt that slavery and colonialism derailed Africa's development, planted and exacerbated the continent's poverty situation. To achieve the wealth they enjoy today, many countries of Western Europe had to use Africans as cannon fodder to get the best of what they could never imagine getting at home in Europe, even if it meant impoverishing the people of Africa. Rodney (1972), the foremost proponent of the view that Africa's poverty and underdevelopment is a result of slavery, colonialism and capitalism acerbically underscores that:

> To achieve economic development, one essential condition is to make maximum use of the country's labour and natural resources. Usually, that demands peaceful conditions, but there have been times in history when social groups have grown stronger by raiding their neighbours for women, cattle and goods because they then used the 'booty' from the raids for the benefit of their own community. Slaving in Africa did not even have that redeeming value. Captives were shipped outside instead of being utilised within any given African community creating wealth from nature. It was only an accidental by-product that in some areas Africans who recruited captives for Europeans realised that they were better off keeping some for themselves. In any case, slaving prevented the remaining population from effectively engaging in agriculture and industry, and it employed professional slave hunters and warriors to destroy rather build. Quite apart from the moral aspect and the immense suffering that it caused, the European slave trade was economically totally irrational from the viewpoint of African development (pp. 108-109).

The forceful removal of the strongest and fittest Africans – through slavery – from the continent had deleterious effects on the development of Africa as it bred and sealed the fate of the African people's poverty and underdevelopment predicament which persists even today. So is colonialism. The colonists exploited not only human resources, but also natural resources such as precious minerals and wildlife, which they carted away to Europe and America willy-nilly. The only investment that colonists "put in place were those absolutely necessary for the exploitation and evacuation of human and natural resources" (Didia 2015: 32). This had long lasting material, physical and psychological effects on the [under-]development and poverty situation of Africa. The same scenario continues obtaining in many African countries where governments are impoverished and incapacitated by the invisible global structural and systemic forces and transnational (neo-)imperial companies, which more often than not siphon out African resources and unscrupulously evade taxes. I underline that where humans are physically and psychologically battered while their [natural] resources are exploited and looted willy-nilly by outsiders, self-esteem and productivity of the subjugated are greatly compromised thereby planting and perpetuating poverty. Scholars like Grier (1999), Price (2003), and Didia (2015) concur that many studies have demonstrated that where a people have been physically and psychologically battered through slavery and colonialism, it may take the same number of years of oppression or even more before the descendants of the once oppressed people can finally overcome the legacies of subjugation and humiliation that their forebears suffered. For this reason, "it would be negligent to talk about the level of economic development of Africa without evaluating the impact of about three centuries of institutionalised slavery and oppression of an entire continent" (Didia 2015: 15), which in fact continue in different forms even today. I therefore argue that due to the asymmetrical nature of the international system, some countries such as Belgium, Germany and France, among others, have never been sued for the genocide they authored and fuelled in Rwanda. This is international political racism which should never be condoned. Such international political racism makes us realise that all types of powers be they political, social or economical in Africa, are still largely artificial and most especially, still controlled by the West which authored colonialism based on the 'divide and rule philosophy'.

More so, the 'hydra-headed monster' of corruption – in all its forms such as rent-seeking, bribery, nepotism and embezzlement etc. – and bad governance should be blamed for Africa's poverty situation. By corruption, I mean "any course of action or failure to act by individuals or organisations, public or private, in violation of law or trust for profit or gain" (Interpol 2014) or the "abuse of entrusted power for private gain" (Transparency International 2004). It is no secret that the unchecked debilitating culture of rampant and insipid corruption in Africa has reduced many countries of the continent into bankruptcy and lawless states deeply impoverished and dependent on donor funds. But why are corruption and bad governance so entrenched in Africa? I note that while corruption is not exclusively a European "child", its badge in Africa was sealed by colonialism. The African colonies that emerged as countries at independence were formed on the basis of the notorious philosophy of corruption where European colonists had to use all corrupt means possible to dominate and expatriate riches from Africa. Most of the African territories were in fact occupied and dominated through gimmicks and corruption. In Zimbabwe, for example, the British South African Company's representative, Charles Rudd (through Francis Thompson) corrupted the Ndebele Induna, Lotshe in order to trick King Lobengula into singing the 1888 Rudd Concession which allowed the company a gain of exclusive mineral rights and occupation of the country (Keppel-Jones 1983). Even missionaries like Robert Moffat practised the corruption and deception of precolonial African rulers. Sadly, the colonies which gained independence from European imperialists did not dissolve the systems and institutions set up by the colonists despite their [Africans] knowledge that the institutions were set up by corrupt figures. Instead of using the opportunity for independence to re-build their respective nations, African leaders and governments adopted their former masters' template of corruption and violence supported by their loop-sided institutions and infrastructures. In many cases, the African leaders have demonstrated even worse off leadership and [poor] governance than that of the former colonial regimes. In essence, many African leaders – such as Mobutu Sese Seko of Zaire, 1965-1977; Sani Abacha of Nigeria, 1993-1998; Idi Amin Dada of Uganda, 1971-79, among others – adopted the despotic and corrupt leadership of the colonial government which was laid on the principle of "what do we get from our colonies rather than what should we do to serve our colonies". In fact, through corruption they became the most exceptionally efficient but destructive vectors for the promotion of poverty and underdevelopment in Africa. The World Bank (2004) estimates that developing countries (especially in Africa) lose between $50 to $100 billion dollars per annum to corruption due to weakened institutions. General Sani Abacha of Nigeria, for instance, is reported to have looted more than $5 billion from the country's treasury before his demise in 1998. Similarly, the late president of Zaire, Mobutu Sese Seko is said to have looted approximately $5 billion from the nation's treasury before he was overthrown in 1997 (Transparency International 2004). In reference to Mobutu, Reno (1997 cited in Wright 2008) points out that:

Social service spending during Mobutu's regime in the former Zaire fell from 17.5% of government spending in 1972 to 2% in 1990, and agricultural spending (mostly subsidies) fell from over 40% of the budget to 11% in 1990. Meanwhile, during that time, the president's share of the budget increased from 30% to 95% (p. 974).

Also revealing a case of corruption of government official by the Cameroonian president, Fombad (2004) observes that:

In 1997, as part of the preparations for elections of that year in which, magistrates, judges and other judicial personnel were to play a key role in various provincial, divisional, and sub-divisional vote-counting commissions, a presidential decree was signed awarding them "hush money" in the form of hefty salary increases and exorbitant allowances (p. 367).

Many other cases of African leaders involved in similar acts of corruption are many. As Transparency International (Ibid) notes, such corrupt acts have destroyed the treasures of their countries while storing the ill-gotten wealth in Western countries and the Americas. I add that such corrupt acts undermine the political, social and economic stability of a country, damages trust in government institutions and authorities, and introduces various forms of distortions such as inefficiency, laziness, apathy, nepotism and mediocrity which compromise enterprise, hard work, creativity and innovation, and lead Africa all the way to the ocean of poverty.

However, for the Euro-American former colonisers, their colonial era corrupt activities [in African colonies] account for their present "riches". In other words, corruption accounts for the "opulence" of Europe and America. In this sense, the major problem is that corrupt African leaders invest their proceeds of corruption in Euro-America rather than in Africa. Whereas Euro-American colonists and enslavers invested the proceeds of their corruption back in Euro-America, corrupt African leaders invest their proceeds of corruption away from home and from the continent. In this sense, the corrupt African officials are as much self-serving as they are serving Euro-America. Africa can neither develop nor eradicate poverty with such self-serving leaders who instead of serving their people and develop their countries make constant efforts to generate African amnesia, which like colonialism set in motion the resilient African impoverishment, as they ruin and suffocate important sectors of the economy such as agriculture, trade, and social services. In fact, such leaders have doused the successful script of development as their acts are at variance with the genuine efforts to eradicate poverty and underdevelopment in Africa.

In the contemporary times, this plundering of African resources by African leaders has become so entrenched and debilitating, aggravated by the continued existence of the Americas, Western and of late Asian countries who, like the insidious empire of the colonial past, shun away conviviality and keep on pillaging and siphoning Africa's resources mainly aided by corrupt African leaders and government officials. Norberg-Hodge (2006:100) captures this scenario even much better when he says:

> In a sense, the countries of the South have subsidised today's globalised economy for the past 500 years, at great expense to their own cultures, their land and their economies. The current dominance of the Western industrial model could never have arisen without prolonged access to the South's raw materials, labour (including slave labour), and markets.

The *Daily Nation* of 29 August, 2016 quoted Zhang Ming, China's Vice-Minister for Foreign Affairs as saying that "there is never shortage of conferences and promises for Africa, and yet action and implementation have not always followed" and even when they followed, there was no gains for Africa. This is a genuine statement that Africa needs to think twice and deeply. The *Daily Nation* went on noting that "China questions Japan's ability to fulfil Ticad promises" soon after Japan convened its Tokyo International Conference on African Development (Ticad VI) on the 27th–28th August, 2016 in Nairobi. Before the Ticad VI, there was China African conference famously known as Forum on China-Africa Cooperation (FOCAC) which was held in Johannesburg from the 3rd to the 5th of December 2015 at which China promised large. Before then, there were other conferences between Britain, France and Africa as well as other bidders such as Turkey. Other "courters" such as Iran, Oman and Qatar have likewise been sending silent emissary to meet different African leaders of the countries that have resources these courters need for their economies and industries. Important to note is the point that all these conferences were, at the core of their objective, aimed at gaining leverage from African countries in a way that would put the courting on a comparative advantage to exploit the continent's resources and further impoverish the people of Africa.

Besides corruption, poverty in Africa is caused by brain drain – what others prefer calling skill flight. Due to poor remuneration, poor working conditions, and political instability in many African countries, many educated and skilled professionals are forced to leave their countries, sometimes against their will, for greener pastures. Fosu (1992, Cited in Didia 2015: 188) is correct to argue that "political instability, as with economic crisis, is likely to lead to brain drain that depletes a given country's stock of highly skilled labour, which emigrates in response to heightened political and economic risks engendered by political instability". Since brain drain literary means talent (or scarce human resource) is leaving for greener pastures where there is comparative advantage, African nations being in a developing state, lose more (than they gain) to the developed nations of the world. Countries such as Zimbabwe, Nigeria Ethiopia, Sierra Leone, Ghana and Kenya have many medical doctors practising in North America and Europe instead of in their home countries where their services are desperately needed. Per capita, World Bank (2011) reveals that the top five destinations of skilled personnel from Africa are Qatar (87 %), Monaco (72 %), the United Arb Emirates (70 %), Kuwait (69 %) and Adora (64 %). As El-Khawas (2004) observed there are more African sciencies and engineers working in the US than there are in Africa. In a study by Clemens and Pettersson (2007) on nine destination countries (USA, UK, France, Canada, Australia, Spain, Portugal, Belgium, and South Africa), it is revealed that at the turn of the new millennium, there were approximately 65, 000 Africa-born physicians and 70, 000 African-born professional nurses working in these nine countries. This represents about one fifth of African-born physicians and one tenth of African-born nurses professional nurses (Ibid). Worse still, the worry for any concerned poverty and development scholar is that if these skilled professionals who are desperately needed in Africa emigrate, who then will develop Africa? Who will fight poverty to make sure that Africa catches up with the rest of the world? In view of this reflection, I argue that brain drain in Africa is exacerbating the widening of inequality in the distribution of income between developed and developing countries, causing Africa to slump back into a vicious cycle of poverty and underdevelopment.

Further, poverty in Africa is caused by culture and attitude of the African people. I should argue that while trans-Atlantic slave trade, colonialism, corruption and brain drain can be blamed for instigating and fuelling poverty and underdevelopment in Africa, Africans' culture and attitude are also to blame. The developments in technology and industrialisation in the Global North – the West and the Americas – today appear as if the Global North keeps on technologically inventing and industrialising while the rest of the world (especially Africa) sits and wait for more to come from the North. The industrial revolution, for example, is historically recognised as a product of the West. Worse still, Europe and the Americas remain in the forefront when it comes to technology and industry. One gets surprised to know that some five hundred to seven hundred years before the European industrial revolution, the civilisations of the Middle East – Asia – were far-ahead those of Europe and the Americas, both in knowledge and wealth (see Landes

2006). The Chinese, for example, are credited for inventions such as the wheelbarrow, textile, printing, iron smelting, gunpowder and paper, among other inventions. Confronted by such reality, one wonders how then was Asia overtaken by Europe and America if it already had such an advantage in science and technology. Also, one wonders how Europe and the Americas managed to catch up if it were some 500 to 700 years behind Asia, to the extent of surpassing the latter. The response to this situation helps us understand why some countries are rich and others poor, at least from a technological view point. The answer to this scenario applies to the African problem too. In view of the question why some countries are poor (e.g. Africa) and others rich (e.g. Europe), I argue that culture and attitude also counts. It can be observed that Europe and America overtook Asia in science and technology for the major reason that there was absence of free enterprise, prevailing autocratic leadership and lack of well defined (or institutionalised) property rights as a result of elements in Chinese culture (Landes 1998). To elaborate this further, Landes makes it clear that around the 13th century, the Chinese government put in place all obstacles that interfered with the development of free enterprise such as taking over all lucrative activities and discouragement of private enrichment or any activity that threatened to widen the income gap amongst the Chinese citizens. Yap and Cotterell (1997) corroborate this assertion when the note that the Ming Dynasty (1368-1644) tried to prohibit international trade and anybody who traded with the outside world or travelled out without permission risked execution. The Ming Dynasty actually described the early Europeans who made contact with China by referring to them as *"Yang kuezi tzu"* which mean "Ocean Devils" (Ibid). This discouragement of accumulation of wealth by individuals in China stifled both innovation, enterprises and instead resulted in corruption as people resorted to unproductive activities such as smuggling, rent seeking and other unproductive activities. In fact, corruption became rampant as government officials enriched themselves with money extorted from smugglers and other illegal dealers. More so, talented people in the society were forced to divert their energies to those activities which enriched them instead of diverting the energies to technology and innovation. Such is the

24

scenario that is obtaining in many if not all African countries. In Africa, this is even worsened by the [cultural] system of extended family which, though with its own merits, dictates that one must share her/his resources with kinsmen. One who opposes the culture is normally berated and labelled as selfish and wicked. This, when integrated with "modern" institutions such as the money economy created by colonialism, fuels the culture of corruption as the appointment of one individual in government, for example, makes the whole family and even ethnic group consider such appointment as their share of the national cake. All this (was and) is contrary to developments that took place in Europe and the Americas where free enterprise has been allowed to be bountiful and innovation and technological progress promoted. To make matters worse, women in the Chinese society (as is still the case in many African countries today) were relegated to the periphery of the national economy as they were only allowed to run homes and were never afforded the opportunity to participate in development activities of the nation outside home. This contributed to the regression of China as is the case with poverty and underdevelopment in many African countries today. Realising the consequences from other countries, Europe and America, though were typically and largely patriarchal, quickly gave their women the opportunity to participate in national economic activities resulting in mass production in the textile industry. The regression of China was further worsened by the secrecy that comes along with Chinese science and technology. The Chinese, just like Africans, have always kept their science and technological development a secret to the outside world. They have also been hesitant to adopt other people's science and technology. This cultural element of Chinese science and technology (as with African science and technology) has made it possible for China to be overtaken and surpassed scientifically and technologically by Europe and America; countries which have become open to plunder other people's science and technology.

Lastly, I argue that poverty in Africa is caused by political instability – the persistent crises in the emergence, tenure, sustainability and succession of leadership in the governance process of a country (Didia 2016: 170). In countries where political instability prevails, the quest to eradicate poverty has not yielded desired results. This is aptly captured by Adedeji (1990) who avers that "the very first and perhaps most basic requirement for Africa to effectively deal with its socio-economic crisis is not in the economic realm but rather in the political sphere of governance". This resonates with Sachs' (1994) later observation that "misrule, disease and civil strife" are foremost factors betraying efforts to eradicate poverty in Africa. As Didia (2015: 170) notes:

> Political instability has numerous socio-economic ramifications which are manifested in myopic policies that result inter alia in neglect of investments in critical institutions, infrastructure and human development, inability to compete internationally, inefficient exploitation of natural resources, corruption and brain drain, and declining productivity.

This is the situation that has plagued many African countries even after independence from the colonial regime. In Egypt, president Hosin Mubarak was forced out of office by mass protests in 2011 due to allegations of poor governance, including corruption. Although there are also allegations that the Arab spring was in fact engineered from outside Africa and by agents and institutions that used action at a distance-social media. In many other African countries such as Mozambique, Eretria, Rwanda, Nigeria, DRC, and Burundi, among others, there have been sprouts of violence and bouts of political instability as a result of a compound of factors. This has always had a net effect of creating and exacerbating poverty levels and underdevelopment in Africa as energy and money are either wasted or diverted away from more productive endeavours and the struggle against poverty. It keeps Africans locked in the chagrins of "survival of the fittest" struggles which do not get them out of the belly of the poverty so easily. The same goes with many longest serving African presidents such as Denis Sassou-Ngueso (Congo), Idriss Derby (Chad), Isayas Afwerki (Eritrea), Paul Kagame (Rwanda), Robert Mugabe (Zimbabwe), Jose Eduardo dos Santos (Angola), Theodoro Obiang (Equatorial Guinea), Yoweri Museveni, and Omar Bashir (Sudan), most of who have prolonged their stay in power through unscrupulous means including rigging elections, nepotism, and bootlicking, among others, thereby fuelling political instability and consequently widening gasps of poverty which cannot be filled-in in a moment.

Having said all this, the million-dollar question that continue boggling our minds is: "What then Africa needs in order to break its cycle of poverty which for years has haunted its people?"

What Africa needs to leap from its debilitating poverty situation

Like a person possessed by a stubborn demon, Africa needs deliverance. However, to successfully save the continent from the demon of poverty, there is need to address the root causes and not only the symptoms of the poverty problem in Africa, as has normally been the case over the years.

To start with, the attempt to resolve Africa's poverty situation should not be executed from outside but from within. Africa needs homemade strategies to save its people from sinking down into the chasm of poverty and underdevelopment. I argue that the push for Western-designed theories – for example, modernisation theory such as Rostow's stages of economic development–, models and even technologies, as the solution for Africa's poverty enigma resembles interventions embedded in colonial practices. It is, in fact, colonialism in its uttermost form; what van Stam and I describe elsewhere as supercolonialism (see Mawere and van Stam 2017). Instead of imposing foreign-made policies on Africa, Africans and their countries need to be first and foremost compensated for enslavement and colonial dispossession and exploitation of the past and present so that they become capacitated to care for their impoverished citizens. In fact, there is need for Euro-American states to account for contemporary global inequalities, let alone to desist from refusing to compensate Africans for the enslavement and colonial dispossession and exploitation they inflicted on Africa. As Franz Fanon (1963) rightly notes, it is necessary to remember that Europe and America were built from the exploitation of [African] slave labour and colonies – Africans who today can barely afford to pay fees for their children. Though [modern] theories of

27

development are celebrated as pushing poverty-stricken societies to the same level with developed societies, there are questions as to whether much of the problems that Africans are encouraged by (neo-)empire to fight for are the real, necessary and indeed original African problems, particularly in a postmodern context of Africa where reality and originality are denied (Nhemachena and Mudimu, this volume). There is need for Africa to focus on the real causes of its poverty and underdevelopment in order for the continent to solve its problem once and for all. As I argued in my book: *Theorising development in Africa…*, Africa should solve its development problems using home-developed theories, models and frameworks, with foreign interventions only coming in as complementors, instead of relying on theories, models and framewoks from Europe and the Americas, which are largely inapplicable and in most cases inconsistent with the realities of the African people. It is for the same realisation that Lynn White (1974: 2) notes that "the technological superiority of Europe was such that its small, mutually hostile nations could spill out over all the rest of the world, conquering, looting, and colonising". Europe did what it did to Africa to solve its own problems at home. There is need, therefore, for a clear focus, contextualisation and alignment of research, policy and agenda by scholars, researchers, policy makers and governments of Africa. In academia, for example, studies in the field of social sciences, and in particular development studies, should never be subject to "disciplinary decadence where universities organise knowledge in narrow terms of rigid disciplines structured into inflexible academic 'tribes' and 'silos' of mono-disciplines" (Ndlovu-Gatsheni 2013: 50). Meanwhile, in most if not all African universities, topics in the field of development and poverty studies are invariably approached from a Western vantage point on scientific assessment, ethics and theoretical construction. Other perspectives that are non-Western and non-American are excluded if not silenced, yet there is need to understand that poverty studies as development studies in general should be approached from different fields and perspectives; otherwise no solution in the field would stand the test of time.

Worse still, a critical approach towards the instrumental meaning and causes of poverty in contexts such as those of Africa, has been little researched. Such research can be regarded by funders, particularly those from the Global North as risky an adventure. Research on society and the causes of poverty (in that order) from African viewpoints is particularly lacking. As a result, many mainstream academic publications on poverty and development studies in general are of questionable relevance for African academics and practitioners (Ndlovu-Gatsheni 2013; Mawere 2017a, b, c). Perhaps, with the exception of Walter Rodney's (1972) infamous "How Europe underdeveloped Africa" and my recent publications on development studies, poverty and development studies (see Mawere 2017a; 2017b, 2017c), critical research and literature on poverty and development cognisant of African worldviews (such as Afro-centric discourses) is scarce. Not only is there a paucity of data set in African concepts of poverty, inequality, democracy, and development, whether in positive or reflective terms. The paucity of data and theory by African scholars relates to the negating of African contributions to the global community (Mamdani 2011). I add that there is a paucity of theory, particularly around issues of poverty and development emanating from African settings because social (or applied) sciences' studies hardly ever incorporate thoughts and practices that are common in African communities, especially those in rural areas. Coming up with a subset of knowledge on development studies and in particular poverty is made more difficult by the challenges involved in obtaining academic inputs grounded in African worldviews. This results in severe challenges to efforts to counter dominant theories, models and frameworks, which emerge mostly from a Euro-American positivist understanding. As a consequent of the institutionalisation of colonial thought inside and outside the academy, many academic definitions and interpretations of poverty, development and other such development related concepts are highly problematic. This is because besides being expressed in the language of former colonists, they tend to embody the values of the people who set them, who unfortunately are outside the contexts where the definitions are applied. This is beyond question if one is to critically explore most of the conceptual definitions in the academy which almost without exception, appear to be set without consideration of African inputs and worldviews. Father Michel (n.d:1), thus, could be correct when he observed:

> There are forms of colonisation that are going on in the world today which are new, not only in the sense of having begun in the recent past, but also in that they differ in some ways from the 'old' or classic forms of colonisation that characterised Africa and world history from the 16th to the half of the 20th centuries.

Now in view of the texts, theories and models used in Africa when they have theoretical foundations informed by the Global North, two critical questions are worth raising: "For whom are all these texts produced? Also, who are these texts meant to benefit?" In view of these questions, I note that solutions developed according to dominant/foreign frameworks, models, theories and philosophical foundations have both an empowering and disempowering effect on communities such as those of Africa, with the latter (disempowering effect) being more pronounced. In other words, imposed solutions on Africa's poverty and underdevelopment problems are not necessarily meant to help Africans escape from the belly of poverty and (neo-)empire; rather the "solutions" are meant to be part of the scheme and engine for moving the mantra of poverty and (neo-)imperial rule forward even as Africans are pushed deep into the turbulent catadromous waters of global (neo-)imperial coloniality and chasms of poverty and underdevelopment.

Besides homemade strategies, Africa needs servant leaders who can boldly shun away corruption and the penchant of plutocracy – "a government of the wealthy by the wealthy and for the wealthy" (Didia 2015: 504) while with open "eyes" always on the ball to detect and cast to the dustbin of political oblivion any (neo-)imperial machinations and shenanigans by the Global North. In other words, Africa needs good governance and leadership to frog-jump from its present poverty predicament. I have already noted that corruption is one of the most severe impediments to both economic development and poverty eradication efforts in Africa. Evidence are bounty to prove this. Clay (2004), for instance, notes that in countries such as Kenya and Nigeria, corruption alone accounts for approximately 8 %

- 12 % of the Gross Domestic Product (GDP). Such high level of corruption thrives in Africa due to a number of factors which include the "the soft state" nature – situation where citizens of a country do not have a strong sense of identity – of African countries (Gould and Mukendi 1989), incompetence and inefficiency of civil servants, high poverty level, widening gap in income inequality, and most importantly weak institutions i.e. judiciary, police and financial audit. What this means is that to successfully curb corruption and ultimately eradicate poverty, African countries need selfless leaders with abilities to unite people and build strong institutions that can stem out corruption and fight poverty from all corners. As Stevensson (2004) suggests, rather than relying on institutions such as judiciary, financial audit and judiciary, which sometimes harass and intimidate opponents, giving citizen more access to information about funds allocated to particular projects by publishing such information in local newspapers has proven to be quite effective in curbing corruption in such countries as Nigeria. Thus, it is critical that "Africans engage in state reconstruction, through democratic constitution making, to provide themselves with institutional arrangements that enhance wealth creation, sustainable development" (Mbaku 2004) and poverty eradication. Otherwise, without such a transformative mode, Africa will continue deteriorating, sinking even deeper into the chasm of poverty and underdevelopment.

More so, Africa needs political stability to come out of its poverty quagmire and underdevelopment jam. Political instability usually results from conflicts. I have already noted that political instability creates impediments to socio-economic development and poverty eradication efforts in any given country. Industrial action at national level, for example, can paralyse economic activities and impose substantial costs on the economy and poverty eradication efforts. Yet, conflicts which normally results in political instability are inevitable in any human society, including in developed countries of the world. The question that arise therefore is: "What should be done to ensure that political stability prevails in Africa?" In view of this question, I note that African countries must have well-established and functioning justice administration system to help adjudicate business litigations at all levels. Such a system must include efficient police, courts, prisons and parole system with well-trained personnel who are frequently retrained as needed. Where such an efficient system exists, rarely can we find maladministration, poor governance, riots, coups d'état, mass protests and therefore political instability. Thus, to ensure political stability, where such efficient systems are non-existent or not properly functioning, need for institutional reforms becomes critical because "the amount of capital, labour and technology dumped in the system will not yield any measurable economic progress" (Didia 2015: 176). Neither would there be poverty alleviation and worse still poverty eradication at any rate. I, thus, submit that without efficient entities and institutions functioning as required, Africa will never break its poverty cycle and unlock its underdevelopment gridlock. Russia is a wonderful example to substantiate my point here. After the demise of the former Soviet Union in 1991, Russia embraced capitalism anticipating that it would instantly achieve the standard of living in established Western systems. Surprisingly, Russia did not automatically realise the anticipated desired dividends as it did not put in place institutional changes and apparatus needed to nurture and sustain capitalism. Africa should take a cue from such historical examples.

Lastly, Africa needs to invest considerably in technology if it ever wants to seriously come out of its poverty and underdevelopment situation. This would boost the continent's output, help create employment, and add value to its products. While this is what Africa needs, the reality is many African countries are still in the rear as far as technology is concerned. This being the obtaining reality, one of the areas Africa needs to invest in is science and technology, to make sure that adequate goods are produced in the right quantities and quality. All sectors, whether formal or informal need to keep abreast with technology in their activities. As to how Africa should engage in such an important journey, countries like India, China, Taiwan, and South Korea, among others, provide an ideal example. Africa needs to first of all make use of its already produced scientists and technologists that are now scattered all over the world, looking for 'greener pastures'. This would require a bold step for Africa to coax and lure them back for its services which are in fact their services too.

With the exception of Mauritius, Africa continue legging behind while other continents shift from resource-based to medium and high technology-based products to produce added value products for exports. This situation needs to be turned around. It is well known that currently Africa depends largely on agriculture, both for subsistence and export. Sadly, while agriculture is the backbone of many African economies, most of the countries on the continent are even struggling agriculture-wise. FAOSTAT (2011) discloses chilling information that in 2007, for instance, Africa's agricultural imports exceeded agricultural exports by approximately US$22 billion. This is shameful for a continent that boasts of vast tracts of fertile soils and where agriculture is the backbone of the economy for majority of the countries. Agriculture has remained both rudimentary and underdeveloped for reasons varying from global warming to poor technology as well as lack of incentives and subsidies. The old hoe that most African countries largely depend on is no longer a viable implement for successful agriculture considering population growth on the continent. Africa, in fact, now needs mechanised farming besides incentives and subsidies for its farmers just the same way the Americas and the West do to their farmers. As Špička, Boudný, and Janotová (2009: 178) remind us, "Subsidies complement the risks farmers may face and reduce farmers' and farm income unpredictability". The trio further argues that this would mean farmers need to be insured in case anything happens to their farms or products. This is how and why farmers in the West and the Americas have always thrived while their counterparts in Africa have always become poorer every year due to lack of subsidies. Similarly, money that Africa loses annually to crimes such as tax evasion, capital flight, embezzlement, under and mispricing, invoice falsification, low prices for its raw materials, huge government expenditure, and corruption should be channelled towards advanced technology to ensure mechanised farming. This resonates with Masha's (2011: 2) argument that "technology should be transferred to end users", in this case, to farmers in the rural areas. In fact for Africa to robustly change and turn things around for its development, there is need to direct technology freely from the academic domain to praxis and the grassroots. This would go a long way to enhance African agriculture as has so far proven by the cell phone use by farmers around Africa.

Conclusion

While agreeing that the slavery and colonial history of the African continent play big as an obstacle to development and poverty eradication efforts in many African countries, corruption, poor governance, and shortage of competent, highly skilled and well-informed professionals (mainly as a result of brain-drain) alongside its cultural institutional arrangements which do not enhance indigenous entrepreneurship have, during the last five decades or so, become the most important contributors to poverty and underdevelopment in Africa. Africa therefore needs a transformative mode to avoid further deterioration of living standards and regression into the chasm of poverty and underdevelopment. I conclude that the poverty trend in Africa raises several challenges, namely the need to address neo-imperialism, brain-drain, corruption and bad governance but more poignant for this study, inequality in all its forms. Inequality in resource access and allocation may further threaten participation in social justice coupled with reduced economic performance and entrenchment of poverty and underdevelopment.

References

Adedeji, A. 1990. The dimensions of the African crisis: Keynote address delivered at the *Conference on the Economic Crisis in Africa at Vassar College*, New York, October 25-28.

Chandy, L. 2015. 'Why is the number of poor people in Africa increasing when African economies are growing?' Africa in Focus.

China Daily, (4 December 2015). "Xi Announces 10 Major Programs to Boost China-Africa Cooperation in Coming 3 Years," China.

Clay, E. 2004. UK envoy's speech on Kenyan corruption, British Broadcasting Company, UK (4 July 2004).

Clemens, M. & Pettersson, G. 2007. New data on African health professionals abroad, Working Paper No. 95, Centre for Global Development. Available at: www.cgdeve.org.

Didia, O. D. 2015. *Ten reasons why sub-Saharan Africa has failed to develop economically: Can Africans succeed by themselves?* Edwin Mellen Press, UK.

El-khawas, M. A. 2004. Brain drain: Putting Africa between a rock and a hard place, Mediterranean Quarterly, Fall 37-55.

Fanon, F. 1963. *The Wretched of the Earth*, New York: Grove Press.

Fombad, C. M. 2004. The Dynamics of Record-breaking Endemic Corruption and Political Opportunism in Cameroon: Cameroon under Paul Biya, *The Leadership Challenge in Africa*, (2004): 357-394.

Fosu, A. K. 1992. Political instability and economic growth: Evidence from sub-Saharan Africa, *Economic Development and Cultural Change* 40 (4): 830-841.

Grier, R. 1999. Colonial legacies and economic growth, *Public Choice* 98: 317-335.

Interpol. 2014. Retrieved from: www.interpol.int.

Keppel-Jones, A. 1983. *Rhodes and Rhodesia: The White conquest of Zimbabwe*, 1884-1902, Quebec and Kingston, Montreal.

Landes, D. S. 1998. *The wealth and poverty of nations*, W.W. Norton & Company, New York.

Landes, D. S. 2006. Why Europe and the West? Why not China? *Journal of Economic Perspectives* 20 (2): 3-22.

Mawere, M. 2011. *Moral Degeneration in Contemporary Zimbabwean Business Practices*, (2011), Langaa RPCIG Publishers: Cameroon.

Mawere, M. 2017a. *Theorising Development in Africa: Towards Building an African Framework of Development*, Langaa Publishers: Bamenda.

Mawere, M. 2017b. (Ed). *Underdevelopment, Development and the Future of Africa*, Langaa Publishers: Bamenda.

Mawere, M. 2017c. (Ed). *Development Perspectives from the South: Troubling the Metrics of [Under-]development in Africa*, Langaa Publishers: Bamenda.

Mbaku, J. M. 2004. *Institutions and Development in Africa*, Africa World Press, Trenton: NJ.

Norberg-Hodge, H. 2006. Sustainable Economies: Local or Global? In: M. Keiner (Ed.), *The Future of Sustainability* (pp. 99–115). Dordrecht: Springer.

Mamdani, M. 2011. The Importance of Research in a University. Accessed 18 May 2016 from http://www.pambazuka.org/en/category/features/72782.

Masha, E. M. 2011. *Assessment of Technology Adoption for Free Range Local Chicken Improvement in Mzumbe Ward Mvomero District Morogoro*, PhD Diss, Sokoine University of Agriculture.

Michel, T. S. J. (n.d.). *New Forms of Colonization in the World Today.* Retrieved from www.bensalemsd.org/cms/lib7/PA01000472/Centricity/Domain/1019/Colonialism Today article.doc

Mutasa, C. 2008. Africa: 'Why the richest continent is also the poorest', Discussion at the Third High Level Forum on Aid Effectiveness (HLF3), Accra, Ghana (2-4 Sept 2008).

Ndlovu-Gatsheni, S. J. 2013. Decolonising the University in Africa. *The Thinker*, 51, 46–51.

Nhemachena, A. and Mudimu, R., (forthcoming) Fighting Fellow Comrades in the Trenches of Poverty in Africa? Interrogating the Fees Must Fall Movement at the University of Namibia, in Mawere, M. (Ed). *The Political Economy of Poverty, Vulnerability and Disaster Risk Management: How Africa can Break the Cycle of Poverty to Unlock its Underdevelopment Jam?* Langaa: Cameroon.

Oktar, A. 7 May 2006. 'The richest continent has the poorest people', Gulf Times. Available at: http:www.gulftimes.com/story/492519/.

Price, G. 2003. Economic growth in a cross-section of non-industrial countries: Does colonial heritage matter for Africa? *Review of Development Economics* 7 (3): 478-495.

Rodney, W. 1972. *How Europe underdeveloped Africa,* University of Dar Es Salaam, Tanzania.

White, L. 1974. The Historical Roots of Our Ecological Crisis [with discussion of St Francis; reprint 1967, *Ecology and Religion in History*, Harper and Row: New York.

Špička, J., Boudný, J. & Janotová, B. 2009. The Role of Subsidies in Managing the Operating Risk of Agricultural Enterprises, *Agricultural Economics–Czech* 50(4): 169-179.

Sachs, J. 1998. A new partnership for growth in Africa, *PROSI Management*.

Stevensson, J. 2004. Eight questions about corruption, *Journal of Economic Perspectives* 19 (3): 19-42.

White, M. K. 1996. The Chinese family and economic development: Obstacle or engine? *Economic Development and Cultural Change* 45 (1): 1-30.

World Bank. 2011. Migration and remittances factbook (2nd end). World Bank Publications, Washington DC. Available at: http://www.worldbank.org/prospects/migrationand remittances.

Chapter 3

Poverty and the Discourses about the Global North's Playing of the Global South

Nkwazi Mhango

> *The North-South conflict also means a cultural division of the world's*
> *societies. It is the division that was defined during the 18ᵗʰ and 19ᵗʰ centuries by*
> *opposing terms such as 'civilization' and 'savagery/barbarism'; later they were*
> *substituted by the binomials 'development' and 'underdevelopment', 'modernity'*
> *and 'tradition', 'domination' and 'dependency', 'metropolis' and 'periphery',*
> *'globalism' and 'localism' (Krotz 1997: 239 cited in Oliveira 2011).*

Introduction

The above quote, apart from being self-explanatory, suffices to answer the question about the origin of the terms of the relationship between the Global North and the Global South dwelling on economic matrices and synergies between the two. So, too, from the quote one can grasp the spirit and intentions of the formulation of these two terms whose major aim is for one side to discriminate against, dwarf and exploit another. Due to its self-explanatory nature, the quote above delivers the message forthrightly. Therefore, this corpus will not dwell on redefining or elaborating more on such terms due to the fact that the provided reading goes even deeper and further as far as the etymology of the terms are concerned. Importantly, some of the terms found in the defining quote above will feature in this chapter.

Nevertheless, we can add something in that the creation, and partly, the conceptualisation of the terms, seems to be more stereotypical, xenophobic and fabricated than logical. It all depends on the lenses one uses to view and analyse them. This is why this chapter suggests that such terms should not be taken for granted so as to be applied blindly without underscoring the ambiguities and the toxicity hidden behind them. Primarily, the corpus takes a deconstructionist slant of scholarship (Jobson 2010) in order to scrutinise; and thereby contribute how these terms can be made right. For, failure to deconstruct and reconstruct the terms, means condoning injustice, hoaxes, and exploitation hidden behind the terms. Arguably, in dealing with the issues this chapter raises, experiential and historical realities will play a fundamental role in devising fair and feasible solutions to the problems resulting from the relationship between two halves of the world however socially constructed. Specifically, this discourse dwells on exploitative and asymmetrical relationship between the Global North and the Global South. Subjectively and objectively, this relationship needs deconstruction and general overhaul in order to serve the parties to it equally and equitably.

Notably, although the chapter is about exploitative and unequal North-South relationship, much emphasis will be on Africa due to experiential and academic, if not, historical reasons. Equally, Africa is the most affected area of the Global South that needs to be given high priority shall the relationship in question intend to be meaningfully constructive. Additionally, Africa is the subset that has more resources than all other areas in the latter which makes it an attraction to economic bullying and exploitation.

Moreover, this chapter briefly dwells on the relationship between the Global North and the Global South namely conflict, poverty and underdevelopment resulting from this relationship with the aim of proving that the said relationship is wanting and unfair. Although, North-South relationship in dealing with various issues such as commerce, conflict and underdevelopment has worked in some places, it is still inequitable; and enables the former to dominate and thereby exploit the former. Thus, this relationship in itself becomes the basis and cause of conflict based on struggle for resource control so as to leave some basic human needs unmet not to mention inequality, poverty, underdevelopment and insecurity in the latter that has led to relative deprivation. This chapter uses theories based on academic, experiential and historical realities to shed light on the ontological nature of the relationship between the two as an extension of colonialism embedded in how the two deal with commerce, conflict and development, among others. By nature, this relationship is built on opposing and dichotomous binary or dualistic paradigm. The major aim of this chapter, *inter alia*, is to earmark some problems resulting from the unequal and unfair relationship to which it will suggest some solutions based on a diagnostic-cum-prognostic approach. I think, through this diagnostic-cum-prognostic undertaking, this discourse will be able to add up to the already-existing literature, and to the dialogue on how the two halves can synchronise and tweak their relationship in order to bear fruits and bring meaningful justice to both sides. It does not make sense, chiefly for the victims, to stay side and look while they are suffering simply because some of the people on the former do not want to see and do justice for all. Importantly, for the latter, justice is not a matter of begging or pleading for it, but instead, it is about facing the former and seek justice based on equitable and equal footings of the relationship between the two.

Furthermore, the chapter briefly and diagnostically, earmarks the areas in which the Global North superimposes its will on the Global South through neoliberal exploitation, exclusion and imposition (Coleman 2007). As well, the discourse touches on the weakness of the latter in dealing with the former. Much evidence will be adduced from academic literature and experiential realities to show how systemic flaws in both sides have contributed immensely; and thus, perpetually sustained the exploitation of the latter by the former. Through this systemic manipulations and collective thievery, the North has gained immensely in terms of wealth and status while the South has comparatively lost hugely almost in everything noteworthy. So, too, the effects of this exploitation, if not addressed now, are likely to take a long time to overcome and redress shall the international system remain archaic, biased and parochial. Primarily, leaving the situation as it is will create more breeding grounds for three central themed facets namely conflict, poverty and underdevelopment. What's more, it is this exploitation that created antithetical duality in which one side is significantly affluent as opposed to the absolutely destitute and dejected counterpart. If anything, this is one of the reasons that pose a challenge to academics, activists and politicians in both sides of this divide asking them to do something about it. Denying or ignoring the existence

41

and consequences of such a situation creates a chaotic and uneven world in which harmony, peace and prosperity for all become seemingly impossible.

Poverty and the North-South Relationship

To address and tackle some academic issues competently and judiciously, sometimes, it is empirical to declare one's interests. At a personal level, I must confess from the outset. I have personal as well as academic interests in the topic. Being a victim of the North-South exploitative relationship, my experience and views can add up to see to it that the said relationship is deconstructed and reconstructed for the justice of the latter and the peace of the world at large. I, therefore, must state it loud and clear that the aim of this chapter, apart from being aimed at contributing to the dialogue academically, proposes some solutions to the problems as seen through my own eyes.

Theoretically, one may comfortably argue that many conflicts, and much poverty and underdevelopment the Global South has experienced for a long time have the hallmarks of colonialism, unfair relationship and coexistence as it was perpetrated by the Global North (Tana 1986; Mark 2005; Mearsheimer 2006) for many years unabated.

Using diagnostic-cum-prognostic analysis, it is easy to note and notice that the Global North has more causation to conflict, poverty and underdevelopment in the latter than solutions. Therefore, it becomes easy to detect the problems and thereby prescribe what should be done to do away with such a catch-22 situation the two are in if we face the truth that they need each other so as to survive. Logically, the wealth that the North enjoys and takes pride in has its roots from the South. Therefore, prescribing the former to redress the latter becomes one of the solutions. For, due to the hegemonic nature of this relationship, the Global North uses its market-oriented neoliberal and scheming policies to control and intervene in commerce, conflict and development in the latter. However exploitative they are, the North regards its interventionist strategies as a panacea while in actual fact they are but a henbane that begs the South to be a misanthrope as far as the former is concerned.

Additionally, after either suffocating and ignoring or side-lining the Global South, the Global North created a paternalistic and clientele system in which the South is at the receiving end while the North is in the position of dictating everything as far as this fatal and toxic relationship is concerned. Agonizingly though, this imbalanced and exploitative relationship has existed for a long time leading to a great loss for the South resulting from the great rip off by the North that has made a killing.

Tjposvold (2006) argues that "conflict is thought to arise from opposing interests involving scarce resources and goal divergence and frustration" (p. 88) in whatever conflicants lay a claim on. In this conflict, the scarce is not about resources but justice. When it comes to poverty, Halsey (cited in Mack and Lansley 1985: 49 as cited in Walker 1987) defines poverty as "being poor based on relation with people as it is socially or cultural conceptualised" (p. 220). Those in the South know too well what poverty means either based on their experiences or definitions from the former. Again, always poverty is defined or measured based on material things while the truth is that poverty transcends material and immaterial things. This is why it is difficult to have a single internationally agreed upon definition of poverty. This is because of the relativity of poverty and the lenses one used to measure or define it. Despite lacking a water-tight definition, this chapter concurs with Robb (2000 cited in Akindola 2009) who defines poverty denoting it to, *inter alia*, imply "vulnerability, physical and social isolation, insecurity, lack of self-respect, lack of access to information, distrust of state institutions and powerlessness can be as important to the poor as low income" (p. 123). Therefore, defining poverty to only revolve around material things makes the concept narrow and materialistic so much that it is likely to exclude other important elements such as the moral wellbeing of those facing poverty.

Essentially, poverty is currently defined by the Global North scholarship as revolving around economic rationale as opposed to natural rationale. One wonders how a person who owns a piece of land in rural Africa can be categorised as impoverished simply because he or she is not a consumer of industrial products and thereby contribute to the existence of capitalism. Some count calories intake and other things without underscoring the fact that the criteria used in measuring such intake was not agreed upon globally. Toye (2007) observes that "the definition of poverty heavily revolves around consumption (or income) so as to ignore both the productive assets of the poor and a range of communal and social resources that the poor use to supplement their consumption" (p. 46).

As for underdevelopment, it is also measured by using only capitalistic and neoliberal yardsticks. Wealth is quantified but not *qualified*. Lall (1975) simply defines it noting that it "equals dependence" (p. 805) based on capitalistic benchmark of income. I would argue that there is no way one can define underdevelopment without considering systemic inequality or manmade inequality resulting from ills such as slavery, colonialism and now neoliberalism embedded in globalism. Again, as it is on poverty, the definition of underdevelopment seems to be constricted and deceptive. For, if we consider underdevelopment to equal dependence, the West is likely to be underdeveloped due to the fact that it heavily depends on Africa for many resources – material and human resources. Thus, going by Lall's interpretation of underdevelopment, Africa is more developed than the North due to the fact that it has many precious resources that capitalistic and colonial definition of wealth tends to purposely ignore in order to make Africa look like poor so as to need saviours from the North. Essentially, this is "the development of underdevelopment" (Scott and Marshall 2009: 169) in which the North has made the South to pointlessly believe that nothing can be done in the latter without necessarily getting a supporting hand from the former. No matter how narrow this definition may sound, it basically is ambiguous. It depends on the lenses one uses and the culture one comes from. Dependence in some cultures, especially collectivistic ones, is wealth based on Social Capital Theory that "suggests that social capital, the network of relationships possessed by an individual or a social network and the set of resources embedded within it, strongly influence the extent to which interpersonal knowledge sharing occurs" (Bandura 1989 cited in Chiu, Hsu and Wang 2006: 1873). However, the same is *vice versa* in individualistic culture in which society is not as important as it is for the collectivistic people. Many concepts are comparatively relative all depending on who defines what and why, and who expounds and for what intention[s] for what purpose[s]. Lall underscores this by equating underdevelopment and dependence as it is defined by the North Arguably, one person may be underdeveloped in one thing and developed in another. Let us use Lall's lenses. Based on this definition the North is rich. For, it does not economically depend on the latter based on who begs and donates. However, when it comes to running its economy, the former more heavily depends on the latter than the latter does on it. For, the South has immense resources and the former has a lot of monies to be able to balance the equation shall it decide to do so. The rationale that applies to this discourse is that the relationship between the Global North and the Global South is naturally conflictual, exploitative and unfair due to having different and opposing goals and interests not to mention power undercurrents. The difference from natural conflict trend is that the scarcity is manmade thanks to greed on one side and sheepishness for the other on the other.

In this theoretical analysis of conflict, poverty and underdevelopment, firstly, the relationship between the Global North and the Global South is treated as conflicting, conspiracy and stumbling block due to its nature of causing conflict, exploitation, inequality, insecurity, poverty and underdevelopment to one side namely the South as it produces pride, wealth and security for the other side namely the North You can see this in policies and practices between the duos.

Secondly, the relationship in question has caused a lot of poverty and underdevelopment in the Global South while it as well has produced wealth and development to the Global North. Applying such two dicta and rationales, we think; the matter in question deserves to be treated as so. In other words, conflict, poverty and underdevelopment in this discourse, among others, have a different nature of being the sources of other many conflicts, exploitation and sufferings that have been going on for a long time. Tjposvold (*Ibid*) goes on arguing that conflict can be seen as a subset, and perhaps, not such a critical one, independent of the major issues of coordination, exchange, support, and decision-making. Essentially, the conflict, exploitation and underdevelopment arising from the relationship between the Global North and the Global South have all hallmarks of this statement in that there is a conflict between two geographical and political entities that has resulted in many conflicts between the elites that form governments in many countries and the majority citizens not to mention poverty and underdevelopment resulting thereof too. Likewise, conflictual are the situations the two found themselves in as they are all manmade thanks to North hegemonic nature and latter's mediocre role.

Going back to basic human needs theory, despite the theory being propounded and expounded by Western scholars, the Global North has never practically and equitably applied its rationale when it comes to dealing with the Global South. The neglect of basic human needs in the South has led to many conflicts, poverty and underdevelopment resulting from uneven and unfair distribution of resources of which many are sold to the former and consumed in the latter through an unfair and injustice trade sanctioned by neoliberal policies as they were enacted and reinforced by the North I can argue under the relative deprivation theory that the former has constantly and systematically denied justice to the latter which in itself is a good source of the three evils or incongruities discussed in this corpus. Under the basic human needs theory, all humans have the same basic human needs that need to be fulfilled. Maslow (1943 cited in Wan and Chiou 2006), under the hierarchy of human needs, did a good job by categorising the needs all humans equally need as they revolve around five hierarches namely self-actualisation, esteem, social, security and physiological needs. I argue that due to colonial nature of scholars from the former, the needs so propounded make sense theoretically due to the lack of one important element of making them attainable and enjoyable namely, justice. I would argue that the lack of justice and unfairness are the major elements the world is lacking now so as to lead to chaos and wars which kill many people besides destroying a lot of property. Arguably, if basic human needs do not include justice, it means all expounded and propounded needs will never be achieve or obtained in the latter, especially due to the fact that there is no mechanism that is supposed to be ingrained in the basic human needs theory itself. Therefore, I can boldly maintain that among basic human needs that every human needs is justice. Moreover, this need must be added to the hierarchy of needs. I know many would argue that the lack of justice cannot kill or cause anybody to lose life. It can. Some view it as a moral thing than a physical thing when it comes to enhancing basic human needs. If you look at this in a short term approach, it is true; but if you look at it in a long term approach, the results become different, particularly if we consider millions of people injustices have already claimed all over the world. What makes us ignore this element is the fact that the consequences of the lack of justice comes either slowly or take long time to surface. Staub (1999) argues that when basic human needs are not met, those lacking them are likely to use destructive means to satisfy them (p. 181) be they legal or illegal due to the lack of trust between each other resulting from the difficulty for them to consider each other's needs (Staub 2006: 871). I think this speaks to the lack of justice which results into conflicts in the latter. You can see this in the relationship between the Global North and the Global South in which many protracted conflicts in the latter are massaged and left to thrive as the people suffer as it is currently in the case in the DRC. Due to prevalence of long-time systemic injustices resulting from perpetual exploitation, the latter seems to have many more conflicts than the former. For, injustices in the South have caused poverty and underdevelopment which force people in the South to seek alternative means of survival through destructive means of satisfying their basic human needs they have been relatively deprived for a long time. Once again, this is why criminality such as bad governance, civil wars and corruption become the means for political opportunists to survive.

Although justice is always politicised, it is supposed to be treated seriously just like any other human rights that humans are supposed to practically and equally achieve and enjoy. Due to politicisation of everything, it has been possible and easy for the former to maintain systemic exploitation for a long time without facing any consequences. However, thanks to globalisation, things are now changing. The North that used to be immune of the sufferings the South faces, is now facing immigration crisis after some of the victims of its policies in the latter decided to follow goodies in the former. Elsewhere I consider this movement of the people as an emancipatory if not a balance act for the duos to address their historical relationship built on exploitation and injustices (cf. Mhango 2015). The arrival of unwanted illegal immigrants to the North will change the habit and habitation there so as to start thinking globally, collectively and gregariously instead of looking at conflict, poverty and underdevelopment as the problem of the South. This is why I call illegal immigrants *modern-time missionaries* reciprocating from the latter to the former just like the first colonial missionaries did when they invaded the latter to lay a foundation of the current unfair relationship. There is no way the economies of the countries in the former will remain in great shape while there are intruders coming every day; and they need to be looked after.

The lack of justice can take away basic human needs which can be seen in negative effects resulting from North-South relationship regulated by capitalistic *diktat*, drive and market only. After dominating and excluding the South the market however has been purposely overlooked as a good cause of conflict, exploitation and underdevelopment in the South by the former. One important question we need to ask is: why does the North relatively deprive the latter its basic human needs by exploiting it while it advocates human rights? What type of human rights are these and for whom? The answer is simple that the former wants to fulfil the basic human needs and even secondary human needs for its population by depriving the South the same right and necessity.

Arguably, such an uneven and unfair relationship has fuelled violent conflicts that have always preoccupied the international community so as to forget production and other aspects of life that are missing in the South *vis-à-vis* poverty and underdevelopment. In a word, the conflicts in case and point seem to have been internalised by both sides so as to be seen as a reality under the international system. This is why it has become a norm for the so-called international community to discretionary deal or ignore the conflicts in the latter while the same acts differently when the ball is in the North's court. Such practices and understanding have enabled such conflicts and other problems resulting from them to not be seen and addressed adequately and timely by those claiming to have what it takes to address them.

Another important area in this relationship is power. The former has absolute power over the South which has always been recipient almost in everything. For any relationship to make sense and do justice there must be the balance of power. If anything, as we will see later, power is one of important things the duos need to adequately address in order to enable each other to be heard and treated with decorum. Here what is needed is the power of balance (Torbert 1991) without with the status quo will always prevail at the detriment of the Global South.

Similarly, the gap and disparity between the duos seems to be accepted as a natural setting-cum-thing while it actually is but a dubiously created-and-nurtured one. Much effort is put on trying to resolve violent conflicts by ignoring the North-South unequal relationship which, in essence, is a major cause of conflicts, poverty and underdevelopment in many countries in the Global South. There are some flaws in Global North's exploitative and prescriptive interventions in conflict, development, democracy, policymaking, executing, funding all projects resulting from its exploitative relationship under its illiberal-neoliberal policies-cum-strategies in post-war, poor and underdeveloped countries. The approaches that the former—under the dupery banner of international community—have taken under its *diktat* to conceal and massage the effects are negative ones. So, too, this seems to be overlooked as the major causations of the many problems in the latter. It is sad to note that even academics have fallen in this trap either thinking they are defending their countries or continent or serving what seems to be their sacred duties as they were handed down depending on how they were brought up. The living example is the fact that all organisations in the former that exploit the latter use academics to formulate their exploitative policies.

The Use of Interventionism as an Exploitative strategy

There are many strategies the Global North has always used to exploit the Global South. I will explore some of these strategies and propose how they can be deconstructed in order to bring about change and equality between the parties to this relationship.

Practically, the Global North has been using interventionist approaches as a pretext or a scapegoat from its original intentions motivated by its self-interests, self-serving and self-preservation under neoliberal development and peace initiatives. Under international relations theory, the state is given the task of protecting its interests by all means even if it means to go to war with another state or suppress its people. Practically, states in the North can go to war with the states in the latter without even following international laws or seeking permission from international organs responsible. Hauss (2010) argues that "the stakes of a conflict can be magnified by security dilemma in which the actions of one state to protect its own security actually serve to weaken its opponents" (p. 30). I must make a distinction here. One should not confuse the state to be homogenous. For, the meaning and powers of the state differ from one state to another depending on where the said state is. If the said state is in the North it has a carte blanche to do as pleased shall the enemy be in the South If the said state is in the latter; and it faces the situation that puts its stakes in danger by another state from the South the offended or threatened state needs to seek permit from the international community. If the said state facing the danger is in the North versus the state in the South, the aggrieved state can proceed with taking whatever action[s] it deems fit without necessarily seeking permission from the international community. Refer to how the US acted when it felt (not evidentially proved) that its interests were endangered by Iraq.

From a practical point of view, international laws and justices make sense for the countries in the North due to the fact that one country or all countries in the North can launch a war against any country or countries when their interests are *threatened* or as they deem fit by any country or countries in the South despite the fact that this right or situation cannot be reciprocated shall the situation imply or say vice versa. Hauss *(Ibid)* makes a good point, mainly when we consider what happened to "rogue" states such as Iraq and Libya where the Global North conspired and cooperated with disgruntled local elites who wanted to settle scores in toppling the governments in these two countries in order to safeguard their hidden interests but not the interests of the citizens without being legally being held accountable. Who would *bell the cats* when the adversaries are good-for-nothings? Therefore, we can vividly see that anarchic and deceitful nature of the international relations–especially the one between the North and the latter–and systems as the former created them after World Wars I and II still serve its interests even at the expenses of other countries in the Global South in particular.

In other words, I can argue that the Global North has always depended on its fashion of the anarchic and dupery international system to commit structural violence based on its norms, *diktats* and unchecked and interventionistic strategies all geared against and towards the South. This becomes eminent due to the fact that under current anarchic international system, the Global North conspires with a few elites from the Global South to safeguard interests of the two conspirators of who the beneficiary is the North. Notably though, while the local elites in the South get satisfied with rat-like-baits on the trap, the North takes a lion share of the loots resulting from this conspiracy. And verily, this becomes a very good causation of backwardness (as the former likes to define it), conflict, poverty and underdevelopment in the Global South. What is currently going on in Syria speaks volume whereby two powerful nations Russia and the United States are waging proxy war on the expenses of Syrian people not to mention Afghanistan and Iraq among others. Who is helping the North to address the real cause of such a problem instead of keeping mum for fear of being retributively dealt with?

Under dependency theory, what is going on in the relationship in question is detrimental to the South and an advantage to the North. Caraveli (2016) notes that the "core-periphery "divide underlines the imbalance between the duo which means the latter is the periphery and the core is the former. I can argue that North-South way of dealing with conflict and development is totally antithesis to dependency theory which is an antithesis of modernisation theory that has always a neoliberal drive to exploiting the Global South. Ever since the time the Global North envisaged exploiting countries in the Global South–through colonialism, and thereafter, through neocolonialism–it has installed its stooges to run some countries for

51

its own benefits as opposed to the interests of the citizens of these countries.

Simmel (1950 cited in Petrocelli *et al.*. 2003) argues that Conflict theory is about power dynamics whereby "power of a given social group dictates social order in that powerful groups not only control the lawmakers, but also the law enforcement apparatus of the state" (p. 2). Likewise, the Global North–through using local elites–does not only control the lawmakers and apparatuses of the state but also the entire state, chiefly in some countries–if not all–in the Global South. By controlling the state, the North gets an upper hand in proxy-decision making in the South By affecting policymaking in the South the North swiftly exacerbates poverty and underdevelopment as it acquires much wealth from the losing South What corrupt local elites do is put their countries to liberal open free market for the North to exploit as pleased provided that they cling to power on the one hand, and safeguard the interests of the North. By so doing, they fully participate in exploiting their countries so as to usher in more poverty and underdevelopment which result into chaos and conflicts in many countries.

Fundamentally, even if we address power dynamics in the relationship between the Global North and the Global South as it is regulated by, and based on what Joana Macy cited in Burrowes (1996) defines as "power over" which–she says "reflects a bias that is characteristic of Western social science" (p. 83) – we can still detect defects and anomalies due to the fact that the North has power over the South and the latter is under the former. The power dynamics in the relationship between the two lacks equity, equality and mutual reciprocity which are fundamental and important in any meaningful relationship which is *sine qua non* in any relationship (Simmel 1950 cited in Komter 2007: 103). Such a situation maintains, and sometimes, causes poverty. On its side, poverty hampers development and fuels conflict as Hauss (2010) notes–as realists put it–that conflict is an inevitable feature of international political life because the international system is anarchic (p. 30), mainly when it comes to the relationship between the Global North and the Global South. On this, the Democratic Republic of Congo (DRC) provides an ideal example in which the Central Intelligence Agency (CIA)–

under the instructions of the White House in conjunction with Belgium–assassinated DRC's first Prime Minister, Patrice Lumumba after disagreeing with the extension of colonialism soon after the DRC gained her political independence. Due to anarchical nature of the international system under which the Global North dictates everything, neither the CIA nor Belgium has ever been forced to redress the DRC or even to face criminal charges. How would the international community have reacted if this crime is treated vice versa? Gerald and Kuklik (2015) note that "after Lumumba's death the United States had propped up Mobutu who ruled Congo for thirty years" (p. 3). Mobutu's corrupt rule ruined and plundered the country for such a long time without being brought to book. Ironically, despite obvious and viable greed that Mobutu displayed, the former supported this albatross. Again, was the former insane or stupid? The answer is clear that when it comes to making quick bucks, the former has no rule except gains. Mac Ginty and Williams (*Ibid*) claim that Mobutu and Ferdinand Marco, former Philippines president, robbed their countries of approximately $50 billion (p. 36). Ironically, despite preaching rule of law and accountability, the International community–which one can argue means the Global North under its neoliberalism–did not have any mechanisms or willingness to hold the culprit accountable as means of resolving the conflict that left millions of people in the two countries poor. How would the international community hold such corrupt dictators accountable while the same Global North was the chief beneficiary of their theft? Moore (2001) notes that "underdeveloped states are too independent of their own citizens ... strong external financial and/or military support for state elites, even when they are in conflict with many of their own citizens; the heavy dependence of states on 'unearned income" (p. 1). How would the North turn the tables against ones of their own? This shows how relationship between the Global North and the Global South is one of major causes of violent conflicts, poverty and underdevelopment in some countries in the Global South. So, too, such unfair relationship has maintained corruption in the latter. This can be mirrored on how many dictators in the South still enjoy the backing of the North provided they vend their people and their resources as we will indicate later.

Another example on how the former has undermined and underdeveloped the latter can be found in Angola's example in which former terrorist group the National Union for the Total Independence of Angola (UNITA) waged a protracted war simply because it openly enjoyed support from the former simply because such a conflict enabled the former to get cheap supply of resources from the latter. Therefore, there was no any international pressure that was timely and equitably exerted on the UNITA to resolve to this conflict during the entire period of the Cold War. How would the international community pressurise the UNITA while the Global North was on the receiving end of the resources looted from Angola chiefly being blood diamond it needed? Sogge (2007) argues that "Angola's long-standing subjugation to a predatory world system" (p. 2) is the cause of such a long war that left the country devastated with destruction. Sogge (Ibid.) goes on showing how the Global North exploits the Global North by saying that in Angola:

Donor agencies have, with few exceptions, been largely irrelevant to citizen empowerment in the post-war period. Most Angolans have relied on their own resources. They are, moreover, captive to configurations of political power built on the basis not of donor power but of international flows of capital, whose deregulated status is protected by Western governments (p. 13).

The help, if any, that the former offered to the warring factions in Angola was nothing but exorbitantly selling them guns so that they can finish each while the former made away with cheap resources. To the former, the blood and resources lost in this war meant nothing but business as usual. Human rights, principally the right to life did not matter then for the Angolan people. And this was not the first of the last time for the former to ignore human rights. Refer to genocides in the DRC under king Leopold, Namibia under German colonial rule and lately in Rwanda. Arguably, the former has always discriminated against the latter almost in everything. This is why it has been possible for it to commit such crimes against humanity without being held accountable for its commission or omissions. Therefore, one of the solutions to the problems in the latter is to stop selling or supplying weapons to the former.

What happened in Angola is a typical replica of what happened in many countries in the Global South, chiefly those facing conflicts geared by the struggle for controlling resources. Resources have become another focal point for academics and practitioners when it comes to predicting where the conflict is likely to happen. It is easy to tell where conflicts will erupt. Wherever there are resources that the former needs, conflicts will surely ensue there. Due to the international conspiracy and discrimination against them, the majority of Angolans are disgruntled (Guimarães 2016). Such a situation is not good for a country to be in. For, it helps opportunistic politicians to capitalise on it; and thereby start civil wars aimed at controlling resources they end up supplying the former. Ironically, the current international superstructure seems to reinforce and support an unequitable relationship between the Global North and the Global South. I would argue that when Peace and Conflict academics do some predictions of conflict, one of the major components to examine should be the abundance of resources in certain countries and the types of the governments such countries have in power. Looking at many countries that have already faced violent conflict such as Angola, the Central African Republic (CAR), the DRC, Ivory Coast, Liberia, Sierra Leone and Nigeria, we find that resources are the major cause of conflict simply because they former needs them; and it supplies weapons to greedy local elites to do its dirty laundry. However, there are countries without resources such as Burundi and Rwanda which also can experience conflict due to the scarcity of resources. Also, such scarcity based on the population explosion can well act as a good predictor for future conflict. It is clear that the relationship between the Global North and the Global South is regulated by who supplies what and who gets what. This is why it has always remained to be clientele and nobody tries to deconstruct and reconstruct it.

So, too, countries without resources supported by the former can cause conflict in their neighbours who happen to have resources. What transpired in the DRC in 1998 and 2000 when Burundi, Rwanda and Uganda invaded it provides an ideal example. Southerland (2011) maintains that the U.S. Geological Survey records of tantalum imports reflect the extra-budgetary system implemented by the Rwandans and the Ugandans for exporting Congolese coltan. From 1998 to 2000, tantalum imports to the United States were specifically listed as originating from the Democratic Republic of Congo. Yet, at that time Rwanda and Uganda controlled the Congolese coltan mines, and the Congolese Ministry of Mines reported zero production of tantalum both in 1998 and 1999, and only 550 metric tons of tantalum in 2000 (p. 15). Ironically, Rwanda and Uganda do not have even single mine for tantalum. I think, to avoid future conflicts, and tackle poverty and underdevelopment, the international community must put a stop on such double standard applied by some industrialised countries. Without doing so, many conflicts will erupt and drag on provided that the wars emanating from such conflicts may take a long time and consume a lot of resources provided that such war are "self-financing" as Kagame cited in Sutherland (*Ibid.*) discloses (p. 15). Such practices and conspiracies need to be stopped if the duo aims at deconstructing their relationship for the benefit of the world peace.

Despite such the double standard that the Global North has been applying over the Global South, many African countries–for example, up until now–still trust the Global North and the International Organisations such as the United Nations (UN) the International Monetary Fund (IFM) and the World Bank (WB) among others the former uses to safeguard its interests as opposed to the interest of the latter. Gerald and Kuklik (2015) goes on arguing that, "the Africans had little knowledge of the UN, did not comprehend its American origins, and had no sense of the dismal weakness of the organisation when it tried to act without the say-so of the powerful" (p. 30). This rationale is in tandem with the aim of creating the North-South polarity of the colonizing and colonised world (Pieterse 2015) whose legacies have gone on in the relationship between the former and the latter. Countries in the North do not respect the mandate of such organisation unless only at the time they stand for their interests but not when they stand in their way. Due to ignoring such malpractices and embezzlement, the Global South–under its neoliberalism policies, apart from showing double standards–shows great weakness and the lack of transparency in process. Again, despite such flaws, still the Global North gets away with murder. Why? Battersby and Siracusa (2009) respond noting that actually, colonial regimes created incongruous colonial states designed to service the economic needs of the colonisers and not the communal or political interests of the colonized (p. 18). Therefore, divisive politics and systems that the former introduced to the latter are still going on up until now. Those who subscribed to such manipulations were able to stay in power even if their people did not want them.

Due to such divisive tactics, many corrupt regimes in the Global South that opened their economies for the Global North's exploitation survived in power for a long time. This is why the so-called free market succeeded in the latter. The Global North made sure that corrupt rulers stay in power so as to protect its interests. However, all this was done on the expense of the citizens of those countries. What such rulers had to do is open their markets ready for the former's exploitation. For neoliberalism opening the market that benefits Western economies surpasses democracy and human rights. Essentially, the notion and lulls of the neoliberalism based on market and personal liberty as solutions to world's problems is wrong. Mac Ginty and Williams (*Ibid.*) note the thinking of the West is that "free markets made free men who would not be foolish to be involved in war" (p. 20). They maintain that free market prevents violent conflict which is they argue is an antithesis of market-induced inequality and causation, escalation and maintenance of violent conflict whereby war was obviously the greatest world's industry in the ascendancy of neoliberalism. It is ironic to note that the former advocated free market without advocating free trade. And all this can be blamed on Global North's predisposition of talking the talk without walking the walk, the move that ignores other mechanisms of dealing with conflicts. I think the latter needs "trade not aid" (Lundsgaarde 2007: 159) trade free of exploitation, and holier than thou mentality that has existed for a long time since the inception of exploitative-neoliberal policies. When it comes to what should be done, Beyerlin (2006) observes that "the industrialized states to take action towards reaching the following seven objectives: opening their markets for the products of developing countries; acknowledging the developing countries' full and permanent sovereignty over natural resources;

increasing the official development aid of industrialized states" (p. 262). Additionally, I argue that the industrialised countries in the Global North must equivocally admit the wrongs they committed to the Global South. Admission will enable the countries in the former to take responsibility for the wrongs they committed to the latter; and thereby devise the mechanism of redressing the former instead of giving it discretionary handouts in the form of aid. This is the way forward given that aid has not solved the problem. Instead, aid has exacerbated the problem due to many reasons such as conditions attached to aid, corruption involving local elites in the South and their counterparts in the North.

Conclusion

In a nutshell, it is important to conceive and entertain the idea of enacting international laws or instruments that deal with all wrongs the former committed and benefitted from through exploiting the former. Why was it possible, for example, to enact international laws to redress the victims of the holocaust while it has become impossible to redress the latter? Isn't this conspiracy and international discrimination against the South Essentially, the twosomes need to deconstruct the laws and regulations by enacting favourable and new laws and regulations governing their relationship in order to do justice for both sides shall they aspire to bring equity and parity in their relationship. This can act as a tool for the emancipation of the Global South while acts as tool for doing justice for the North By enacting laws that force violators of others to clean up their deeds, the two halves will be inculcating global rule of law that binds both equally. There is no way the North can teach the South rule of law without upholding it in their relationship. This is hypocritical and a double standard by all standards.

Abbreviations

UN–United Nations
CAR–Central African Republic
DRC–Democratic Republic of Congo

CIA–Central Intelligence Agency
IMF–International Monetary Fund
WB–World Bank
US–United States
UNITA–União Nacional para a Independência Total de Angola

References

Akindola, Rufus B. 2009. Towards a definition of poverty: poor people's perspectives and implications for poverty reduction, *Journal of Developing Societies* 25(2): 121-150.

Battersby, Paul, and Joseph M. Siracusa. 2009. *Globalization and human security*, Rowman & Littlefield Publishers.

Beyerlin, Ulrich. 2006. Bridging the North-South Divide in International Environmental Law, *Heidelberg Journal of International Law 66* (2006): 259-296.

Burrowes, Robert J. 1996. *The Strategy of Nonviolent Defence: A Gandhian Approach*, SUNY Press.

Caraveli, Helen. 2016. Global Imbalances and EU Core-Periphery Division: Institutional Framework and Theoretical Interpretations, *World Review of Political Economy* 7(1): 29-55.

Chiu, Chao-Min, Meng-Hsiang Hsu, and Eric T. G. Wang. 2006. Understanding knowledge sharing in virtual communities: An integration of social capital and social cognitive theories, *Decision support systems* 42(3): 1872-1888.

Coleman, Lara. 2007. The gendered violence of development: Imaginative geographies of exclusion in the imposition of neo-liberal capitalism. *The British Journal of Politics and International Relations* 9(2): 204-219.

Gerard, Emmanuel, and Bruce Kuklick. 2015. *Death in the Congo: Murdering Patrice Lumumba*. Harvard University Press.

Griggs, Richard. 1996. The Great Lakes Conflict and Spatial Designs for Peace: A Neorealist Analysis. *Boundary and Security Bulletin*: 68-78.

Guimarães, Fernando Andresen. 2016. *The Origins of the Angolan Civil War: Foreign Intervention and Domestic Political Conflict, 1961-76.* Springer.

Hauss, Charles. 2010. *International Conflict Resolution* 2nd Ed. A&C Black, 2010.

Jackson, Stephen. 2006. Sons of Which Soil? The Language and Politics of Autochthony in eastern DR Congo, *African Studies Review 49* (02): 95-124.

Jobson, Ryan. 2010. Afrocentricity and Commodity Fetishism: Cultural Objectification and the "New" African Diaspora, *Penn McNair Research Journal* 2(1): 3.

Komter, Aafke. 2007. Gifts and social relations the mechanisms of reciprocity, *International Sociology* 22(1): 93-107.

Lall, Sanjaya. 1975. Is 'Dependence' a Useful Concept in Analysing Underdevelopment? *World Development 3* (11-12): 799-810.

Lundsgaarde, Erik, Christian Breunig, and Aseem Prakash. 2007. Trade versus aid: donor generosity in an era of globalization, *Policy sciences* 40(2): 157-179.

Mac Ginty, Roger, and Andrew Williams. 2009. *Conflict and Development,* Routledge.

Mark, Clyde R. 2005. *Israel: US Foreign Assistance.* Library of Congress Washington, D.C, Congressional Research Service.

Mearsheimer, John J., and Stephen M. (2006). Walt. The Israel Lobby and US Foreign Policy, *Middle East Policy 13*(3): 29-87.

Mhango, Nkwazi Nkuzi. 2015. *Africa Reunite or Perish,* Langaa RPCIG, Cameroon.

Moore, Mick. 2001. Political Underdevelopment: What Causes 'Bad Governance', *Public Management Review 3*(3): 385-418.

Oliveira, Frederico César B. 2011. O projeto das Antropologias Mundiais diante dos desafios da alteridade no mundo globalizado, *Revista Anthropológicas-ISSN: 2525-5223* 18.1.

Petrocelli, Matthew, Alex R. Piquero, and Michael R. Smith. 2003. Conflict Theory and Racial Profiling: An Empirical Analysis of Police Traffic Stop Data, *Journal of Criminal Justice 31*(1): 1-11.

Pieterse, Jan Nederveen. 2015. *Globalization and culture: Global mélange,* Rowman & Littlefield.

Scott, John, and Gordon Marshall. 2009. *A dictionary of sociology*, Oxford University Press, USA.

Sogge, David. 2007. *Angola: Empowerment of the Few*. Fundación para las Relaciones Internacionales y el Diálogo Exterior (FRIDE).

Staub, Ervin. "The Roots of evil: Social Conditions, Culture, Personality, and Basic Human Needs," *Personality and Social Psychology Review 3*(3): 179-192.

Staub, Ervin. 2006. Reconciliation after genocide, mass killing, or intractable conflict: Understanding the roots of violence, psychological recovery, and steps toward a general theory. *Political Psychology* 27(6): 867-894.

Sutherland, Ewan. 2011. *Coltan, the Congo and your cell phone.*

Tana, Fabio. 1999. US military Aid to Israel, *The International Spectator 21*(1): 3-11.

Tjosvold, Dean. 2006. Defining Conflict and Making Choices about Its Management: Lighting the Dark Side of Organizational Life, *International Journal of Conflict Management 17*(2): 87-95.

Torbert, William R. 1999. *The power of balance: Transforming self, society, and scientific inquiry*, Newbery Park: Sage.

Toye, John. 2007. Poverty reduction, *Development in practice* 17(4-5): 505-510.

Vlassenroot, Koen, and Chris Huggins. 2005. Land, Migration and Conflict in Eastern DRC. *From the Ground Up: Land Rights, Conflict and Peace in Sub-Saharan Africa*, pp. 115-195.

Walker, Robert. 1987. Consensual Approaches to the Definition of Poverty: Towards an Alternative Methodology, *Journal of Social Policy 16*(02): 213-226.

Chapter 4

Breaking the Cycle of Poverty: Rethinking Africa's Socio-political Economy

Aluko Opeyemi I. & Munyaradzi Mawere

Introduction

Poverty flows in a vicious cycle! The wind of poverty blows like a cyclone with a heavy tide of hardship, melancholy, acrimony and socio-political anarchism sweeping violently along its pathway. This tide makes the pathway difficult to travel, overcome and manoeuvre. Several policy actors and researchers have made attempts to proffer determined solutions to this tenuous situation which has however defy most implementations and workability. No doubt, many countries of the world especially in the developing countries of Asia, Africa and Latin America, have been entangled and some mangled by the tide of poverty while an others have been swept away into an unknown destination or better still a "dustbin of oblivion" (Mawere 2014). This, as well, has rendered such countries the tug "third world nations" among the comity of state that is languishing in hopelessness, helplessness, 'moneylessness', powerlessness and above all abject poverty.

Any country that has the manifestation of such tide will no doubt witness slaggish economic growth and high dependency on other countries for basic amenities of life for livelihood and survival. The rate of social instability and mental unsteadiness in such countries is normally high resulting in socially unacceptable upbringing, indecent family lives, rampart community violence and high rate of juvenile delinquencies (Sen 1981; Morduch and Siwicki 2017). On the other hand, the extent of puppet political structures masquerading as humanitarian organisations under the manoeuvring operations of the donor countries will be glaring, political mishaps and economic dwarfism ladled with poor gross domestic product (GDP), while very low income per capita and mundane technological and infrastructural facilities are experienced. Africa is within the circumference of the heavy tide of poverty that has gripped many communities of the world.

The continent of Africa has come of age as far as poverty and underdevelopment are concerned. There is a need to understand the nature of the poverty in the continent, the causes, the symptoms and how to come out of the poverty quandary. The nature of poverty in Africa is operating on the principle of totalitarianism in so far as it haunts almost the entire African populace. It will gradually and over a period of time, overturns all the sectors of the continent's development wheels to a less productive type. This wind has blown harshly across the social, cultural, political and economic sectors of the continent. The deleterious net impacts of poverty are evident in the social structure of the continent. There are very large proportions of the lower class development strata, a relatively or somewhat large middle class of the development strata, and a small proportion of the upper class of the development strata. Invariably, the income distribution is lopsided to the rich minority. The poor working class are getting poorer while the rich few are getting richer.

The elite groups are being circulated in the political structure using patron client principles, while the vast majority are subjected to social hardship, dumpsite survival strategy and subjection to the uncertainty and tantalising political propaganda of better tomorrow. This chapter examines three cycles of poverty, its components, manifestations and regeneration strategies in Africa. The cycle of poverty here examined include the Social Cycle of Poverty (SCP), Political Cycle of Poverty (PCP) and the Economic Cycle of Poverty (ECP). Further, the chapter explores strategies that can be used to break the cycle of poverty in Africa and other developing countries across the globe.

The research methodology adopted in this chapter is largely qualitative but utilises data from Africa Development Bank (AFDB) Socio Economic Database, 2000-2016 and Afrobarometer socio-political and economic database round six data. A descriptive overview analysis is adopted to present and express the poverty and development status in Africa and its implication on the continent.

The findings explain why poverty still persists in the African continent and the challenge it posses to Africa.

The chapter argues that poverty is evil and atrocious as it renders human life inhumane, solitary, nasty and short-lived. It further argues that poverty will remain an endemic disease in the African continent until the cycle, the cycler and the cyclone are carefully dealt with.

The elusiveness of poverty

Poverty like many concepts in the social sciences did not avail us of a single perspective of conceptualisation. There are several interpretations of the concept as there are scholar. In their interpretation, both the scholars and the different schools of thought are highly influenced by the exact definition of the concept that each of them utilises. This is so owing to the multi-dimensionalism and variability associated with poverty. The difficulty in pinning down with precision is aptly explained by Mawere (2017: 96) when he argues "the difficulty in unpacking what poverty entails mainly emanates from the fact that although many people are said to be living in or under poverty conditions, what to one is poverty is in fact not poverty to another". The "understanding of poverty thus, largely depends on who defines it and how" (Ibid). Adam Smith, for example, interpreted poverty as the inability to purchase necessities required by nature or custom (Smith 1776; Anyawu and Erhjakpor 2010). This view, is however too generalised to encapsulate the entire sphere which poverty covers because nobody is self-sufficient by nature and might not be able to get a basic necessity at a particular time though s/he has the wherewithal.

As one of the authors of this chapter notes "the variation of definitions of poverty could be explained in terms of history" (Mawere 2017: 98). He (Ibid) furthers to note that "Rowntree's 1901 study marks the first step towards the development of a poverty standard for individual families, based on estimates of nutritional and other such requirements he deemed necessary for a 'steady' life". Thus, perhaps noting limitations of Smith's interpretation, Sen (1983) has come to understand poverty as the absolute deprivation in terms of a person's capabilities to get a basic necessity of life which emanates from relative deprivation in terms of commodities, incomes and resources. Sen is one of the most important contributors to poverty and development discourse. His view implies that relative deprivation is a stage of poverty that if undisturbed matures to absolute deprivation, which is now full-blown poverty. This assertion corroborates what Townsend (1979) notes of poverty when he notes that poverty starts as a pure relative measures of deprivation or lack of the resources necessary to permit participation in the activities, customs and diets commonly approved by community.

Other contemporary scholars view poverty as a relative phenomenon where someone's resources are so seriously below those commanded by the average individual or family that they are, in effect, excluded from ordinary living patterns, customs and activities (Seymour 2009). This view strongly emphasises social exclusion as a fundamental yardstick for relative poverty. Further, the view stresses that resources which are seriously below average are a symptom of relative poverty. However, there may be situations of below average livelihood which is better than some other categories of the two poverty situations, yet they are below the third category which may still be within the below average category. One would wonder if the three categories can be classified as living in poverty. The answer to this question is somehow tricky, but what needs to be born in mind is the fact that not all those in the three categories are in the 'serious' below average poverty as Seymour would claim.

The World Bank notes that a common method used to measure poverty is based on incomes or consumption levels. Following this characterisation, a person is considered poor if his or her consumption or income level falls below some minimum level considered as necessary to meet basic needs. When estimating poverty worldwide, the same benchmark poverty line has to be used, and expressed in a common unit across countries. For the purpose of global aggregation and comparison and due to depreciation of the US$, the World Bank uses reference lines set between $1.25 and $2 per day. This minimum level is usually called the poverty datum line (Ravallion and Chen 2008; Mawere 2017). However, this measurement might not be pronounced in the developed countries like United Kingdom (UK) and United State of America (USA), among others, as compared to the developing countries of Africa and the world. Besides, we argue that this characterisation of poverty is narrow and exclusionary as it fails to account for other forms of wealth – material wealth – which is not purely monetary. There are certain contexts, for example those of many African rural areas, where people do not rely much on money for their daily sustenance as they have almost all the basics they need for their daily living. Such people cannot be considered as poor for the sole reason that they do not use $1. 25 per day even though the material things they use on daily basis may be far much above the stated amount if converted to monetary value.

The European Commission's view of poverty seem to be equally narrow as to emphasise more on money in its characterises poverty, thus: People are said to be living in poverty if their income and resources are so inadequate as to preclude them from having a standard of living considered acceptable in the society in which they live. Because of their poverty they may experience multiple disadvantaged through unemployment, low income, poor housing, inadequate health care and barriers to lifelong learning, culture, sport and recreation (*Joint report by the Commission and the Council on social inclusion*, 2004).

This perception of poverty might entirely be a Eurocentric view of poverty but a more comprehensive and balance view of poverty is the United Nations' (1995) perception published in the Copenhagen Declaration of the United Nations of 1995. It attempts to encompass both the developing and developed country contexts in its characterisation of poverty. At the summit it was agreed that poverty should be understood to include:

> Lack of income and productive resources to ensure sustainable livelihoods; hunger and malnutrition; ill health; limited or lack of access to education and other basic services; increased morbidity and mortality from illness; homelessness and inadequate housing; unsafe environments and social discrimination and exclusion, it is also characterized by lack of participation in decision making and in civil, social and cultural life (United Nations 1995).

The Declaration also highlights how poverty occurs in all countries not only in the so-called developing countries, most of which who do not rely much on monetary economy. In The Declaration further notes that in many developing countries it occurs as mass poverty, in developed countries, it occurs as pockets of poverty amid wealth, loss of livelihoods as a result of economic recession, sudden poverty as a result of disaster or conflict, the poverty of low-wage workers, and the utter destitution of people who fall outside family support systems, social institutions and safety nets. Poverty, thus, is multi-dimensional and should be characterised in view of context, especially owing to the fact that "the conceptualisation of poverty in the African framework, for example, may differ from the conceptualisation of the same in the European framework. So is how poverty is measured in both the African and the European frameworks" (Mawere 2017: 96). What remains characteristically loud and clear of poverty in all contexts is lack of some sort, which means there is no way we can talk of poverty without talking of lacking. Mawere (Ibid: 98), thus, is apt to say "poverty is the partial or complete lack of access to all – resource capitals – that makes human life worth living". Yet the Eurocentric characterisation of poverty explained above seem to have influenced how poverty should be conceptualised and what has come to be understood as the theory of poverty. We elaborate on the theory in the section below.

The theory of poverty

The notion of theory of poverty has been discussed under various platforms. These include the Marxian point of view, the moral point of view, and the liberal point of view, among many others. The view that no one should suffer from want or deprivation when others have the means to prevent it, or that a community should take care of its own is a moral view. This notion only assumes that poverty is inevitable and requires ongoing remediation, compassion, and charity. It also recognises the claim that those in need –the poor, the sick, the very old, and the very young –have a moral claim against the larger community. The moral duty to the

68

poor is an obligation of one individual to another, rather than an obligation of the state to an individual. The obligation is therefore, voluntary and moral. If the donor declines to give, there is no legal claim or entitlement besides moral claim. Moral arguments appeal to the would-be benefactor because they are not coercive. They seek to evoke compassion and empathy.

Taking it from an economic point of view, Townsend (1979) opines that poverty is about much more than simply a lack of economic resources. For him, poverty should be understood as 'the experience of lacking resources to obtain the types of diet, participate in the activities and have the living conditions and amenities which are customary, or are at least widely encouraged and approved in societies to which they belong'. Townsend who hails from the nineteenth century behavioural school perspectives, thus remarks that poverty was necessary because otherwise the labourers would not be motivated to work. Poverty Policy was therefore interwoven with notions of laissez-faire.

From the sociological point of view, Welshman (2013) identified six variations in the terminology used to describe disadvantaged groups: the social residuum of the 1880s; the social problem group of the 1930s; the problem family of the 1950s; the culture of poverty thesis of the 1960s; the cycle of deprivation thesis of 1970s; and the underclass debates of the 1980s. During the late 1990s the less stigmatising and pejorative term 'social exclusion' took centre stage as a way of talking about those individuals (or groups) experiencing multiple disadvantages. Furthermore, the notion gets better with the views of factors beyond individual behaviour analysis viewed as important in understanding poverty, to the point that by the early 2000s the idea had become common part of the political debates in Europe and especially in Britain (Burchardt, Le Grand and Piachaud 2002; Aluko 2017).

In his theory of the culture of poverty, Lewis (1961) has also noted that being in state of poverty tends to create a way of living which becomes a culture of its own. This culture is mostly learned, shared and socially or generationally transmitted as a form of behaviour of the concerned social group. People living in this culture perceived themselves as a separate part of society. This is evident in their utilisation of the basic amenities for the elites. Lewis furthered to note that the urban poor make little use of institutions such as banks, hospitals, museums and art galleries. In this way, Lewis argues that the poor segregate themselves from mainstream society. This gives rise to two distinct schools of thought on poverty. The first school perceived poverty as an individual phenomenon – belonging to an individual – while the second school perceived poverty as a structural phenomenon – belonging to a group.

The first school of thought notes that poverty is an individual causative phenomenon (Ryan 2014; Bruenig 2014). It opines that people are in poverty because they are lazy, uneducated, ignorant, or otherwise inferior in some way. Thus, for this school, poverty is a self-inflicted hardship by an individual on himself resulting from laziness, uneducatedness, ignorance or inferiority of an individual. If this theory were true, it would follow that impoverished people are basically the same people every year. Their poverty will become perpetual and forever in their generation without any improvement in their lives. By implication, the government and other international communities have no apportioned blame as to who caused the state of the poverty. The whole duty of escaping poverty resides on the individual even though the government and the international community have provided some palliative measures against the individual poverty. The individual therefore needs to break-off from being lazy, uneducated, ignorant, or otherwise inferior to the rich in the community in order to shake-off the chains of poverty. The second school of thought notes that poverty is a structural phenomenon (Ryan 2014; Bruenig 2014). This school argues that people are in poverty because they find themselves in holes in the economic system that delivers them inadequate income (Ryan 2014). However, because individual lives are dynamic, people do not remain in those holes forever. One year they are in a low-income hole, but the next year they have found a job or gotten a promotion and become rich or not poor anymore. The poverty holes that they were in the previous year do not go away. Others inevitably find themselves in those same holes because they are caused by a persistent defect in the economic structure of the society. Therefore, the structural school of poverty believe that impoverished people are not the same people every year. Besides, the school believes that the only way to reduce poverty is to alter the economic structure so as to reduce the number of low-income holes in the society.

Cycles of poverty in Africa

Poverty moves and trans-generate and regenerate in a cycle. The cycles have their catalyst that activates the poverty reaction and lifespan in a country, group or individual. In Africa, there are many reasons that make some countries in the continent to be poor while others are somewhat rich. Many of such factors are more of domestic policies – institutional – which the foreign policies externalities capitalises upon so as to override the domestic economies and cyclically inflict poverty. There may be many of such possible cycles but there are three most prominent cycles which inflict and regenerates poverty if the catalysts are activated in any country's economy. The three cycles of poverty have their components, manifestations and regeneration strategies in Africa. The cycle of poverty include the Social Cycle of Poverty (SCP), Political Cycle of Poverty (PCP) and the Economic Cycle of Poverty (ECP). The strategies to break the cycle of poverty in Africa and other developing countries are as well analysed and articulated.

The Social Cycle of Poverty (SCP) operates in a culture milieu of life patterned around neglect of basic work ethics and regular duties so as to boost personal and national income generated. The major component of social cycle of poverty is the Culture of Excessive Public Holidays (CEPH). The Culture of Excessive Public Holidays in the Social Cycle of Poverty is the catalyst that promotes absconding and neglect of duties by public and private workers. The CEPH that leads to poverty prominent in Africa and other developing countries manifests in six cyclical ways. The CEPH leads to Reduce Work Input (RWI). The time taken off the duty post is lost in the productive sector, if the time off is excessive then the work input will be far lesser than expected. The Reduce Work Input (RWI) therefore leads to Reduce Work Output (RWO). As every working system always have inputs and outputs, if the input is reduced, the output will be reduced and if the input multiplies, the output also multiplies. Once there is a reduction in work outputs, there will be a definite decline in the net growth; this implies a Reduce Net Growth (RNG).

Reduce Net Growth (RNG) in the economy is a factor of poor input and non-commiserating outputs over a period of time. Net growth covers round all the sectors of the economy such that development will be retarded and ascetic. At this point of development, there will be glaring increase in the poverty rate and high rate of dependency on externalities (outside donors) for aids and bailouts. In essence, Reduce Net Growth (RNG) in the economy results in Increase Poverty and Dependency (IPD). At this point of the social poverty cycle, there is need for drastic government policy and interventions so as to correct the anomalies. If the intervention(s) results in poor policy or no policy to reduce the CEPH, then the cycle regenerates and poverty continues taking its toll. The Poor/No policy to Reduce CEPH (PNP-CEPH) is the regenerating stage in the SCP. This simply continues the old status quo of culture of excessive public holiday as is diagrammatically explained below.

The Political Cycle of Poverty (PCP) is a political institutional cycle that determines policies, growth and development. The PCP indicates how poverty is permitted and accommodated in a political institution. PCP has seven components and it starts with Government Policy (GP). These include regulatory, directional and other types of policies. The policy statement will indicate the commitment of the government to solve a societal problem. The level and the political will to implement such policies are also vital in curbing poverty. The next component is the strength of the policy. A Weak Government Policy (WGP) will encourage laxity and lackadaisical attitude to policy statement and the policy makers. There, the other determining component of PCP will become weak. This is to say a Weak Government Institution (WGI) has emerged. WGI will further endanger the level of implementation of the policy. Porosity in the government policy will be capitalised on, leading to the next component which is the Unethical/Corrupt Political Environment (U-CPE). This type of environment endangers the entire society and determines whether the government policy will succeed or not.

Culture of Excessive Public Holidays

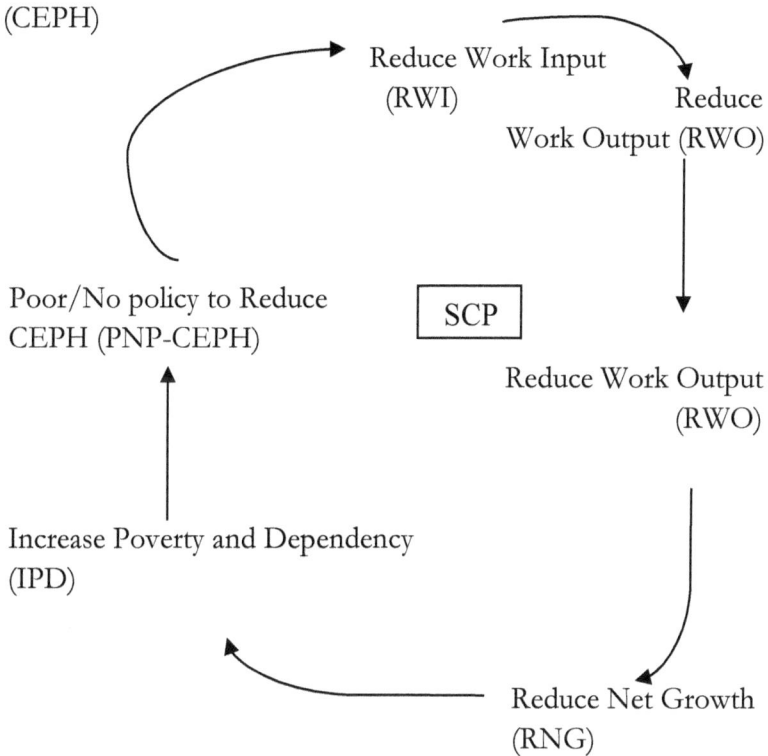

(CEPH)

Reduce Work Input (RWI)

Reduce Work Output (RWO)

Poor/No policy to Reduce CEPH (PNP-CEPH)

SCP

Reduce Work Output (RWO)

Increase Poverty and Dependency (IPD)

Reduce Net Growth (RNG)

Figure I: *The Social Cycle of Poverty (SCP)*

A U-CPE will therefore encourage the environment of secrecy in public transactions and non-transparency. This leads to and makes up the next component of PCP which is Increase in Back Door Politics (IBDP). Back Door Politics is a kind of patron client relations, patrimonial politics and prebendal activities. The rich will be getting richer due to the circumventing of the entire national wealth into the covers of a group of people. The resultant effect is the poor attitude to work and this leads to Low Commitment and Productivity (LCP). LCP is a great challenge to national development because it will endanger the per capita income, the gross domestic product (GDP) and the net income of the country. When all of the economic growth indicators are low, Increase in Poverty (IP) as the final component is inevitable. The IP can be curbed as fast and effective as possible if Government Policy (GP) is strong. See fig. 11 below:

**Government Policy
(GP)**

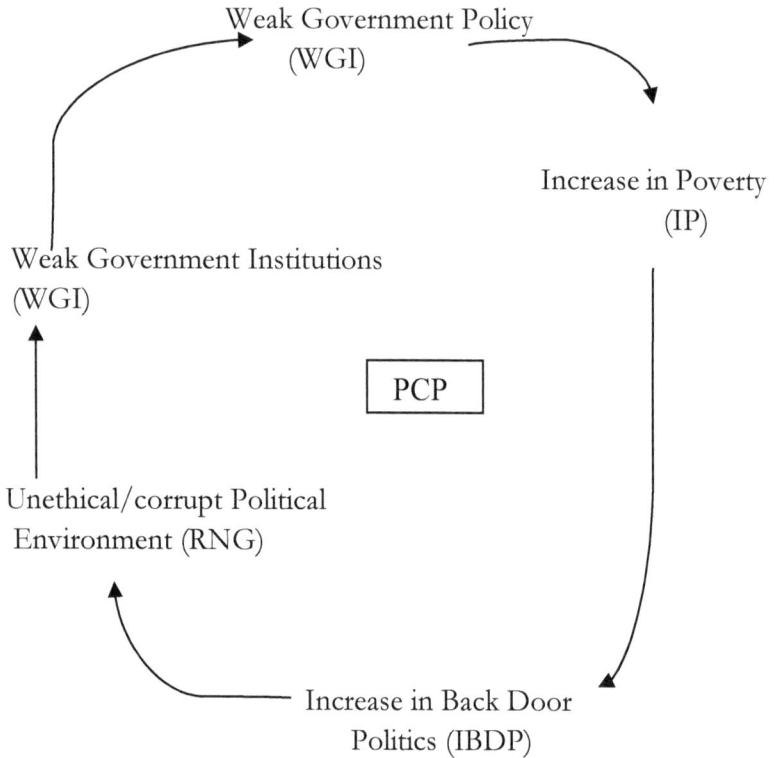

Weak Government Policy
(WGI)

Increase in Poverty
(IP)

Weak Government Institutions
(WGI)

PCP

Unethical/corrupt Political
Environment (RNG)

Increase in Back Door
Politics (IBDP)

Figure II: *The Political Cycle of Poverty (PCP)*

The Economic Cycle of Poverty (ECP), on the other hand, is a major cycle which encapsulates major economic activities of a country, and thereby dictates the pathway to growth, development, dependency and or poverty. ECP has eight major components that hamper a country from adequate growth and development. The first and major catalyst is the government economic plan/policy. A Weak

Economic Plan/Policy (WEP-P) will endanger the nation leading it into weak strategies and implementations. This will lead to the dependence on the externalities and foreign governments for help, aid or assistance. This leads to Excessive External Dependency (EED) which dictates what posture the local economy of the country should take. Over time, this will result into an External Control of the Economy (ECE). The major sectors of the economy will be dominated by the external governments and the price and products of the local industries will not be able to compete favourably with those of the foreign goods. This as well leads to Reduced Indigenous Industries/Experts (RII-E).

Many of the indigenous industries will fold up and become moribund. The expertise will be out of business because foreign expatriates have dominated the country's economic sector. Therefore, there will be a drastic repatriation of the profit from the host country to their homeland. This component of ECP is called External Profit Repatriation (EPR). No doubt, EPR will eventually lead to Shortage of Economic Capital (SEC) in the economy of the country. The shortage of capital will prevent major and important developmental activities to take place. This will lead to the next component of Stagnant Economic Growth (SEG). At this level in the economic cycle of poverty, a drastic measure is required to curb serious crises in the country, especially if the stagnation lingers for a long time to the extent of dilapidation of government infrastructure, wind up of private investments, famine or even war in the country. At this critical stage, the last effect in the ECP is Increase in Poverty (IP). A drastic measure from the government is needed to curb this menace. If the response from the government is another weak economic plan or policy, the cycle will be *ad infinitum*, entrapping the people in the vortex of poverty for even longer. Find figure 111 below which tries to explain this scenario.

Weak Economic Plan-Policy (WEP-P)

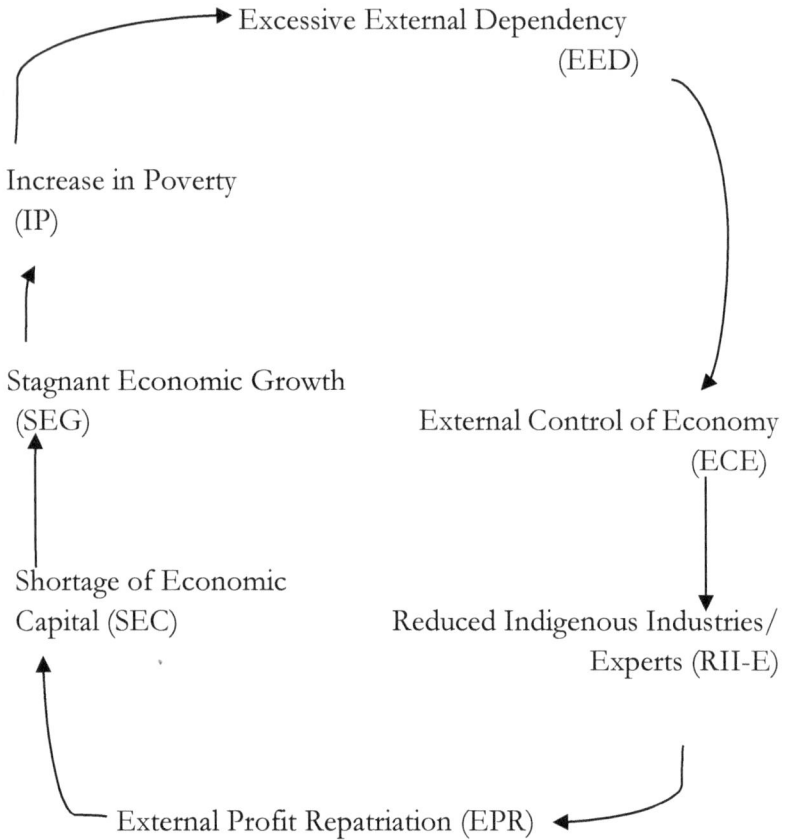

Figure III: *The Economic Cycle of Poverty (PCP)*

Interrogating poverty in Africa

We have already argued in this chapter that poverty should be better understood in context. For this major reason, the research methodology adopted for this chapter mainly utilises data from Africa Development Bank (AFDB) Socio-economic Database reported of 2017 and Afrobarometer socio-political and economic database round six of 2014-2015 data. The Africa Development Bank data presents the years 2000 and 2005 summary of the socio-economic indicators such as total population in Africa and the economically active or viable population, Gross Domestic Product, debt and financial flow. The Afrobarometer research network surveyed 37 countries in Africa. This covers about 76% of the entire African population. A total of socio-political and economic data centres about 54,000 survey responses on the present economic condition of Africa were obtained. A descriptive overview and analysis are adopted to present and express the poverty and development status in Africa and its implication on the continent.

Data in context
Africa's Economic Active Population

Population	2000	2005
Total Population (millions)	812.9	918.8
Female (% of active population)	41.5	42.2
Male (% of active population)	58.5	57.8

Table I: *Africa's Economic Active Population* Source: *AfDB Statistics Pocketbook 2017*

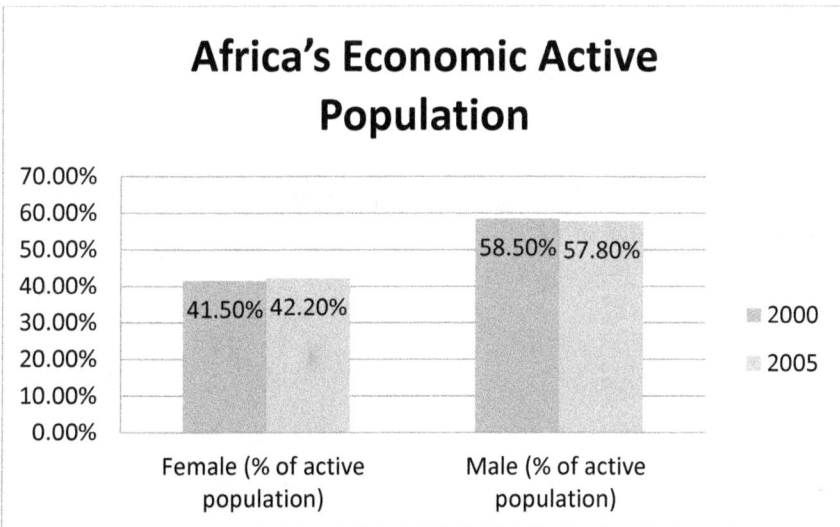

Figure IV: *Africa's Economic Active Population*

77

In data presented above, poverty does not reflect itself in Africa's total population for the reason that the population of the continent keeps growing from year to year. This means that more and more human capital – able bodied men and women – is ejected time and then with the possibility of increasing productivity and working against poverty. However, Africa's economic active population in terms of female gendered people is below average and not significant with rate of about forty-two percent (42%) while that of the male gendered people is slightly significant at about fifty-eight percent (58%). This implies that economically active population in Africa is very low on the average and their contribution to economic growth and development is expectedly low as well. Also, population's input and capability to reduce poverty in Africa is undoubtedly low.

Africa's Demographic and Education Growth

Demographic and Education Indicators 2000		2005
Annual Population Growth Rate-Total %	2.5	2.5
Life Expectancy at Birth- Total (years) %	53.7	55.8
Infant Mortality Rates (per 1000) %	87.7	74.1
Crude Death Rate (per 1000) %	13.5	12.2
Gross Education Enrolment Ratio		
Primary - Total %	87.0	96.4
Secondary – Total %	38.0	39.8

Table II: *Africa's Demographic and Education Growth* Source: *AfDB Statistics Pocketbook 2017*

Africa's Demographic and Education Growth

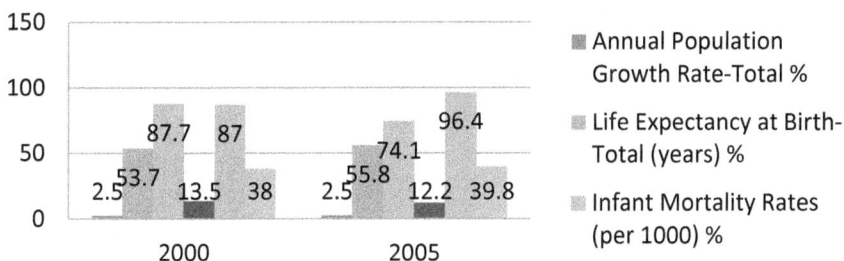

Figure V: *Africa's Demographic and Education Growth*

The table II and figure V above reveal Africa's demographic and educational growth. The tabled data reveals that the manifestation of the cycle of poverty in Africa may not be easily broken given that the annual growth rate is stagnant at about three percent (exactly 2.5%) while the life expectancy at birth stands at below sixty years with infant mortality rate of about seventy-five percent (75%) per one thousand births and the crude deaths per one thousand people being approximately twelve percent (12%). The percentage of the total secondary education enrolment is about forty percent (40%). All these data imply that there is a limited or insufficient human capital to cater for the health and the education sectors in African states, hence making it difficult for the continent to break its cycle of poverty.

Africa's National Accounts

National Accounts	2000	2005
Real GDP Growth Rate (%)	4.5	6.0
Gross National Savings (% GDP)	20.3	27.2

Table III: *Africa's National Accounts* Source: *AfDB Statistics Pocketbook 2017*

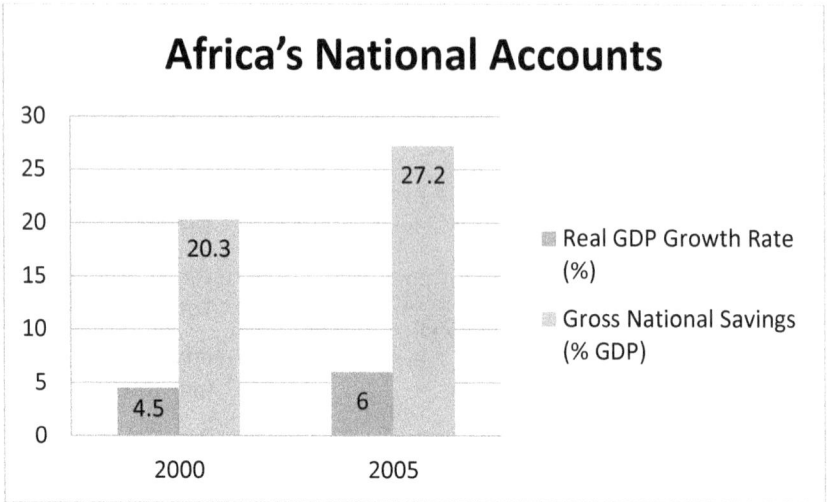

Figure VI: *Africa's National Accounts*

The picture of African countries' net national account is a real image of the growth and development tendencies of the continent. The Africa Development Bank 2017 Report shows that the real gross domestic product (GDP) and growth rate in Africa is very low and not rapidly growing. In the space of five years (2000-2005), for example, it only increased by less than two percent (2 %). In the year 2000, the real GDP was about five percent (exactly 4.5%) and it increased to six percent (6%) in 2005. These have it turn impacted on the gross National savings which stood at twenty-seven (27%). All of this reveal clear signs of poverty and underdevelopment in the continent of Africa.

Africa's Prices and Money

in % unless otherwise specified		
Prices and Money	2000	2005
Inflation (CPI)	9.1	7.7

Table IV: *Africa's Prices and Money* Source: *AfDB Statistics Pocketbook 2017*

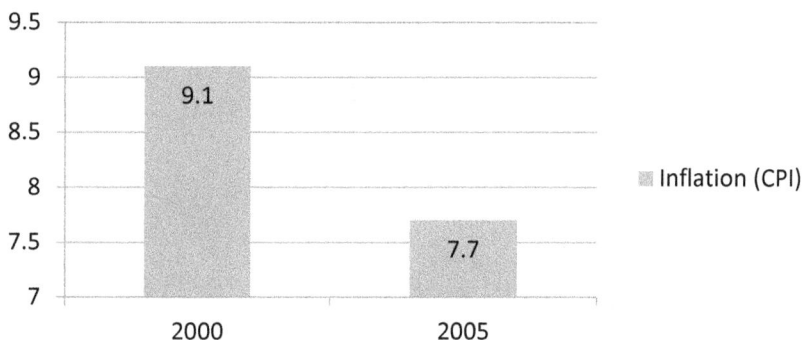

Africa's Prices and Money: Inflation (CPI)

Figure VII: *Africa's Prices and Money*

The rate of inflation in Africa is another yardstick to measure the extent of poverty on the continent. The cost price inflation in Africa is still moderately high as compared to the cost price inflation in other continents of the world such as Europe and the United States of America. It was above five percent (exactly 9.1%) and (exactly 7.7%) in the years 2000 and 2005, respectively. This indicates that goods on the continent remain relatively scarce, which means industries are not well capacitated to revamp and turn-around Africa's economy by producing en masse such goods needed for daily survival and exportation.

Africa's Trade and External Sector

in % unless otherwise specified		
External Sector	**2000**	**2005**
Exports Volume Growth (Goods)	0.4	13.2
Imports Volume Growth (Goods)	0.9	17.1
Terms of Trade Growth	28.6	15.8
Current Account Balance (% GDP)	3.5	5.2

External Reserves (months of imports)	5.7	8.1

Table V: *Africa's Trade and External Sector* Source: *AfDB Statistics Pocketbook 2017*

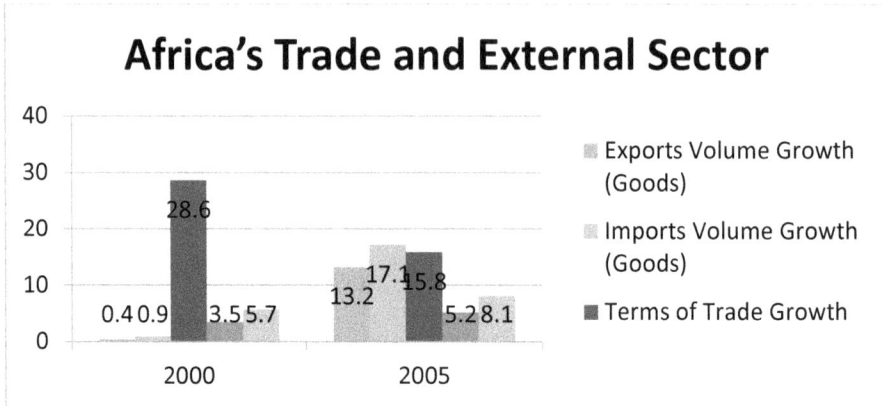

Figure VIII: *Africa's Trade and External Sector*

Africa's trade and external sector involves the import and export volume growth, the difference in trade growth, the current account balance and the external reserves volume. The export volumes for the years 2000 and 2005 were below fifteen percent from the 2017 Africa development bank's report. In exact terms, these were 0.4% and 13.2% in year 2000 and 2005, respectively. This shows a very slow and less significant export volume. The import volume also is higher than the export volume with about five percent (5%) growth volume in the year 2000 and 2015, respectively as shown in the 2017 Africa development bank's report. The terms of trade growth are therefore below thirty percent (30%) trade growth. In the year 2000 it was about twenty- nine (29%) while in the year 2005 it was about sixteen percent (16%). This indicates that there is an unfavourable balance of trade and market forces in Africa's socio-political economy.

The current account balance from Africa's gross domestic product (GDP) is about four percent (exactly 3.5%) and about five percent (exactly 5.2%) for the years 2000 and 2005 respectively as indicated in the 2017 Africa Development Bank's report. This shows that Africa's current account is very low and insignificant for rapid industrial development to take place. It is more of a maintenance ration for the continent and not a development account balance. With such a scenario, it remains a dream to talk of industrialisation in Africa. This also affect the external reserves as it is below ten percent, about six percent (exactly 5.7%) and about eight percent (8%) in both 2000 and 2005 respectively. These external reserves are not adequate enough for significant developments which have the capacity to alleviate poverty and worse still to promote development in the continent.

Africa's Debt and Financial Flows

millions of US$ unless otherwise specified		
Debt and Financial Flows	2000	2005
Debt Service (% exports)	27.5	19.4
External Debt (% GDP)	53.6	31.5
Net Total Financial Flows	14 805.4	53 358.6
Net Official Development Assistance	14 237.6	33 383.5
Foreign Direct Investment Inflows	9 628.3	29 505.4

Table VI: *Debt and Financial Flows* Source: *AfDB Statistics Pocketbook 2017*

Africa's Debts

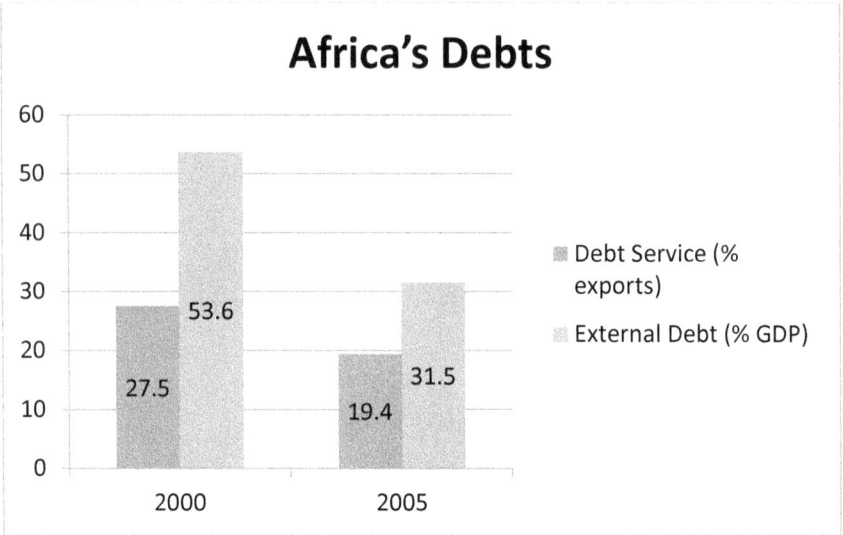

Figure IX: *Debt and Financial Flows*

The poverty streak in Africa is further expressed in the debt services of the continent as a whole. A huge percentage of the account balance in Africa is used to service debts. About twenty-eight percent (28%) and nineteen percent (19%) of the account balance goes into debt servicing in the years 2000 and 2005, respectively. The external debt as well stood at a high level of about fifty- four percent (54%) and was reduced to about thirty-two percent (32%) in the years 2000 and 2005, respectively. This external debt and debt servicing has usurp major part of the capital meant for development. It is important to note that the foreign direct investment inflows difference increased with about twenty million US Dollars. This has no major impact on poverty eradication in Africa because of the level and depth of underdevelopment inherently prevailing in the continent.

Africa's present economic condition

Africa's present economic condition- Afrobarometer Round Six 2014/2015 ("In general, how would you describe: The present economic condition of Africa?")	Total- Africa
Very bad	23.9%

Fairly bad	27.9%
Neither good nor bad	14.9%
Fairly good	26.7%
Very good	5.0%
Missing; Unknown	*
Don't know	1.5%
(N)	(53,932)

Table VII: *Africa's present economic condition Source: Afrobarometer Round 6 data (2014/2015)*

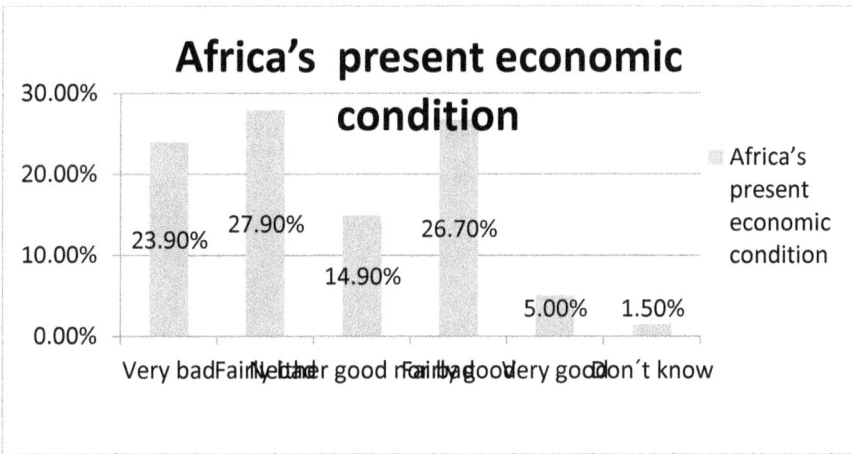

Figure X: *Africa's present economic condition*

The Afrobarometer (2015) data presents the present economic condition in Africa as shown above in figure x. It is observed that about twenty-four percent (exactly 23.9%) of Africans opined that the present economic situation in Africa is very bad. About twenty-eight percent (exactly 27.9%) of Africans perceived the economy to be fairly bad. This implies that a total of about fifty-two percent (exactly 51.8%) of African population opined that the present economic condition of the continent is bad. Also, about twenty-seven percent (exactly 26.7%) of Africans opined that the present economic condition of the continent is fairly good while a less significant five percent (5%) perceived that the present economic situation is good. This implies that about thirty-two percent (exactly 31.7%) of Africans opined that the economic condition of Africa is good. About fifteen percent (exactly 14.9%) opined that it is neither good nor bad while about two percent (exactly 1.5%) do not know what the present economic situation of Africa looks like.

Breaking the cycle of poverty

The data presented above and the attendant analysis show that poverty has ravaged all the sectors of economy and spheres of life in Africa. The cycle of poverty must be broken at all cost if Africa is to be freed from the shackles of poverty. For the cycle of poverty to be effectively broken and development be rapidly ensured, the three cycles of poverty must be inhibited by key inhibitor of the cycles. This is primarily the political will of the leaders to formulate relevant policies that will address directly the socio-economic and political problems (Alkire, Housseini, and Series, 2014; Morduch and Siwicki, 2017) that hamper development and perpetuate poverty on the continent. Yet, we should be quick to caution that the implementation will of the citizens, who in an case are critical stakeholders should never be compromised. This calls for the need for servant leaders and not rulers with the penchant for plutocracy – "government of the wealthy and for the wealthy" (Didia 2015: 504). This is critical as the actions of overbearing government elite members and the disempowerment of the masses create distrust of the government and a vicious cycle which hampers economic development.

The social cycle of poverty (SCP) can be broken when the culture of excessive public holidays, abuse of office, casual absconding of duties, and unethical relaxation during work time which has the capacity to hinder the work outcome is eradicated. As Mhango (forthcoming) rightly in view of public holidays and abuse of office notes:

> there is another aspect of lossmaking in this corruption resulting from selfishness and self-services that many African presidents and their appointees enjoy. Ironically, in some countries, such power abuses are backed by constitutional provisions. Aged and sick government officials are always accompanied by their doctors, relatives not to mention who's who that go to see them in hospitals they are oft-

86

admitted. Furthermore, apart from paying for their medical and lodging expenses, governments pay for their air tickets and those of those who accompany them which in most cases are in the first class not to mention being paid *per diem*s for the whole time they spend in hospital abroad where they go to seek better medical services after sabotaging the same in their countries.

The eradication of such a culture will increase work input and work output respectively. This will positively affect the net growth rate of the country and the poverty and dependency levels on external countries will as well gradually reduced (Demery, and Squire, 1996; Justesen, and Bjornskov, 2014). Therefore, the government policy should be formulated in such a way that it helps reduce the unethical practice of work absconding and excessive public holidays so as to increase productivity and eradicate poverty.

More so, the political cycle of poverty (PCP) can be broken when the government shows the political will to make and implement public policies that are strong enough to drive the various institutions of governance so as to eradicate the unethical practices which are corrupt and sanitise the political environment from political mishaps (Sahn, Dorosh, and Younger 1999). Then back door politics will be reduced, government transaction transparency will increase, commitment to work will increase also the level of productivity will increase. At this level the expanse of poverty in the countries will be drastically reduced and the wealth of the nations will circulate among all the citizens.

The economic cycle of poverty (ECP) can be broken as well when the government's economic plan and policies are environmentally sensitive and indigenously (or contextually) planed. Home-grown strategies have the net effect that they limit the reliance on external government to the minimum or to near 'zero' in socio-economic and political issues. This allows the country to control its own economy and the destiny of its people. Zimbabwe's 2008 Indigenisation and Economic Empowerment Policy is a good example. The policy gives indigenous Zimbabweans the right to take over and control many foreign owned companies – mainly by former colonists – in Zimbabwe. Moreover, the policy affords indigenous companies the opportunity to operate and drive the economy so as to retain and reinvest the gains lost during colonialism within the country. This will boost the capital base of the local economy. Yet, if non-indigenous companies are dominant in the economy of the country, the profits are repatriated and other such resources siphoned to the homeland of the foreign companies. When we thus argue that where indigenous companies have sufficient capital to reinvest in the country, the economy will without a doubt make positive gains while food and livelihood will be adequate for all and poverty level maintained minimal.

Conclusion

The cycle of poverty in Africa cut across the entire socio-political and economic terrains. Poverty has become so entrenched in all sectors to the extent that it has become a culture or a way of life. Although the rich and political elite are getting richer in the same terrain thereby impoverishing many by enacting policies that are egocentric, the 'political will' to implement such policies remain obscure. Therefore, poverty is on the increase across the social, political and economic circles in Africa.

The economy indicators as presented in this chapter revealed that the educational sector of Africa is lagging behind the expected level. So, is the health sector. A few are being empowered in the secondary education level while the infants' mortality and the crude death rates are on the rise. The trade indexes also show an unfavourable balance of trade as the percentage net imports exceed that of the exports. The rate of cost price inflation is also on the rise while external debts are insurmountable. The foreign direct investments to the continent have little or no effect on the affected countries because of the extent of damages incurred in poverty terrains.

We conclude that poverty is evil and a 'hydra monster' as it renders human life unworth living, solitary, nasty and short-lived. Yet, though all might be yearning for the eradication of poverty, the phenomenon is likely to remain an endemic disease in the African continent until the cycle, cycler and the cyclone are meticulously dealt with. The cycles include the social, cultural, political and economic cycles, their cycler are the weak government policies, weak socio-political, cultural and economic institutions and low political will to implement the policies while the cyclone are the corruption, bad governance, unethical workplace practices, excessive culture of public holidays and work absenteeism, among others. It must therefore be curbed with the application of right and adequate dose of political will by the concerned stakeholders. A sincere, appropriate and swift approach should be adopted in each country so as to mitigate the spread of poverty to other upcoming generations across the African continent.

References

Africa Development Bank (AfDB). 2017. *Africa Development Bank Statistics Pocketbook, Statistics Department Economic Governance and Knowledge Management Complex, African Development Bank,* Abidjan, Côte d'Ivoire.

Afrobarometer. 2016. Country´s present economic condition –Total for Africa Round 6, 2014/2015
http://www.afrobarometer.org/online-data-analysis/analyse-online assessed on 4/7/2017.

Alkire, S., Housseini, B., and Series, O. S. 2014. Multidimensional Poverty in Sub-Saharan Africa: Levels and Trends, *OPHI Working Paper* 81.

Aluko O. I. 2017. Political Economy of Crony Inequality among Nations: A Study on Capitalism and Socialism, *Journal of Community Development Research-Humanities and Social Sciences* 10(2).

Anyawu, J. C. and Erhjakpor, A. E. 2010. Do International Remittances affect Poverty in Africa? *African Development Review,* 22 (1).

Arndt, C., McKay, A., and Trap, F. 2016. *Growth and Poverty in Sub-Saharan Africa,* Oxford University Press.

Bluemenstock, J. E. 2016. Fighting Poverty with Data, *Science* 353(6301) 753-754.

Bruenig M. 2014. "Two Theories of Poverty"
http://www.demos.org/policy-shop/Matt%20Bruenig on July

28, 2014 http://www.demos.org/blog/7/28/14/two-theories-poverty Assessed on 12/6/2017.

Burchardt, T., Le Grand, J. and Piachaud, C. 2002. 'Degrees of exclusion: developing a dynamic multidimensional measure'. In: J. Hills, J. Le Grand and D. Piachaud. (Eds). *Understanding Social Exclusion*, Oxford University Press: Oxford.

Demery, L. and Squire, L. 1996. Macroeconomic Adjustment and Poverty in Africa: An Emerging Picture, *The World Bank Research Observer* 11(11).

Didia, O. D. 2015. *Ten reasons why sub-Saharan Africa has failed to develop economically: Can Africans succeed by themselves?* Edwin Mellen Press, UK.

Justesen, M. K., and Bjornskov, C. 2014. Exploiting the Poor: Bureaucratic Corruption and Poverty in Africa, *World Development* 58.

Lewis, O. 1961. *Five families: Mexican case studies in the culture of poverty*, New York: Basic Books.

Mawere, M. 2017. *Theorising development in Africa: Towards building an African framework of development*, Langaa Publishers: Bamenda.

Mhango, N. (forthcoming). *Africa's dependency syndrome: Still Africa can turn around things for the better*, Langaa Publishers: Bamenda.

Morduch J., and siwicki, J. 2017. In and Out of Poverty: Episodic Poverty and Income Volatility in the US, *Financial Diaries 1*.

Musterd, S., Murie A. And Kesteloot, C. 2016. *Neighbourhood of Poverty*, Palgrave Macmillan.

Ryan P. 2014. Do Not Block Grant and Expanding Opportunity in America
http://budget.house.gov/uploadedfiles/expanding_opportunity_in_america.pdf
http://www.demos.org/blog/7/24/14/response-paul-ryan-expand-eitc-do-not-block-grant-anything Assessed on 12/6/2017.

Sahn, D.E. Dorosh, P.A. and Younger S. D. 1999. *Structural Adjustment Reconsidered: Economic Policy and Poverty in Africa*, Cambridge University Press.

Sen, A. 1981. *Poverty and Famines: An Essay on Entitlement and Deprivation*, Oxford University Press.

Townsend, P. 1979. *Poverty in the United Kingdom: A survey of household resources and standards of living*, London: Penguin.

Chapter 5

Resorting to Illegality: The Illicit Shangwe Cannabis Trade as an Anti-cotton Response to Agrarian Policy in Colonial Zimbabwe, c. 1962-1979

Simeon Maravanyika & Harro Maat

Introduction

This chapter examines the nexus between colonial agrarian policies and African responses with particular reference to Shangwe anti-cotton production in colonial Zimbabwe. Colonial states in Africa often tried to alter local agrarian ethos by introducing new commercial crops and production cultures, while local farmers strived to maintain their autonomy and indigenous crops and forms of production. African farmers generally felt disempowered, impoverished and suffocated by colonial regimes and their agricultural policies. These policies were, in the majority of cases, top-down in approach and backed by state instruments of force such as the police to ensure their uptake. African farmers were seldom consulted in their formulation and implementation, and their indigenous knowledge systems were often disregarded on account of a general misconception that they were informed by ignorance and lack of civilisation. The impoverished African farmers, comparatively powerless against the might of coercive state apparatus, have generally been cast by scholars as having been hapless victims of colonial agrarian policies.

This instalment takes a different approach by examining local counter-movements against commodity policies in Mbumbuze, located in the Gokwe Region of colonial Zimbabwe, where Shangwe farmers (heretofore referred to as the Shangwe) sought, with relative success, to shake-off pressure exerted by the colonial administration to make them produce cotton. The Shangwe cleverly came up with an alternative commercial crop, cannabis (*Mbanje* in the Shona language), which yielded better returns than cotton in terms of profit margins. In addition to this, they also resorted to an array of other measures, considered illegal by the state, to maintain their autonomy in their communities, and to maintain their way of life. Some of these illicit activities included but were not limited to illegal harvesting of resources from the Mafungautsi state-protected forest, poaching small game, stealing from government installations, brewing and selling banned "kaffir beer", squatting in protected areas, and gambling.

While the introduction of cotton in Gokwe in 1962 is often considered to have gainfully served the colony and Madheruka Shona immigrant farmers who, unlike the majority of the Shangwe, generally embraced the crop, cotton pushed the Shangwe into a huge economic predicament characterised by poverty. Some Shangwe farmers reacted to the introduction of cotton and their consequent impoverishment by turning to illegal activities for subsistence. Resorting to illegal activities was one avenue through which the Shangwe sought to address this economic situation. These anti-commodity expressions shed light on how local farmers were not just victims of colonial agrarian policies and the poverty induced by such policies by showing their agency and creative capacity whose net effect was to negate colonial design and, in the process, create parallel socio-economic structures to those the colonial state sought to establish.

This chapter focusses on only two of these responses – gambling and illegal production and marketing of cannabis – to shed light on the poignancy of anti-commodity expressions in negating colonial design. The chapter does two things. Firstly, it examines interventions by the colonial state in peasant agriculture through its transformation of Gokwe from a sparsely populated forest region into a cotton-growing enclave where ethnic labels and a spurious, adulterated and rather extraneous concept of "modernity" were utilised to entrench commodification. Secondly, it examines one component of Shangwe anti-cotton and anti-market responses - illegality - with particular focus on cannabis production and gambling and argues that illegal activities, apart from negating colonial agrarian design, provided Shangwe families with alternative sources of livelihood which enabled them to avoid cotton production and to resist "modernity" in preference of the old Shangwe way of life.

A momentous era of tremendous change

Shangwe anti-commodity production must be understood in the context of the post-1945 political and socio-economic environment in colonial Zimbabwe. The post-Second World War period ushered in an era of change for the Shangwe communities in Gokwe as the state sought to restructure management praxis in all sectors of the economy – among them agriculture, wildlife, forestry, fisheries and water resources – to make them more productive and responsive to post-war socio-economic and bipolar world governance dynamics characterised by Cold War politics (Worby, 2000). Prior to 1945, Gokwe had largely been secluded as it was unpopular for its infestation with wild animals, tsetse-flies and malaria (Worby, 1998). After the Second World War the state embarked on a programme to resettle Africans resident on land reserved for white occupation. Gokwe and other areas were identified as suitable areas for African relocation.

The resettlement programme accelerated in the 1950s, particularly from 1953 onwards (Maravanyika, 2009). Parallel to the resettlement of Shona migrants from land reserved for white farms in areas such as Rhodesdale Estate - a huge swath of land which shared a boundary with Gweru on the south and covered parts of Kwekwe and Kadoma to the north and Chivhu and Gutu - to Gokwe, Shangwe relocation was also taking place in Gokwe (Nyambara, 2005). The Shangwe were being relocated from the Mafungautsi Forest in Gokwe, a place the Shangwe of Mbumbuzi had called home for time immemorial, which was proclaimed (gazetted) a state-protected zone, leading to eviction and resettlement of the Shangwe adjacent to the forest in new villages such as Mafa, Maruta and Matashu (Mutimukuru-Maravanyika, 2010). This deprived the Shangwe of their source of livelihood and cast them into a poverty net as, apart from their inability to continue to subsist from their old forest home, they now had to embrace large-scale agriculture. That proved to be a tall order for a former forest community whose crop production had always been at a small, insignificant scale (Maravanyika, 2012).

Dispossessed of their Mafungautsi forest home, hemmed in by the *en masse* resettlement of Shona farmers, derogatorily nicknamed *Madheruka* by the Shangwe, and confronted by the introduction of cotton, the Shangwe found themselves between a rock and a hard place. Their options, according to the state's logic, were limited to just one turn; quickly adjusting to their new economic reality by embracing cotton in order to make a living. The Shangwe communities found themselves in deep swirling economic waters characterised by widespread poverty and the possibility of acute hunger. The majority of the Shangwe, however, did not respond to this situation in the manner that the state had anticipated; they did the opposite by coming up with an array of creative measures, which this article terms anti-commodity responses, to sustain themselves without having to produce cotton (Maravanyika, 2016). Though illegal, these anti-cotton expressions enabled Shangwe communities to raise financial resources with which they were capable of earning a living in the new market-based economy characterised by the utilisation of money as the predominant medium of exchange.

Confronted by such tremendous changes in the post-Second World War period, which required quick adjustment, Shangwe responses are remarkable in that they elected not to comply with state socio-economic engineering. Shangwe communities were therefore not mere victims of colonial planning and colonial processes, but were prime movers and shakers in their own right in these colonial discourses. They had their own agency, as demonstrated by their coming up with innovative and creative ways to continue with their lives on a parallel path to what the state desired.

Cotton growing: A worship of foreign material gods?

Commodification has had a debilitating impact on many African communities from the early colonial period. "The African is really helpless against the material gods of the white man, as embodied in the trinity of imperialism, capitalistic-exploitation, and militarism", wrote Edmund Morel in 1920. Morel, a leading voice in awakening

96

public opinion in the West to what Africans in Southern Rhodesia and the Belgian Congo, among other colonies, were being subjected to under colonial administration, further observed, "If the white man retains these gods and if he insists upon making the African worship them as assiduously as he has done himself, the African will go the way of the Red Indian, the Amerindian, the Carib, the Guanche, and many more" (Ibid: 9). African exploitation at the turn of the 20th century was taking place in the context of industrial expansion in Europe and the consequent insatiable thirst for inputs such as agricultural commodities and other natural resources. Almost the entire African continent had been parcelled out to European countries by 1900, who viewed their new overseas territories as having enormous economic potential. The production of agrarian commodities for consumption and value addition ranked high among the colonies' perceived potentialities (Isaacman *et al*, 1995; Robins, 2009).

Cotton was in huge demand in the European textile sector and its downstream industries – spinners, manufacturers, shippers, merchants, and retailers, to name only but a few. Cotton supply from the southern states of America, which had traditionally accounted for above seventy-five percent of the world's cotton crop, was dwindling due to interruption by the American civil war, labour challenges as slavery reached its twilight, continued increases in prices and a raft of other bottlenecks (Hose, 1970). There was optimism that African cotton, together with supplies from other colonies outside Africa such as India, would bring dependence on American cotton to an end. This optimism was echoed in 1910 at the International Cotton Federation in Brussels. The Director of German Cotton Association (KWK), Moritz Schanz, declared that cotton cultivation in Africa would be a success story. His catalogue of reasons for bright prospects for the crop included "suitable climate and soil" and "sufficient supply of cheap native labour" (Robins, 2009: 3). Similarly, colonial officials in Africa shared and, by their periodic reports, fuelled this optimism.

"Cotton," one Southern Rhodesian official wrote, "being an indigenous plant, is sure to thrive; it is quickly and cheaply grown, it yields a crop every year, while the market of course is inexhaustible."

(National Archives of Zimbabwe, hereinafter NAZ, A11/22/2/9, British South Africa Company Reports, Correspondence, 1890-1923, Letter from Percy Inskipp to W. H. Milton dated 8th of September, 1902). This line of thinking was informed by the fact that cotton is indigenous to the country and the perceived abundance of African labour. However, the optimism of the early colonial period was not matched by developments on the ground. African farmers took long to embrace cotton (Nyambara, 1990), preferring instead to grown food crops, principally maize, which had a huge market because of the rise and growth of new towns, mines and other settlement centres. Maize production during the early colonial period, characterised by Palmer as an "era of peasant prosperity" (Palmer, 1977: 71 – 73) increased significantly in parts of Mashonaland where "better-off Shona farmers" bought ploughs and extended the number of acreages under the plough by selling their "ploughing capacity" to neighbours (Phimister 1985: 247).

It was only in the second half of the 1960s and in the early 1970s that African cotton production picked up, in part because of African maize marketing difficulties and restrictions put in place by the Native Land Husbandry Act (NLHA) OF 1951 (Machingaidze, 1991). The cotton boom of the late 1960s and early 1970s may, from a distance, give the false impression that cotton production played a poignant midwifery role to the birth of an entrenched, generally-accepted, all-encompassing and across-the-board cotton-culture or cotton movement; what has been represented, in Eric Worby's words (1992), as a "miracle of agrarian transformation, a frontier of commoditisation, and more broadly, as an exemplifier of the transition to modernity." At a closer look, however, it becomes glaringly apparent that commoditisation in Gokwe was not an all-inclusive process. Some locals, particularly the Shangwe, were left behind – paradoxically on their volition.

While the Shona (*Madheruka*) master-farmers overwhelmingly embraced and profited from cotton, a significant proportion of Shangwe people resisted subordination of their economic, social and religious organisation to commoditisation and the dictates of the colonial regime and commodity market (Nyambara, 2002). This story of Shangwe resistance to cotton cultivation, resorting instead to what the state classified as illegal for a living, has for long been overshadowed by narratives about what has been termed the pre-independence "cotton miracle", and therefore needs to be told to demonstrate that cotton, which for the Shangwe was a 'foreign material god', was not able to successfully proselytise and propagandise in Shangwe strongholds.

No escape for the African?

There is a huge body of literature that examines the complex processes through which agriculture in the colonies was tailored to suit colonial design (Curry-Machado, 2013, Hazareesingh and Maat, 2016). The production of agricultural commodities ranging from foodstuffs, stimulants and industrial crops was fuelled by the industrial revolution in Europe. Reorientation of agriculture in the colonies, according to the Commodities of Empire Project, "brought vast spatial, social, economic and cultural changes" to people in colonised regions of the world. Morel (1920), after observing the ferocity of industrial revolution-inspired change in Africa at the beginning of the 19th century, wrote in 1920, thus:

> What the partial occupation of his [African] soil by the white man has failed to do… what the maxim and the rifle, the slave gang, labour in the bowels of the earth and the lash, have failed to do; what imported measles, smallpox and syphilis have failed to do… the power of modern capitalistic exploitation, assisted by modern engines of destruction, may yet succeed in accomplishing…there is no escape for the African… it kills not the body, but the soul (p. 7).

For reorientation of African agriculture, and other changes to happen, the colonial states had to, in the majority of cases, utilise their political and military might and an array of non-market and extra-legal instruments (Arrighi, 1967).

The use of "coercion, indirect pressures and material inducements" by colonial administrators, in the majority of cases, effectively "smashed the self-sufficiency of indigenous pre-capitalist societies", which, in many cases, spelt poverty for African communities (Berman, 2008:161). Collin Bundy (1979), Ian Phimister (1974), Paul Mosley (1982), and Robin Palmer *et al* (1977), among others, have investigated in detail how subordination and reorientation of local agricultural systems led to the "fall of the peasantry" in central, southern and east Africa, in the majority of cases with ghastly consequences for African farmers and communities. African non-commercial forms of production were subordinated to the colonial produce market system. Isaacman (1996) has examined forced cotton production in Mozambique during the era of the Salazar Regime in Portugal and come to the conclusion that "cotton is the mother of poverty." This is because cotton production in Mozambique, as was the case with commoditisation in other regions of Africa, was, in Isaacman's words (1980: 592-4) "both predictable and disastrous" as local food-self-sufficiency was lost:

> Their [African farmers] tattered clothing symbolized the impoverishment of the cotton producers who, forced to meet state-imposed work schedules, also found it difficult to satisfy their own food requirements… In 1953, for example, between 3,000 and 4,000 cotton producers were reported to have died of famine in Mogvolas in northern Mozambique… Many peasants supplemented their meagre diets by eating roots and tubers and planting manioc which, though of lower nutritional value than other food crops, required only a minimal amount of labour.

This account by Isaacman demonstrates that the colonial farming system in Mozambique, by emphasising the production of commercial crops such as cotton at the expense of foodstuffs, impoverished African farmers and brought widespread deprivation and suffering.

African colonial agrarian history is replete of similar accounts, with varying impacts on African people and communities, in French Soudan (Roberts, 1996), the Belgian Congo (Likaka, 1997), the Gezira Scheme in Sudan (Barnett, 1975), among others, where local agricultural production was – with varying degrees of intensity - suppressed, labour was exploited and a new colonial market-based agrarian ethos was introduced. This was not limited to cotton, but extended to other commercial crops such as tea in Zimbabwe's eastern highlands regions such as Chipinge and Nyanga where a combination of land alienation and coercive labour mobilisation devises impoverished African communities, leaving them at the mercy of the state and agrarian capital (Nyaruwata, 1984).

Illife (1990) has revealed the extent to which intervention impacted on African communities; it resulted in high mortality. State-instigated famine, to illustrate this point, ravaged Ndebele communities between 1890 and 1960. Food scarcity in Matabeleland, Illife argues, was primarily a product of state-induced violence and intervention in African food production, which resulted in the death of thousands of Ndebele people. Legislation, such as the Orders-in-Council (1894 and 1898), the Land Apportionment Act (1930), the Native Land Husbandry Act (1951) and the Native Land Tenure Act (1969), was a major asset in the colonial tool kit used to alter peasant land-holdings and to shape and redirect production patterns, often with disastrous consequences for African farmers.

Though it is accurate to say that colonial states used political and military force, in concert with an array of other extra-legal and extra-market interventions, the characterisation of the colonial state as an all-powerful coercive apparatus is somewhat problematic, as colonial states were, in many instances, either weak or fraught with contradictions. Weakness manifested itself in a number of ways, among them being "constantly strapped for resources, plagued by poor communications and inadequate information, and at times possessing limited coercive force" (Berman, 2008: 162). Geoffrey Kay (1972: 9) has observed that British colonial administrators and officials in Ghana, for example, carried out their duties,

>...with extreme caution... instinctively aware, if not fully conscious, of the frailty of their position and knew they could never maintain their power in the face of organised opposition among the mass of the Ghanaian people...The attempt, wherever possible, to avoid such opposition by exercising deliberate restraint, runs like a thread through official actions and statements.

Colonial rule in Mozambique illustrates another weakness of colonial regimes.

The scramble for Africa put some countries, such as Portugal, in a place where their economies could not sustain the occupation of large territories in Africa all at once. This duty was sub-contracted to chartered companies. Leroy Vail (1976) has characterised governance by two of the companies that were given the mandate by the Portuguese government to govern Mozambique from the 1890s till the late 1920s namely, Companhia de Niassa (the Niassa/Nyasa Company) and Companhia de Moçambique (the Mozambique Company), as "the rule of the feeble." These companies were very exploitative to the extent that their economic activities pushed Africans into abject poverty.

Rethinking African agency

In addition to inherent weakness of colonial states and contradictions in their *modus operandi*, a generalised characterisation of colonised people as mere victims of colonial processes is also ahistorical. Apart from the stories of peasants' victimhood; how their labour was exploited, how local knowledge systems were often disregarded (Mawere, 2012), how they were forced to grow commercial crops at the expense of their own agrarian preferences, among other narratives, there is also the story of their creative potential and resilience in the face of colonial pressure. There were instances where locals found ways of resisting the imposition of commodity production. This was achieved through a number of ways including, but not limited to, adapting commercial crops to local conditions to suit or further the local economy, establishment of alternative commercial crops and lifestyles, and resorting to "illegal" practices for survival, which negated colonial commodity policies. If these local expressions and production are not documented, it is not possible to get a wholesome picture of colonial agrarian and commodity history.

Janet MacGaffey's research (1983) on what has come to be known as the black or parallel market in Zaire (now Democratic Republic of Congo) elaborates this thinking. She argues that in Zaire and other African countries, a lot of economic transactions are carried out in the "second" or "backyard" economy. The "second" or "backyard" economy, in this context, mean the same as the black market or parallel economy. These activities, though not included in the calculation and determination of gross domestic product (GDP), have resulted in some people getting massively wealthy. There are instances, MacGaffey argues, when black market activities have accounted for more than half of the monetary GDP of their countries. Unless these activities are encapsulated in calculating GDP, it is not possible to get accurate economic data in developing countries. In the same vein, unless the story of anti-commodity production is told alongside that of colonial commodity production for the market, this important piece of the picture will remain unknown, regardless of its undisputed importance in Africa's colonial commodity histories. It is for this reason that the present chapter focuses on one aspect of anti-commodity processes in Zimbabwe's agrarian history; a group of Africans turning to practices that the state considered illegal for survival in the face of the introduction of cotton in Gokwe. Villagers in Mafa, Maruta and Matashu, Mbumbuzi, resorted to a number of "illegal" activities to cope with changes brought to their area since the 1950s.

There is no doubt that colonial states in Africa utilised the law to promote "capitalist transformation" (Merry, 1991). Africans were not mere victims of this process as they have traditionally been cast by scholarship on African commodity histories; they opposed laws that they viewed as unjust (Benton, 2002). This created two dichotomies; the state, on one hand, which strove to "command and demand", while Africans, on the other, responded by "speaking back" (Comaroff, 2001:307). This process of "speaking back" took many forms. From the early colonial period for example, Africans resisted land alienation by continuously trekking to zones not yet under the tentacles of the state (Punt, 1979). With the enactment of the Land Apportionment Act in 1930 Africans defiantly continued to settle on land designated for white use, often times in cahoots with poor white farmers with whom they entered into tenancy and share-cropping agreements (Memorandum on Land Occupied by Natives, 1943).

George Karekwaivanane (2011) has examined how state authority was negotiated in the legal arena from the mid-1960s. While the Ian Smith-led Rhodesia-Front government "increasingly relied on repressive legislation", a number of Africans, such as Mqibelo Dube of Gokwe District (also see Mawere, 2013) and in the Chamburuka Case – a border dispute between two chieftaincies in Bikita and Zaka Districts – resorted to the same colonial justice system for recourse. In the case of the Shangwe of Mbumbuzi, they resorted to doing what was, in the eyes of the colonial state, outside the law to fight cotton cultivation which, apart from being labour intensive, was described by local spirit mediums as "a white man's crop" whose cultivation did not have the blessing of the ancestors (Maravanyika, 2016). In addition to this, cotton brought with it many developments that buttressed the cash economy. Illegal activities helped to raise money needed for survival in this new dispensation.

Introduction of cotton in Gokwe

Southern Africa was one of the regions in Africa where a lot of potential for cotton was seen, especially in the wake of writings by missionaries such as David Livingstone. Livingstone had, as he travelled in present day Zambia and Zimbabwe, characterised the territories as the place that could "make Lancashire independent of the United States of America" (Nyambara, 2000: 81, Prentice, 1972). The British Cotton Growers Association (BCGA), formed in Britain in 1902 by Manchester and Liverpool merchants and other cotton interests immediately set out on a mission to encourage and promote the cultivation of cotton in British colonies, including Southern Rhodesia (Himbury, 1927). A sample of local cotton was sent to London in 1902 where it got a good report: "The "staple" is …of good strength, and if obtainable in sufficient quantities would be saleable at about the equivalent of American cotton", Percy Inskipp, a British South Africa Company (BSC Co.) official wrote in September 1902, adding that, "The class of cotton is much superior to what is known as East India cotton…" (Nyambara, 2000: 86). This was welcome news for the BSC Co. as it had become clear that there would not be gold discoveries in anticipated quantities in the colony.

The British South Africa Company had, in the wake of discovery of gold at Witwatersrand, South Africa, in 1886, acquired a Royal Charter from the British Crown, on the basis of which Zimbabwe was occupied in 1890. There was a general expectation that a second gold Rand lay somewhere in the colony (Phimister, 1976: 465). By 1902, it was becoming apparent to the Company officials that the prospect of building a colony on the basis of the mining industry were dim and untenable. Cotton was, thus, welcomed as the crop that would, together with other crops such as maize, tobacco, tea, coffee, and sugarcane, open a new vistas for this young colony, only 12 years old then. A number of companies rushed to register in response to news of the prospects of cotton in the colony, among them, the Rhodesia Cotton Syndicate. From 1904, cotton seed was distributed to Africans. An experimental target of between 50 and 100 acres was set for each African District in the 1904/5 farming season (Nyambara, 2000: 86-7). The uptake of cotton by Africans was lower than expected.

The Department of Agriculture reported in 1916: "There is little hope of the native being induced [to take up cotton]. All efforts in this direction have...proved futile" (Southern Rhodesia Department of Agriculture, Annual Report for the Year 1916). This trend continued into the 1920s. "Mere talk will be of no use whatsoever", the Native Commissioner for Sinoa observed in 1923, "The natives will agree to all that is said and do nothing" (Nyambara, 2000: 91). Lack of enthusiasm by Africans to grow cotton did not, however, discourage colonial officials. In July 1936, Government Notice 557 announced the creation of the Cotton Research and Industry Board with a mandate to "carry out cotton research, to promote cotton production in the colony and to establish and operate cotton ginneries" (The Cotton Research and Industry Board (CRIB), First Annual Report for the Period ending 31 March, 1937, p. 1). The Board set out to reverse declining cotton output by making it "a serious and sustained branch of its activities" (CRIB, Second Annual Report for the Period ending 31 March 1938, p. 2). By 1943, the Board's research unit had discovered a new strain of high-yielding cotton, called the 9L34, which became dominant from the second half of the 1940s well into the 1960s (Matowa, 1996). The discovery of this high-yielding variety of cotton resulted in Gokwe being opened up as a new frontier for cotton production at an accelerated pace from the 1950s, with enormous implication on the inhabitants of the region.

The 1950s were an era of change for Shangwe communities of Gokwe. This was because the region, formerly sparsely populated, experienced massive demographic changes as Shona farming communities were relocated by the state from prime land that had been set aside for white agriculture by the Land Apportionment Act of 1930 (Floyd, 1962). Most of the Shona immigrants were transported by huge haulage trucks provided by the government from Rhodesdale, a massive portion of land designated for white settlement (Nyambara, 2005). The migrants were derogatorily termed *"Madheruka"* or *"MaRhodesdale"*, terms used to depict the sounds made by the huge trucks which brought them to Gokwe, as well as the place from which they were being ejected (Nyambara, 2002). Relocation of *Madheruka* farmers, long exposed to Europeans and European culture, prepared the Gokwe region for conflict between the two groups as their cultures and backgrounds were remarkably different.

The immigrants, large-scale farmers in their own right, had gained a lot of farming experience from their contact with the white agricultural sector. Madheruka farmers gladly embraced cotton.

As for the Shangwe, uptake of cotton was very slow. There was also a perception that illness and death had increased in the area, especially among people who grew cotton because of poisonous chemicals used for pest-control and diseases such as malaria and because of lack of respect for traditions by Madheruka. There was also a religious dimension: Shangwe spirit mediums encouraged them not to grow cotton, arguing that it did not have the blessing of the ancestors (Maravanyika, 2016). The combination of these factors made a good proportion of Shangwe people elect to continue with old ways of life such as hunting (including poaching and illegal harvesting of forest products from Forestry Commission-protected areas), gathering and animal husbandry. Others embarked on gambling cultivating *mbanje* for the market; the crop was in high demand among African labourers on mines.

The rise of the underground cannabis trade

The cultivation and use of tobacco and marijuana (cannabis) in Gokwe dates back to the 20th century. It has not been possible to date exactly when these activities commenced. Weinmann (1972) has argued that colonial Zimbabwe was famous for its widespread production of tobacco. Tobacco cultivation in Shangwe areas of Gokwe was very logical; though the area's alluvial soils were suitable for crop cultivation, erratic rainfall patterns in the area made it unsound to cultivate crops on a very large scale, except on river banks and wetlands, called *mativi* by the Shangwe (Interviews with Kevias Mhanqwa, Mafa village, 13 February and 15 February, 2011). The area also had a high population of crop-destroying wild animals such as elephants, wild pigs, and other wild animals (Interview, Mutimba Khohliso Weresi, Mafa village, 16 February, 2011). The Shangwe could also not do animal husbandry (e.g. cattle, goats, and sheep) on a large scale because of tsetse-fly infestation and malaria (Interview, Marabu Sibanda, Mafa village, 22 October, 2011). Kosmin (1974:557) has argued that apart from the tsetse, which "preclude[d] cattle holding", the nature of the forests in the area (their being dominated by *Mopani* trees) "inhibits grass cover, which causes grazing problems, particularly in winter."

All these factors favoured the production of African tobacco, which Kosmin (1974:557) describes as being "very similar to Turkish varieties." It is surprising that the colonial administration did not push for the area to become a commercial tobacco-growing zone from the early colonial days. The reason, however, could be that the state wanted tobacco to be a preserve of the white commercial sector, and that local varieties of tobacco would be difficult to market and sell profitably in international markets. What is known is that by the 1960s, when cotton was introduced to Gokwe, "all traces of the Inyoka (Shangwe) tobacco industry had disappeared and the Shangwe *nyika* was regarded as one of the most backward of the tribal trust lands" (Kosmin, 1974: 575).

What cannot be disputed is that from the 1930s there was an increase in the production of cannabis in Shangwe areas, or at least there was an increase in documentation of cases where Shangwe men were arrested for either growing or peddling *mbanje* as the colonial administration spread its tentacles deeper into the Shangwe hinterland. The Native Commissioner for Sebungwe (the name for Gokwe in the colonial period) wrote in his report for 1935, "The number of convictions… for being in possession or cultivating 'Dagga' (marijuana) [has] begun to form no insignificant feature of the crime returns" (Kosmin, 1974: 575). Cultivation and use of cannabis was not a phenomena of the colonial era. It was prevalent even before the occupation of the country. In the early colonial days – in the 1890s - the administration largely gave a blind eye to tobacco cultivation and consumption by Africans. Cultivation of cannabis was for consumption, not for sale. This, in the eyes of the administration, did not constitute a major offence as there was no evidence of a direct relationship between its consumption and crime. In 1912, the Chief Native Commissioner reported that African cannabis consumption was, in fact, on the decline (NAZ, A3/18/20, Responses to the Chief Native Commissioner's Circular dated 1912).

In this context, the increased cultivation and use of cannabis in the mid-1930s came as a surprise for the Native Department officials in Gokwe. Needless to say, because of the poor accessibility of large areas in the forested district, tsetse-fly, mosquito and wild game infestation, these officials did not have a comprehensive picture of what was taking place in the entire district. The officials' influence was only confined to areas close to the district centre and those located on road networks, such as on the road to Que (now Kwekwe). In the case of Gokwe, it was not that consumption of cannabis was on the increase. Rather, it was that the Native Department was coming into contact with more and more Africans in the area, especially because of the discovery of coal deposits in the 1930s at Kadzviti, Mashami and Goredema Kraals, Malahla Hill, Katsanga River, at Sengwe and at Mafungabusi Mountain, among a number of other places, and consequent increased prospecting (NAZ, S2090, Memorandum on Coal in the Sobungwe District, 1937). As such, contact was taking place. The Department came to know more information of the lives and customs of the Shangwe people, such as the murder of twin children which was also prevalent in other parts of the country besides the Shangwe communities

(NAZ, S2091, Circular Newsletters to Native Commissioners). Knowledge about the Shangwe also increased as communities close to the district native administration centre increasingly turned to the colonial systems, such as the legal system. Between 1937 and 1949, for example, the court at Gokwe presided over more than 100 African divorce cases (NAZ, S1947, Civil Cases, Sobungwe District).

Cannabis was widely used in Gokwe from the pre-colonial period. Among the Shangwe and the Tonga People in the Zambezi Valley, it was used for traditional ceremonies (Interview, Samson Kohwapakuru Msanika, Mafa village, 20 November 2012). At traditional ceremonies, spirit mediums would, while under the control of the spirit of a dead relative (*mudzimu*), smoke *mbanje* (Interview, Silas Mapfumo, Matashu village, 26 November, 2011 and Vincent Sibanda, Mafa village, 2 December 2011). Married men also smoked *mbanje*, but *Shangwe* customs did not allow this to be done in public. As a result, most *Shangwe* men grew their *mbanje* in the forest or in and around their cattle kraals, where access by small children and women was restricted. Men would deep into the forest to smoke, or would do it at their cattle kraals in the morning and in the evening (Interview, Liza Jojo, Mafa village, 12 January, 2012).

Apart from use at religious ceremonies, smoking *mbanje* had other purposes in *Shangwe* lives; it was believed that it had the power to chase away evil spirits. If, for example, an owl, which was believed to be an evil bird used by witches, hooted outside a *Shangwe* home at night, a fire would be started and *mbanje* would be burnt. It was believed that its smell chased owls away (Interview, Angeline Mafa, Mafa village, 18 November 2011). Cannabis production was carried for consumption and for use for religious purposes, not as a commercial proposition. This state of affairs changed in the 1960s. The change towards commercial production was a reaction to actions of the colonial state from the 1950s. With their eviction from the forest and with the squeeze on their old way of life owing to their relocation, the Shangwe discovered that they could make money through growing and selling *mbanje*.

Transcending gender barriers: The changing uses of *mbanje* from the 1960s

The "opening up" of Gokwe exposed the Shangwe, a previously secluded community, to the vagaries of the colonial markets and the cash-based economy. There was resistance to this new order, as many aspects of it negated the Shangwe customs, especially Christianity and the church. There were aspects of the new order that were not resistible, though. The "opening up" of Gokwe brought with it a number of sweeteners, such as Coca-Cola and other such soft drinks and other ingredients with the "sweet" sugar. Ideas about cleanliness and beauty also began to evolve among the Shangwe women in the 1950s. Timothy Burke's book, aptly titled *Lifebuoy Men, Lux Women: Commodification, Consumption and Cleanliness in Modern Zimbabwe* (1996), shows how commodities (cosmetics) such as soaps, skin-lightening creams, Vaseline and other body lotions and hair creams (commodity culture in general), have played a huge role in defining and shaping not just ideas around fashion and cleanliness, but also gender relations.

A good example about the evolution of ideas about fashion is the transformation of *mbanje* into a beauty product. Commodification brought with it previously unknown soaps and skin and hair products. The majority of the Shangwe, at this early point, could not afford most of these products. But there were creative attempts to substitute these commercial products with what was available. Honey, for example, which was widely available in Mafungautsi Forest and other forested areas, found a new use. Honey had previously been considered as a medicine that would be given to sick people, but now began to be used as a sweetener for tea. Men and women had to take a risk and venture into the protected forest in search of honey (Interview, Eunice Mafa, Mafa village, 10 March 2011). The new commodities, rather than facilitating a migration by local people from old ways to new, in some ways helped buttress old ways.

The same happened with *mbanje*. *Mbanje* seeds began to be used by Shangwe women as a substitute for hair creams. Young girls got pre-occupied with gathering *mbanje* seeds which were utilised to make a powder for hair care. The seeds would be roasted and ground into a fine powder. The powder would be mixed with water or other products in certain quantities, depending on what the user intended to do with her hair. The powder could be mixed in a certain way for washing one's hair with. It was believed that this would prevent the hair from breaking. The powder could also be prepared in a certain way to dye hair to make it darker (Interview, Angeline Mafa, 14 July, 2011). As was the case with the example of honey mentioned above, this new development in a way buttressed old traditions. The girls learned about their culture, which the colonial system sought to undermine, from their interaction with elders as they sought *mbanje* seeds. In societies where there is no or little Western education, as was the case with the Shangwe, learning about traditions and matters such as marriage was passed by word of mouth from one generation to another.

"To get access to *mbanje* seeds", Angeline Mafa recalled (on 14 July, 2011), "we really had to have good relations with our older brothers, uncles and other elderly people like *sekuru* (grandfather) VaOne. We would sometimes go to help them with small chores just to stay in their good books to keep the supply of *mbanje* seeds flowing. We would sometimes just go to listen to *sekuru* VaOne's stories – Eustina (now Masora's wife), Pauline, Sifile, Hleiwe, Tendai, and many other girls - some of the stories were quite interesting and educative, while some were boring. Of course with time some stories were retold over and over, so it became quite boring. But it was important to have good relations with these people grown-up people who cultivated and consumed *mbanje*." It is quite fascinating that in spite of the illegality of the crop, its use increased with the introduction of cotton, to the extent of transcending gender barriers.

Mbanje production also increased significantly as it assumed the position of a commodity sold illicitly on the market. Because of its commercial value, villagers from Mafa and Matashu began to grow bigger patches of *mbanje* in Mafungautsi Forest to avoid detection. Because of the eviction from the forest and its protection by Forestry Commission of Rhodesia officers (who did not have the capacity to maintain their presence in all parts of the 101 hectare forest), very few people would venture into the forest. When the mbanje was ripe, it was harvested, packed into sacks and transported by night to the villages where it was stored in granaries, usually underneath produce such as maize or groundnuts (Interviews, Mafa village, September 2011). Villagers would take their *mbanje* to mining centres in Gatooma (now Kadoma) and Que (now Kwekwe), around 100 kilometres away. Empress Mine was one of the centres that were supplied with the product from Mafa Village. "We would take our crop to Empress Mine in Kadoma to sell it to the mines. We sold it for the equivalent of about one American dollar per 'twist.' A 'twist' is only a few grams. This was a lot more remunerating than cotton. Cotton farmers used to get only one shilling and six pence per kilogramme delivered. Mbanje growers did not need to grow much to get better returns than cotton farmers", one villager stated.

The *mbanje* growers came up with their own "underground" routes from the village to the mining centres to avoid detection by police. They would leave the village on bicycles and cycle on forest tracks and remain in the forest till they reached Sikhombela Farm, where they would branch into rural routes in the Chidoma Reserve till they reached Kadoma. "We would at all costs avoid the main road, where police mounted roadblocks. People would be made to disembark from buses with all their possessions to be searched", a villager recalled. At the mines, they had their friends and "business partners" who would house them for days as they sold their stock. Because of the fear of getting caught and imprisonment for a long time (as duration of sentences depended on quantities of mbanje one was caught in possession of), they carried their mbanje in many small instalments. "We would carry a maximum of three or four gallons per trip, 15 to 20 kilogrammes", he stated. "This would yield anything between £50 and £100."

Gambling among the Shangwe

Gambling emerged as a big activity in Mbumbuzi from the 1960s. Gambling was done utilising playing cards, and many Shangwe men made a fortune through the activity, while, needless to say, some men were impoverished because of the vice. With the coming of Madheruka in the 1950s, accompanied by the introduction of bus

112

services, opening of the first schools, opening of shops and infrastructural development projects such as the construction of gravel roads, dip tanks and boreholes, a new dynamic was introduced to Mbumbuzi and the surrounding areas.

While in the past it had been possible to subsist without use of money, these developments made money an everyday essential to meet daily needs. Whereas in the 1940s and 1950s the majority of the Shangwe wore animal hides as their clothing, the 1960s brought with them material changes; clothes, tennis shoes, soap, skin and hair creams, soft drinks, sugar, among a list of other manufactures, which became popular in Mbumbuzi. In the early 1950s, the Shangwe would derogatorily call new *Madheruka* settlers as *vanhu vasinamabvi* (those with no knees) because of the trousers they wore. By the mid-1960s, this perception was changing, as more and more Shangwe men also began to wear trousers. Journeys that would take days to complete on foot could now be undertaken in a matter of hours, cumbersome chores such as preparing mealie-meal (corn flour) could be done quickly by new mechanical devices such as grinding mills.

While in the past successful hunters, traditional healers, those with more cattle and the few migrants who had trekked to mining, commercial farming and urban centres were the most prosperous people in Shangwe society, the new order opened the door to everyone who had the means to get an extra farthing to prosper, by local standards. Gambling among men soon became an important economic activity as Shangwe men sought to make more money and quickly get rich. Many men, among them Limon Lunga, Lot Sidhakwa, Kefas Ncube, Nyakasaka Fute, Kevias Mhanqwa, Sizeboy Mafa, Mavhurasaga Ncube, Mhedge Sibanda and Sodaka Sibanda, Thomas Dilivera Bhunu, among many others, earned popularity for their gambling (Interviews in Mbumbuze, 2011-2012, Interview with Regina Lunga, Matashu village, 26 September, 2011). He proceeds from the activities would then be used for bride price to marry more wives (as the Shangwe were and are still very polygamous), to buy cattle (a symbol of wealth by which one got a higher status in society), to buy clothes, among other needs. Though gambling was illegal, men carried out the activity in broad daylight. The gamblers would go away for long periods of time to gamble, sometimes up to three months at a time (Interview with Regina Lunga, Matashu village, 26 September, 2011). Gambling was a self-reinforcing vice; those who would have lost would borrow from fellow gamblers, hoping to recoup their losses. Some would sell their cattle and other valuable possessions for gambling purposes.

Many gamblers found themselves neck-deep in debt. Because of addiction to gambling, many men married off their daughters to get money for the activity, and to settle their indebtedness. "At one time", one interviewee stated, Nyika Kucha gambled away his own wife, Mtshado Nkiwane. The wife refused to go to her "new husband", opting to go and stay with her brother. The brother brought her back to Kucha, seeing nothing wrong with the deal (using the woman to settle indebtedness)." Nyika finally used his donkeys and some of his land to repay his debt, leaving his family more impoverished. There were many instances when men gambled away their wives. Gambling often resulted in family problems. Many men lost significant numbers of their cattle in their gambling escapades, often resulting in conflict between them and their wives, and, in some instances, with their older children. "Gambling is a very evil practice", Emily Mafa (Mafa village, 2012) stated, "In the 1960s my father used to get quite a bit of money from gambling. But in later days, as he got older, he lost a significant amount of his money to gambling. He even sold our cattle to settle debts incurred from gambling."

Conclusion

Cotton production in pre-colonial Zimbabwe is often cited as a case of an example of a success story, an "agrarian miracle", where peasants rose to the occasion and improved their lot by producing for the market. As the cotton story gets told, one gets an impression that this was an all-inclusive agrarian revolution. This view is ahistorical. Cotton was only introduced in Gokwe in 1960 in a fashion typical of colonial top-down management; there was no consultation and there were no attempts to understand the sensibilities of Shangwe people. The Shangwe, who had lived in harmony with nature in the Mafungautsi Forest for a long time, were suddenly told that the forest had been demarcated for [colonial] state use and that they had to vacate. The same process happened in relation to Madheruka farmers; they were settled on land designated for white farms where they were accused of being responsible for massive degradation of the soil. Madheruka were forcibly resettled in Gokwe in 1953, the year Shangwe relocation also began after Mafungautsi was gazetted a state-protected forest. It was against such a background that cotton was introduced. While transition to cotton was not a relatively easy process for the Madheruka, the same cannot be said of the Shangwe.

Old habits die hard. Deprived of their old livelihood, the Shangwe were left with no choice but to embrace cotton production, but along with their old forms of livelihoods. As far as the state was concerned, that shift to producing cotton for the market, together with other crops, was what would bring "modernity" to the so-called "backward" Shangwe people. They had adequate land for cotton production, and because of their polygamous marriages – colonial agricultural officials often reasoned - they also had a lot of labour force to utilise for commodity production. They did not have to worry about capital for farming; there were facilities to provide seed, chemicals, fertilizers and other such inputs on credit. The money would be redeemed upon selling the cotton. This promised to be difficult from the onset. The Shangwe were not agriculturalists at any significant scale. Though they had always cultivated crops, it was at a very small scale, for household use rather than for the market. In addition to this, the Shangwe did not view these events as modernising; rather they were an onslaught on their way of life and culture. Because of this, the initial response to the shift to cotton production was to frown on this new system, with its churches, schools, crops, agricultural officers, loan schemes and *Madheruka* immigrants.

The response to these developments was an array of anti-cotton measures meant to ensure survival in this new environment. Among these reactions were illegal actions such as illegal harvesting of forest products, poaching, gambling, brewing of illicit beer, and growing of *mbanje* for the market. This chapter has shown that illegal activities helped some Shangwe to earn money with which to subsist in the newly introduced money economy brought forth by the colonial government in Gokwe. These responses were important as far as they demonstrate that Africans were not mere victims of the colonial system. They evaluated each colonial action or onslaught and came up with responses that they deemed, in their own specific context, appropriate for their sustenance. These responses have shaped Gokwe today, where the Shangwe are still being derogatorily considered "primitive" and "backward" by their fellow Madheruka countrymen.

References

Archival Sources
National Archives of Zimbabwe (NAZ), A3/18/20, Responses to the Chief Native Commissioner's Circular dated 1912.
NAZ, S2090, Memorandum on Coal in the Sobungwe district, 1937.
NAZ, S2091, Circular Newsletters to Native Commissioners.
NAZ, S1947, Civil Cases, Sobungwe District.

Interviews
Angeline Mafa, 61, Mafa village, 18 November 2011.
Brown Kufa, Matashu Village.
Dhara Msanika (also known as Kohwapakuru) of Mafa village.
Eunice Mafa, mid-60s, Mafa village, 10 March 2011.
Isaac Gavaza, 85, Rumhumha village.
Kevias Mhanqwa, 66 years old, at Mafa village, 13 February and 15 February, 2011.
Killion Lunga, 72, Matashu village, 26 October 2012.
King Moyo, 70, Mafa village, 12 February 2012.
Liza Jojo, 65, Mafa village, 12 January, 2012.
Mabheu Senzela, 70, Matashu village, 26 October 2011.
Manhamba Sande, Sande village, Nemangwe, 66, 10 October 2011.
Marabu Sibanda, 63, Mafa village, 22 October, 2011.
Mutimba Khohliso Weresi, around 85 years old, at Mafa village, 16 February, 2011.
Regina Lunga, 81, Matashu village, 26 September, 2011.

Samson Kohwapakuru Msanika, 87 years old, Mafa village, 20 November 2012.

Shadrick Silemba (a Shangwe spirit medium), Mandava village, Svisvi, Nemangwe.

Silas Mapfumo, mid-80s, Matashu village, 26 November, 2011

Tafirenyika Tafirei Shumba, 71, Takaendesa village

Vincent Sibanda, 69, Mafa village, 2 December 2011.

Unpublished Sources

Alvord, E. D. (1958). "Development of Native Agriculture and Land Tenure in Southern Rhodesia", Unpublished Manuscript, University of Zimbabwe Library.

Hose, J. (1970). "Britain and the Development of West African Cotton, 1845-1960", PhD thesis, Columbia University.

Maast, M. (1996). "The Harvest of Independence: Commodity Boom and Socio-Economic Differentiation among Peasants in Zimbabwe", PhD thesis, University of Roskilde.

Worby, E. (1992). "Remaking Labour, Reshaping Identity: Cotton, Commoditization and the Culture of Modernity in North-western Zimbabwe", Doctor of Philosophy thesis, McGill University.

Published Sources

Agriserve (Pvt) Ltd. 1986. *The Impact of the Sanyati Gin on Small-holder Cotton Production*, Harare, Agriserve.

Arrighi, G. 1967. *The Political Economy of Rhodesia*, Vol. 16, The Hague, Mouton.

Barnett, T. 1975. "The Gezira Scheme: Production of Cotton and the Reproduction of Underdevelopment", *Beyond the Sociology of Development*, London, Routledge and Kegan Paul.

Benton, L. 2002. *Law and Colonial Cultures: Legal Regimes in World History, 1400-1900*, Cambridge, Cambridge University Press.

Berman, B. 1984. "Structure and Process in the Bureaucratic States of Colonial Africa", *Development and Change*, 15, 2, 161-202.

Bundy, C. 1979. *The Rise and Fall of the South African Peasantry*, Vol. 28, Los Angeles, University of California Press.

Burke, T. 1996. *Lifebuoy Men, Lux Women: Commodification, Consumption and Cleanliness in Modern Zimbabwe*, Durham, Duke University Press.

Comaroff, J. 2002. "Governmentality, Materiality, Legality, Modernity: On the Colonial State of Africa" in Deutsch, Schmidt, H. and Probst, P. (Eds), *African Modernities, Entangled Meanings in Current Debate*, Oxford, James Currey.

copied Worby, E. 1998. Inscribing the State At the "Edge Of Beyond:" Danger and Development in Northwestern Zimbabwe, *Political and Legal Anthropology Review, 21*(2): 55-70.

Cousins, B. (1993). "Debating Communal Tenure in Zimbabwe", *Journal of Contemporary African Studies* 12 (1): 29-39.

Cousins, B., Weiner, D. and Amin, N. 1992. "Social Differentiation in the Communal Lands of Zimbabwe", *Review of African Political Economy* 19 (53): 5-24.

Curry-Machado, J. (Ed.) 2013. Global Histories, Imperial Commodities, Local Interactions, Basingstoke: Palgrave MacMillan.

Floyd, B. 1962. Land Apportionment in Southern Rhodesia. *Geographical Review, 52*(4): 566-582.

Hazareesingh, S. and Maat, H. (Eds). 2016. *Local Subversions of Colonial Cultures: Commodities and Anti-Commodities in Global History*, Cambridge, Palgrave Macmillan UK,

Iliffe, J. 1990. *Famine in Zimbabwe, 1890 – 1960*, Gweru, Mambo Press.

Isaacman, A. *et al.* 1980. "Cotton is the Mother of Poverty: Peasant Resistance to Forced Cotton Production in Mozambique, 1938-61", *The International Journal of African Historical Studies* 13 (4): 581-615.

Isaacman, A. F. 1996. "Cotton is the Mother of Poverty: Peasants, Work and Rural Struggle in Colonial Mozambique, 1938-61", *Social History of Africa*, Portsmouth, Heinemann.

Isaacman, I. and Roberts, R. 1995. *Cotton, Colonialism and Social History in Sub-Saharan Africa: Introduction*, Portsmouth, Heinemann Educational Publishers.

Karekwaivanane, G. H. 2011. "It Shall be the Duty of Every African to Obey and Comply Promptly': Negotiating State Authority in the Legal Arena, Rhodesia, 1965-1980", *Journal of Southern African Studies*, 37, 2, 333-349.

Kay, G. B. and Hymer, S. 1972. *The Political Economy of Colonialism in Ghana, A Collection of Documents and Statistics, 1900-1960*, Cambridge.

Kosmin, B. 1977. "The Inyoka Tobacco Industry of the Shangwe People: the Displacement of a Pre-colonial Economy in Southern Rhodesia, 1898 – 1938" in Palmer, R. 1977. *Roots of Rural Poverty in Central and Southern Africa*, Berkeley, University of California Press.

Likaka, O. 1997. *Rural Society and Cotton in Colonial Zaire*, Madison, University of Wisconsin Press.

MacGaffey, J. 1983. "How to Survive and Become Rich Amidst Devastation: the Second Economy in Zaire", *African Affairs*, 82, 328, 351-366.

Machingaidze, V. 1979. "Company Rule and Agricultural Development: The case of BSA Company in Southern Rhodesia, 1908-1923", *Collected Seminar Papers: Institute of Common wealth Studies*, London.

Machingaidze, V. E. M. 1991. "Agrarian Change from above: The Southern Rhodesia Native Land Husbandry Act and African Response", *The International Journal of African Historical Studies*, 24 (3): 557-588.

Mapedza, E. 2007. "Forestry Policy in Colonial and Post-colonial Zimbabwe: Continuity and Change", *Journal of Historical Geography* 33 (4): 833-851.

Maravanyika, S. 2012. "Local Responses to Colonial Evictions, Conservation and Commodity Policies among Shangwe Communities in Gokwe, 1963 – 1980", *African Nebula*, 5, pp. 1 – 20.

Maravanyika, S. 2016. "Shun the White Man's Crop': Shangwe Grievances, Religious Leaders and Cotton Cultivation in North-Western Zimbabwe" in Hazareesingh, S. and Maat, H. (Eds), *Local Subversions of Colonial Cultures: Commodities and Anti-Commodities in Global History*, Cambridge, Palgrave Macmillan UK, pp. 187 – 209.

Maravanyika, S., & Mutimukuru-Maravanyika, T. 2009. Resource-based Conflict at the Local Level in a Changing National Environment: The Case of Zimbabwe's Mafungautsi State Forest. *African Economic History, 37*, 129-150.

Mawere, M. 2012. *The Struggle of African Indigenous Knowledge Systems In an Age of Globalisation – A Case for Children's Traditional Games in South-eastern Zimbabwe,* Langaa RPCIG.

Mawere, M. 2013. A critical review of environmental conservation in Zimbabwe, 2013, *Africa Spectrum,* 48 (2): 85- 97.

Merry, S. E. 1991. "Law and Colonialism", *Law and Society Review,* 25, 4, 889-922.

Morel, E. D. 1920. *The Black Man's Burden: The White Man in Africa from the Fifteenth Century to World War 1*, London, Monthly Review Press.

Mosley, P. 1982. "Agricultural Development and Government Policy in Settler Economies: The case of Kenya and Southern Rhodesia, 1900-1960", *The Economic History Review,* 35, 3, 390-408.

Mufuka, K. 1991. "The Weak Link in Zimbabwe's Agricultural Miracle, 1980-1990: A Case Study of Masvingo Province Resettlement Projects, *Development Southern Africa,* 8, 3, 293-304.

Mutimukuru-Maravanyika, T. 2010. *Can we Learn our Way to Sustainable Management? Adaptive Collaborative Management in Mafungautsi State Forest*, Zimbabwe, PhD Thesis, Wageningen University.

Nyambara, P. 1990. "The Origins and Development of the Cotton Industry in Colonial Zimbabwe, 1903 – 1935", *Eastern Africa Social Science Research Review* 6 (2): 141 – 156.

Nyambara, P. 2000. Colonial Policy and Peasant Cotton Agriculture in Southern Rhodesia, 1904-1953. *The International Journal of African Historical Studies, 33*(1): 81-111.

Nyambara, P. 2005. "That Place was Wonderful!" African Tenants on Rhodesdale Estate, Colonial Zimbabwe, c. 1900-1952. *The International Journal of African Historical Studies, 38*(2), 267-299.

Nyambara, P. S. 2000. "Colonial Policy and Peasant Cotton Agriculture in Southern Rhodesia, 1904-1953", *The International Journal of African Historical Studies* 33 (1): 81-111.

Nyambara, P. S. (2001). "The Politics of Land Acquisition and Struggles over Land in the Communal Areas of Zimbabwe: the Gokwe Region in the 1980s and 1990s", *Africa-London-International African Institute*, 71, 2, 253-85.

Nyambara, P. S. (2002). "Madheruka and Shangwe: Ethnic Identities and the Culture of Modernity in Gokwe, North-western Zimbabwe, 1963-79", *Journal of African History*, 287-306.

Nyaruwata, S. (1984). Eastern Highlands Tea Estates: "A Case Study of the Historical Development of a Tea Estate", *Geographical Association of Zimbabwe*, 7, 1.

Page, S. L. J. and Page, H. E. (1991). "Western Hegemony over African Agriculture in Southern Rhodesia and its Continuing Threat to Food Security in Independent Zimbabwe", *Agriculture and Human Values* 8 (4): 3-18.

Palmer, R. 1977. *Land and Racial Domination in Rhodesia*, California, University of California Press.

Palmer, R. H. and Parsons, N. (Eds.). 1977. *The Roots of Rural Poverty in Central and Southern Africa*, Vol. 25, Los Angeles, University of California Press.

Phimister, I. 1987. "Zimbabwe: The Combined and Contradictory Inheritance of the Struggle against Colonialism", *Transformation*, 5, 51-59.

Phimister, I. R. 1974. "Peasant Production and Underdevelopment in Southern Rhodesia, 1890-1914", *African Affairs* 73 (291): 217-228.

Phimister, I. R. 1976. "The Reconstruction of the Southern Rhodesian Gold Mining Industry, 1903-10", *The Economic History Review*, 29, 3, 465-81.

Phimister, I. R. 1988. *An Economic and Social History of Zimbabwe, 1890-1948: Capital Accumulation and Class Struggle*, London, Longman.

Prentice, A. N. 1972. *Cotton, with Special Reference to Africa*, London, Longman.

Punt, E. 1979. *The Development of African Agriculture in Southern Rhodesia with particular reference to the Inter-War Years*, Master of Arts (MA) Thesis, University of Natal.

Roberts, R. L. 1996. *Two Worlds of Cotton: Colonization and the Regional Economy in the French Soudan, 1800-1946*, Stanford, Stanford University Press.

Robins, J. 2009. "The Black Man's Crop: Cotton, Imperialism and Public-Private Development in Britain's African Colonies, 1900-1918", *Commodities of Empire Working Papers*, Working Paper No. 11.

Vail, L. 1976. "Mozambique's Chartered Companies: the Rule of the Feeble", *Journal of African History* 17 (3): 389-416.

Worby, E. 2000. 'Discipline without Oppression': Sequence, Timing and Marginality in Southern Rhodesia's Post-War Development Regime. *The Journal of African History, 41*(1): 101-125.

Chapter 6

Political Naivety, Corruption, and Poverty Promotion in Africa: Riding the 'Poorest-ugliest French' Bijuralism Horse from Cameroon to Canada via Britain

Peter Ateh-Afac Fossungu

I will comfort the powerless people. I will pull them out of the affliction of so painful a colonial yoke. The world must hear their story through me. There has never been a time like this fitting for this challenge. My defence for a fatherland is put on this context. In fact, preaching to empty stomachs without showing them how to come out of misery is as worthless as saying Mass to dogs. Go grant them the secrets to improve on their standards of living and conscientization to bring down the tyrant who has held their progress hostage. Go tell it on the mountain that injustice has been practiced on depraved peoples for the whole length of fifty-six years (Jumbam, 2017).

Introduction

Professor John Mukum Mbaku's *Institutions and Development in Africa* makes a significant contribution to the debate on poverty alleviation in Africa. It contains a refreshing, rigorous and informative analysis of underdevelopment in Africa using the tools of public choice theory and provides practical and effective policies and institutions to economic growth and development. While agreeing that the shortage of competent, highly skilled and well-informed bureaucrats has been a major development obstacle in many countries in Africa during the last forty years, the author argues that the most important contributor to poverty and deprivation in Africa is the absence of institutional arrangements that enhance indigenous entrepreneurship and wealth creation. As Africans complete several years in the new millennium, the continent remains the poorest and most deprived region of the world. Mbaku theorizes that the abrogation of economic freedoms has stunted entrepreneurship and prevented the creation of the wealth that the continent needs to deal with poverty and underdevelopment. It is critical, then, that Africans engage in state reconstruction, through democratic constitution making, to provide themselves with institutional arrangements that enhance wealth creation and sustainable development. This transformative mode, he concludes, is so vital that living standards in the continent will continue to deteriorate, unless and until these institutional building blocks are in place (Mbaku, 2004).

Using Cameroon (Professor Mbaku's country of origin, which also perfectly makes the case for 'brain-drain') comparatively as a classical case-study "of poverty and vulnerability which create disaster risks and foment and perpetuate different faces of poverty among African communities" (Professor Mawere, chapter 1: this volume), this chapter argues essentially that politically naïve, corrupt, and corrupting administrators – and other 'elites' in Africa – have been exceptionally efficient vectors for the promotion (rather than the eradication) of poverty in the continent. That modus operandi has so easily turned Africa into what one critic has protractedly described as *Quagmatickism* – which is actually just a cloaked means of continuing the trans-Atlantic slave trade and colonialism in Africa under innocuously new names like 'brain-drain' or '*voluntary* slavery'[1] – before appositely querying: "Now, just seeing how someone (like Odilia) can be so easily frustrated in their relentless efforts to have a better life in Africa by things that are not supposed to stand in someone's way, why wouldn't there be this mad rush to rush away from the quagmaticking African show and into the so-called Western world? Why wouldn't anyone be right in saying we greatly contribute to, if not actually creating, our own problems?" (Fossungu, 2016: 37).

This chapter comes to further show just how we do this problem-creation to Africa and its inhabitants; exposing the new or so-called modern drivers of modernized (or *voluntary*) slavery to be the

---

[1] "Voluntary slavery is worse than the other well-known type, just as Native Reserves is worse than the well-known Apartheid: if you correctly put the 'borderless doctors' slant on them, as you should. It is a long story trying to specifically detail all that out right now but cut it short and clear with this brief *Ignorance Theory*. The worst thing that can happen to you is to be ignorant of your ignorance. As a teacher, my task is often made easier if my students know what they do not know. He who does not know what he does not know will never know" (Fossungu, 2015b: 5, original emphasis).

"mounting oddifacism and enduring resilience of 'African poverty' as well as the politics, controversies, and events which surround, stymie and constrain poverty and vulnerability reduction efforts by poverty and vulnerability professionals" (Professor Mawere, chapter 1: this volume). It is very hard to proffer a generally accepted definition of poverty, especially as "[t]hey say Africans don't usually need humourists because they are always happy and laughing even in their poverty or moneylessness" (Fossungu, 2015b: 6);[2] let alone assign one particular cause to it. Hawker and Waite (2007: 703) give poverty the following three connotations: '1) *abject poverty*: pennilessness, destitution, penury, impoverishment, neediness, hardship, impecuniousness; 2) *the poverty of choice*: scarcity, deficiency, dearth, shortage, paucity, absence, lack; and 3) *the poverty of her imagination*: inferiority, mediocrity sterility.' What these specialists give as the opposites of poverty are 'wealth, abundance [and] fertility.' All these meanings of the terminology come into play throughout this chapter. What is clear though is that poverty is not merely a natural phenomenon, but it is also anthropogenic as it is political, economic, and socio-cultural. This chapter hinges on the funny neo-colonial politics of the duality of legal systems (bijuralism) in Cameroon, forcefully bringing out the two most bedevilling candidates of political naivety and of corruption as an unholy pair of the most proficient poverty promoters in Africa. The glaring evidence for this observation is the existing worrisome human rights violations and nation-building situation rampant in Cameroon. The carnage going on in the two 'English-speaking' regions (Debundschazone and Savannazone) is brought out with the aid of Reverend Gerald Jumbam's thought-provoking open-letter to the head of the National Episcopal Conference of Cameroon (NECC), in the person of Archbishop Samuel Kleda:

---

[2] And especially also if one also diligently considers Momany's May 2006 message to *The Lion of Judah* called Nginyam: "Please, the word POVERTY has no place in your vocabulary because you have what no amount of money can fetch for a lot of others – responsible and well-behaved daughters, four in number, and deserving sons-in-law especially championed by no other than Solomon E. Tatah, the one man I have come to consider [as] one of the luckiest guys on earth" (Fossungu, 2016: 177).

Your Grace, I wish to conclude here by saying that the capacity for self-determination is Christian. No one can conquer the British Cameroons. You can't extinguish the fire that led our forebears out of Nigeria. That fire burns! If our effort is not enough to win the battle, our children will win it with better effort. But it shall not be postponed this time around. And yet, the cry of the agonizing British Cameroonian has fallen on deaf ears around the globe. For them, the pogrom in the British Cameroons is only some localized problem. The abductions and butchery of humans are hidden, ill-reported. Along with the nonstop infiltration of our land with armed killer squads and military bastards criminally excused from any probe, query or answerability, we are witnessing an experiment with "ethnic cleansing" authorized and sustained by the French Cameroon psychopath, Paul Biya. Strange that those that obtain the just publicity of terror in our land are only the French Cameroons controlled media. A military selected for the assignment of absolute "pacification" of the British Cameroons is doing its work unopposed. Where is Britain's assuagement in this matter? It is impossible to believe these things are happening under the nose of international human right bodies and the silence of Great Britain in this carnage in its trusteeship territory it sacrificed its independence in the altar of De Gaullism (Jumbam, 2017).[3]

---

[3] *According to Tatah Mentan (Theodore Lentz scholar of Peace and Security Studies and Professor of Political Science),*

Merely urging the Cameroonian government to exercise the "utmost restraint" in dealing with the aggrieved Anglophone people, as people-centered governments around the world do, is far too weak a response. The international community, beginning with the United Nations and other international organizations like the African Union, as well as individual countries, should use every means possible to step up pressure on the blood-thirsty Cameroon thugtatorship to:

• allow foreign media, as well as international fact-finding missions, into the country in order to enable objective investigations of what has been happening;

• release all those who only peacefully exercised their internationally guaranteed human rights, and guarantee that no one is subjected to hostage taking, torture, and unfair trials;

• enter into a meaningful dialogue with the representatives of the Anglophone people, not bribed gangsters.

Unless these conditions are fulfilled, the United Nations should seriously reconsider whether restoring the botched independence of the former British Southern Cameroons in a country that includes a peaceful graveyard is not the best idea (Mentan, 2017).

126

It is truly an atmosphere that cannot fail to attract the attention of anyone who at least has an ephemeral idea of what multiculturalism, federalism, judicial independence, and democracy do signify. Some political economists have already postulated that Cameroon, with far more natural resources and other aspects favouring speedy development, is not leading the advancement game in Africa solely because of the schizophrenic drive aimed at "Turning the English-speaking into the French" (Fossungu, 2013a: 209-218). This chapter seeks to also strengthen this theory that was posited in the context of the political economy by using the burning issue of bijuralism – dualism of legal systems. In countries like Cameroon and Canada, the approach to some of the issues surrounding legal and education systems and equality cannot exclude the requirement of the twins of bijuralism and bilingualism. Being from one of the most prominent candidates of multiculturalism, this chapter seeks to throw light on the darkness that has been cast by tracing the root causes of the persisting quagmire in relation to legal dualism.

"At unification in 1961 of anglophone and francophone Cameroon, each with a distinct legal system," writes Dr Joseph Temngah Nyambo, a law professor at the University of Yaoundé II, "the idea of the co-existence of two legal systems was born" (cited in Fossungu, 2013a: 173). With this poor kind of intellectualism,[4] the miseducated public cannot see and detect the difference between camouflaged unijuralism and effective legal pluralism. Would anyone then be wrong in linking economic poverty in Africa to poverty in constitutional scholarship? Innovative poverty is deep down in matters of legal pluralism in Cameroon and the easy creation of penury and underdevelopment would greatly be enhanced by it. I would like to avoid delving into the controversies and conflicts about the "folly" of legal pluralism, said to be so much loved by postmodern jurists, by simply using bijuralism in this chapter. It is already well known that in countries like Cameroon and Canada, bijuralism and bilingualism are linked not only one to the other, but

---

[4] According to the dictionaristic experts mentioned earlier, poor is an adjective signifying '1 having very little money. 2 of a low standard or quality. 3 (poor in) not having enough of something. 4 deserving pity or sympathy' (Hawker and Waite, 2007: 697).

as well to the systems of education. This intimate connection would thus make Fossungu's (2013a: 95-110) elaborate and critical discussion of "The Philosophy of the [1998] Education Law" to already determine the fate of the others. Yet, to the foregoing thesis on bijuralism, has also been added that of Dr Dan Lantum, a professor at the University of Yaoundé I, which is acclaiming the Foumban actors/architects for the "bilingualism which was enshrined into the Federal Constitution of 1st October 1961" (cited in Fossungu, 2013a: 169). This claim is anchored on Article 59 of the Federal Constitution;[5] the chapter not specifically looking in details into this claimed bilingualism until its tail end where it is sparingly examined.

Some of these intellectuals have gone as far as justifying their dishonesty (or poverty in intellectualism) on the basis of national unity. Cameroon's contradictory One-Party Federation (or Advanced Democracy) was actually given its impetus by the Anglophones. These momentum and inauguration had been lacking on the eastern side of the Mungo River where a 1962 Opposition Manifesto very clearly affirmed (in the face of the ceaseless drive to create the single party) that:

> National unity such as is defined by certain people is a myth, and this myth borders on utopia. If we were really animated, all of us, by a desire for unity, one would employ a different language than the one we are used to hearing from Radio Yaounde and the officials. As for ourselves, we believe that unity supposes a minimum of courtesy towards those one wants to unite: but we observe, to our great regret, that this unity will come about only when the holders of power have reduced the other Cameroonians to the rank of slaves....
>
> National Unity with effective competition and activity among all the political and spiritual families of Cameroon. Yes!

National Unity in the uniformization of the single party which will lead necessarily to dictatorship. No! (Translated and quoted by

---

[5] See *Loi N° 61-24 du 1er septembre 1961 portant révision constitutionnelle et tendant à adapter la constitution actuelle aux nécessités du Cameroun réunifié* (hereinafter Federal Constitution).

Johnson, 1970: 263; original omission marks). This Manifesto is lengthily discussed in Anyangwe (1989: 64-65) and it evidently means that National Unity, if that is actually the goal (it is strongly submitted here), must not only tolerate dissent; it has to also, in countries like Cameroon and Canada, properly address important questions such as that suggested by Enonchong (1967: xii): "What common ground exists between the Cameroon common-law and civil-law approaches and what is their point of departure?" Questions like this one must be properly addressed to give any meaning that is not offensive to the acclaimed bicultural and bilingual nature of Cameroon. Doing so, I think, will also mitigate the crisis that is now threatening Cameroon's very existence. I think the current stalemate in Cameroon has emanated directly from the drive to uniformize that was inaugurated and confirmed by the 1961 One-Hour-35-Minute Foumban Conference[6] (a pitiable gathering that is falsely considered to be Cameroon's version of Canada's very lengthy and purposeful Confederation Debates, and which is also being unnecessarily acclaimed as Cameroon's Philadelphia!). Yet, a lot of Cameroonians – mostly Anglophones, for that matter – have been applauding this erratic Foumban 'federal'-Unitary arrangement for having institutionalized the rule of law, democracy, bilingualism, and legal pluralism in Cameroon. This is unfortunate intellectualism creating indescribable deprivation for the masses that would be eagerly looking up to the 'intellectuals' for salvation! Although they are strongly connected, this chapter critically and extensively examines only bijuralism.

Though the chapter does not join in the making and/or unmaking of the legal pluralism 'folly', its employment of bijuralism is in agreement, at least, with Sally Engels Merry's definition of legal pluralism: "a situation in which two or more legal systems coexist in the same social field" (cited in Tamanaha, 1993: 193). To the Amsterdam University professor, the definitions of the concept,

---

[6] See *Record of the Conference on the Constitutional Future of the Southern Cameroons, Held at Foumban 17th to 21st July 1961* (Buea: West Cameroon Government, 1961). The close to two hours duration given here is in relation to the actual period of meeting between the two delegations of East and West Cameroon. See Anyangwe (1987: 128) and Johnson (1970: 188).

"unobjectionable" as they are, would only be a starting point (Tamanaha, 1993: 193). Professor Tamanaha is not incorrect, especially in the context of Cameroon's confusion that I propose to examine and expose its poverty creation and stifling of development within two main issues: (1) whether or not there is an 'Anglophone Cameroon' in a Cameroon which conspicuously has only (2) a common Civil-Law system.

Distinguishing God From God: Is There An "Anglophone Cameroon"?

'Distinguishing God from God' is just a neat and tidy philosophical way of saying 'it is a needlessly senseless distinction'. The title is an essential question because of several reasons, one of which enormously justifies a critic's 1998 theory on the 'mocking of the bilingualism and bijuralism birds' that "any discussion of Cameroon's bilingualism/bijuralism, to my mind, is like discussing an invention that is yet to be realized as if it were already real. In short, it is like talking about a nothing. But, as there has already been too much talk about a *nothing* as if it is a *something*, I have now got something to discuss about nothing" (cited in Fossungu, 2013a: 171, original emphasis). The Mungo River is traditionally considered as the dividing line between the two colonially imposed legal systems and cultures. Furthermore, it is claimed that the constitutional changes in Cameroon brought about by the 1972 Constitution[7] destroyed the bicultural nature of the country and thence moved its development gear into the reverse. The authenticity (or otherwise) of these claims, together with their impacts on the facilitation of poverty creation and underdevelopment, can be comprehended by thoroughly examining (1) the Mungo River distinction and (2) the related issue of Cameroon's Commonwealth membership.

The Mungo River Myth and the Quebec Analogy

If making *something* out of *nothing* is not a myth, then it is hard to comprehend what would constitute a falsehood. Myths about

---

[7] See 2 June 1972 Constitution of the United Republic of Cameroon.

something have been defined as "false and stereotyped views or beliefs about" that something.[8] 'Stereotyping' itself is defined as "a misuse of the naming process; a reduction of considered dimension rather than an expansion" (Williams, 1987: 414).[9] The Mungo River is still said to be the division between *former* Anglophone (West) and Francophone (East) Cameroon. The use of italicized 'former' here is not only to allude to the "defunct" but existing federation. It applies also to the very concepts following the word "because the concepts (or categories) of 'Anglophone' and 'Francophone' have been so politicized and twisted in Cameroon that they most often have no sensible meaning; being employed in situations that are very far from those that they actually should be referring to" (Fossungu, 2014: 60). Wealth creation obviously requires straightforward and untwisted rules. Twisted rules can only be good for under-developing a community. In fact, it is even wondered if there is any sense at all in talking of Cameroon as bijural, let alone trijural. I cannot even help wondering at times if it is not nonsensical to distinguish "Anglophone Cameroon from Francophone Cameroon"[10] except for historical purposes. And what is even the sense in it when history – an indispensable part of development – is being denied in

---

[8] Richard.T. Andrias, "Rape Myths: A Persistent Problem in Defining and Prosecuting Rape" 7/2 *Criminal Justice* (Summer 1992), 2 at 3. For further discussion of how some of these 'myths' work in Cameroon, see J.T. Ayeh, "The Political Origin of Hate Myths in Cameroon" *Cameroon Post* (2-9 May 1991), 6; and for how they operate even in so-called "developed" societies, see, S.M. Corbett, "Book Review of *George Grant: a bibliography* (Toronto: University of Toronto Press, 1993) by William Christian" 20/2 *Queen's Law Journal* (1995), 611-627 at 622-625 (Canada); and R.N. Stone, "The killing of Charles Walker: Racial Bias and the Death Sentence" 7/2 *Criminal Justice* (Summer 1992), 22 (United States).

[9] For more extensive studies on the stereotyping of Africa in the western world generally but the United States in particular, see Emmanuel Fru Doh, *Stereotyping Africa: Surprising Answers to Surprising Questions* (Bamenda: Langaa RPCIG, 2009) and Peter Ateh-Afac Fossungu , *The HISOFE Dictionary of Midnight Politics: Expibasketical Theories on Afrikentication and African Unity* (Bamenda: Langaa RPCIG, 2015) chapters 6 & 5.

[10] See Anyangwe (1989: xi); Andrew Sone Ewang, "Can the Prosecutor Discontinue a Private Prosecution by Entering a *Nolle Prosequi?*" 31 *Juridis Péridique* (1997) 39 at 40-41; and Michael Akomaye Yanou, *Practice and Procedure in Civil Matters in the Courts of Records in Anglophone Cameroon* (Bamenda: Langaa RPCIG, 2015).

Cameroon? Is developing without authentic history regression or advancement? What is in fact and in law an "Anglophone Cameroon" in a highly centralized unitary Cameroon? Belgium can quickly vouch that multiculturalism and development can have no place in such a state. Or can they possibly flourish there? It is not clear what 'Anglophone Cameroon' is, especially in a Cameroon with a unified criminal code and practice, and, moreover, with a single magistracy and administration school in which the English system of justice administration is completely put at naught. In short, "Anglophone Cameroon" can signify nothing sensible in a Cameroon with no effective sub units, with a unified and personalized political structure and management that is not only punctuated by "sa *Constitution monarchique*" but also littered with *'tous ces vandales, ces démagogues, ces intoxicateurs, ces bons à rien.*"[11] Are all these people and constitution that Rim is describing and condemning appropriate vectors of development and wealth creation or those of poverty and underdevelopment?

One is even talking of unified codes and the like, but it is indeed helpful at this juncture to highlight the fact that such codes or constitutions are not even an attempted blend of the two inherited systems (to talk less of the indigenous) but simply entire French transplants. It is truly and wholly a "unique sort of mental laziness and... anti-intellectual tendency" (Maneli, 1994: 6) which Professor Carlson Anyangwe says is the inevitable result of "Some lazy, petty and misguided minds [who] would rather choose the road of ease, wholly inappropriate in our national context which consists of taking the French Civil Code [for example], tinkering with it, having it translated into English and presenting it as a 'Cameroonian Civil Code'" (cited in Fossungu, 2013a: 174-75). How is that to facilitate development and poverty eradication in 'bijural' Cameroon? And these are the same gangsters and their ploys that are to take Cameroon to emergence in 2035? Talking of emerging, I will prefer to let the following powerful *Cameroon Journal* Editorial better tell not

---

[11] Daniel Rim, "Petits mots, grands maux... " *Le Messager* (12 janvier 1998), 2. For the constitution being ably described by Daniel Rim, see *Loi N° 96-06 du 18 janvier 1996 portant révision de la Constitution du 02 juin 1972*(hereinafter 1996 Constitution).

only the poverty-underdevelopment tale but as well the pitiful story of Africans and the 'foreign' dictators they do have as leaders:

> President Biya after hearing of the national disaster that visited the nation in the Eseka train accident, declared a day of national mourning for Monday October 24. Then, he hastily flew back into the country – and you did think he was coming to personally participate in the mourning. That wasn't the case.

The President was absent from events marking the national day of mourning. Events which took place in various corners of the nation especially the nation's capital, Yaoundé, Douala and Eseka where the accident actually took place did not see the participation of President Biya.

At Our Lady of Victory Cathedral in the epicentre of Yaoundé, where Biya, from time-to-time is known to worship, especially on special occasions, he was only represented; even when he was right there in Yaoundé. In his characteristic cavalier attitude, he chose to have Martin Belinga Eboutou, Director of cabinet to represent him. Belinga did not disclose the whereabouts of the President who had jetted into the country a day after spending 37 days out of the country. At Eseka where there was a similar ceremony, no member of government bothered to show up. The highest authority there was the SDO for the Nyong et Kéllé division, Aboubakar Iyawa.

This snobbish and shameful attitude of Biya is not new to Cameroonians who have learned to live without their President. Since Biya himself declared war on Boko Haram in May 2014, he has never visited soldiers at the war front, nor the affected population. Moreover, he has never been present at the military headquarters when military honours were given to fallen soldiers in spite of the fact that he is their Commander-in-Chief.

In responsible governance like what obtains in countries like the United States, France, Great Britain, among others, the President personally would visit soldiers at war front to shake hands, encourage and sometimes like in the case of George W. Bush during the Iraq war, even share meals with the soldiers.

But in Cameroon, Biya has always remained indifferent when it concerns incidents of national disaster. Consider Lake Nyos in 1986, the Kenya Airways plane crash near Douala in 2007. When news of the visit of Fru Ndi to victims of the Buea mountain eruption in 2000 was leaked out, it was only then that President Biya hurriedly made an impromptu visit to the South West to save his name. In the days of the Bakassi conflict, Biya never for once saw the need of meeting with victims. He has reigned for almost 35 years. Did he say he's the one to take Cameroon to emergence? At the *Cameroon Journal*, we suggest that the President emerge himself before trying same for a whole nation.[12]

Does that nation properly have an 'Anglophone Cameroon' as a distinct part of it? If not a distinct part of it (as it is), how does that create poverty and underdevelopment? Going to Canada would help understanding of the issues of poverty of the law and of judicial politics engendering deprivation and vulnerability. The Canadian Bar Association, for instance, can be correct in their recommending "a standard curriculum of subjects for Canada's *common law provinces* [my emphasis]."[13] Canada's 1867 *British North America Act* effectively preserved the existing pre-Confederation "systems" in its Section 129. As two McGill University professors competently tell us:

> Upon Confederation, the entire panoply of legal rules applicable in Canada East were carried forward as 'law in force' within the territorial division of the new colony of Canada thereafter known as the Province of Quebec. This law in force was neither the law of the new legislature of Quebec, nor the law of the new Parliament of Canada. It was simply pre-Confederation law originating from one of: (1) the law of the Parliament of England or the Imperial Parliament; or (2) the law of the legislature of lower Canada (prior to 1838) or the Special Council (from 1832-1842); or the Parliament of the United Canadas (from 1842-

---

[12] "Editorial: What a Heartless, Shameless President Cameroon Has?" @ http://cameroonjournal.com/2016/10/26/editorial-what-a-heartless-shameless-president-cameroon-has/

[13] Andrew J. Pirie, "Objectives in Legal Education: The Case for Systematic Instructional Design," 37 *Journal of Legal Education* (1987), 576-597 at 578.

1867); or (3) unenacted law received, resurrected or continued by the *Quebec Act, 1774* (Macdonald and Scott, 1997: 32).

Canada's Section 129 contrasts very vividly with the Cameroonian Federal Article 46 by which "Previous legislation of the Federated States shall remain in force in so far as it does not conflict with the provision of this Constitution" – a constitution "Most of the articles of ... [which] were directly taken from the French Fifth Republican Constitution, 1 958" (Enonchong, 1967: 81). We visualize immediately from Cameroon's concerned federal enactment that "it is pure madness to be talking of the birth at Foumban of the idea of the co-existence of the two legal systems" (Fossungu, 2013a: 174). There poverty of the law and the judiciary, a branch of government generally associated with human rights respect, rights that are clearly the invisible hand behind meaningful development. Why and how? First, we can note that it is not the *legal* system of the said states that have to remain in force. Second, in the stark absence of an independent judiciary (with Federal Article 32 making the president the guardian of judicial independence), who else but the President of the Federal Republic (a Francophone psychopath, as Reverend Jumbam calls them), decides if there is conflict? And, third, how on earth is the common law not going to conflict with a French-civilian Constitution?

This third point is very important since both legal systems seem to be opposites in almost every sense. Dr HNA Enonchong posited in 1967 that "Common law is of course to be distinguished from 'civil law', the Roman law based system, where uniformity is the fundamental objective by the promulgation of presumably all-inclusive Codes... Needless to say that these two legal systems differ not only in concepts but also in approach" (cited in Fossungu, 2013a: 174). In further illustrating the point, Enonchong indicated how "droit constitutionnel has one connotation to the French civil-law trained lawyer and another to the Anglo-American trained lawyer" (cited in Fossungu, 2013a: 174). An established expert on Cameroon constitutional law, Dr Enonchong has poignantly pointed out that the "differences between the French-trained lawyer and the English-trained lawyer in what is and what is not constitutional law are not

135

trivial. They range from the form to content of the entire spectrum of constitutional law" (cited in Fossungu, 2013a: 106). This sharp contrast in perspectives, the doctor concludes, would thus turn the issue of 'What Cameroon Constitutional Law is' into one which "is certainly a difficult question to answer because it bristles with a multiplicity of complex problems which are of historical origin" (Fossungu, 2013a: 106). How then, once more, are West Cameroon's common law legislation and principles not going to "conflict with the provision of this [1961] Constitution" in order to co-exist with it? This folly would duly account for Dr Anyangwe's indication in 1987 that "it is in the civil law area that law reform [in Cameroon] encounters the stiffest test – test of will, test of national interest, test of intellectual integrity and honesty" (Fossungu, 2013a: 174).

The difficulty involved perhaps justifies Prime Minister Pierre-Elliott Trudeau's invaluable messages to both the Quebec separatists and the 'Perfect Nation' seeking "Anglo-conformists" (Driedger, 1989: 39-42 & passim) of the rest of Canada. As the first minister is said to have stated: "The die is cast in Canada: there are two main ethnic and linguistic groups; each is too strong and too deeply rooted in the past, too firmly bound to a mother culture, to be able to engulf the other" (Driedger, 1989: 193). Some experts like Professor André Morel have therefore sagaciously suggested that, in countries like (Cameroon and) Canada where two cultures are deeply entrenched, a proper situation of bijuralism must entail the equal respect of both legal traditions (Morel, 1997a: 28).[14] As a means to further these noble objectives of multiculturalism, refashioning of the rules (rather than overturning everything) has then been proposed by Morel (1997a: 27).[15] The message is simple and clear. Is this what West

---

[14] As the Université de Montréal professor has put it, it entails *l'application des lois et l'administration de la justice qui sont en cause. C'est aussi le respect de la tradition civiliste à l'égard de laquelle les deux Chambres du Parlement [canadien] ont pris l'engagement solennel que l'on sait. C'est enfin le respect de l'égalité entre les collectivités francophone et anglophone qui toutes deux relèvent indépendamment leur langage, soif de la common law soir du droit civil.*"

[15] "*Revoir le langage du Législateur fédéral pour qu'il s'accorde avec celui du droit civil; revoir les normes législatives à la lumière des règles et des institutions que le nouveau Code a réformées ; revoir la version anglaise des lois et régiments pour qu'elle tienne compte de la tradition civiliste; revoir en fin le droit préconfédérale qui survit pour refléter les valeurs de la société d'aujourd'hui et s'intégrer sans heurtes au droit commun du Québec.*"

Cameroonians have been ineffectively demanding? And can their analogy with Quebec be helpful and not expose poverty in constitutional scholarship as well as poverty in human rights discourse: all of which engender deprivation and regression?

Which Cameroon Is which Cameroon?

The responses to the questions raised above would boil down to the central question regarding the existence of an 'Anglophone Cameroon'. It is also greatly assisted by the answer to this other issue of what does actually give force to Cameroon being Cameroon *(Le Cameroun c'est le Cameroun,* as the leadership is known to always go about boasting). What does make Cameroun to be (which?[16]) Cameroon, I think, is the somewhat unholy utilization of the double-edged Anglophone Sword. The first side of this sword has to do with Anglophones back-stabbing themselves, the documentation of which alone some critics like Frank Stark say would fill several small volumes (cited in Fossungu, 2013b: 89-90). Just get a minute taste of it from what is happening within the Anglophone Diaspora in the United States in relation to the ongoing 'schools-lawyers' impasse at 'home'. The Cameroon Journal (online) is the best place to get this instruction from.

As to the second side, most moves towards stamping out human rights and freedoms in Cameroon often take off as aimed at the "worrisome Anglophone minority"[17] and most of the "majority" will quite unthinkingly join hands (as they usually say) in 'teaching these Anglos a lesson'. But, as it is usually the case, the very next minute the same measures are directed at everyone else. At this time, it is often too late. Divide and oppress is an entrenched rule in Cameroon's advanced democracy. Some have termed this second

---

[16] See below: 'Idiotickering and Validating the Two-Cameroon Theory or Emulating Canada?'

[17] "Since the Biya regime is ill at ease with Anglophones," *The Herald* has editorialized, "every opportunity is now used by the regime to prove to the wider public that it is Anglophones causing trouble - not the regime." Boniface Forbin, "North West Terrorism: Gov't Provokes Anti-Anglophone Violence" *The Herald* (18-20 April 1997), 4. Mr. Biya is also quoted as saying *"Malgré nos efforts. .. ce sont les Anglophones qui gâtent le pays."* Ntemfac Ofege, "Mr Biya's Evil Government" *The Post* N° 0040 (23 December 1997), 7.

side the 'Anglos War-Cry' (Fossungu, 2013a: 24-25). According to some critics, the two edges of the Anglophone Sword which actually fortify each other are clearly the result "of much uncritical support from politically naive students [or people], excited more by the superficial appeal of agitprop slogans and images than the content of their actions."[18] This is what some other human rights experts would see as naively confusing the wrappings with their contents.[19] These are clearly instruments of regression; not of development or wealth creation.

Having surveyed the use and effect of this double-edged Anglophone Sword, some critics have postulated their interesting theories on Cameroon. First, there is the one from Frank Stark that "An analogy which suggests that West Cameroon is the 'Quebec of Cameroon' has limited value" (cited in Fossungu, 2013b: 184). Multiculturalism in Canada is fortified by the federal structure that allows each national subgroup to develop or realize its potentials to the fullest and thereby enrich the entire country. It is the reverse in Cameroon. Such a questionable analogy is made in a piece ("A Quiet Revolution" in *West Africa* of 27 April-3 May 1992) which would be solely harping on the so-called Anglophone infiltration into the reins of power in Cameroon because of the appointment of one of them as the president's prime minister. As a critic has put it: "It would appear, from the very brief discussion of the prime ministry here, to be abusing Quebec's splendid Quiet Revolution to describe the Cameroonian farce as such. Quebec within Canada clearly cannot be reasonably made analogous to 'Anglophone Cameroon' within Cameroon or vice versa" (Fossungu, 2013b: 184-85, note omitted). There are a lot of other reasons for the assertion, all of which would also be attesting to why Cameroon and Canada are not on the same regression plane.

To begin with, while Canadian entities moved from separateness to *unity in diversity* (Quebec's splendid resistance to English Canada's uniformization drives is not being ignored in any case), Cameroon

---

[18] Stephen Segaller, *Invisible Armies: Terrorism into the 1990s* (London: Sphere Books Ltd, 1987) at 277.

[19] Peter Archer and Lord Reay *Freedom at Stake* (London: The Bodley Head, 1966) at 12.

moved, first, from unity to division, and then strangely to *divergence in unity* rather than unity in diversity. All this will seem quite fascinating. But this "fascination" will properly explain how Cameroon has come to be denied responsible government: with the initial shaky denial (through the acquisition of *Pleins Pouvoirs* in 1959 in East Cameroon) being firmly confirmed in 1961 at Foumban where it is claimed that plenty of guarantees for human rights were instituted. All this is just as questionable as the equation of Quebec with the so-called 'Anglophone Cameroon'. The real problem has to do not so much with these claimed institutionalized guarantees as with the praise-singing from some of us in the academia about the intellectualism of people who came up with the Foumban arrangements. The more especially when the youths who do not seem to understand and ask to know (e.g., "How do we cone to be ruled directly from Yaoundé?") are rather miseducated and/or told to shut up and just know that the brilliant show-up of certain "inte1lectuals in politics" at Foumban in 1961 led to the achievement of future self-government, independence and fuller freedom for them (see Fossungu, 2013b: ix & 82); thus putting them in the same wealth creation position as Quebec in Canada. There is a Quebec government in Canada but is there a West Cameroon government in Cameroon? Is it poverty in intellectualism or deliberate confusion and emasculation of the issues?

Second Fiddle Syndrome and Irrational Pride

Quebec cannot be reasonably made analogous to the so-called "Anglophone Cameroon" for yet other significant reasons that all pave the way to poverty and vulnerability in Africa.[20] One of their principal differences is that, unlike in Cameroon's so-called "Solid Federal Edifice" (see Fossungu, 2013b: 19-37), Canadian Confederation guaranteed the cultural rights of the francophone minority (Bissonnette, 1963: 23; Tremblay, 1993: 27-29). To be specific, Bissonnette points out, for instance, that "*Les droits des habitants [francophones] étaient sauvegardes: Langues, religion, institutions,*

---

[20] For more ethnographic demonstrations of the poverty-vulnerability spiral (that is not necessarily provoked by the bijuralism 'war') in Cameroon, see Heum (2016: chapter s 5 & 3).

coutumes, même si le pouvoir et l'autorité étaient exercés par une autre hégémonie. " These guaranteed cultural rights are the locomotion for development in Canada, thus separating it from Cameroon where assimilation of the minority is the rule. Resources that would have gone into some development projects are instead being fed into the brutalization machine. Moreover, even before Confederation, Quebec completely met the definition of a "people" which Bissonnette (1963: 20) defines as *"Une société commune formant un atout moral et attachée à un territoire determine.'* One must note the difference here with Cameroon's "Perfect Nation" that can only be productive of poverty and helplessness. As defined by President Biya, it is "[t]he nation... [which] is characterized by a partial or total combination of certain specific material and spiritual elements which reinforce its homogeneity and its members' awareness of unity. It is a union of communities with one race, language, territory, economic life and history" (cited in Fossungu, 2013a: 61-62). That simply means assimilation or annihilation of anything 'outside the box.' Period. Good only for poverty creation. Period. And back to prosperous Canada.

Quebec also succumbed to no statutory inferiority or subordination since, from the outset, the 1867 *B.N.A. Act* and other documents such as the *Quebec Act,* 1774, all provided French or Lower Canada and its citizens with equal rights and political institutions. As a Quebec Court of Appeal justice has indicated, there were *'droits égaux pour ses habitants comme pour ceux du Haut-Canada; libertés politiques et parlementaires analogues; en un mot, coexistence des deux nationalités distinctes, homogènes, vivant sur un territoire propre et déterminé, sous l'égide d'instituions politiques similaires"* (Bissonnette, 1963: 25).[21]

On the other hand, non-development or stagnation has been the case in Cameroon because of poverty and dishonesty (corruption) in institutional framework. Not only did Cameroon's "Federal" Constitution of 1961 deliberately, at the outset and in several significant ways, subordinate Anglophones and their language to a second place. By this document, for instance, West Cameroon's prime minister was automatically put in second place in the

---

[21] See also Maurice Lamontagne, *Le fédéralisme canadien: évolution et problèmes* (Montréal: Québec Presses Universitaires, 1954).

Federation (Article 52) and also "The revised Constitution shall be published in French and in English, the French text being authentic" (Article 59). West Cameroon, furthermore, did not have its own established autonomous institutions before, during, and after the Foumban Conference (see Fossungu, 2013b: 37-39 & 85-86). It is even the Constitution of East Cameroon that graduated into the Federal Constitution that, paradoxically, came to concentrate rather than to separate power centres in Cameroon. Development is promoted more by decentralized local governance than by a unitary centralized government. No one, therefore, a final thesis of the critics (like Patrick-Thomas Eyoum'a Ntoh) then goes, can doubt that Cameroon is a wonderful country inhabited by a wonderful people. But very serious doubts are cast on everything, these critics have concluded, when real issues (among which are federalism, multiculturalism, and human rights defence) are carefully examined. On such an insightful inspection, one would find that Cameroonians are only 20 million proud rascals (see Fossungu, 2013b: 146) who, according to J.T. Ayeh, "pride themselves of many things which, on the basis of existing evidence, are genuine for the most part; but if, by some remote coincidence, rationality is one of them, it raises an eyebrow for a people who easily consume myths" (cited in Fossungu, 2013a: 232).

This easy consumption of myths in a country full of rascals is what gives impetus to the widespread poverty in Africa, but especially in Cameroon which has swirling dangerous waters that people have been warned against attempting to cross. Some Englishmen like Geoffrey Moorhouse (perhaps knowing exactly what they left behind) would even have warned that the breadth of the *Advancing Confusion* Ocean in West-Central Africa "is much wider, say some who have made the crossing, than you ever expect beforehand" (cited in Fossungu, 2013a: x).[22] But it seems this warning has hardly been heeded. A law and language researcher then – either oblivious of the warning or thinking perhaps that Canada, in having just two legal systems and official languages, was not the right place to go to –

---

[22] Other colleagues of Moorhouse's would also join in describing it as a "very wide gulf" – Norman St. John-Stevas, "Foreword" to Humphry. Berkeley, *The Power of the Prime Minister* (London: George Allen and Unwin Ltd., 1968) 7-11 at 11.

actually did the fatal crossing. But, according to the reports, he had to quickly depart from the West-Central African law-language *Towering Laboratory* not as the enthusiastic apostle sent out by the Master to go and spread the Word to all the corners of the earth. Apostle Peter, we are told, very quietly escaped from Cameroon, being more dismayed by the strange discovery that the country's *École Nationale de l'Administration et de la Magistrature* (ENAM) – the school where both judges and other top-ranking civil administrators are trained – "is run mainly by French professors and practitioners of law; [and that] the West Cameroon 'English' law and legal practice seem to be widely neglected. When I visited the library of that school in May, 1978, I could not find one single English book" (Bringer, 1981: 8-9).[23] Professor Peter Bringer was reporting in 1981 but his visit to the ENAM was done 17 years after the 1961 Foumban Union. The question is: Where then are the entrenched legal dualism and bilingualism? Is this not a true testimony of the poverty in institutional framework (and in scholarship) that Professor Mbaku would be talking about as responsible for Africa being the poorest and most deprived continent of the world?

Having learnt about this exasperating Apostle-Peter tale, some professors of Quebec universities have, understandably[24] joined Dale

---

[23] See also Richard Bjornson, *The African Quest for Freedom and Identity: Cameroonian Writing and the National Experience* (Bloomington & Indianapolis: Indiana University Press, 1991) at 114; and Anyangwe (1989: 4-5). The notorious case in S0.NA.R.A (the oil refinery in Limbe in Debundschazone) also brings the folly of "Anglophone Cameroon" to the forefront. The fraud and the Douala state counsels' "Questionable Releases" in this particular case apart, it is being questioned [for example] why a matter involving SONARA in Fako division should earn but the attention of Douala, a different judicial division.

The running of the refinery itself [solely] by ...Francophones and the criticism that SONARA pays its taxes in Douala instead of Limbe continues to strengthen the suspicion of Anglophone annexation and exploitation by Francophones.

See "SONARA buys water for 40 M" *Cameroon Post* N° 0274 (11-18 December 1995) 12 & 10 at 10. The author of this piece generally reports the fraud of top officials in "a hush-hush transaction that has caused the National refinery company SONARA ... over CFA 40 million." *Ibid.*

[24] See generally Justice Canada (1997). *"Il est probablement normal que ce soit un Québécois qui se penche b premier sur le son des Camerounais occidentaux, <<les choses étant ce qu'elles sont> >, disait le Général de Gaulle Il st d'ailleurs peut-être symbolique que* care *recherche sur le terrain ait été menée alors qu'd cinquante milles plus b l'ouest la minorité biafraise*

142

Gibson of the University of Manitoba in trenchantly condemning Cameroon for not training its judges in particular in both legal traditions like Canada.[25] Is it not obviously very strange that only others (outsiders), and not Cameroon's citizens generally, and Anglophones especially, should have been worrying about all this (until lately)? Or are Cameroonians even now doing so? If they (the minority) are, do they know and understand the how and why of their excruciating problems?

It is thought that Cameroonians cannot know most of these issues until they can grasp the essence of both federalism and decentralization as they ought to affect both inherited cultures, as well as the indigenous one. All this entails that they can clearly not be able to master the subject with the unnecessary invention of entrenched legal "pluralism and bilingualism" that is characteristic of Cameroonian intellectuals. Officially and otherwise, I think Cameroon is basically a unijural and unilingual state, explaining the government's brutal reaction to a simple exercise of 'multicultural rights.[26] Consequently, anyone referring to common-law provinces or "Anglophone provinces" in Cameroon must now have to do so with adequate (historical) qualification. Otherwise, one cannot at all (by the open-ended employment of those terms) be helping those that President Biya calls "the poorly-informed foreign visitors" (Biya, 1986: 10) to be able (in Michael Wheeler's apt words) "to peer behind

---

tentait *de faire sécession, et que la première version de cet ouvrage ait été rédigé alors que les Pakistanais orientaux tentaient d'affirmer leur autonomie. C'est instinctivement que le Québécois se sent concerné. L'exemple camerounais est peut-être le plus près du sien: un régime de type fédératif, une majorité groupant 70% de la population totale et une minorité de l'ordre de 30%, le français étant la langue officiel de l'une des entités - de la majorité (au contraire du Canada) - et l 'anglais la langue officiel de l'autre."* (Benjamin, 1972: 1).

[25] See Dale Gibson, "Judges as Legislators: Not Whether But How" 25/2 *Alberta Law Review* (1987), 249 at 253

[26] "The reaction of the Cameroon authorities to the protests evokes echoes of the totalitarian practices that many of us remember from the days before communism in Central and Eastern Europe collapsed in 1989: harsh censorship of the domestic media led by Senior Peter Esoka and Minister Issa Tchiroma, blackouts of reporting by foreign media, refusal of visas to foreign journalists, and blaming the unrest on a conspiratorial clique of manipulators and other unspecified dark forces supposedly manipulated and sponsored from abroad. In fact, it is like shaming heaven for its peaceful purity" (Mentan, 2017).

the curtain and see ... [Cameroon] as it really is. The practice is a far cry from what ... [its administrators] would have us believe" (cited in Fossungu, 2013a: 2). Not even the country's belated and contested Commonwealth membership could have changed this far cry in Cameroon. It rather worsened it by corruption.

Commonwealth Membership and the Advanced Corruption of Multiculturalism

Cameroon's five neighbours (Central African Republic, Chad, Congo-Brazzaville, Equatorial Guinea, Gabon, and Nigerian) speak three foreign languages. These are English, French, and Spanish. As indicated by some researchers cited in Dr Fossungu's work, Cameroon properly belongs to both West and Central Africa, although the country's authorities will prefer to be seen as belonging to the latter. This preference, the critics have pursued, can also help to explain why Cameroon is a member of Central Africa's mono-cultural UDEAC (French acronym) but not of West Africa's bicultural ECOWAS. Dr Fossungu's critical report goes on to explain how Cameroon has traditionally avoided the English-speaking world and particularly Nigeria. This perhaps also elucidates why it has always been active in *La Francophonie* but only controversially became member of the Commonwealth in 1995 (Fossungu, 2013a: 32-38). This is quite interesting for a country claiming cultural dualism. For decades, Cameroon has avoided the English-speaking world and persistently refused to join the Commonwealth, despite clarion calls from its Anglophone community. But Cameroon then hastily joined that organization despite all the campaigns from that same Anglophone community to foil its admission. How does one explain all this except with corrupting Advanced Multiculturalism?

The Corrupted Gentlemen and the World's "Number One Corruptor"

Since the 1970s, most countries in Africa have failed to make any significant improvements in the standard of living of their citizens. One of the most important reasons advanced to explain continued poverty and deprivation in the continent is pervasive corruption.

Corruption, the subject of most of John Mukum Mbaku's books, has become quite pervasive in Africa and now constitutes an important development constraint. Mbaku's *Bureaucratic and Political Corruption in Africa* emphasizes the public choice perspective to corruption clean-ups and thus, also presents the international dimension of corruption along with global efforts to tackle the problem (Mbaku, 1999). M.L. Lokanga, in writing about the refusal of the Cameroon Students Leader to talk to the Endeley Commission in 1991, declared that "there is a growing disenchantment about commissions of inquiry in the Biya regime. For one thing, they have always symbolised official deception at its most treacherous stage... [G]overnment sponsored commissions of inquiry have always tended to cloak rather than shed light on issues....Since he [Biya] came to power...[34] years ago, he has contrived to create commissions [and universities and/or constitutional organs] only when he intends to shelve an issue" (cited in Fossungu, 2013a: 186-87).[27]

Lokanga's theory applies with a lot of force to the Commonwealth palaver that was intended to shelve the burning issues of multiculturalism and its corollary, equality. For instance, Barrister Charles Achaleke Taku sent a letter in December 1995 to them clearly and far-sightedly informing the 'money-grabbing' British government of the accelerated dismantling of Commonwealth institutions in Cameroon after barely two months of its admission into their *club of gentlemen*, concluding that "the most important problem that must be resolved and quickly too is the Southern Cameroons problem. No admission into the Commonwealth, no media campaign will side track this basic problem. It is the resolution of this problem that will guarantee durable peace [real development and poverty eradication] in the sub region" (cited in Fossungu, 2013a: 36-37). The ongoing impasse in the country twenty years after Charles Taku's declaration solidly proves the barrister and many others 200% correct. In another open letter to the British High

---

[27] This theory helped R.B. Sanjo to easily answer his own question ("Did Ahidjo and Biya Suppress Foncha's Plan for an Anglophone University?") in the affirmative by declaring that "Cameroon is a nation where, deliberately or otherwise, the political cart is placed before the horse." Cited in Fossungu (2013a: 184).

Commissioner in Cameroon, Ngwa Ntonufor seriously critiqued, with ample evidence, Cameroon's application and admission into the Commonwealth in 1995, firmly charging that "Mr. Biya, it would seem, had, true to type, bribed his way into an organization whose members are supposed to be gentlemen. Yes, he might have bribed his way through because even onto this day no possible reason exists for Cameroon's admission" (cited in Fossungu, 2013a: 34). In December 1995, the editors of the *Montreal Gazette* asserted that these were quite serious allegations and, "[i[f true, the accusations made…demonstrate how money has become ruinously pervasive in a movement that is supposed to be about higher ideals" (cited in Fossungu, 2013a: 34).

In the public sense of the term, according to J.S. Nye, corruption is said to be "behaviour which deviates from the formal duties of a public role because of private-regarding (personal, close family, private clique) pecuniary or status gains; or violates rules against the exercise of certain types of private-regarding influences."[28] John Mukum Mbaku's *Corruption in Africa* makes a significant contribution to the study of the impacts and eradication of corruption in African societies. Mbaku offers a comprehensive analysis of the causes of public malfeasance in African countries and provides a number of practical and effective policy options for change. His book demonstrates the destructive relationship between corruption and the abrogation of economic freedoms and entrepreneurship, a system that has clearly left Africa as one of the most deprived regions in the world. Utilizing the tools of public choice theory, Mbaku emphasizes the important role that institutions have in corruption control and he recommends reconstructive democratic constitutions as the most effective means to development and poverty eradication. Until African states provide their people with institutional arrangements that adequately constrain the state and enhance wealth production, the living standards in the continent will continue to deteriorate. *Corruption in Africa* is a fascinating and informative text that will appeal to those interested in African studies and developmental policies (Mbaku, 2012). Bribery, nepotism, and misappropriation

---

[28] J.S. Nye, "Corruption and Political Development: A Cost-Benefit Analysis" 61 *American Political Science Review* (1967) 419, cited in Coldham (1995: 115 n.1).

have been identified as the main types of corrupt behaviour (Coldham, 1995: 115 n.1).

Revolving-Door Denrée Exportation à la Camerounaise

Support for Ntonufor's Cameroon-Commonwealth bribery theory appears to be legion. Corruption in Cameroon has attained that level where there is no place and/or area of exclusion. Thus, we hear it being mentioned and condemned even at the topmost level of the church by a cleric reproaching the silence of the church on the carnage that is going on in Cameroon:

We know very well that when the National Episcopal Council (NECC) speaks out, it is listened to by the political powers in Cameroon. When tinged by the inspiration and endorsement of Cardinal Christian Tumi in 2000, the NECC spoke against the canker warm of bribery and corruption. The whole world listened and the government of Cameroon adjusted. Those were prophetic times for the clergy. Spiritual leaders the world over are always pace-setters; their intervention on socio-political disasters has always been prototypical, precisely because it sets the tyrants quaking. With the retirement and deaths among your circles, of names like Ndongmo, Tumi, Etoga, Wouking, Verdzekov, Awah, the national Episcopal Council all this while has been a sleeping bag. Today, NEC has been a fiasco, if we must speak the truth.

Cameroon[ians] should be courageous to accept they are flawed and stop blaming France or Britain. The [b]ribery and corruption that we have been African champions for more than a decade, is self-inflicted. Bribery and corruption are a moral and spiritual problem [in as much as it is a legal economic problem]. And therefore the moral and spiritual authorities [along with the judiciary and politicians] are to blame. If the Church truly cared for its members, the problem will not be happening every now and then. And the oppressed people of British Cameroons are undergoing something of genocide now because the National Episcopal Council (NEC) is on holidays, and the world knows that too well.

We know what the bishops of the British Cameroons have gone through from the national episcopacy because they kicked up the storm in the daring letter they wrote (despite earlier hesitations) not because they were hoping the leadership of NEC would notice, but precisely because they knew that with the 2016-2017 NEC leadership in charge, … raped, maimed and unjustly imprisoned British Cameroonian[s] might as well add NEC to their laundry list of Do-It-Yourself. The bishops of the British Cameroons came up with another communiqué by the very [moment] to the effect that they have not closed down their schools and that they are waiting for the Catholic pupils and students to return to school. But right up till now, the pupils and students have not returned, meaning that the parents have lost faith in the Church's hierarchy. It is precisely because the Cameroon National Church lacks the courage to support what is right that people are going their own sweet ways. Is it asking too much from Church leaders to say good shepherds must lay life for flock? (Jumbam, 2017).

For another church example, after citing the case of late President Mobutu (of former Zaire), Reverend Suh Niba of Santa went further to elucidate how (in Cameroon) "even within the ranks of the Church, there are priests, catechists, church presidents, secretaries and even treasurers, who, because of egoism, *chop broke potism* or the desire for cheap popularity, end up like the '*ngong dog*' (or useless dog) or the foolish juju" (Panky, 1997).[29] It is because of these *chop-broke potism* and the egoism syndromes which have implanted themselves so firmly in most Cameroonians that the country is now cracking. As the Santa priest is said to have observed, were it otherwise, then Cameroonians could no longer be suffering under the weight of dictatorship because "[w]hen a particular juju refuses to quit the dancing ground, after dancing for too long, it hinders the others from exhibiting their own talents and capabilities and, therefore, must be forced out" (Panky, 1997). What else but the unsurpassed degree of corruption in Cameroon can explain the fact that the Zairian juju has long been forced out but Cameroon's foolish juju stays comfortably on?

---

[29] See also Ngah Christian Mpipgo, "CBC Boss Laments Vice in Church, Promises Sanctions for Wayward Pastors" *The Herald* (10-12 July 1998), 2; and Ambe Michael, "The Biblical Cure for Corruption" *The Herald* (18-19 July 1998), 4.

Other critics now even wonder whether there is any living Cameroonian who is not corrupt. They tie this phenomenon to the means by which modern corruption was entrenched in the country. They have thus posited that "modem corruption was legalized in Cameroon when the first state servant [the president of the republic] asked the question, 'Monsieur Eric Chinje [an Anglophone journalist], *est-ce* que *vous avez des preuves?*' during a TV interview. What Cameroonians [especially the president and his appointed officials] do now is to corrupt and be corrupted to the fullest and make sure there is no proof."[30] That no court can question any of these acts was very clearly indicated in the same TV interview by Paul Biya who was so, so crossed because of the unexpected question from the English-speaking journalist that he "had told Cameroonians, but the judges and journalists in particular (through Mr. Eric Chinje, a journalist whose 'slip of the tongue' let him to ask the president a not-on-the-list question) that 'It only suffices that I shake my oblong Head and any of you would no longer be judge'."[31] Yes, you got that perfectly right. No court can question the Cameroonian emperor – proof or no proof. And this is a country that is claiming development, democracy and multiculturalism? In short, according to the critics, all this aptly explains why there are so many corrupt people in Cameroon and why corruption has become a very profitable or saleable commodity for Cameroonians who know exactly how to export it.[32] Could Cameroon then have successfully exported this

---

[30] Joe Bashi, "Who Is Corrupt in Cameroon?" *The Herald* (18-19 march, 1998), 10 (italics added).

[31] Peter Ateh-Afac Fossungu, "Doing Politics without Politics = Lords in Place of Servants" *The herald* (5-7 June 1998), 10.

[32] "*Il y en a tellement d'hommes et de femmes véreux dans ce pays que le Cameroun est aujourd'hui le premier exportateur africain de cette denrée, loin, très loin devant le Nigeria. Et c'est une activité extrêmement rentable. Rentable pour ceux des Camerounais véreux qui ont su exporter ce know-how bien de chez nous.*" Patrick-Thomas, Eyoum'a Ntoh "13 millions de voyous!" *Le Messager* (12 septembre 1996), 2. See also N. Joseph, "The Extent and Implication of Corruption in Cameroon" *The Herald* (20-21 April 1998), 10; Asong .S. Ndifor and Peter .Ngea Beng, "Gov't Threatens Court Action as Biya Regime Is Rated Most Corrupt in The World" *The Herald* (28-29 September, 1998) 1 & 3; and Herald Editorial, "Biya Regime: Fight Corruption, Not Transparency International" *The Herald* (28-29 September, 1998), 4. Some critics have concluded

denrée to the Commonwealth, as *Kontchoumeter* had proudly said the Biya regime was ready to do?

The response is affirmative, if you consider the fact that both RHS Crossman and Geoffrey Moorhouse "would think the corruption check is now otherwise in Britain" (Fossungu, 2013a: 125 n.125). According to a very authoritative report, a surprising number of people from other countries' delegations and media leaders abroad spoke with intensity and awareness (at the Edinburgh Summit) of what has been happening in Cameroon. Cameroon was not suspended at that Commonwealth Summit, the report states, simply because, if done then "only two years after being admitted, went the argument, it might raise questions about the integrity of the organization and how in the first place Cameroon should have been admitted."[33] Some critics have somewhat corroborated by further indicating how all that *cunny-door* getting in might have been done, while at the same time putting those hoodwinked *gentlemen* on guard. Here is the way Taku (1995: 3) put it to them: "Be informed that the decree calling for elections for January 1996 and the purported debate on the constitution are political gimmicks intended to deceive the international community and the purpose is to hoodwink Commonwealth leaders into thinking that Mr. Biya is a democrat." Other critics have denied that the Commonwealth was deceived because the fact that the Edinburgh meeting insisted on only the so-called Economic Charter "emphasized the comfort that members like Nigeria, Cameroon, Sierra Leone and several others with a permanent record of human rights abuse and faltering democratization will have when attention turns away from Harare [dealing with Declaration on Good Governance]."[34]

---

that "We [Are] Becoming a Nation of Embezzlers." N. Jaspan with H. Black, *The Thief in the White Collar* (Library of Congress, 1960) chapter 1.

[33] Boniface Forbin, "Commonwealth Summit: Cameroon Escapes Suspension. But Is To Be Watched By Action Group – Biya's Absence Embarrasses Observers and Upsets Protocol; Musonge Arrives Late" *The Herald* (27-28 October 1997), 1 at 3.

[34] Boniface Forbin, "Commonwealth Summit (CHOGM) Edinburgh: CHOGM to Adopt Economic Declaration and Keep Away from Divisive Issues" *The Herald* (27-28 October 1997), 3.

The Harare Principles were again idly reasserted in Botswana,[35] reflecting well what you find happening in 'Commonwealth-buying' Cameroon today. Indeed, the so-called Constitutional Reforms (that is, Cameroon's 1996 Constitution), Barrister Taku did maintain in his letter to the British government, is intended to ridicule all that the Commonwealth stands for, concluding that "[t]he admission of *La République du Cameroun* into the Commonwealth has been portrayed invariably as a victory of that country over the Southern Cameroons National Council (SCNC), and [that] even Commonwealth admission is perceived as another tool in the hands of the Oppressor" (Taku, 1995: 3). The barrister is quite correct, if you realize that the same 1996 Constitution has been described by Ntemfac Ofege as "this anti-Anglophone heathen document [that even] *forgets* to dedicate Cameroon to God" (cited in Fossungu, 2013a: 79). Charles Taku, the Buea-based lawyer and leading human rights crusader, then proceeded to exemplify how the dismantling of institutions associated with the Commonwealth is very visible in the field of education and law, stressing how "Attempts by us to form a Cameroon Common Law Bar have been frustrated. The practice of the Common Law as it were has been systematically invalidated by piecemeal legislation and what is left is a mockery of the system. Anglo-Saxon qualifications are still being subjected to the equivalence of inferior certificates from France" (cited in Fossungu, 2013a: 175).[36] What is bijuralism in Cameroon that does not tolerate a Common Law Bar? Who would still be arguing then that there is only a common Civil-Law in Cameroon?

---

[35] See "Democracy and Good Governance: Challenges and Solutions Reflecting National Circumstances" (being a report of heads of governments of Commonwealth African states adopted after a roundtable conference on Democracy and Good Governance in Africa in Gaborone, Botswana, on February 23-25, 1997), as reported in *The Herald* (3-4 March 1997), 6.

[36] Sylvanus Ezieh on February 27, 2015 wrote in an article, stating that "The Common Law practice in Cameroon has again suffered a major setback. After Common Law Lawyers protested an attempt by the Biya's regime to impose notaries on the English Legal System last year, Anglophone Lawyers in the North West Region are now being compelled to make their court submissions only in the French language." Cited in Fossungu (2015a: 132).

Common Civil-Law: Rootless Education and the Idiotickerizing Leadership

The concept of *idiotickerization* is borrowed from an *Afrikentication* specialist who describes Africa's so-called "'leaders' that do nothing other than going around the world *idiotickering* Africans"[37] as well as those other Africans who "would hide their personal stupidity through aiding to *idiotickerize* the continent."[38] To answer the last-posed question thoroughly and thoughtfully, I propose to do two main things. First, I attempt to eliminate the claim of trijuralism in Cameroon by seeing how the apex court views the matter of *droit coutumier*. Second, I tackle the issue of whether or not Cameroon should emulate from effectively bijural and bilingual polities like Canada. The meticulous examination of both issues facilitates deep comprehension of the confusion being called bijuralism in Cameroon.

Droit Coutumier's Illusory Choice in the Cameroon Supreme Court

The question of "Anglophone Cameroon" so far demonstrates the absence of bijuralism. Will trijuralism exist when or where bijuralism is impossible? In other words, "How does the Cameroon customary law, that is, the indigenous unwritten and uncodified customs and traditions of the people which have crystallized into legal norms, [even] fit into the common-law and civil-law federal scheme?" (Enonchong, 1967: xii). In answer, some experts in the

---

[37] Peter Ateh-Afac Fossungu, "African Democracy vis-a-vis Western Democracy: Afrikenticating, Follyfying, Expibasketizing, and Reversing the 'African Democracy' Debate" in Munyaradzi Mawere and Tendai Rinos Mwanaka (eds.), *Democracy, Good Governance and Development in Africa* (Bamenda: Langaa RPCIG, 2015), 71-124 at 82 (original emphasis).

[38] *Id* at 112 (original emphasis). As Jumbam (2017) has also put it, "In a nation where silliness is given a standing ovation and fools ride on royal horses, a sell out like PM Philemon Yang who shamelessly takes himself a dishonorable recent trip around the North West, should be taken critically. Cameroon's false impression of greatness and self-styled portrayal as the island of peace in a sea of troubled Africa has been exposed for what it truly is."

field think that there is only a "tenuous co-existence of the common law and civil law traditions in Cameroon" (Anyangwe, 1987: xiii). The civil law tradition is not only predominant (if not exclusive) but there is nothing like customary law. Cameroon, contrary to the generally held belief, is not bijural let alone trijural. Trijuralism has been defined as meaning that three systems of law – customary or "native" law, English-derived laws (common law), and French-derived laws (civil law) – coexist in Cameroon (Anyangwe, 1987: 263). Is that really the case in Cameroon?

My response is NO! The first thing to note is that there is no teaching and study of Customary Law which the Foumban Enterprise grossly ignored. This has not failed to have some negative effects on national unity and development. Poverty production rather than eradication has thus been the result. Customary law as such is not taught in the country's law faculties: some critics would want to add perhaps 'with the possible exception of certain aspects of Dr Ephraim Ngwafor's family law.'[39] But I still doubt that because even here as elsewhere (exemplified by the other French-speaking authors claiming it[40]), it is merely a matter of adding to or substituting the English or French cases with a few locally-decided cases. Marriages, for example, not "officially" (that is, according to the Western concepts) valid are completely left out although being traditionally or customarily valid. It is the traditional methods (neither studied nor taught) that have to govern them. However, do these untaught "customary" or "traditional" rules and methods even govern such marriages purportedly entered into under such system(s)? In other words, is Cameroon even trijural or bijural?

---

[39] See, for example, Ephraim N. Ngwafor, "Family law trends in Cameroon: a non-developmental process" (1985) 8 *Annual Survey of Family Law* as discussed in Nyambo (1997: 895).

[40] For some persistent claims to there being a so-called "droit coutumier" in Cameroon, see, e.g., Francois Anoukaha in *Juridis Info* (*Revue de Législation et de Jurisprudence Camerounaises*) N° 0 (décembre 1989) 29-30; Christine Youengo in: *Juridis Info* N° 8 (1991) 65-59; *Juridis Info* N° 1 (1990) 39; *Juridis Info* N° 7 (1991) 40-41; and Lisette Elomo Ntonga & Christine Youengo in *Juridis Info* N° 5 (1991) 60-61.

The Modern Educated Illiterates

The appetizer to the folly of *"droit coutumier"* in a unijural state is not even hard to find. This illustration (though focusing on customary law) is indicative as well of the case of civil law and common law. The matter is effortlessly taken off the table with one critic's "Confused Cameroon Law" of 1998 in which he argued at length against the claim that *trijuralism* exists in Cameroon:

Well, I don't know how correct that claim [of *trijuralism* and of the courts upholding it] is, but I think I have a small story that can help us [to] find out. There is the case of this [University of Yaoundé] law graduate whom villagers would consider (and rightly so) as... [a culturally certificated] illiterate. He happens to be in the village when a land dispute arises. The village council and chief settle the case as is usual for them to do.

But the law graduate gets up (full of his empty University of Yaoundé Law) and challenges the decision on the basis that, as none of the two disputants could produce a land title (*titre foncier* as he would prefer to say in order to bamboozle those unschooled villagers), the said land becomes village property. Perfectly the right thing in the wrong place. Hardly is customary law as such taught in the country's law faculties. [41] There is then tension between these 'customary lawyers' and the customary-law illiterate 'modern lawyers'.

The examples could be endless; and there would be no need trying to multiply them here. But the question is: how is this *trijuralism* operating here? I should like to take time to draw your attention to the fact that this is the same person who will tomorrow be sitting on our bench and applying the only law he knows to all the cases: after having bribed his way into and through ENAM. Such schizophrenic drive to apply only the 'judge's law' to all situations would also help in its own way to divide rather than integrate Cameroonians. *Trijuralism* indeed! Would *bijuralism* also stand?" (Cited in Fossungu, 2015a: 131-32).[42]

---

[41] More on this vexing issue could be pursued further in Aquiline Tarimo S.J., *African Land Rights Systems* (Bamenda: Langaa RPCIG, 2014).

[42] For more classical cases of communal tensions between the 'certificateful' (city) and 'certificateless' (village) intellectuals, see Peter Ateh-Afac Fossungu,

Finding the Right Judge: **'Getting It All Wrong'** *with* *Equality in the Cameroon Supreme Court (CSC)*

In easing your comprehension of the nonsense in Cameroon, I must first take you to Ecuador in South America where you would find the right judge. Ecuador is a country with several normative systems coexisting within the same territory. Having a multiplicity of systems facilitates the clashes of jurisdiction among them. Oswaldo Ruiz-Chiriboga's invaluable contribution has studied the applicable rules Ecuador has to allocate jurisdiction among different legal systems, and how these rules advance or compromise human rights. One particular way the country deals with conflicting jurisdictions is the request to relinquish jurisdiction that indigenous authorities may submit to ordinary courts if the former believe that the latter have no jurisdiction to hear a case. Ruiz-Chiriboga analyses the decisions of ordinary courts on the request to relinquish jurisdiction, as well as the impressions and opinions on the matter from academics, ordinary judges and prosecutors, indigenous authorities, activists and lawyers, all of them collected during three field research trips conducted in the country. His paper concludes by arguing that jurisdiction has a human rights impact. Every person has the right to be heard by a competent court, and barring that person from his/her natural judge is a fair trial violation (Ruiz-Chiriboga, 2017).

When one carefully examines the discussions of the authors claiming the existence and operation of "droit coutumier" in Cameroon, one cannot but wonder if they actually do grasp what they are talking about. It is surely not only poverty in scholarship but also a case of "going alanu" (or getting it all wrong) like Dr Fossungu has shown the Obamas to have done with *Michelleobamalism* and 'legacy preservation' (see Fossungu, 2017: chapter 1). It is doubted what exactly the place of "droit coutumier" is in a society where the judges (especially at the apex – Supreme Court) must apply no other law than the civil law that they appear to know. For concrete illustration, let's study the Cameroon Supreme Court's *Arrêt N° 16/2 du 17 Mars 1988* otherwise known as *Affaire P.G.C.S. Yaoundé c/ Baninga Paul Frédéric* (hereinafter *Affaire Baninga*). It is a case which revolves around

---

"Challenging Intellectuals in Politics: The Village Experience" *The Herald* N° 598 (22-23 April 1998), 10,

succession and custody of minor children under the Baya custom in Cameroon's Guinea-Savannazone (with Bertoua as the capital).[43] These matters devolve on the deceased husband's brother and not the surviving wife. But the deceased's wife went to court when the customary successor and guardian of her children began exercising those rights. Both the Court of First Instance and the Bertoua Court of Appeal, applying the rules of the Baya custom, ruled against the wife who then appealed to the CSC. To this CSC, however, this customary practice must be struck down in favour of written law which guarantees equality of the sexes (my translation).[44] One wonders where this CSC goes to hide when, to leave out 'The Anglophone Problem', there is clear "Sexing [of] Patriotism and Equality" (Fossungu, 2013a: 115-121) by what B. Chinje calls "discriminatory provisions in the laws of the land." (Fossungu, 2013a: 117). I would not want to delve much into the sex equality behind which the CSC is attempting to hide its naked denial of freedom of choice and common sense, but continue to concentrate on the question of *droit coutumier* passing through *droit écrit*.

Whatever can be said about the sanity or otherwise of the Baya custom is not what one is concerned with here. The point is simply that of whether or not one can be entitled to talk of the existence of the customary law system if its every rule must be judged only in the light of conformity with "modern" or "official" law standard: the more especially when the parties to the contract of marriage are "legally" left with the choice of either contracting it under any of those "systems."[45] Now, with this *Affaire Baninga* decision (which is not the only in the Class Naught in the School of Multi-legal

---

[43] Bangwa land in Debundschazone (with Buea as capital) would certainly furnish more intriguing and much more complex African (royal) succession and inheritance *bangwalangwalism* (or Bangwa philosophies) that would surely be completely beyond the comprehension of these judges of the CSC.

[44] "*La coutume qui prévoit qu'en matière de succession et en cas de minorité des enfants du de cujus, la tutelle de ceux-ci incombe à un proche parent mâle et jamais a la mère des enfants, est contraire au principe d'ordre public de l'égalité des sexes proclamée par la constitution. Par conséquent, elle doit être déclarée inapplicable au profit du droit écrit qui reconnait au conjoint survivant (l'époux ou l'épouse) le droit a la tutelle de ses enfants mineurs. Doit être cassé l'arrêt qui viole ces principes.*" Cited in Anoukaha, *supra*, note 40, at 29.

[45] As to this choice, see *Civil Status Registration Ordinance N° 81-02 of 29 June 1981*; and Fossungu (2014: 114).

Litigation[46]), how and when are 'de mécanismes juridiques differents' applying 'à des situation identiques' here, as demanded by legal pluralism experts? *"Une définition du pluralisme juridique,"* according to Jacques Vanderlinden, *"[c'est] l'existence, au sein d'une société déterminée, de mécanismes juridiques différents s'appliquant à des situations identiques"* (cited in Fossungu, 2013a: 8).

What one does actually have here in the CSC can only be likened to a case that arises from Quebec's civil law in Quebec, reaching the Supreme Court of Canada and being decided according to rules of common law: simply because the civil law rule in question 'smacks of injustice' to the common law "backwoods lawyers who would serve on the new court in Ottawa."[47] Should that then fall in line with regarding Canada as bijural? The experts are all saying not at all, since in such a scenario, as they have pointed out, it is only tantamount to the 'teaching of civil law through the common law' – what some critics have considered to be assimilation or the "taking of charge."[48] This assimilationist drive in Canada is even very easily seen in what a Université de Montréal professor denounces as *"les contestations judiciaires, comme on en voit occasionnellement au Québec, où l'on tente – non sans succès parfois – de faire prévaloir le recours aux règles ou aux concepts de la common law aux dépens du droit civil, le plus souvent sous prétexte de devoir assurer l'uniformité d'application des lois fédérales"* (Morel, 1997a: 25). If this propensity to uniformize is present even in federal Canada, it is perforce overwhelming in a highly centralized polity like Cameroon; thus according a lot of credit to "The Belgians [who quickly] realized the folly of multiculturalism in a unitary state and made adjustments

---

[46] Several other examples on adoption can be found in Nyambo (1997). See also Décret N° 69/DF/544 du 19 décembre sur les juridictions traditionnelles; Cour Suprême du Cameroun 21 octobre 1978, as reported in *Panant Revue de Droit des Pays d'Afrique* (1978) 253 at 253-54 (here the CSC annulled the Bafoussam Court of Appeal decision because of irregularities of the marriage certificate. Why should a marriage certificate – meant for 'official' marriages – be required in the first place for a customary marriage?); *and Cour Suprême du Cameroun 21 janvier 1977*, as reported in *Panant Revue de Droit des Pays d'Afrique* (1978) at 90-100, with *note* by P Lampue at 100-102.

[47] Peter H. Russell, *The Judiciary in Canada: Third Branch of Government* (Toronto: McGraw-Hill Ryerson Ltd., 1987) at 336.

[48] See Donald Poirier, "La common law en français: outil d'assimilation ou de prise en charge?" 1/2 *Revue de la Common Law* (1997), 215; and Morel (1997b).

by adapting to federalism" (Fossungu, 2013a: 6). Just how then is there bijuralism if not unity poverty operating in Cameroon? Has it not even been very clearly indicated by some experts that the Foumban Enterprise paid no attention to customary institutions? To one of these experts, "the Federal Constitution excludes these [indigenous law and customs] and several other vital questions some of which are, in a metaphorical sense, jigsaw-puzzles not only to Cameroonians themselves but also to foreigners interested in Cameroon progress" (Enonchong, 1967: xii).

Canada Looking to Cameroon or Cameroon Learning from Canada?

Assuming even that Cameroon were really that trijural, there could be difference in this respect with Canada which, through its obstinate refusal to accommodate Aboriginal legal institutions, remains effectively bijural (common law and civil law). Notwithstanding that "*bi*culturalism is *multi*culturalism at least" (Fossungu, 2013a: 155), there is a report that has strongly recommended to Canada, to no avail, the change of its deplorable attitude towards its Native Peoples, especially by adopting a separate justice system for them.[49] "To this effect," therefore, a multiculturalism expert has concluded, "Canada is also guilty of confusing or ambivalent multiculturalism" (Fossungu, 2013a: 151). Canada is nonetheless further pulled away from Cameroon in being stiffly confronted with (1) the presence of indigenous peoples and their claims; and (2) the competing influences of many intellectual traditions, economic philosophies and interests and regional identities[50] that obviously go into the prize-winning portrait of peace.[51] Canada may become effectively trijural if it adopts the

---

[49] See *Justice on Trail Vol. I: Report of the Task Force on the Criminal Justice and its Impact on the Indian and Métis People of Alberta* (March 1991) at 1-7.

[50] See Arthurs Report. *Law and Learning: Report to the Social Sciences and Humanities Research Council of Canada* (1983) at 4; and J.R. Mallory, *The Structure of Canadian Government* (Toronto: Gage Publishing Company, 1984) at vii.

[51] The butchers in Cameroon obviously justify the dictatorship with the attainment of peace; but experts on peace studies tell us plainly that "Peace does not mean to be in a place where there is no noise, trouble, or hard work. Peace

separate justice system for its Aboriginal (or "Native") peoples, which is being constantly proposed to it. But as previously said, Cameroon's unity and judiciary poverty is neither of what Canada is nor what it may become on adopting the recommendations of *Justice on Trial.*

Endangering the Endangered Species by Side-by-Siding Discrimination in Africa?

Cameroon is only what can be conveniently termed a common Civil-Law country: although being confused for a bijural one even by its own highest judges (Oh! these CSC judges!) and other legal academics. The doubts cast on the so-called bijuralism or trijuralism are buttressed, first, by some utterances at an inaugural dinner of the nascent Common Law Society of Cameroon held in Limbe (formerly Victoria) in June 1996. Banister Luke Sendze, then president of the Cameroon Bar Association, at this dinner, plainly christened the common law system and its lawyers "an endangered species in the French legal system" (Sunde, 1996). The mere change of that city's name (from Victoria to Limbe) is a whole story of its own in the assimilation process (see Fossungu, 2013a: 166-168). Barrister Bernard Muna is also said to have distributed a pamphlet entitled: "the Fate of Common Law in Cameroon, its Origin and its Concepts" during this same inaugural dinner (Sunde, 1996).

The second, and perhaps much more compelling, buttressing factor is from Justice Nyo'Wakai who Carlson Anyangwe describes as one of 'two of Cameroon's ablest and finest judges'. This very able

---

means to be in the midst of all those things and still be calm in your heart. That is the real meaning of peace. Peace can mean different things to different people. It is the way freedom struggle and terrorism are used for same types of acts. One can be a freedom fighter for one and a terrorist for another. But we have to distinguish between the two. Same is the case in different parts of the world. For uncouth oppressors, those fighting are terrorists, for people of these areas they are freedom fighters" (Mentan, 2017). Thus, "As I listened to the children of Ngaoubela singing the phrase '*Let's always move forward in peace*', I wondered: What does peace mean to Cameroonians in their everyday lives? And, what does it take to live and move forward in peace? During my fieldwork I discovered that people in the field had many perspectives and concerns of their own about the topic of peace. Not everyone agreed to the state-centered focus of understanding peace as merely the absence of war" (Heum, 2016: 5).

and fine CSC justice seems to have clearly divined (without, perhaps, actually knowing it[52]) the entire civil law dominance when he commended Dr Anyangwe's book. "One cannot help but be impressed with some features of the book. Among these are: The clarity of expressions in the presentation of the subject to the extent that even where French expressions are used, *and these could not be avoided when you are dealing with or treating a bi-jural system*, they have in no way obscured their meaning."[53]

There is a significant contradiction in this speech which seems to only indicate the absence of the bijuralisrn/bilingualisrn that it is acclaiming. A Francophone writer simply confronts no English expressions (let alone their inevitability). The question then becomes that of where the bijuralism is. There will even be no question of inevitability in situations where both legal (language) systems are effectively operating; since, both being side-by-side, the equivalent words or expressions in either system will be readily available to the reader of whichever of the said legal or language systems. Some experts have however concluded that this side-by-side appearance of texts is somewhat incompatible with effective bilingualism, thus:

> Were all judges to be fluently bilingual, dual versions of judgments would be rare. Typically, judges would write only in one language, choosing that language on the basis of the total context – language of pleadings, language of litigants, predominant language of external

---

[52] But this ignorance is hard to defend in view of the central theme (civil law overwhelming common law) of his recent book: Nyo'Wakai, *Under the Broken Scale of Justice: The Law and My Times* (Bamenda: Langaa RPCIG, 2008).

[53] Justice Nyo'Wakai, "Foreword II" to Carlson Anyangwe, *The Magistracy and the Bar in Cameroon* (Yaoundé: PANAG-CEPER, 1989), xix at xix (emphasis added). The other of the 'two ablest and finest judges' who wrote the first Foreword of this same book, on his part, also stated that "Upon the birth of the re-united Cameroon Republic, the harmonization of the laws which were to govern it became a pressing necessity. To meet that necessity, a number of commissions of experts were created and placed under the tutelage of the Ministry of Justice which was enjoined by Government *to guard strictly against imposing the legal system of one state over the other*. The guiding principles for these commissions w[ere] to be harmonization, and harmonization at its strictest sense." Chief Justice S.M.L. Endeley, "Foreword I" to Carlson Anyangwe, *The Magistracy and the Bar in Cameroon* (Yaoundé: PANAG-CEPER, 1989), xvii at xvii (emphasis added).

audience, character of justificatory sources material and rhetorical and syntactical properties of a language – of their literary endeavour (Macdonald, 1997: 164, note omitted).

What Professor Roderick Macdonald suggests here is very academic. But it has been challenged from many angles. Viewing that we are talking majority/minority cultures, some think his theorization could only facilitate what has been castigated by the experts as the majority's *l'unijuralisme* (see Morel, 1997b: 320-321), which is evidenced by the fact that the camouflaged legal system(s) can only exist through one legal system – common Civil-Law (for Cameroon) or civil Common Law, for Canada. Quite apart from what can be considered as the last straw that broke the camel's back and sparked off the current gridlock in Cameroon,[54] André Morel has specifically kicked against this unijuralism which is *"encore plus évidente lorsqu'on est en présence des dispositions législatives qui, même dans leur version française, adoptent une formulation qui n'a de sens qu'en fonction du système de common law"* (Morel, 1997b: 320).

Furthermore, research in most effectively bijural/bilingual entities has indicated, first, the need for using juridically neutral and formally bijuridical language.[55] The language's neutrality in this instance must result from the fact that it is not exclusively derived from only one of the legal systems in question.[56] Second, it has been discovered that the technique of side-by-side bilingual texts not only

---

[54] See C Caffey, "Understanding Cameroon's Anglophone Protests" on 2/13/17 at 12:27 available at http://www.newsweek.com/cameroon-anglophone-problem-paul-biya-556151 (last accessed on 20 April 2017); and "Anglophone Problem Rocks National Assembly" (December 2016) available at http://bamendaonline.net/blog/anglophone-problem-rocks-national-assembly/ (last accessed on 20 April 2017).

[55] A further exposition on 'L'utilisation d'un langage juridiquement neutre' and 'L'utilisation d'un langage formellement bijuridique'is offered by Morel (1997a: 19-20 & 20-21, respectively). For more extensive discussion of both conditions, the reader could consult Morel (1997b: 332-338 & 338-346, respectively); and Macdonald and Scott (1997) generally.

[56]*"Un tel langage est neutre en ce qu'il n'est exclusive ni au droit civil ni à la common law; et il est bijuridique en ce qu'il permet néanmoins de designer, sans les nommer, des notions ou des institutions appartenant en propre à chacune des deux traditions juridiques"* (Morel, 1997a 19).

161

promotes effective bijuralism.[57] It has also been shown to even enormously enhance bilingualism among citizens in general and public officials in particular. That is probably why most, if not all, Canadian Supreme Court decisions (especially as reported in the *Supreme Court Reports*) assume this side-by-side form – not to overemphasize that this Canadian apex judicial institution itself is bijural and bilingual.[58] As one editor-in-chief has forcefully put the point, "we occasionally receive notes thanking us for printing each article in English and French [because] most readers [say they] use our 'side-by-side' bilingual format to practice the other language. Bravo!"[59] That is indeed what promoting bijuralism/bilingualism (or multiculturalism) and justice or equality should entail.

The country's institutions particularly have to be bicultural (bilingual and bijural). Otherwise, what happens to a student or litigant who can only comprehend one of these languages? There is obvious poverty in justice administration, in communication, and in education. Carry it specifically to the courts and one can only imagine, for instance, what it is like for an English-speaking common-law oriented accused to be tried by the one-man French-speaking civil-law oriented judge. The puzzle here becomes even greatly magnified in these courts if one appreciates (as experts like Peter Bringer have indicated) that most of Cameroon's current top judges are ex-officers

---

[57] "*[R]ecourir à des dispositions parallèles* " according to one expert, "*permet de conserver aux textes législatifs la clarté et la lisibilité qui sont souhaitables. Il offre au surplus et surtout la possibilité d'énoncer une norme dans des formulations qui respectent le génie de chacun des deux systèmes, ce qui ne peut que contribuer à harmoniser les rapports entre la loi fédérale et le droit civil.*" (Morel, 1997: 20 & 21).

[58] See Peter H. Russell, *The Supreme Court of Canada as a Bilingual and Bicultural Institution (Documents of the Royal Commission on Bilingualism and Biculturalism)* (Ottawa: Queen's Printer for Canada , 1969).

[59] Lise Ravary, "Bourquets and brickbats" Air Canada's *enRoute* (December-Décembre 1996), 8. And, of course, the French text is right there, side-by-side: "*nous recevons a l'occasion du Courier nous remerciant de publier tous nos articles en français et en anglais: bien des lecteurs se servent de notre mise en pages bilingue en parallèle pour travailler leur langue seconde. Félicitations!*" *Id.* One can mention, for further cases of commendable texts in English and French on facing pages, the Canadian Prime Minister's Statement given at the Constitutional Conference, held in Ottawa, February 5, 6, and 7, 1968. See *Federalism for the Future: A Statement of Policy by the Government of Canada/ Le fédéralisme et l'avenir: déclaration de principe et exposé de la politique du Gouvernement du Canada* (Ottawa: Queen's Printer, 1968).

of the colonial administration with no legal knowledge. And – here further comes the most awkward and bewildering part of the whole confusing arrangement, namely – that:

Most trial courts in Cameroon and other parts of French Africa [a]re one-man courts. Not only did the bench consist of one magistrate, but this one man, also called a 'polyvalent magistrate', performed in addition to his judicial task the functions of the 'procureur de la republique' and 'juge d'instruction' or 'examining magistrate'. These two posts can only be imprecisely translated as 'prosecutor' and 'examining magistrate'. The non-adversarial French procedure assigns them functions and positions which are quite different from the English procedural system (Bringer, 1981: 3).

That explains it all. That is, why Southern Cameroonians are being ferried to Yaoundé for kangaroo trial rather than in the place of supposed crime. "The heart of our people is bleeding. They are carted away like cattle in groves into prison yards away from homeland to Yaoundé. In a country where you are arrested because you are poor, in a country where you go to prison because you have no godfather to back you up, in country where you are put behind bars because you stand for justice and freedom – in such a country, good men must rise up to say Enough is Enough" (Jumbam, 2017). What kind of justice is an English-speaking litigant in, say, the capital of Yaoundé, going to obtain by being tried before one of these unilingual and unijural judges and prosecutors? Or even a bilingual litigant before this unilingual and unijural judge?[60] Is the bilingualism/bijuralism position, especially in Cameroon's capital, any better now with the newly trained young *magistrats* from ENAM?

On the whole, the language and justice situation would seem to be still the same as before or even worse. It could be said that the University of Yaoundé and Cameroon seem to be the inverse situation in effectively bilingual countries. About President Ahmadou

---

[60] For possible answers to these associated issues, see Linda Friedman Ramirez, Leslie Nori Kay, and Katherine Weber, "When Language is a Barrier to Justice: The Non-English-Speaking Suspect's Waiver of Right" 9-2 *Criminal Justice* (1994), 2 at 2-4 ('When officer and detainee are monolingual'), at 6 (Anxiety and language proficiency), at 4 (when only the detainee is bilingual), & at 5 (Defending Culture).

Ahidjo's "dualism culturel", therefore, Jacques Benjamin (having more elaborately canvassed the centralizing effects of unilingualism in Cameroon, especially in the capital and the unique University of Yaounde until 1974[61]) concluded that it consists *"uniquement en terme d'adaptation du modèle universitaire Français au contexte africain"* (Benjamin, 1972: 127). Even the use of 'adaptation' here is doubtful. Blind copying is the correct expression, as further seen below. It does not also mean that, since that year (1974), the situation has ameliorated. Far from it.

It is encouraging that some Cameroonian texts (laws) are already being printed in the side-by-side fashion in both English and French.[62] One of the laws in question is the Private Security Companies Law (PSCL).[63] This PSCL could have appeared in both languages, side-by-side, perhaps, because most of those involved in this business in Cameroon are foreigners from English-speaking countries, notably the USA. However commendable the side-by-side bilingual appearance of this particular law may be, it is still very questionable that "Security establishments and companies shall be subject to constant control [when] The conditions of such control shall be laid down by the [president's] decree to implement this law" (PSCL, Article 15). What is even more astonishing is the fact that, as discriminatory as several critics (including the supposed law-makers themselves) see it, this law was still passed.[64] Although bilingual and side-by-side, this PSCL does not deserve any applause since it is arbitrary and discriminatory. Graphically though, it brings to the forefront the issue of whether or not the Cameroon Supreme Court (CSC) will unfalteringly apply its *Affaire Baninga* equality decision

---

[61] See Benjamin, 1972 : Part II, chapitre 2 ('L'Influence Centralisatrice de la Langue et de la Présence Française au Cameroun').

[62] See *Juridis Périodique* (*Revue de Droit et de Science Politique*) N° 31 (1997) at 19-33.

[63] *Id* at 19-24: *Loi N° 97/021 du 10 septembre 1997 relative aux activités de gardiennage/Law N° 97/021 of 10 September 1997 Relating to Private Security Companies.*

[64] *"Jugée discriminatoire par nombre d'observateurs et de députés, la loi sur les sociétés de gardiennage a cependant été votée."* Michrl Mombio, "Gestion des sociétés de gardiennage: des conditions draconiennes" *Le Messager* N° 662 (10 septembre 1997), 5.

should it be challenged in that court. Must emulation from Canada not be the rule?

Idiotickerizing and Validating the Two-Cameroon Theory or Emulating Canada?

A Canadian minister has stated that "[m]ulticulturalism is an affirmation of our commitment that Canadians of all ethnic ... backgrounds have the right to equal recognition and equal opportunity in this country."[65] The right to equality must also capture that of the sexes in all sectors of national life. I think Cameroonian administrators really need to visit Canada to learn some of these things just like the Israelis and other Africans are doing. There are reports indicating several factors that have led Israeli judges and other legal scholars to consider Canadian constitutional models and legal precedents. Hillel Neuer, for example, declares notably in bold print that "In several key recent decisions, direct Canadian influence is evident in Israel's approach to a variety of separate issues, including gender equality, the application of constitutional remedies, and even in the area of procedure" (cited in Fossungu, 2013b: 158). Ethiopians are doing the same, as reported by Paul Pelletier (ibid). 1s there any compelling reason why Cameroon, of all countries, should not do this learning? Perhaps there is absolutely none for persisting in turning the English-speaking there into (artificial) Frenchmen. The more especially as "Cameroonians should be encouraged to imitate the catalyst models that mankind has known in order to survive" (Biya, 1986: 99). Those catalyst models that Cameroonians need to adapt to their situation, it is submitted, have been very plentifully designed in Canada. Canada must be emulated, or should it not?

The response of some Cameroonians to this question, according to some critics, clearly "appears to have been instinctive rather than conscious and deliberate" (Anyangwe, 1987: 264). It is no secret that most instinctive acts have been decried for their potential to obliterate distinction or differentiation and, therefore, rigorous

---

[65] See *Operation of the Canadian Multiculturalism Act – Annual Report 1988/89* (Ottawa: Minister of Supply and Services Canada, 1989) at ix (omission as in original, and bold taken off). The minister in question was/is Gerry Weiner, Minister of State for Multiculturalism and Citizenship.

analysis of relevance and purpose. Instinctive tendencies create more confusion and problems rather than tackling existing ones. "This so-called... [instinct] is unprincipled and unstructured. If it is permitted to gain credence, any principled analysis will disappear, problems will multiply, and difficulties of differentiating when... [to emulate] will be compounded. It is, in fact, merely an excuse for not undertaking a rigorous analysis of relevance and purpose and, as such, is to be deplored."[66] The instinctive response of some Cameroonians to the question at hand proves these critics. "From this point of view, it is important... [that some of these greatly emulated Canadian concepts] which are vital vehicles of human values, are no longer merely Cameroonized but Cameroonian" (Biya, 1986: 99). It is in the same line of reasoning, perhaps, that an unthinking reliance on Bagehot's notion of parliamentary sovereignty (meant for unitary states) by the Canadian Supreme Court to deny certain rights of provincial governments and other interest groups, has been trenchantly criticized by the executive director of the University of Alberta's Centre for Constitutional Studies.[67] These arguments are good and fine indeed; but not when we leave the realms of instinct to that of principled analysis in Cameroon. At that point one must wonder if transplanting wholesale from France does indeed meet the "Cameroonian" requirement. That can only be if we go by the insurmountable thesis that there are in fact two Cameroonian territories separated by the wide Atlantic Ocean. Let us now take this to the task of rigorous analysis of relevance and purpose.

The refusal in Cameroon to emulate from Canada is that "our concern is not to identify Cameroon with any ideology whatsoever, however fascinating it may be" (ibid: 12-13). That was in 1986. Nine years later President Biya stated on 31 December 1995 how Cameroon has resisted copying blindly from other nations, instead preferring authentic democracy that is based upon truly Cameroonian institutions that have been fashioned by free and

---

[66] Alan W. Mewett, "Editorial: Statements Admissible In Narrative" 38 *The Criminal Law Quarterly* (1996) 385 at 386.

[67] See David Schneiderman, "The Market and the Constitution" 3/2 *Constitutional Forum Constitutionnel* (Winter 1991), 40 at 44.

independent Cameroonians (my translation).[68] Another reason, the principal one, is the unsuitability of the borrowed rules. Cameroon has its own uniqueness that dictates that it should not copy things that would not fit in. "Cameroon has its own values and peculiarities from which we try to learn the lessons needed to guide our actions, instead of borrowing from other countries rules of conduct and actions which are not easily adapted to the life of the Cameroonian nation" (Biya, 1986: 13). There is every reason for saying many positive things about suitability and adaptability of borrowed rules.

But just take the French Constitution of 1958 and substitute 'French' with 'Cameroonian' and the so-called 'Cameroonian Constitutional Council', for instance, is found in it (see 1996 Constitution, Articles 46-52). Thereafter one must find it really hard not to charge both Professors M. Cappelletti and Dallis Radamaker with discussing Cameroon's constitutional organ and calling it French.[69] France is thus not "another country" as far as Cameroon is concerned? This dishonest act is, first of all, a glaring shame to Cameroonian intellectualism. The intellectuals of this country are thus being enormously idiotickerized. And those that refuse to be so demeaned are forcefully cowed or cut off the world that must not hear their story. "The Internet blockage and the mass abduction of the British Cameroonians to Yaoundé by the republican forces of lawlessness and disorder, expose them as a flimsy country pretending to be tough. Our people say that there is no greater injustice than

---

[68] *"Avec méthode et détermination, nous avons résisté à la tentation des solutions toutes faites et des raccourcis faciles. Nous avons choisi la voie de la vraie démocratie en nous appuyant sur les institutions de la République que le peuple souverain s'est librement données."* Quoted in *Cameroon Tribune* N° 6574-N° 2853 (8 avril-April 8, 1996), 1.

[69] See M. Cappelletti, *Judicial Review in the Contemporary World* (New York: The Bobbs-Merrill Company Inc., 1971) especially at 2-5; and Dallis Radamaker, "The courts in France" in Jerold L. Waltman and Keneth M. Holland (eds.), *The Political Role of Law Courts in Modern Democracies* (New York: St. Martin's Press, 1989), 129-152. The only slight shifting in the two organs will be to render the African counterpart even much more omnipotent than its original European version, in order, perhaps, that it be befitting for the advanced state that the Yaoundé gangsters have happily defined as a "State [which] is the best politically organized human grouping and the most complete from the standpoint of its system of authority...and a concentration of the most imposing deterrent forces (army, police, prisons) in order to ensure order." Paul Biya, as cited in Fossungu (2013b: 26).

when anus farts, head receives a knock. The tyrant who is oppressor has engaged in placating international eyes that he is the oppressed. What a shame!" (Jumbam, 2017). Second, by shamelessly transplanting French models to polyethnic so-called bijural and 'officially' bilingual Cameroon – done without at all considering if they fit in or not; not bothering at all whether or not there are some *Cameroonians* who are not used to them – one can only be led to one thing that begins with France not being a different country from Cameroon. That is, one must end up in the legitimate theory of there being either (1) two Cameroonian territories – one in Africa and the other in Europe; or (2) two French territories, one European and the other African. Which of the alternatives is the correct one?

Closing Observation

At this point it is better to simply avoid any prioritization between the two alternatives. But one is here writing about rnulticulturalism and poverty creation in "Cameroon". The answer to the questions is properly reflected in the prevailing poor political tendency in Cameroon. It is well known that ideology does not always represent an inverted picture of reality; it merely operates with half-truths, even though the intention may not be deliberately to deceive. This is because, more often than not, one can be the victim of one's own conviction and the first object of one's own intellectual and manipulative bias (Maneli, 1994: 48). It is thus especially important for one to be able to assess whether the ideas (ideology) of one's interlocutor are on the conservative or the progressive side. Are they innovative, reformist, or are they a part of an ideological tradition? And, most importantly, is the interlocutor in favour of democratic freedom and elections? All these, the experts have concluded, can only be evaluated primarily from the viewpoint of the prevailing political tendency and atmosphere (ibid: 48-49).[70]

---

[70] Can the fact that Cameroon is a member of the European Economic Community (EEC) also help? See Harold D. Nelson, Margarita Dobert, Gordon C. McDonald, James McLaughlin, Barbara Marvin and Philip W. Moeller, *Area Handbook for the United Republic of Cameroon* (Washington, D.C., 1974) at vii; and Rome Treaty of 1957 by which:"the HIGH CONTRACTING PARTIES

If they had turned to and meticulously scrutinized that political atmosphere, 1 think the intellectuals in Cameroon who are advancing baseless theories must, of course, have very easily deciphered the 'new Hobbesian Kingdom of Darkness' which is presenting itself as a realm of reason (ibid: 23). In short, therefore, they should have realized that what is involved in Cameroon is only what Justice Oliver Wendell Holmes in 1952 termed the naive state of mind that accepts what has been familiar and accepted by them and their neighbours as something that must be accepted by all people everywhere (ibid: 27 n.6). This naive state of mind is precisely what is at the heart of the current crisis in Cameroon. It is not the country's legendary diversity. 'Advanced Democracy' is merely using this characteristic feature as a suit to cover to its nakedness. Its success in this nudity-hiding business is greatly assisted by the cow dung journalism and intellectualism that often quickly convert important issues to petty ones of cultural supremacy. I think turning some of these issues into a mere fight for supremacy between the two inherited cultures is a "shameless exhibition of myopia, bigotry and regionalism [and] accounts for the sometimes violent and acrimonious arguments that have occurred [within the legal profession and academia and] during working sessions of the commissions. This is a retrograde attitude which deserves utter condemnation from any *right-thinking educated and sincere person*" (Anyangwe, 1987: 269, *emphasis added*).

Are there many of such right-thinking educated and sincere people in Cameroon? If there were, surely Cameroon could not still be the inversion of Canada that it currently seems to be. Choked full with poverty in all its ramifications; right and left, up and down, east and west, north and south! Otherwise, is it not solely to bijural and bilingual Canada (and not to unijural and unilingual France nor Britain exclusively) that Cameroonians should be looking, if they are really interested in doing just what is being supposedly desired? That is, working for national progress and eradication of abject poverty and vulnerability in the community? To close it up in the pertinent words of Fossungu (2013a: 3), "would the current nation-building malaise be resolved through putting all the facts (bitter and

---

establish[ed] among themselves a EUROPEAN ECONOMIC COMMUNITY", Article 1.

169

embarrassing as some of them are or may be) on the table for open, frank and seasoned discussion; or will it be through the ongoing farce of emasculation and refusal to recognize that serious national unity problems do exist? Shouldn't the guiding philosophy in every action in Cameroon be a very genuine *Quel Cameroun pour nos enfants* (What kind of Cameroon is to be passed on to our children)?" 0783205007

References

Anyangwe, Carlson. 1989. *The Magistracy and the Bar in Cameroon,* Yaoundé: PANAG-CEPER.

_____ 1987. *The Cameroonian Judicial System*, Yaoundé: CEPER.

Benjamin, Jacques. 1972. *Les camerounais occidentaux: la minorité dans un état bicommunautaire,* Montréal: Université de Montréal.

Bissonnette, Bernard. 1963. *Essai sur la constitution du Canada,* Montréal: Les Éditions du Jour.

Biya, Paul. 1986. *Communal Liberalism*, London: Macmillan.

Bringer, Peter. 1981. The Abiding Influence of English and French Criminal Law in One African Country: Some Remarks Regarding the Machinery of Criminal Justice in Cameroon, *Journal of African Law* 25(1): 1—13.

Coldham, Simon. 1995. Legal Responses to State Corruption in Commonwealth Africa, 39/2 *Journal of African Law* 115.

Driedger, Leo. 1989. *The Ethnic Factor: Identity in Diversity,* Toronto: McGraw-Hill.

Enonchong, H. N. A. 1967. *Cameroon Constitutional Law – Federalism in a Mixed Common-Law and Civil-Law System,* Yaoundé: Centre d'Édition et de Production de Manuel et d'Auxilliares de l'Enseignement.

Fossungu, Peter Ateh-Afac. 2017. *Frantalkist Dictionary of Community and Family Politics: Africa's Immaculate Unity and Development Theory without Africa?* Bamenda: Langaa RPCIG, (forthcoming).

_____ 2016. *The Expibasketics and Intrigues of Love*, Bamenda: Langaa RPCIG.

_____ 2015a. *Family Politics and Deception in Northern North America and West-Central Africa: Litigating God's Marriage Intention?* Bamenda: Langaa RPCIG.

_____ 2015b. *Africans and Negative Competition in Canadian Factories: Revamping Canada's Immigration, Employment, and Welfare Policies?* Bamenda: Langaa RPCIG.

_____ 2014. *Africa's Anthropological Dictionary on Love and Understanding: Marriage and the Tensions of Belonging in Cameroon,* Bamenda: Langaa RPCIG.

_____ 2013a. *Understanding Confusion in Africa: The Politics of Multiculturalism and Nation-building in Cameroon,* Bamenda: Langaa RPCIG.

_____ 2013b. *Democracy and Human Rights in Africa: The Politics of Collective Participation and Governance in Cameroon,* Bamenda: Langaa RPCIG.

Hawker, Sara and Maurice Waite. 2007. *Oxford Paperback Dictionary & Thesaurus,* Oxford University Press, Oxford.

Heum, Audhild Steinnes. 2016. *"They Say We Have Peace": Perceptions and Practices of Peace in Northern Cameroon,* Master's Thesis in Social Anthropology, University of Bergen, Norway.

Johnson, Willard R. 1970. *The Cameroon Federation: Political Integration in a Fragmentary Society,* Princeton, N.J.: Princeton University Press.

Jumbam, Fr. Gerald. 2017. An Open Letter to the President of the National Episcopal Conference of Cameroon (NECC) – Archbishop Samuel Kleda, (sent to SobaAmerica on 8 May 2017 at 12:11 PM by Oben Besong obensong@yahoo.com).

Macdonald, Roderick. A. 1997. Legal Bilingualism 42, *McGill Law Journal* 119—167.

Macdonald, Roderick A. and F.R. Scott, 1997. "Harmonizing the Concept and Vocabulary of Federal and Provincial Law: The Unique Situation of Quebec Civil Law", In: Ministère de la justice Canada (Ed.), *L'harmonisation de la législation fédérale avec le droit civil québécois et le bijuridisme canadien,* Ottawa: Ministère de la justice Canada.

Maneli, Mieczyslaw. 1994. *Perelman's New Rhetoric as philosophy and Methodology for the Next Century,* Dordrecht: Kluwer Academic Publishers.

Mbaku, John Mukum. 2012. *Corruption in Africa: Causes, Consequences, and Cleanups* Lanham, MD: Lexington Books.

_____ 2004. *Institutions and Development in Africa*, Trenton, NJ: Africa World Press.

_____ 1999. *Bureaucratic and Political Corruption in Africa: The Public Choice Perspective* (Malabar, Florida: Krieger Publishing Co).

Mentan, Tatah. 2017. "Shaming Heaven: Peace of the Graveyard in Cameroon" available @ http://cameroonjournal.com/2017/04/11/commentary-shaming-heaven-peace-of-the-graveyard-in-cameroon/

Morel, André. 1997a. "L'harmonisation de la législation fédérale avec le *Code* civil du Québec. pourquoi? comment?" In: Ministère de la justice Canada (Ed.), *L'harmonisation de la législation fédérale avec le droit civil québécois et le bijuridisme canadien,* Ottawa: Ministère de la justice Canada, 1—28.

_____ 1997b. "La rédaction de lois bilingues harmonisées avec le droit civil", In: Ministère de la justice Canada (Ed.), *L'harmonisation de la législation fédérale avec le droit civil québécois et le bijuridisme canadien,* Ottawa: Ministère de la justice Canada, 309—363.

Nyambo, Temngah Joseph. 1997. Adoption of Children under Customary and Statutory Law in Cameroon, 9 *Revue Africaine de Droit International et Comparé* 894—904.

Panky, Wamey. 1997. Santa Priest Attacks Chop Broke Potism" *The Post* (24 October), 8.

Ruiz-Chiriboga, Oswaldo. 2017. Finding the Right Judge: Challenges of Jurisdiction between Indigenous and Ordinary Adjudicators in Ecuador, 49 *Journal of Legal Pluralism and Unofficial Law* 3-33.

Sunde, Lucas. 1996. Execution of Bad Laws: Anglophone Lawyers Told to Blame Assembly Not Supreme Court, *The Herald* N° 322 (24-26 June), 3.

Taku, Charles Achaleke. 1995. Lawyer Alerts British Gov't: C'wealth Systems Are Being Destroyed in Cameroon, *Cameroon Post* N° 0274 (11-18 December) 1.

Tamanaha, Brian Z. 1993. The Folly of the 'Social Scientific' Concept of Legal Pluralism, 20/2 *Journal of Law and Society* 192—217.

Tremblay, André. 1993. *Droit Constitutionnel: Principes,* Montréal: Les Éditions Thémis.

Williams, Patricia J. 1987. Alchemical Notes: Reconstructing Ideals from Deconstructed Rights, 22 *Harvard Civil Rights-Civil Liberty Law Review* 401—433.

Chapter 7

Poverty and Environmental Degradation on a Large Scale: The History of the Establishment, Operation and Management of a Multinational Mining Enterprise at Mashava, 1903-2015

Davidson Mabweazara Mugodzwa

Introduction

This chapter seeks to demonstrate that the establishment, operation and management of a multinational mining enterprise at Mashava since 1908 ushered in not only poverty, but underdevelopment and environmental degradation on a large scale in a formerly rural enclave of Chivi District. Mashava (formerly known as Mashaba) is a mining town in Masvingo Province, Zimbabwe. The town is located 40 km from Masvingo along the Bulawayo-Mashava Highway. During its heydays, from 1970s to the early 1990s Mashava was once a thriving and booming mining town comprising urban communities of both white and black mine workers who derived their livelihood by selling their labour power to the Multinational Associated African Asbestos Mining Company. Asbestos was mined three places, namely Gaths Mine, King Mine and Temeraire Mine. Since the late 1990s, Mashava has been suffering from environmental neglect characteristic of a shanty town as the Zimbabwean Government has failed to channel in infrastructural and maintenance development programmes to keep the town on a sound footing. Sadly, clean water is not available on a regular scale and electricity supply to the town is chaotic and sometimes major areas of Mashava are cut-off for more than four or even five days a week. Water comes only twice a week, on Tuesdays and Thursdays and worse still this water is always filthy from the rusty pipes (Interview with Gandiwa Tariro, Temeraire resident, 6 February 2017). This deplorable situation has caused illnesses amongst the Mashava civilians, and to make matters worse

175

underground water is heavily polluted by the dumping of mine waste into the nearby rivers and streams.

At Gaths Mine, for example, asbestos mining operations have stopped though the place remains important as the headquarters of the mining corporation. Some of the major buildings are located here such as the General Administration Office, the Mine General Hospital, Mine Training Centre and the Chemberi High and Low density residential areas for the workers. Temeraire Mine has also stopped operations and was until recently a services area with some of the departments still operating from there such as transport including the garage, laboratories, mechanical machine shop, electrical and civil departments. The High density Mupatagore and Low density suburbs; Temeraire, Eastvale and Westonlee are located at Gaths Mine. It is only at King Mine that some small-scale mining operations continue taking place but only run by a skeletal staff at Mine Shafts One and Two. Besides the aforementioned suburbs, the Asbestos Mine Mill and the Stores Department are also located here. Mambo High residential suburb and King Mine Low density residential areas are also domiciled at King Mine.

The Mashava Mines were up until the early 1990s part of Shabani and Mashaba Mines owned by the Turner and Newell Multinational Corporation who then sold both mines to Zimbabwean business mogul, Mutumwa Mawere for sixty million British pounds (£60 000 000.00) in a deal sponsored by the World Bank. The Zimbabwean Government was the sole guarantor of this World Bank loan (Gaths Mine Report, 1990:1). Both mines are now under the Zimbabwean Government control after Mutumwa Mawere fled the country, fearing for his life when trumped up charges were levelled against him by some members of the current ZANU (PF) Government. The two mines produced asbestos and Gaths Mine supplied the longer fibre, which was very popular on the international market. There are also other private mining enterprises in the surrounding area but they have also now all ceased operations due to escalating functional costs as well as unprofessional government interferences linked to the demand of a 51% to be surrendered to indigenous Zimbabweans. These are D.S.O. Mine, Boss Mine and Reedbuck formerly Lennox (Rex) Mine (Interview with Gutu Onias, former employee at Lennox

Mine, 6 February 2017). Bere Township is also a Mashava High and Low density residential area and was created to supply cheap labour to the once flourishing mines (Interview with Yepe William, former mine employee, King Mine, 4 February 2017). Little development has taken place in Mashava despite operating for nearly a century: the town centre is occupied by Balmain Supermarket which is the main shopping centre, a single private petrol station which also ceased operations many years ago and a sub-police station built of wooden structures.

In the light of this background, this chapter seeks to demonstrate that the establishment, operation and management of a multinational mining enterprise at Mashava since 1908 created not only the development of underdevelopment but poverty and environmental degradation on a large scale in a formerly self-sufficient and self-sustaining rural enclave. More precisely, the chapter argues that both the local Karanga people and Malawian migrant labourers domiciled in Mashava were systematically underpaid, overworked and later abandoned by this European capitalist oligarchic mining enterprise. Both working and living conditions amongst labourers in Mashava drastically deteriorated to appalling subhuman levels. These struggling workers were owed thousands of US Dollars in salary and pension arrears by both the former European capitalist oligarchic mining enterprise and the Government of Zimbabwe which subsequently took over the ownership of Mashava Mines from business tycoon Mutumwa Mawere who had purchased the mining company. The workers retaliated by occupying all available housing units scattered all over Mashava at King Mine, Gaths Mine, Temeraire and refused to leave or pay any rent until they received their salaries and pensions stretching over twenty years. Most of these workers have sublet their housing units to the newly arrived Great Zimbabwe University employees and students in order to earn an extra income.

This chapter further argues that Mashava has suffered environmental deterioration and degradation because of the persistent Government neglect and lack of capital injection into the mining operations and general day to day up keep of the town and its environs.

177

The chapter adopts both a historical and political economy approach and was also informed by oral evidence collected from selected male and female informants living at King Mine, Temeraire Mine and Gaths Mine. I also targeted mine management and political leadership for selected questionnaires. Documentary evidence from published sources such as archival colonial documents stored at the National Archives in Harare, mine publications, books, booklets and newspapers were also consulted to capture corroborative data relevant to the subject under discussion.

Historical background of asbestos mining at Mashava 1903-2015

The history of asbestos mining at Gaths Mine commenced in 1903 as recorded in the Mining Commissioners' Annual Report (Gaths Mine Report, 1981:1). However, asbestos production at Gaths Mine only started at a significant scale in 1908 and continued progressively until 1983 when the mining operations were temporarily suspended due to financial challenges (ibid). As already noted above, currently King Mine is the only section which is partially functional with all other mines having fully closed down their operations. In 1983, the Gaths Mine Mill was suspended due to the decline in demand of asbestos on the World market. Both underground operations and Gaths Mill are only operating on a care and maintenance basis. This also applies to the Temeraire Asbestos Mill.

From as early as 1908, mine employees were allocated accommodation according to race, rank and skill at King Mine, Temeraire and Gaths Mine housing complexes. Employees were housed in four main residential areas, namely Gaths High and Low density suburbs, Temeraire High and Low density suburbs, Westonlee Low density suburb and at King Mine High and Low density suburbs (Gaths Mine Report, 1981:2). Before 1980, Low density suburbs were strictly reserved for European personnel regardless of skill or rank because the Gaths Mine administration followed the racial segregation laws of the then political order and any European was always accorded high status for this reason. As such there were no middle suburbs for blacks (Interview with Amos Mabhande, former underground mine employee, King Mine, 22 January 2017).

The Gaths Mine Report (1981:2) notes that various mining methods have been in use at King Mine. According to the same report, in selecting the correct method for a particular ore body, "...geological and geomechanics assessment were considered in conjunction with required production rates, loading methods and costing" (ibid). Results from observations and experiments on caving angles, draw control crown pillar design, support and rock strength were utilized in deciding on the optimum mining method for a given set of conditions. The information from the science of geomechanics was applied to determine the type of support required for all excavation prior to mining (Gaths Mine Report, 1981: 3).

According to Sayce (1986:171), "...mining at Gaths Mine was executed using the opencast method but the last ore obtained by this method was in 1971." From 1980 onwards new methods were employed to extract asbestos from underground. Underground mining originally involved open slopping with back-filling, leaving pillars to support the surrounding rock (ibid). However, after a number of pillars collapsed, the current method of sub-level caving and block-level mining were introduced (Sayce, 1986). Later, the extraction of asbestos at King Mine was done using the vertical shaft method. King Mine was served by two vertical shafts and the first one was completed in 1965 and increased demand led to the opening of a second shaft whose operations started in late 1975 but was commissioned in 1978 (ibid).

At independence in 1980, Gaths Mine produced an average of 170 000 metric tonnes per annum, making Zimbabwe the third largest producer of the mineral in the world after China and Italy (Sayce, 1986). Weiss (1992) has argued that in the early 1980s, asbestos was Zimbabwe's largest foreign income earner. Furthermore, Mashava Mine was the only mine in Africa which produced and processed pure Chrystotile fibre which was considered safe for both industrial and domestic use (Interview with Mawere Dave, Health and Environmental Manager at Gaths Mine, 21 January 2017). Therefore due to the high demand for the Chrystotile variety produced in Zimbabwe, the country exported the mineral to over ninety countries worldwide. Following increased demand for asbestos at home and on the international market, asbestos production at Mashava Mines required an equal expansion in the labour force of more than 5 000 skilled and semi-skilled workers. This reverberates with Weiss's observation that a major asbestos mining enterprise usually needs more than 11 000 employees. Mashava Mines only employed 4 000 permanent workers and another one hundred contract labourers by 2000 (The Chronicle, 28 September, 2007).

Peasant livelihoods and mode of production in pre-colonial era Mashava

This section investigates the socio-economic environment in Mashava in the pre-colonial era. I will give a brief description of the environment on the eve of colonial rule in order to enable a comparative analysis with the situation now prevailing in the same area, nearly a hundred years after the mining economy was introduced. Mashava was originally a rural enclave where the Karanga ethnic group pursued a vibrant peasant economy largely based on agriculture and livestock keeping (NI/1/2, NC Chibi to CNC Mashonaland, 13 May 1897). It was part of Chibi District (now called Chivi) and largely inhabited by the Karanga people. Mashava was bordered to the north by Charter District which was also inhabited by Karanga speaking people.

Mashava had generally a Savanna woodland type of vegetation and the north - eastern part of the area was a dense forest where many varieties of trees thrived (NSKI/1/1, NC Chibi to CNC Salisbury, 31 May 1899). Mashava shared the northern border with Charter District and the Mashava Range marked the geographical boundary between the two districts which were both occupied by Karanga speaking people. On the watershed of Mashava, the *Musasa* tree grew in great abundance and the bark of this tree species used for multi-purposes by the local population, such as making blankets (called *daunha*), fish and game nets (called *mambure*). The Karanga people also used the same bark for making very strong rope used for thatching huts and other similar purposes. The north-eastern part of Mashava is what local people called Mutao forest. In the Mutao Forest, the *Mopani*, the black olive tree naturally thrived (ibid). See picture below showing a natural landscape undisturbed by mining intrusion existing in some portions of Mashava.

Figure 1: Picture showing a natural landscape undisturbed by mining intrusion existing in some portions of Mashava

Mashava had a generally mild climate except in June and July which had cold winds, often accompanied by frost (ibid). However, the climate varied slightly in different parts of the area under research. Rainfall was heaviest between November and January. Chibi District was however notorious for periodic droughts (ibid). The principle grain cultivated by the Karanga people of the area included finger millet [called *rukweza*], and this was grown mostly in the wetter Highveld areas, bulrush millet (*mhunga*) and sorghum (*mapfunde*) The indigenous people also grew subsidiary crops such as rice (called *mupunga*), groundnuts (*nzungu*), ground beans (or *nyemba*), cowpeas (*nyimo*), maize (*chibage*), and some different types of vegetables including pumpkins (*manhanga*), cucumbers (*magake*), gourds (*matende*) and many others (ibid). *Mhunga*, a drought resistant cereal crop was the staple food for the Karanga and it was grown in large quantities in the drought-ravaged Chibi District. Maize, introduced later into the country by Portuguese traders, did not become a staple crop until the twentieth century because it was said to be difficult to reduce it to mealie-meal (N3/1/5, NC Chibi to CNC Salisbury, 26 August 1903).

Documentary evidence suggests that the Karanga people in Mashava were basically agriculturalists and thus agriculture was the most important economic activity before colonial rule. However, there were also other economic activities such as hunting, gathering, fishing, manufacturing, [making bark clothes, blankets, fish and game traps, ropes, baskets, pottery etc.], building [huts, cattle pens, fencing homesteads and fields], iron smelting and trade (NSKI/1/1, NC Chibi to CNC Salisbury, 31 May 1899). These were however, only secondary economic activities which were done during the agricultural off-season or when there was drought (called *shangwa*). Available written evidence shows that the Karanga agricultural system in Mashava was relatively successful but the major constraint was periodic droughts (N3/1/5, NC Chibi to CNC Salisbury, 5 December 1899*)*. Iron hoes (*mapadza*) obtained from trade with the Njanja people of Charter District were used on a large scale and this boosted agricultural production. The Njanja traders preferred to receive cattle in exchange for their hoes (Mackenzie, 1975). Iron hoes were also exchanged for goats and sheep at the rate of two or three hoes for a small goat/sheep and three or five hoes for a large one (NSKI/1/1, NC Charter to CNC Salisbury, 31 May 1899).

The iron hoes revolutionised food production. The hoes together with axes [*matemo*] were used to great effect in preparing new and old fields for cultivation. Agricultural land was abundantly available and was communally owned. There was plenty of land for everybody, however only married male persons had access to such land. Women owned small gardens where they cultivated mainly vegetables such as *manhanga, tsunga, nyevhe* and many others. However, upon the death of the spouse, the surviving female owned and cultivated the fields of her deceased husband (Interview with Chinoti Pfunye, peasant farmer, Handikori Village, 12 January 2017). Land was distributed by the chief (*mambo*) to his respective headmen (*masadunhu*) who in turn distributed it to male family heads. Chief Bere was the local chief of Mashava area (Interview with Chief Bere, Bere area, Mashava, 24 January 2017).

Cattle-keeping was also a major source of wealth for the Karanga people of Mashava and during years of drought cattle were sold in order to procure grain from those families who had surplus (N9/1/8, Annual Report, 31 March 1903). During the colonial people, cattle were also sold to meet tax obligations (N9/2/1, Half-yearly Report, 30 September 1897). It is thus my argument that the introduction of taxation by the BSAC marked the beginning of a long period of systematic impoverishment of the peasantry by a colonial economic administration. The Karanga people of Chivi seem to have had large herds of cattle as observed by NC Taylor (N9/1/7, Annual Report, 31 March 1901). Cattle were also important as baggage animals. They were also crucial in bride wealth [*lobola*] payment (NSKI/1/1, Monthly Report, 31 March 1899). Therefore cattle played an important part in the Karanga economy during both the pre-colonial and colonial periods. Cattle were also used as a form of exchange in the procurement of hoes, axes and other daily needs (Mackenzie, 1975). The Karanga people of Mashava were also engaged in local internal trade to obtain essential commodities like salt and hoes from Charter District. Beach (1977:40) has noted that, "...the best known salt-producing area was the middle Sabi valley." The Hera people of Nyashanu were involved in salt manufacturing in this area and they sold it in areas such as Bikita, Mashava and others were it was scarce (ibid).

Availability of land accompanied by a successful agricultural and animal husbandry system meant that poverty on a large scale was non-existent amongst the peasantry Karanga speaking people of Mashava before the advent of colonial rule. My argument is that poverty and the subsequent environmental degradation occurring at Mashava were the creation of the establishment, operation and management of a European capitalist oligarchic mining enterprise there. On the whole, available evidence suggests that the economy of Mashava during the pre-colonial era was independently developing. Mashava area also corresponds with Rodney's definition of development, because the Karanga people were independently, "...increasing their capacity to extract a living from the natural environment and ability to support a growing population" (Rodney, 1980: 51).

Establishment, operation and management of a capitalist oligarchic mining enterprise and its impacts on Mashava rural enclave

This section examines the economic situation prevailing in Mashava area after the introduction of colonial rule and the subsequent operation of European capitalist farming and mining activities which shattered the existing robust peasant economy. The traditional land tenure system operating in Mashava before the advent of British colonial rule was effectively shattered by this capitalist economic system leaving the peasantry fairly dislocated and underdeveloped. According to Chief Bere, it is taxation and loss of land which greatly contributed to the impoverishment of the Karanga peasants (Interview with Chief Bere, Bere area in Mashava, 24 January 2017). All adult males were forced to pay tax which initially they met by selling grain to local dealers but during periods of drought, the Karanga sold off their cattle to European commercial ranchers at next to nothing prices in order to raise the money to pay taxes. The European ranchers deliberately under-priced the cattle bought from the Karanga in order to fleece the peasantry and reduce them to beggars (ibid). The Karanga were not at all enthusiastic to register for any farm or mine labour on European capitalist enterprises because they could easily meet their taxation obligation through agricultural and livestock production. According to Mackenzie (1970:43), BSAC officials and European settlers argued very strongly that the, "...development of Southern Rhodesia was being retarded by the reluctance of the African population to go to work".

In an attempt to resolve the perennial labour shortage in the colony, the British South African Company (BSAC) initially introduced various mechanisms such as boosting the population of Africans in Rhodesia by inviting foreign Africans from South Africa to come and settle in Rhodesia (ibid). The Fingos were targeted for this promotional immigration into Rhodesia. Mackenzie states that other African groups were also invited from Portuguese East African territory, the Northern Transvaal and Bechuanaland. Some of these arrangements were said to have been secretly made (ibid). The Chamber of Mines in Southern Rhodesia also encouraged immigrant labourers from Northern Rhodesia and Nyasaland to bring their wives and children to settle permanently in Southern Rhodesia (ibid). All these attempts to have foreigners to settle in Southern Rhodesia to act as labour reserves proved a complete failure for a variety of reasons. The Somalis and South Arabians who arrived in Rhodesia in 1900 and 1901 proved unsuitable for mine labour, in fact one group rioted in Beira and the whole exercise was scrapped (ibid).

As a result of this labour shortage some European mining companies were employing Africans from Nyasaland (now Malawi) registered by Recruiting Agents operating there. NC Chibi observed that, "…the Nyasa labourers with the exception of a few are giving satisfaction, the employers experience some difficulty with their language otherwise the relations between master and servant are satisfactory…" (N9/1/12, Annual Report, 31 December 1909). I must state that despite the introduction of African labourers from Nyasaland the labour shortage still remained unsolved. Even NC Chibi noted that, "…local employers were very short of labour…" (N9/1/14, Annual Report, 31 December 1911). I must also mention that even migrant labourers from the Cape in South Africa did not prove useful because of the poor working conditions on mines in Southern Rhodesia where the workers were subjected to long working hours and grossly underpaid. Furthermore workers were starved on poor diet and housing conditions were appalling (N9/1/16, Annual Report 31 December 1913).

This chapter now wishes to state that Malawian migrant workers were thus recruited and resettled in Mashava as cheap labour reservoir for the asbestos mining enterprise. I seek to establish that the response of local peasants in the surrounding Mashava area of Southern Rhodesia to labour recruitment for mines was not initially positive. Pertinent to this investigation is the view that, in fact there was no labour shortage in Southern Rhodesia at all: but rather the colonial capitalist enterprises were financially handicapped to enable them to pay adequately and fairly for African labour. At the same time I must state that African peasants in most of Southern Rhodesia region were in fact producing surplus grain and livestock for sale at a profit and did not need to work for Europeans to accrue cash (N9/1/17, Annual Report, 31 December 1914).

The NC of Chibi District noted the reluctance of Karanga peasants into registering for labour. The Native Commissioner however completely missed the point when he interestingly attributed the lack of interest to work amongst the peasants as due to sheer laziness. Even as late as 1914, South Rhodesian peasants in general did not show any slight inclination for working for the European capitalist enterprise. NC Chibi reported that, "…although a substantial increase in the number who want to work can be shown over last year there is no doubt that a general reluctance exists among natives to go and work at all…" (N9/1/17, Annual Report, 31 December 1914).

NC Chibi described this labour as being of an 'inferior' quality only suitable for surface mine work. He also warned that "…as long as the natives have no pressure they will not and need not work…" (ibid). NC Chibi attributed this reason to economic factors such as the possession of, "…unfortunately unlimited ground for cultivation, unlimited food supplies…" (ibid). Europeans were thus generally angered that Africans had adequate food and farm lands which enabled them to pursue a semi-luxurious peasant existence which was both self-sufficient and self-sustaining. My argument from the outset is that European enterprises deliberately set forth mechanisms which destroyed peasant production in order to force the Africans into the European capitalist labour market. This they did with remarkable success and, thus, ushered in an era of rapid impoverishment, underdevelopment and environmental degradation of a formerly rural self-sufficient peasantry economy.

The proletarianisation of Karanga peasants and the development of systematic poverty and environmental degradation in Mashava

In this section, I investigate the environmental impact of asbestos mining on Mashava. By environment, I mean the natural surroundings especially as they affect peoples' lives, animals and plants and also the non-living physical matter such as water, air and soil. I will attempt to demonstrate that asbestos mining activities impacted negatively on the natural environment of Mashava in various ways: the physical environmental, that is, water bodies, air, flora and fauna were greatly affected when excavation commenced in 1908. Various photographs presented below will give a graphic representation of the extent of land waste and degradation of the Mashava environment. Open pits were created haphazardly as the prospectors selected and tested the best sites to launch their mining enterprise (Interview with Takura Magwizi, former mine employee, Balmain Shopping centre, 28 January 2017). Most of these pits presently are not covered up as shown in the photographs below and are a health hazard to human beings and animals that may accidentally fall into the deep pits. Most are filled up with dirty stagnant water where now mosquitoes breed at will unabated (Interview with Norman Chadya, former mine employee, Bere Village, 26 January 2017). The old quarries and opencast pits scattered all over Mashava are dangerous traps to human and animal lives. They have also been filled with water and have become havens for bilharzias and mosquitoes which cause malaria. However, one such quarry, located a few metres from D.S.O. high density residential suburb has found usefulness as an alternative source of water to Mashava during periods of drought when water from Muzhwi Dam runs dry. Muzhwi Dam is the chief source of water for Mashava. See below a mountain of quarry at D.S.O Compound where the Great Zimbabwe University is harvesting water.

187

Figure 2: Mountain of quarry at D.S.O Compound where the Great Zimbabwe University is harvesting water

The mining operations at Mashava commenced in 1908 as explained above and 55 tonnes of hand-cleaned asbestos were shipped overseas (Gaths Mine Report, 1954:1). By the 1980s Mashava Mines had expanded to increase productivity to 1 680 000 metric tonnes of asbestos per annum (Gaths Mine Report, 1981:1). I must state that this asbestos mining at Mashava has caused visual pollution through creation of dumping sites which now appear everywhere and stand out like artificial mountains (Interview with Angeline Rugweda, teacher at Temeraire High School, Temeraire, 9 February 2017). To an ordinary visitor in Mashava, the dumping sites really appear like some mountains because now they have been overgrown with acacia bushes and merge with the natural environment in a very ugly manner, especially during the dry season when the bushes dry up because of the summer heat.

The dumping of mine waste affected fertile agricultural land which has now been covered up by acidic waste material (Interview with Ismael Muti, teacher at Temeraire High School, Temeraire, 9 February 2017). The surrounding vegetation cover was subsequently destroyed by the dumpsites and the natural flora and fauna suffered similar fate. Middleton (1990) has argued that when ores are washed, the water which has been used is drained into the local rivers and streams, poisoning the brooks and destroying marine life, wildlife and vegetation. Mashava landscape has lost its naturally beautiful scenery because of dumping sites which are an eyesore (Interview with Tariro Gandiwa, Temeraire resident, 6 February 2017). Middleton (1990) has stated that, waste dumping produces a devastated landscape of heaps, tips and logons with disused land between them. This situation describes the environmental impact of asbestos mining at Mashava. Below is a picture showing barren land as a result of mining activities.

Figure 3: Picture showing barren land as a result of mining activities

On a national scale, such waste land created by mine dumps can cover a significant portion of the productive national land. For example, the Motora Dump Mountain which is located between Gaths Mine low density suburb and the Gaths Mine high density suburbs covers a lot of useful land that could have been used for agricultural purposes. It is my argument that these dumps starve the local people of fertile farming land and, thus, contributes to poverty creation. Weiss (1992) has observed that, no minerals could be quarried or mined without some cost or damage to the local community and the environment. The argument is that the spoiled land could have been put to better use for farming, building houses or factories. Land that is used for mining is rendered spoilt and cannot be used for other useful purposes unless it is reclaimed. Below is a picture showing dump sites which now appear like a chain of mountains.

Figure 4: Picture showing dump sites which now appear like a chain of mountains

Asbestos mining at Mashava has also resulted in the dereliction of land. According to Leong and Morgen (1990), derelict land is theoretically that land which has been abandoned as useless or as too badly damaged that it cannot be repaired. This scenario describes Mashava landscape where mining has long stopped due to financial constraints and yet large stretches of land lie idle whereas it could have been reclaimed for other useful purposes. Leong and Morgen (1990) have argued that, in many underdeveloped countries, the financial advantages of exports, employment opportunities and economic growth encourage the government to exploit mineral resources but rehabilitation legislation is often not strict enough or is not strictly enforced. Instead of rehabilitating land at Gaths Mine which ceased functioning in 1983, the mining corporation opened up another mining venture at King Mine thus laying to waste large acreages of land which could have been used for agricultural purposes (Interview with William Yepe, former mine employee, King Mine, 21 January 2017). Mine dumps and open pits are scattered all over Mashava whilst poor former mine employees languish in abject poverty whereas they could have used the same land for agricultural and animal husbandry purposes.

I must argue that asbestos mining caused irreparable damage to the formerly beautiful lively forest of Mashava. Leong and Morgen have argued that minerals often occur in mountainous areas or other areas of great natural beauty and if mines are not properly rehabilitated much beautiful scenery may be permanently spoilt. This scenario closely relates to Mashava where the asbestos seams are confined to rocks embedded in mountainous areas. Mining of asbestos thus devastated not only the beautiful landscape scenery of Mashava but also had destructive effects on animals and vegetation (Interview with Morris Purazeni, former mine employee, Eastvale, 10 February 2017). Below is a picture showing failed revegetation programme on dumpsites.

Digby (1996) has argued that, overburden stock piles have no soil, appear barren and invegetated and in most cases the land is stripped bare of vegetation. This closely resembles the mine dumps in Mashava where toxic materials in the waste have rendered the land useless for plant cultivation. Usually the landscape scenery looks beautiful when furnished by plant and tree growth, albeit this is no longer the case in Mashava where the scenery is irritably damaged. See the disturbed scenery at Mashava.

Figure 5: Picture showing failed revegetation programme on dumpsites

Pollution from asbestos extraction, transportation and processing has also presented serious environmental problems affecting soil, water and air quality in Mashava. Most of the streams and rivers are heavily polluted especially now when *Makorokoza* (Illegal and unregistered miners) have descended on Mashava to excavate for gold and chrome all over without due supervision or care (Interview with David Mawere, Health, Safety and Environmental Manager, King Mine, 3 January 2017). Water pollution is one of the serious threats to the environment caused by mining. Weiss (1992) has argued that the problem with mining which is more frequent with sub-surface mining is run-off acids, eroded soil toxic substances into nearby surface and ground waters. The mine waste material is drained into rivers thus polluting the environment. Furthermore, at Mashava the eroded soil containing toxic waste from the dumps is washed down into the nearby Shashe River, Tugwi River and Muzhwi Dam. Below is a picture showing a large heap of quarry on the road to Balmain Shopping Centre. The quarry is very deep and cattle have drowned in this pool when they have ventured to drink water

Figure 6: Picture showing a large quarry heap on the road to Balmain Shopping Centre. The quarry is very deep and cattle have drowned in this pool when they have ventured to drink water.

Dust and gases that are produced during the mining process are also a major atmospheric pollutant and they poison the environment. Chenje and Johnson (1994) have stated that pollution is the poisoning of the environment with anything that reduces its ability to support life. During asbestos mining, when the Chrystotile fibre is being extracted, the air quality is affected by rock and fibre dust, fumes and gases which thus pollute the atmosphere. Mine workers suffered most as they were continuously exposed to inhaling mine gases and dust as a result respiratory and other related mining diseases such as bronchitis, lung cancer, tuberculosis, asbestosis and others spread widely amongst the mine employees (Interview with Elmore Chikuvire, retired nurse, Westonlee, 10 February 2017). Tuberculosis became the most common disease amongst many miners who came for treatment at the Gaths Mine Hospital from the late 1900s onwards (Gaths Mine Report, 1981:2). According to Chenje and Johnson (1994), asbestos is made up of thin fibre which cause scarring of the lung tissue, leading to asbestosis which is a lung disease, bronchial *caranoma mesothelioma* (cancer of the chest or abdominal lining) Moreso, the surrounding residential areas which unfortunately were located in close proximity to the mining complexes also suffered negatively from the mining daily operations through dust, noise and gases which were emitted into the atmosphere (Interview with Ambrose Phiri, former mine employee, 13 January 2017).

It is my argument that the externally recruited Malawian proletariat has also been trapped in this cycle of poverty and environmental degradation occurring at Mashava since their arrival in Southern Rhodesia in the 1970s. The former mine employees have been reduced into poverty and destituteness by both the former European employers and the Government of Zimbabwe. Most of their children have dropped out of school and many go hungry days on end because of lack of financial resources to enable purchasing of food in Masvingo City (Interview with Agatha Jaravaza, housewife, King Mine, 12 January 2017). As a result teenage pregnancies and child prostitution are the order of the day in the former mining town and as expected venereal diseases and HIV and AIDS are on the increase in this town.

Water, which is polluted by the rusty old pipes only flows through the tapes mounted on communal points on Tuesdays and Thursdays every week (Interview with Morris Purazeni, former mine employee, Eastvale, 10 February 2017). Therefore, most families have to do without clean water and have to rely on nearby rivers which are heavily polluted by affluent from the mining dumps. Pre-paid Electricity has now been installed in most houses in Mashava and as expected most poor families do without electricity because they cannot afford it (Interview with Asande Vivian, former mine employee, Temeraire, 14 January 2017). The once thriving beer halls and community halls where televisions and other entertainment facilities were once installed have been privatized and leased to the Great Zimbabwe University (Interview with July Moyo, former mine employee, Gaths Mine, 24 January 2017). Below, see a picture with a quary mountain behind, showing the Great Zimbabwe University Learning Centre established as Mashava, where the buildings were once used as the Headquarters of Mashaba Mines.

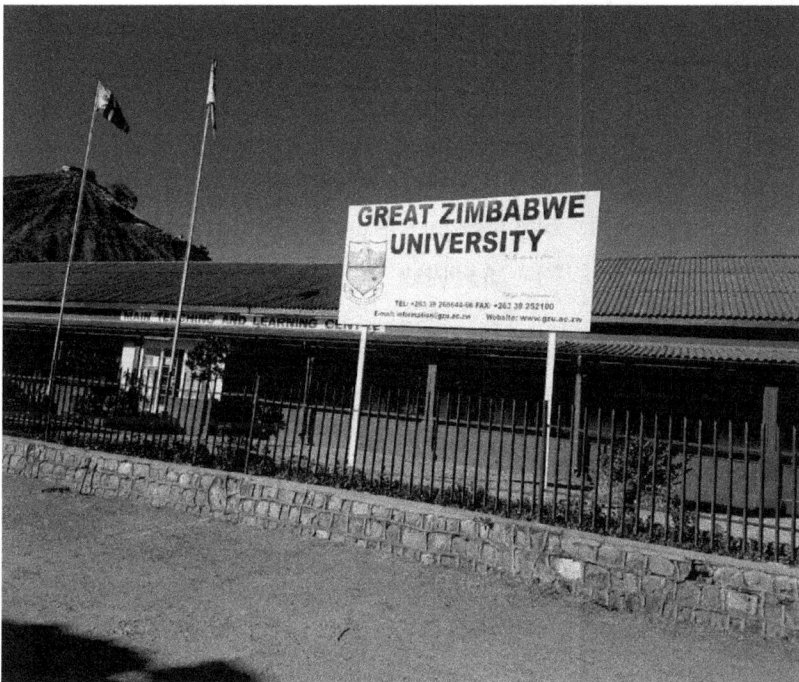

Figure 7: Picture with a quary mountain behind, showing the Great Zimbabwe University Learning Centre established as Mashava where the buildings were once used as the Headquarters of Mashaba Mines

Children from the Gaths Mine compound spend their part time roaming around the streets, poorly dressed and visibly malnourished in a sea of well-dressed and well-fed university students who stay only a stone's throw from these broken-down shackles inhabited by children, descendants of migrant Malawian workers. The Great Zimbabwe University has refurbished the old mine houses allocated to the institution under a private agreement with the Government of Zimbabwe and installed private bathrooms, electricity and geysers to the same houses which are now rented out to university students who live in luxury in a sea of poverty and environmental degradation (Interview with Mutambirwa Simon, political activist, Westonlee, 21 January 2017).

My research is guided by the Marxist thinking that urban dwellers mostly derive income from selling their labour power to the capitalist enterprises in order to survive and the situation in Mashava indicates that no industrial production seems to be taking place on a significant scale and thus I state that poverty and hunger is the order of the day in Mashava. This urban population in Mashava is surely subject to the vagaries of a Capitalist cash economy affecting the rest of Zimbabwe and since the available waste land does not allow them to eke out a living from utilization of such land for agricultural purposes then procuring their daily food needs and other basic needs is clearly a major challenge for most families. Presently, Mashava is a place characterized by abject poverty, prostitution, large scale land degradation, crumbling suburban houses in Chemberi, King Mine and Gaths Mine and the notorious *Makorokoza*, the illegal gold and chrome hunters, rule the sleeping town. Thanks to the arrival, settlement and occupation of most disused infrastructure by the Great Zimbabwe University at Gaths Mine the place would have totally fallen apart.

Many former male mine employees have turned to gold panning when the economy nose-dived but currently there is not much gold left in Mashava and people are getting very desperate (Interview with Marime A, retired teacher, Temeraire, 23 January 2017). Thabani Ncube said young men were now resorting to stealing and his shop had been broken into recently (Interview with Thabani Ncube, Businessman, Balmain Shopping Centre, 28 January 2017). Prostitution has also taken root and the few bars that are dotted around Mashava have become popular spots for men. The business however is not as lucrative and the commercial sex workers have been forced to charge very low fees for their services. As Lucy revealed, "for casual sex we charge as little as a dollar: that is how desperate the situation is" (Interview with Lucy Moyo, commercial sex worker, Upperdeck Bar, Bere suburb, 22 January 2017). Women in their fifties have literally been reduced to beggars by day and commercial sex workers by night.

Some women now survive by selling live chickens which they rear in their backyards. Loveness Banda reiterated that, "people do not pay cash for the chickens and it takes most customers two months to pay off the US$7 that I charge for one bird" (Interview with Loveness Banda, housewife, King Mine, 10 January 2017). Her occasional customers are students from Great Zimbabwe University campus. Mariana Chuma stated that, "I have become very poor indeed and to supplement for the meagre income, I go to a farm commonly known as Kwa Peter and enlist for food for work" (Interview with Mariana Chuma, housewife, Gaths Mine, 10 February 2017). At Kwa Peter the women are allocated large pieces of land to till and in exchange for their hard labour they only receive a bucket of maize in return. "It is quite a feat to complete the task and at times I spend two days working on the allocated piece of land…they count 85 by 85 strides to demarcate the area to be tilled in return for a bucketful of maize" (ibid).

In Mashava, some women now spend time manufacturing reed mats which they sell for as little as US$2. "Collecting the reeds is a difficult task…I get bitten by mosquitoes and my body is ridden with scars from the bite marks" (Interview with Tambudzai Banda, 34 years old, housewife, King Mine, 8 February 2017). The mats are bought in bulk by cross border women traders who take them for resale into neighbouring South Africa and Botswana. "For six reed mats they give me three bars of soap and for 15 mats I get a two litre bottle of cooking oil" (ibid). Other women take part in cleaning private houses and yards to earn money for food. Melody Chakawa reported that, "…sometimes I clean people's houses and yards in exchange for a bowl of mealie-meal… am not ashamed of what I do because I just want to survive and be able to send my children to school" (Interview with Melody Chakawa, commercial sex worker, Gaths Mine, 9 February 2017).

The poverty and environmental degradation is worse in Village Three of Mashava where electricity was never installed and the residential area resembles a dumping area. The old houses are coated with grime and barefoot children run around the squalid dwellings that are depressingly run down. Dirty, torn curtains that adorn most house windows amplify the level of poverty in the area. Young women, no more than 20 years of age have more than one child, are single and unemployed. Asked how they survive in these squalid conditions they become evasive but elderly residents tell the sorry story of rampant prostitution in the area which the women engage in so as to make ends meet. Ezekiel Banda confirmed that, "…our young girls now help us to survive by engaging in prostitution in the local bars" (Interview with Ezekiel Banda, former mine employee, Village Three in Mashava, 13 February 2017).

Fortunately, the Ministry of Education passed a resolution that no child would be sent away from school for failing to pay school fees. According to Professor Paul Mavhima, the Deputy Minister of Education, "…it is a criminal offence for any school headmaster to turn away children who have not paid fees" (Interview with Professor Paul Mavhima, Deputy Minister of Education, Munhu Mutapa Building, Harare, 14 June 2017). Allowing children into classes does not however cancel out the fees arrears: the fees debt continues to accumulate every time and sometimes debt-collectors are sent in to confiscate property from outstanding debtors. Bishion Banda reiterated that, "…debt collectors are hot on our heels and we are constantly afraid that we might lose our property" (Interview with Bishion Banda, 58 years old, mine employee, Lennox Mine in Mashava, 13 February 2017).

Kiki Yepe lamented that, "When the government took over and operations ceased in 2008, we were thrown into poverty's deep end" (Interview with Kiki Yepe, former mine employee, King Mine, 22 January 2017). "Nobody cared about us anymore…there were no salaries from then, nothing. We were just staying here and surviving by the grace of God…but since 2008, life for us former workers has been hell" (ibid). Social and economic problems have dogged families. Some male former employees travel to neighbouring rural areas to work on the farms in return for food handouts. According to Leonard Mwaira, "We usually travel on foot as far as Bhuka rural area which is about 40km to do menial jobs…sometimes we spend the whole day working in villagers' fields for a single bucket of maize" (Interview with Leonard Mwaira, Gaths Mine, 24 January 2017).

As a result of the desperate economic conditions, the former mine workers are also exploited for cheap labour by companies located around Mashava. According to Takawira Chirodzo, "There are small companies mining mostly gold and chrome around this place including some Chinese companies and they engage us on a part-time basis as casual workers…sometimes we are forced to work from 7am to 6pm for only US $5 a day" (Interview with Takawira Chirodzo, former employee, King Mine, 26 January 2017). "It is ironical that the Chinese, although they make us work for many hours for paltry allowances, seem to understand our plight and are more sympathetic than other capitalist enterprises. They make us rotate so as to give everyone a chance for survival. They also engage each one of us for not more than four days" (ibid).

Poverty generally gives rise to serious social problems. According to Shirley Wenge, "Many marriages have fallen apart since 2008…married women are openly selling sex to workers from the small companies mining around Mashava…some desperate women are even being taken for a packet of maize-meal" (Interview with Shirley Wenge, commercial sex worker, Gaths Mine, 28 January 2017). Lenard Mwaira also concurred when he indicated that, "A number of married men and women ditched their spouses and escaped to the diaspora, mostly to South Africa, Namibia or Botswana…we have lost a generation due to the financial crisis" (Interview with Leonard Mwaira, former mine employee, Gaths Mine, 24 January 2017).

As a result of massive poverty and hunger most children in Mashava have dropped out of school to eke out a living as beggars or workers at neighbouring farms. Leonard Mwaira confirmed that, "We have a lot of children who have turned into street kids in Mashava who because of hunger and poverty they failed to go to school…they were attempting to escape from the hunger that is gnawing at the roots of our existence" (ibid). Child labour has become the norm in the small mining town of Mashava as former mine-workers' children carry out manual chores for meagre pay-outs to supplement their parents' income. Children as young as nine are tilling the fields in the neighbouring resettlement farms, cutting and selling firewood, selling sweets and doing other odd jobs. Chipo Chirwa has reiterated that, "The level of poverty since the closure of the mine has drastically increased…most of our male relatives have relocated to neighbouring countries, such as South Africa and Botswana in search of greener pastures that are proving not to be green after all. This has left the remaining parents with no option but to team up with their children to raise money" (Interview with Chipo Chirwa, housewife, Gaths Mine, 24 February 2017).

In a nearby resettlement farming area called Kwa Peter, 13-year-old Thresia Maucha has been doing manual jobs since she was ten years old. "I started cutting and selling firewood and also tilling the fields at Kwa Peter...life is not rosy for my mother after my father who is a former worker walked out of the family due to economic challenges" (Interview with Thresia Maucha, child labourer, Kwa Peter Farm, 12 February 2017). "While my mother sells fruits and vegetables at Gaths Mine's Chemberi compound, I am busy with some of my friends cutting and selling firewood or doing other manual work to contribute to the family income...I earn about $10 a week...for tilling the fields, I am given a bucket of maize meal or sorghum." *[ibid]* Twelve-year-old Leroy Maredza has stopped going to school and spends his days fishing at nearby Muzhwi Dam instead. "Since the mine closed, we have become very poor...I team up with my father, who is now a full-time fisherman...my mother sells the fish we catch" (Interview with Leroy Maredza, juvenile fisherman, Muzhwi Dam, 21 February 2017).

Scores of young girls, together with their mothers, sisters and older girls, gather elephant grass that is common in Mashava area, weave it into brooms and sell the products in the local residential areas. School attendance in Mashava has dropped as the children have to think of survival rather than their future prospects. Mary Rugweda, primary teacher at Temeraire School indicated that children's performance had declined in recent years. "When all was well at the mine, we had excellent passes...now children's concentration has been compromised by the need to fend for their family...the pass rate at our school has plummeted" (Interview with Mary Rugweda, teacher at Temeraire Primary School, Temeraire, 25 February 2017).

Conclusion

This chapter has attempted to demonstrate that the establishment, operation and management of a European capitalist oligarchic mining enterprise at Mashava since 1908 ushered in not only poverty, but underdevelopment and environmental degradation on a large scale. Both the local Karanga people and Malawian migrant labourers resident in Mashava were systematically underpaid, overworked and later abandoned by this European capitalist oligarchic mining enterprise and presently suffer magnified levels of the same fate under the Robert Mugabe government which inherited political power from the minority European regime of Ian Douglas Smith in 1980. Both working and living conditions amongst the local Karanga and migrant Malawian proletariat in Mashava has drastically deteriorated to appalling subhuman levels. Migrant Malawian former workers are the worst affected since they do not have rural homes in Zimbabwe where they could relocate to start farming as an alternative means of livelihood. Many have succumbed to poverty, illness and even death as they have been pushed to the margins. Female children of these migrant workers survive entirely through prostitution or small scale economic projects such as poaching for fish at Muzhwi Dam or running poultry projects. Most elderly Karanga former employees have retreated to their local rural homes and have rented out their houses to Great Zimbabwe University students and staff. The Mashava Mine management are said to have currently rented out the whole of Gaths Mine to the Great Zimbabwe University under a Government brokered agreement and this has triggered a wave of forced mass removals of the Malawian emigrant population from Gaths Mine to King Mine or Temeraire suburbs. At both Temeraire and King Mine these former workers cannot find any person interested in renting out their houses because so many such houses are empty as there is absolutely no demand for accommodation at both these suburbs.

References

Primary sources: Oral interviews conducted in Mashava.
Asande V, former mine employee, 14-01-2017.
Banda E, former mine employee, Village 3, 13-02-2017.
Banda L, former mine employee, 10-01-2017.
Banda S, housewife, 12-01-2017.

Banda T, housewife, King Mine, 08-02-2017.

Chadya N, former employee, Bere Suburb, 26-01-2017.

Chakawa M, commercial sex worker, 09-02-2017.

Chikuvire E, retired nurse, Westonlee, 10-02-2017.

Chirodzo T, former mine employee, King Mine, 26-01-2017.

Chirwa C, housewife, Gaths Mine, 24 February 2017.

Chuma M, housewife, Gaths Mine, 10-02-2017.

Gandiwa T, former mine employee, Lennox Mine, 06-02-2017.

Gutu O, former mine employee, Lennox Mine, 06-02-201.7

Jaravaza A, housewife, King Mine, 12-01-2017.

Mabhande A, former mine employee, King Mine, 22-01-2017.

Mahamba T, retired nurse, Westonlee, 22-01-2017.

Maredza L, juvenile fisherman, Muzhwi Dam, 21-02-2017.

Marime A, retired teacher, Temeraire, 23-01-2017.

Maucha T, female child labourer, Kwa Peter Farm, 12-02-2017.

Mawere D, Health, Safety and Environment Manager, Gaths Mine, 03-01-2017.

Moyo L, commercial sex worker, Bere Suburb, 22-02-2017.

Moyo J, former mine employee, Gaths Mine, 24-01-2017.

Mutambirwa S, political activist, Westonlee, 21-01-2017.

Muti I, teacher at Temeraire, 09-02-2017.

Mwaira L, former mine employee, Gaths Mine, 24-01-2017.

Ncube T, businessman, Balmain shopping centre, 28-01-2017.

Paradzai T, retired teacher, Westonlee, 24-01-17.

Phiri A, former mine employee, Gaths Mine, 22-01-2017.

Phiri M, housewife, Gaths Mine, 13-01-2017.

Professor Mavhima, Deputy Minister of Education, Munhu Mutapa Building, Harare, 14 June 2017.

Purazeni M, former mine employee, Eastvale, 10-02-2017.

Rugweda A, teacher at Temeraire School, 09-02-2017.

Rugweda M, teacher at Temeraire Primary School, 25-02-2017.

Vheremu T, former mine employee, 21-01-2017.

Wasosa T, retired teacher, Westonlee, 23-01-2017.

Wenge S, commercial sex worker, Gaths Mine, 28-01-2017.

Yepe K, former mine employee, 22-01-2017.

Yepe W, former mine employee, 04-02-2017.

Published sources: Newspapers and Mine Publications
Daily News, Harare, 20 November 2013.
Gaths Mine Reports, [1954, 1981, 1990 and 1990.
The Chronicle, 28 September 2007.
The Herald, Harare, 16 November 2013.
The Herald, Harare, 2 February 2015.
The Zimbabwean, London, 20 June 2008.
The Zimbabwean, London, 3 December 2013.
Voice of America on Zimbabwe, 2 February 2015.
Archival sources: All Archival Documents based on Files kept at the
    Zimbabwe National Archives, Harare.

Monthly Reports
1. N9/4.
2. N9/4/1-45. [Up to 1923].

Quarterly Reports
1. N9/3.
2. N9/3/1-3. [Up to1900].

Half-yearly Reports
1. N9/2.
2. N9/2/1-3. [Up to 1913].

Annual Reports
1. N9/1.
2. N9/1/1-26 [Up to 1923].

Native Department Files [Charter and Chibi]
1. NSK Files.
2. NSK1/1/1-3 [1898-1905].

D. Published sources: Books and Journals
Mackenzie, J. M. 1974. African labour in the Chartered Company
    period, *Rhodesian History*, 1.
Mackenzie, J. M. 1974. Colonial labour policy and Rhodesia, in
    Rhodesian Journal of Economics, 8.

Onselen, V. C. 1976. *Chibaro, African mine labour in Southern Rhodesia, 1900-1933*, Pluto Press, London.

Phimister, I. 1977. "Peasant production and underdevelopment in Southern Rhodesia 1890-1914, with particular reference to the Victoria District", In: Palmer R and Parsons N, [Eds], *Roots of rural poverty*, Heinemann.

Sayce, K. 2000. [Ed], *Geography: an integrated approach*, Nelson House, London.

Weiss, P. 1992. *The Human Environment of Southern Africa*, College Press, Harare.

ABREVIATIONS USED IN THE TEXT

A.N.C -Assistant Native Commissioner.

B.S.A.C -British South African Company.

C.N.C- Chief Native Commissioner.

MDC-Movement for Democratic Change.

N.A.D.A-Southern Rhodesian Native Affairs Department.

N.C-Native Commissioner.

ZANU [PF] Zimbabwe African National Union [Patriotic Front].

Chapter 8

Ethnographic Monitoring Through Phone-in Radio Programs: An Example from Ankore, Uganda

Clementia Murembe Neema, Jenny-Louise Van der Aa,
Sjaak Kroon & Veerle Draulans

Introduction

In this chapter, we present and discuss the use of radio shows as a new approach to ethnographic monitoring. The approach stems from a study on women's empowerment and decision making at the household level in Ankore families in Uganda that was conducted by the first author between 2006 and 2009 (see Neema, 2015). A phone-in radio talk show, hosted by the first author, was used to return the research outcomes to the participants in the study (and to other listeners as well). The study explored married women's decision-making power regarding family resources' use, control and ownership relative to that of their husbands. It investigated how a range of empowerment measures and strategies have contributed to the empowerment of women and more equal power relations in the family institution. It did so by tapping into men's and women's own experiences, deploying a variety of methods, ranging from written questionnaires to interviews, observations and focus group discussions. The study's main focus were women's experiences regarding negotiations with their husbands at the household level as well as their position towards traditional family systems and societal initiatives implemented to promote equality in gender and power relations. A main outcome of the study was that women's empowerment in Ankore families turned out to be more of a myth, than an achieved reality, irrespective of all the initiatives that were taken at the national, regional or local level.

Since one of the main aims of the study was the valorisation of its findings, ways and means were sought to share these with the participants in order to contribute to their empowerment. Two different methods for doing so have been used. These are focus group feedback conferences as a more traditional way of valorisation during the study and the use of radio programs during and after the study, as a more innovative way of valorisation that perfectly fits the approach of ethnographic monitoring as proposed by Hymes *et al.* (1980). In what follows we will first present the original Ankore study and briefly introduce Hymes *et al.*'s approach to ethnographic monitoring. After that, we will introduce and discuss the ongoing radio programs on family development as a form of ethnographic monitoring. Using the tape recordings of these radio programs as new data we will then analyse the way in which this approach of ethnographic monitoring can contribute to more awareness of the participants in the field of gender relations and decision making at the household level. In the final section of the study, we will draw some conclusions and suggest future activities, in particular a more systematic methodology for using the radio as an instrument for ethnographic monitoring in developing countries of the Global South.[71]

Women's empowerment and decision-making at the household level in Ankore

As previously noted, the study that served as a starting point of this article was conducted by the first author. It addressed women's empowerment and decision-making at the household level in families in the Ankore region in South-West Uganda including the districts of Bushenyi, Mbarara, Ibanda, Kiruhura, Isingiro and Ntungam. The study included extensive fieldwork using questionnaires, interviews and focus group discussions with 660 respondents. The study's main aim was to find out "how (…) women in Ankore families perceive their experiences with decision-making processes in the use, control and ownership of family resources" (Neema, 2015:20).

The report of this study included three empirical chapters, which are worth overviewing here briefly. The main purpose of the first empirical chapter was to examine whether "oppressive" and

---

[71] In the following when referring to the specific activities carried out by the first author we will use 'I' instead of 'we'.

"insensitive" traditional practices, i.e. "practices (directly, subconsciously imparted or in the form of rituals) considered to be placing a woman secondary and subordinate to a man or depriving women of an opportunity to realize their full potential after what they have consciously or subconsciously gone through" (Neema, 2015:97) had been done away with or whether they still existed in Ankore families. These traditional practices included male headship and hierarchical family structures, marriage practices (especially the giving and returning of *enjugano*, bride wealth) and polygamous relations. The chapter also examined whether the increasing number of women employed in strategic sectors related to empowerment had improved the general position of women in Ankore family relations. The guiding research question in this chapter was therefore whether eliminating or changing traditional practices had led to a change in decision-making processes and to an improvement of the position of women in Ankore family relations. The study concluded that the country's official empowerment mission of doing away with cultural practices that work against women's emancipation has largely not been achieved. Married women in Ankore either do not have the possibility to change the practices that disadvantage them or have accepted the status quo.

The second empirical chapter examined whether women's increased opportunities and improved incomes in Ankore families had also improved or enhanced their possibilities regarding their decision-making power relative to their husbands. In order to understand how women's empowerment in Ankore families was evaluated from the participants' own perspectives, participants' experiences and opinions were presented in their own voices. The income-generating activities and projects (IGA/Ps) from which the participants shared their empowerment experiences included livestock, piggery, poultry and beekeeping (in rural areas), shop keeping, food and beer selling, selling of clothes, saloon work, tailoring and professional careers (in urban areas). The views that individual women held on the outcomes of these IGA/Ps and their evaluation of family relations before and after IGA/P participation highlighted their own experiences with respect to work negotiations (compromise, acceptance, resistance, opposition) as personal struggles involved in addressing gender inequalities in decision-making at the household level. The stories told and explanations given during interviews and focus group discussions, in addition to the answers given in the questionnaires, brought out the hidden and silent realities of family relations in the women's day-to-day experiences and activities. Moreover, home visits to married women interviewees offered an added opportunity to see some of the IGA/P-related improvements made in terms of purchased family assets, changed home environment, welfare and livelihood.

The focus of the third empirical chapter was on married women's awareness and use of established legal institutions for women's protection and on whether gender parity and women's protection had been achieved in Ankore family relations. Consequently, the participants' personal shared views, stories and experiences illustrated the degree of success in women's empowerment in family relations, protection and well-being. This chapter therefore examined whether the strategies and institutions in place had improved the protection and position of women in family relations in Ankore families. It presented married people's experiences of conflicts in their families. On the same note, the chapter explored the causes of conflicts and how they were resolved in the traditional Ankore context before discussing the current problems together with the new mechanisms that were applied and the implications on women in family relations.

The study concluded that the achievements associated with women's empowerment in Uganda, namely increasing the number of women in the education sector, increasing women's income levels, increasing women's participation in policy and political decision-making processes and increasing the awareness of established intervening institutions for family protection and women's rights, although no doubt contributing to achieving general development goals (e.g. UNDP, 2012), had not substantially changed women's decision-making possibilities at the household level regarding the use, control and ownership of family resources relative to their husbands (Neema 2015, 221-231). Moreover, in reference to the working definition of women's empowerment introduced in the study (Neema 2015: 171), namely as "the process and outcomes of the efforts of women and men (as partners), playing complementary roles in family activities and decisions regarding the use and control of family resources, taking the lead (individually and collectively) to change existing power relations in the family structure and in society that disadvantage them and that they have reasons to change," such a relationship status had not been attained in the majority of the studied families.

Ethnographic Monitoring

In ethnographic research, the concept of 'voice' or 'hearing the ethnographies on their own terms' is central. Here we revisit the practice of ethnographic monitoring as a way to disclose stories, beliefs and motifs that often get lost in macro-analyses (Hymes *et al.*, 1981). A brief definition of voice is "who says what in which way to whom" (Juffermans & Van der Aa, 2013). Voice, however, is not similar to language; neither does it refer to vocal characteristics. Voice is about being heard on one's own terms (Blommaert, 2008) and not on the terms of the other. The concept touches upon linguistic inequality: the opportunities to a successful outcome of the communication process are limited when the demanded resource is not in one's repertoire (see Blommaert, 2008 for insights in how far-reaching the consequences may be). Voice as an "analytical heuristic" (Hornberger, 2006) allows us to search in our data for instances of conflict, inequality and power as well as resistance, creativity and counter-hegemonic practices. Voice provides a tool for finding and dealing with alternative understandings of language, education and society. It is a heuristic that shapes our research both as conceivable problem and as key to a growing epistemology. As a possible problem, it is an area of interest: how do people produce voice, what opportunities to produce voice do they get in a particular area, what factors prevent them from producing voice? When voice is considered as key towards a growing epistemology, the importance of listening to the people's voices in the field becomes clear and peremptory. Carefully listening to voice is essential in obtaining ethnographic knowledge: only the people engaged with the field enable access to emic knowledge, which is acquired through in-depth interaction with ethnographies, combined with observational research. Taken together, this leads to a fieldwork-based perspective that is guiding during all stages of the research process: from collecting our data to formulating theory. We can only realize the full democratic potential of this perspective when we succeed in incorporating the voice of the people we work with into our research. A practice that can do this is ethnographic monitoring.

Ethnographic monitoring testifies to the fact that the fundamental position of the researcher as an actor of change, as someone who automatically "intervenes," did not become mainstream but remains a position for which elaborate and precarious argumentation is required. The distinction, for instance, made in Cameron *et al* (1992:52), among research on, for, and with others, obviously recalls many of the aspects of ethnographic monitoring. Rampton (2011:1) similarly developed an empirically driven trajectory, which "follows the analysis of [...] data into an academic argument, into a research training program, and into professional development materials for teachers".

The practice of ethnographic monitoring is political, theoretical, and methodological. Its insistence on collaboration between the researcher and his/her interlocutors offers ideal circumstances to observe and understand voice. It creates this opportunity through: (1) listening to what the real problems are, as worded by real people in real situations, (2) carefully observing the semiotic resources that are at play in the participants' lives, and also in the wider community, and (3) offering collaborators a place to reiterate their voice through making known their concerns with the way the work was conducted, through its subsequent analyses or through any other issues. In other words, ethnographic monitoring is the basis for analysing voice in any situated discourse: voice as an opportunity and a target for participants, and also as an obstacle and constraint for many individuals and groups (Van der Aa & Blommaert, 2011).

Ethnographic Monitoring is not only the process of bringing back knowledge to the people involved in a study – those that gave it to the researcher in the first place – it also includes having a firmly established relationship with these research participants as subjects rather than objects right from the start of the enterprise in order to guarantee their perspectives and questions to be included and considered as guiding principles in the design of the study at hand.

In social sciences research, from a valorisation perspective it is increasingly becoming necessary for researchers to improve the quality of their relationship with the study participants as beneficiaries. As Van der Aa and Blommaert (2011) and Van der Aa (2012) note, rather than having the researcher as a mere observer to simply describe the study scene, there is more of a need for him or her to become an active participant. In such instance, the researcher is at the same time the observer and part of the observed and his or her participation can partly be analysed in order to improve the quality of the interaction and the relationship with the research participants for better understanding each other. Furthermore, the quality of interaction and relationship reduces the danger of working on generalized assumptions. Moreover, as Van der Aa (2012) notes, this quality forms ground for the researcher in consultations with the participants to identify and understand underlying real issues in the context and concerns of the latter.

Additionally, with several researchers in the field sometimes investigating the same people, the participants seem to get tired being treated as study objects only with little or no gains at all for themselves. Therefore, it is pertinent to give feedback to the participants as stakeholders of the study to which they contributed, but also as an opportunity to verify that what is described in the research report represents what they said (Van der Aa, 2012). In an elaborate triple volume, Hymes *et al.* (1981) identify four steps as part of what they coined as 'ethnographic monitoring' (EM). As a first step, ethnographers consult participants to identify what issues concern them most. A second step is to observe behaviour relevant to that issue in a series of contexts in and out of the research site. A third step is to share back the findings and feedback of the observations at different levels and at different times. A final step is to take stock of the whole process and to check whether all cooperative possibilities have been maximally explored, and, we might add to Hymes' four-step procedure, if needed engage in another EM loop.

211

In this way, it is guaranteed that research plans and programs are developed organically, and in close consultation with all participants involved. In other words: static, often top-down solutions are being replaced by complex dynamics, because understanding the world involves changing it and being changed in the process as participants. Therefore, when deploying ethnographic monitoring, one can speak of epistemic solidarity: building shareable knowledge together during a long-term commitment to the field where researchers together with social actors observe change and operationalize particular (academic) concepts and practices relevant to them.

Understanding Ankore family relations through ethnographic monitoring

In the context of the Ankore study (Neema, 2015), a radio based approach of ethnographic monitoring was used. It aimed at feeding the findings of the study back to the participants in order to contribute to their awareness and empowerment by communicating and discussing these findings through a series of phone-in radio programs in which the first author took the role of a talk-show host. We will describe this new EM method below based on the first author's account and analyse some of the data that it provided.

Description

In the Nyamitanga-Mbarara Municipality plenary session, following the focus group discussions that I organized during my PhD-study, a Radio West program director participated who offered me the opportunity to host a radio program. This program on marital and family relations, entitled Nyamunyonyi or "Lovebirds", was aired every Saturday morning on Radio West, from April 2006 up to June 2012. It allowed its listeners to phone in for asking questions and contributing their views on the topics being discussed.

The radio program offered me an opportunity to fulfil the EM-related social responsibility of giving feedback to the research participants and other people in society at large. In what follows I describe how a typical talk show would run, combined with a discussion of this event as a form of EM.

After an opening in which the moderator introduces me and the topic to be discussed for two hours this Saturday, I explain that I am going to share with my listeners the outcomes of my study that was conducted between 2006 and 2009 in a number of sites in the Ankore region. I would, for example, talk about women's participation in income generating projects and the way in which at the household level, that is, between husband and wife, decisions are made about the spending of the incomes thereof. I would give examples from my individual interviews and focus group discussions and would then ask for comments and additions. After my talk, the listening audience is then given the opportunity to phone-in for contributions, sharing experiences and examples, for illustrations or comparisons and questions for clarification. Even before inviting them to do so, listeners generally would already phone-in to the radio station to contribute. After this round of listeners' contributions I would deal with possible solutions to the problem under discussion based on my research outcomes, for example, problems encountered by women who earned their own money but generally had to leave spending decisions to their husbands. The solutions that I proposed again led to new callers offering their views and experiences. After about two hours, I would round up, formulate kind of a conclusion and thank the listeners for having joined the program.

We need to delve a bit more into EM in order to understand what is happening here. Van der Aa & Blommaert (2015) discuss different types of feedback, which occur during the third phase of EM, i.e. sharing back the findings and feedback of the observations to the participants (see Section 3). These are instant, intermediate and long-term types of feedback, all of which take place during the radio show described above. Instant feedback happens usually during the ongoing study in which preliminary results are immediately communicated to and discussed with participants in the field. Intermediate feedback usually takes place when a study is completed or when a significant part of it is ready to be fed back into the participating community. Long-term feedback consists of more structural mechanisms of feedback, usually also set-up after or during the last phases of a project in order to guarantee its continuity. The first author makes use of all these three mechanisms of feedback during the radio show in a rather creative way: by feeding back the study's results at an intermediate level through the medium of regional radio, she allows for spontaneous issues from listeners, freely associated with the study, to come in. She then gives instant feedback to these issues which also enlighten some of the study's results. The fact that these radio shows occur regularly and that she has been a regular guest, opens up possibilities for making these kinds of feedback more structural, and thus long-term. Let us now continue with the first author's description of what happens during the radio show to highlight some of the issues described above.

In the studio, I generally stick to the research rule of confidentiality and safeguarding my research participants' privacy. Phone-in radio participants, however, usually give their names and place of residence without any reservation. They find it fulfilling to do so and consider it a way of showing ownership of their opinions on the topics being discussed.

Such phone-in discussions are very useful means of feeding back research outcomes to my research participants. Particularly, in a society that severely lacks the availability of and access to written sources and in which quite some people are still illiterate, creating a new, quick and practical form of spreading and discussing information through radio programs and thereby giving people the possibility to learn about their own situation on the basis of their own shared experiences and insights, in my opinion can be considered an important contribution to, in this case, the raising of awareness and empowerment of women.

It was not my intention to discuss during the radio programs the topic that I encountered in my study afresh in order to get new information or opinions. Essentially, the purpose was to give back a report to my participants and to create an opportunity to a wider community outside my study sites to get informed. The wider community's acknowledgement of the shared information can be considered an indication of the fact that my study outcomes were not totally idiosyncratic but on the contrary were recognized by others and therefore to a certain extent can be considered generalizable not only within the Ankore Region but also outside.

The topics that I introduced in the radio-talk-shows were based on the issues that I discussed with my participants during individual interviews with key informants and during focus group discussions. The topics introduced by myself and discussed on air included:

traditional family practices and family development;
women in politics and policy making positions and their family relations;
women's income generating projects;
women entrepreneurial and family relations;
women with formal education and formal employment;

women with higher education, incomes or social status than their husbands and family relations;

bride wealth (enjugano) and family relations;

match-made and self-found spouses and family stability;

traditional rural marriage ceremonies and urban planned marriage ceremonies and family relations;

legal institutions and enhancing position of women in family relations;

traditional methods and family conflict resolution;

legal institutions and family conflict resolution;

women's empowerment and gender based violence in families;

government strategies and their success in improving status of women relative to men at national and household level;

parenting roles and out of homes mothers;

expected qualities of an ideal wife/husband in the context of Ankore families.

Several other topics of discussion came from listeners and Radio program managers. These included:

Role of women in family food security (seen as core in-charge);

Why some husbands oppose/resent women's empowerment;

Women's voice in men's space and emerging issues on power relations at family level;

Women's shift to men's roles and persistent traditional gender dichotomous roles;

Role of relatives/ bigger family members and stability of the nuclear family;

Implications of sending children to relatives in parenting roles;

Issues of food discipline at parties, bodily hygiene and family/marital relations;

Communication in the family and its development in power relations;

Role of media in homes and family relations.

Although Radio West was my entry point to share my study findings as a form of ethnographic monitoring with listeners through radio talks, I have since had more opportunities on other radio stations, more specifically Vision Radio and Radio Maria, all in Mbarara Town. I ended up using Vision Radio more regularly than the other studios because of its Saturday 7: 30 am to 9: 30 am program Entunguka y'eka or "Family Development". These stations are also listened to in the south western parts of Uganda and beyond. All radio talk shows had more or less the same content and format as the one described above. The phone-in calls asking me to have family relations workshops in my study sites, but also in new areas that were not part of the sampled places of my study have been increasing. All radio discussions and dialogues are recorded and kept in the radio archives to be re-run when the need arises. As such they form an important new source for studying the contents and discourses that were shared.

An ideal couple in the traditional Ankore family

Here we will further discuss and analyse one of the topics that appeared in the radio shows described above, i.e., the qualities of an ideal wife and husband in the context of Ankore families against the background of measures taken for women's empowerment. It is worth noting that the opinions put forward in the radio phone-in discussions were similar to those that had been shared during focus group discussions when exploring the position of married women in the Ankore family structure and systems. The discussions indicated a resilience of traditionally expected virtues in a wife and a husband, which in turn influenced women's decision-making possibilities at the family level. However, such traditional expectations were not necessarily considered significant and that remained a constraint in the process of women's empowerment. The views reported here in English translation were originally shared in Runyankore, the native language of the Ankore ethnic group, in September 2011. Table 1 presents an overview of the expected qualities of an ideal wife as brought forward by men and women respectively.

An ideal wife according to men	An ideal wife according to women
Is loyal and faithful to her husband and his relatives	Is hospitable and welcoming to husbands' relatives
Is respectful and supportive to her husband and his relatives	Is hard working
Is working for her family to be well endowed with food	Is keen on her husband's and children's meals
Is not loving her job at the cost of her family and children	Knows what pleases or upsets her husband

Is listening to and accepting her husband's word	Accords her husband high esteem and value
Is submissive and not big-headed	
Has time for her husband	Is able to satisfy her husband in bed
Is willing to produce 'enough' children (not one or two), preferably boys	Is able to produce boys as heirs to guarantee her status and strong ground in the family
Is cleanly with respect to body and homestead	Is cleanly with respect to body and homestead
Is hospitable and welcoming	Keeps family secrets
Is not a rumour monger	
Is soothing	
Makes wise discernment	

Table 1: Image of an ideal wife expressed by phone-in participants (Source: compiled views of FGD participants and phone-in radio program participants, September 2011).

Before we have a closer look at Table 1 it has to be noted that although the traditional practice of family heads giving women new names on their marriage is dying out, phone-in participants made reference to such names as latent guidelines for women's behaviour in marital family relations. Some of the names that were mentioned were *bayoroba* (being submissive), *bashorora* (making wise discernment), *batatsya* (hospitable), and *bahuumura* (being soothing). These qualities are also reported in Table 1.

A first observation regarding Table 1 is that the qualities of an ideal wife mentioned by men outnumber those mentioned by women. In the list of wives' qualities as produced by the men we can roughly distinguish four types:

    qualities related to husband and relatives (nr. 1-2);
    qualities related to work (nr. 3-4);
    qualities related to the husband (nr. 5-8);
    qualities related to the wife herself (nr. 9-13).

In the first three categories, all qualities that were considered to make a woman an ideal wife refer to her relationship with others: her husband, his relatives, her family and her children. An ideal wife was defined by men not in terms of her personal qualities but in terms of her usefulness for others, especially her husband. The fourth category at first sight includes mainly qualities of the wife herself. A closer look at the qualities included in this list however shows that these are in fact also formulated in a way that makes them mainly profitable for others. Quality nr. 14 'makes wise discernments,' in fact, is the only autonomous quality of an ideal wife mentioned by the men. Given the first twelve qualities of an ideal wife, one might suspect that 'wise' here most probably is meant to mean 'according to the husband's judgment'. An interesting observation finally is that physical features of beauty were not mentioned by men as a strong trait for an ideal wife.

If we then look at the qualities of an ideal wife put forward by the women, we see the same four categories. What is immediately clear, however, is that the husband's family, except for the fact that an ideal wife is hospitable and welcoming to them (nr. 1), just as to other people, do not play a very prominent role. Most of the qualities that were put forward deal with the ideal wife's relationship with her husband (nr. 4-7). These qualities, however, seem to be formulated in a less submissive way than those put forward by men. Furthermore, an ideal wife was expected to be hard-working and caring for feeding her family (nr. 2-3) as well as being cleanly and keeping family secrets (nr. 8-9). Also, these qualities were formulated in an autonomous way, as qualities so to say, of an independent wife, not a wife that totally depends on her husband.

All in all Table 1 on the one hand, seems to be an indication of the fact that as far as women are concerned an ideal wife can be defined in an autonomous way, i.e. having features that are not necessarily formulated in dependence of their husbands. Men on their part seem to stick to a more top-down perspective in which the qualities of a wife were mainly defined in terms of the extent in which she pleases her husband, mainly in the sense of being subordinate to him and his relatives. On the other hand, however, it can also not be denied that most of the women's views and expectations seem to be geared towards supporting the wellbeing of their husband, his status and his family. The wife, as a matter of fact, seems to consider herself as a means for the wellbeing of herself and mainly others: husband, his relatives, her children and society. In that sense, women's empowerment has still a long way to go.

Table 2 presents an overview of the expected qualities of an ideal husband as brought forward by men and women respectively.

An ideal husband according to men	An ideal husband according to women
Heads, fends and provides for the family	Heads, fends and provides for the family.
Is able to protect his wife and children	Is able to protect and defend his wife and children
Has voice in his family (decision-making)	Has voice in the home and in society
Has good stature that commands respect	Is loving and respectful to his wife
Has respect in society	Can satisfy his wife's needs and desires
Has a well-built home in terms of structure, people, resources, assets and the future in form of children.	Supports his wife in her activities: physically, financially, and morally
Can satisfy his wife or wives' sexual desires	Has time for the family
	Has his own job
	Is not dependent on the wife's income
	Is autonomous in thinking not decided for by his parents, relatives or society
	Is not violent and is willing to have a dialogue
	Is not wasteful, alcoholic or workaholic

Table 2: Image of an ideal husband expressed by phone-in participants (Source: compiled views of FGD participants and phone-in radio program participants; September 2011).

Before we have a closer look at Table 2, it has to be noted that in the conversations with the phone-in participants, especially rural women, when referring to the status of their husbands, mentioned the following names to express such status: *owangye* (mine), *ibanye* (my husband), *isheka* (head of the family), *mukamangye* (my lord), *ishe abangye* (father of my children). Urban wives or wives with professional husbands called their husbands dad, boss or used their job title or their Christian names.

Generally speaking, Table 2 shows that here it's the women who put forward much more qualities of an ideal husband than the men. Categories that can be distinguished in these qualities include:

> the protective function of husbands regarding their wives, children and family (nr. 1-2);
> having authority (nr. 3);
> being supportive to his wife and family (nr. 4-7);
> being autonomous and independent (nr. 8-10);
> positive qualities related to the husband's character and behaviour (nr. 11-12).

The main category in terms of the number of expected qualities mentioned clearly was the ideal husbands' (physical, moral and financial) support for their wives in a variety of contexts including respect, love, needs, desires, activities and time. Second came the husband's independence in terms of work, income and decision making. Noticeable here is the explicit mention that was made of an ideal husband's independence of his wife's income and work and his expected independence of others in thinking and decision making. Being the head, provider and protector of the family came third, a number of positive personal features that make family life easier (and at the same time reveal some of the problems that women struggle with at the household level) came fourth and finally, husbands should not only have a position in the family but they should also have voice, i.e., be respected in society. The image that women gave of an ideal husband clearly showed a critical perspective on marital relations. They explicitly referred to qualities that contributed to independence and equality of husband and wife at the household level and rejected women's subordination to their husbands or their husbands' relatives.

Men on the other hand provided a much more limited number of qualities of the ideal husband. Their main category referred to the husband's headship, providing and protection of his family (nr. 1-3). This is followed by some qualities that defined his position in society at large (nr. 4-5). After that followed qualities of wealth an property (nr. 6) and finally his ability to satisfy his wife's of wives' sexual desires. This final qualities was the only one that the participating men explicitly formulated with reference to their relationship with their wives. Most other qualities, except for nr. 2 that among other things referred to wives, were not necessarily related to men in their role as ideal husbands but rather to (married) men in general. It seemed as if men took their central position in, and headship of, the family as a given, not as something that required specific qualities and certainly not qualities that paid special attention to their women – except for the field of sexuality.

Comparing the contents of the two tables, a first conclusion has to be that women as well as men were apparently more able to come up with qualities regarding their ideal counterpart than regarding themselves. This might have been a consequence of the fact that thinking about oneself required a higher level of abstraction than thinking about someone else. Men as well as women had a clear image of their wives and husbands respectively. A second conclusion is that the level of thinking of women about their ideal husbands was much more sophisticated, personal and critical than the other way around. Women expected their ideal husband to not only be the head of the family that cared for his family and protected it; they also expected them to respect and support their wives and their wives' activities and they finally wanted them to simply be nice and caring husbands.

All in all, the women's image of an ideal husband seemed to be clearly influenced by contemporary ideas, discussions and measures that contributed to women's empowerment at the household level. Men on the other hand, seemed to formulate the qualities of their ideal wives without paying much attention to such developments, thereby mainly focusing on their own central and leading position in the family and their dominance over their wives. For them, women's empowerment seemed to be not really an issue that they have thought about a lot and they certainly didn't reflect a clear consciousness of the changes that (at least some of) their wives went through as a consequence of their participation in, for example, income generating activities or the higher educational level they achieved. The men still seemed to conceive their position as it always had been, i.e. being the undisputed centre of the family and the world. Women's empowerment for them certainly seemed to be more of a matter of rhetoric than actual fact.

Conclusion

In this chapter, we have demonstrated how a phone-in radio talk show was innovatively used not only as a channel through which feedback was given to research participants and research outcomes were shared with other members of the community, but also as a means to once again tap into rich information from the participants' own voices and viewpoints on the position of married women in Ankore family relations. The radio program was available free of charge and was therefore much cheaper as a feedback instrument than, for example, re-mobilizing the participants in their research sites (often in remote areas) for giving them feedback information. Using the latter approach, it would moreover not have been possible to reach an audience that was broader than just the study participants. The radio approach requires willingness on the part of the researcher to engage with hitherto unknown people in the exchange of views and to also learn from them as they might have very different understandings of the world, different practices, beliefs and values, and hence quite often different viewpoints. Connecting this new information with what was already known and shared on the basis of the earlier study can be challenging, especially if there might appear really big differences in perspectives.

From the interviews and focus group discussions in the study but even more so from the phone-in radio programs and the large number of phone calls received afterwards, it became clear how peoples' cultural values, deeply entrenched in patriarchal attitudes

(Neema, 2015:61), consciously or unconsciously, influence family socio-economic and political systems and relations and how these relate to women's empowerment. It also became clear that there is a big need to have more studies as well as more sensitizing and developmental activities in the field of gender and family relations in the Ankore region. This can be attained through initiating new research[72] and designing programs or projects for sensitizing men and women to learn about these issues. The availability and use of family resources being a common problem for families in general, constitutes an excellent starting point to coordinate families and sensitize them to learn or improve their practical life skills for better and sustainable livelihoods. By reducing the costs of teaching and learning, e.g. by the use of radio programs, men and women can learn from each other and form networking groups for projects in the fight against poverty at the household level. In addition, there is a need to introduce family studies and design training curricula for higher learning institutions, with a different approach to gender studies in consideration of people's cultures, capabilities and capacity (Freire, 1970; Rowlands, 1998; Sen, 1999; Kabeer, 1999; Nussbaum, 2000).

For making what was done through using phone-in radio programs really a form of ethnographic monitoring, interactions with married couples in the region will have to be continued, tapping from their talents and building on what they already know and would still wish to know about family relations and parenting roles.

Finally, from an ethnographic monitoring perspective it can be concluded that the radio phone-in talk shows, apart from being used as a feedback instrument, can also be considered constituting the first step in a consecutive or ongoing EM process. Through the (new) information provided by the phone-in talk show participants and the people who made phone calls after the show, new issues of interest for the participants related to the position of women in the Ankore family relations could be identified. In a second EM step, these issues could be more thoroughly investigated by using the information provided by the callers as data, i.e. participants' texts that can be

---

[72] An example here is a study into the influence of traditional and new marriage rituals as an impediment to women's empowerment that is currently developed by the first author.

subjected to analysis, leading to new insights in the position and empowerment of women at the household level. These findings then, in a third step can be again fed back to the participants, ultimately leading to joint conclusions regarding the cooperation between researchers and participants and the rewards of this process for especially the participants in terms of improving the position of women.

References

Blommaert, J. 2008. Bernstein and poetics revisited: Voice, globalization and education, *Discourse and Society, 19*(4), 421-447.

Cameron, D., *et al.* 1992. *Researching language: Issues of power and method,* London: Routledge.

Freire, P. 1970. *Pedagogy of the oppressed.* Harmondsworth: Penguin

Hornberger, N. H. 2006. Voice and biliteracy in indigenous language revitalization: Contentious educational practices in Quechua, Guarani, and Maori contexts, *Journal of Language, Identity and Education, 5*(4): 277-292.

Hymes, D. *et al.* 1981. *Ethnographic Monitoring of Children's Acquisition of Reading/Language Arts Skills In and Out of the Classroom,* Volumes I, II, and III. Final Report, Graduate School of Education. Philadelphia: University of Pennsylvania.

Juffermans, K. and J. Van der Aa. 2013. Analysing voice in educational discourses, Special Issue of *Anthropology and Education Quarterly* 44(2).

Kabeer, N. 1999. Resources, agency, achievement: Reflections on the movement of women's empowerment, *Development and Change* 30(108): 435-464.

Neema, C. M. 2015. *Women's empowerment and decision-making at the household level: A case study of Ankore families in Uganda,* Doctoral dissertation, Tilburg University.

Nussbaum, M. C. 2000. *Women and human development: The capabilities approach,* Cambridge: Cambridge University Press.

Rampton, B. 2011. A neo-Hymesian trajectory in applied linguistics. *Urban Language and Literacies Working Papers 78.*

www.kcl.ac.uk/projects/ldc/LDCPublications/workingpapers/download. aspx (accessed: November 1, 2011).

Rowlands, J. 1997. *Questioning empowerment: Working with women in Honduras*, London: Oxfam.

Sen, A. 1999. *Development as freedom*, Oxford: Oxford University Press.

Van der Aa, J. 2012. *Ethnographic monitoring: Language, narrative and voice in a Caribbean classroom*, Doctoral dissertation, Tilburg University.

Van der Aa, J. & Blommaert, J. 2011. Ethnographic Monitoring: Hymes' Unfinished Business in Education, *Anthropology and Education Quarterly* 42 (4): 319-344.

Van der Aa, J. & Blommaert, J. 2015. Ethnographic Monitoring and the study of complexity, *Tilburg Papers in Culture Studies 123*, Tilburg: Babylon.

UNDP. 2012. *The millennium development goals*, New York: UNDP.

Chapter 9

Fighting Fellow Comrades in the Trenches of Poverty in Africa? Interrogating the Fees Must Fall Movement at the University of Namibia and Universities in South Africa

Artwell Nhemachena & Romeo Mudimu

Exactly how the Rhodes Must Fall Movement quickly turned into Fees Must Fall provides an interesting case study into the behaviour of colonial and oppressive systems when they encounter [local] resistance. The ability to narrow the struggle from the call to decolonise the university in Africa to simply asking for fees to be abolished is classic abilities of the system to invent smaller struggles for its enemies so as to protect its loot. No wonder, Fees Must Fall protests are so well funded, with sympathetic old white professors, from their pockets supply bottled water, food parcels and ice cream to the protestors. Philanthropic NGOs also appear with goodies to lubricate the struggle, a privilege that Rhodes Must Fall struggles did not enjoy… For empire, however, Fees Must Fall is a safe struggle. Away from the Rhodes Must Fall, the struggle is now opposing poor black students to a black government. For that reason, the same old white professors whose presence in the universities is proof of lack of transformation and decolonisation can sponsor Fees Must Fall. The NGOs that feed from the Ford Foundation and from the estates of Cecil John Rhodes are willing to offer "generous" donations and field support to Fees Must Fall. Expensive law firms are willing to donate legal representation to those Fees Must Fall students who find themselves in court for burning lecture-rooms and setting vehicles alight…Fees Must Fall has narrowed from fighting the World System to fighting an order that the system can do away with after all and still remain alive. Fees Must Fall has lost the potential and the world systemic potency that Rhodes Must Fall carried…Today, every South African university, on 24-hour basis, is guarded by poor black police officers who wait to arrest poor black students… (Cetshwayo Mabhena in The Sunday Times, 10 April 2016).

Introduction

This chapter is based on research carried out in 2016 at the University of Namibia, Main Campus where students engaged in 'Fees Must Fall' protests against the university and the government of Namibia. Students protested against fees increases which they considered to be too steep for them. Although Namibia is considered to be an upper-middle income country, the students considered themselves to be impoverished and hence, to be unable to pay the fees that the university charged. On the other hand, the university considered the fee increases as necessary for the operations of the financially embattled institution. In essence, both the students and the university were pleading impoverishment and incapacitation. The scuffles between the students and the university can be understood as a battle between the [impoverished] tussling for survival, though sadly the issue of commonality of impoverishment between them has been conveniently ignored by proponents and drivers of the protests as noted in the vignette above. Thus, students and their leaders were determined to fight for reduction in fees while on the other hand, the university was determined to ensure that students paid the gazetted fees so that the institution would be able to subsist and survive in the embattled African economic environment. So, in February 2016 students and their protest leaders at the University of Namibia's Main Campus struggled against the authorities of the university whom they shut outside the university premises. All gates of the university were closed by the protesting students and no one was allowed to enter the university, even the staff members. This chapter interrogates the positions of the students and the university; it concludes that both the students and the university were impoverished by the invisible global structural and systemic forces yet, the impoverished in Africa often do not notice that global structural and systemic impoverishment sets one African against the other such that comrades in trenches of poverty paradoxically resort to fighting one another instead of fighting the global (neo-)imperial root causes of their impoverishment.

The scenario with respect to the Fees Must Fall Movement can be contextualised in the broader occurrences in Africa where

Africans paradoxically often tenaciously fight their states and leaders for perceived absence of democracy yet the same Africans unquestioningly tolerate the international economic dictatorships, including sweatshops of Western transnational corporations and impoverishing economic programmes such as the Bretton Woods Institutions' Economic Structural Adjustment Programmes (ESAP). Instead of fighting transnational corporations some of which evade paying taxes to Africans and their African governments, indigenous Africans often fight one another in the trenches of poverty. As Nhemachena (2016) argues, Africa is characterised more by violence of absence than violence of the present. In this sense, the World Bank and the International Monetary Fund foisted market reforms, the commercialisations of higher education and introduction of cost-recovery measures which have turned African universities and scholars into the marketplace (Mamdani, 2007). Africans are now turning against one another including against their states and leaders because of the World Bank's marketisation of higher education on the continent, which is fast becoming unaffordable to the majority of Africans. Instead of turning against the World Bank and International Monetary Fund which introduced the lethal market reforms and capital friendliness in African universities, Africans paradoxically choose to fight one another because of problems which have been placed in their midst by Western institutions, states and individuals. Mamdani (2007: 8, 9) aptly captures the challenges of Africa when he argues that the market reforms were guided by the World Bank's conviction that higher education is more of a private than a public good and that the market should define the priorities of a public university including giving maximum freedom to revenue-earning units.

Having destroyed [via colonial dispossession and the introduction of neoliberal reforms] the economic bases or foundations of African states and universities, Western institutions, organisations and states resorted to celebrating postmodernism in Africa, including postmodern revolutions in the forms of the May 1968 postmodern revolutions by students and workers in Europe (Call, 2002: 23). Such postmodern revolutions involve the impoverished students [denied their economic bases and foundations

229

by Western capital] who are being prodded by agents of capital, often via social media, to engage in revolutions against their states, governments and leaders in the (neo-)colonially dispossessed states. The postmodern revolutions are also targeting transformation of African universities in ways that result in loss of control over the universities by Africans and their states and governments. In South Africa, for example, there was use of postmodern deterritorialising and decentring media, which are not territorially controlled, (Peterson *et al*, 2016: 1) in the Fees Must Fall Movement which some have simplistically claimed to be spontaneous while others have noted [surreptitious] support and prodding from agents of (neo-)apartheid and (neo-)imperialism who sought to deflect the activism initially directed at the Rhodes Must Fall Movement.

Situating Poverty and Fees Must Fall Movements in South Africa and Namibia within the Global Context

Some scholars have argued that the Fees Must Fall Movement was informed by historical 'antiapartheid' black consciousness movements wherein student challenged 'hierarchical top-down leadership systems of university management' (Booysen, 2017; Hefferman *et al*, 2016). However, it is important to note that the movement is different from colonial 'apartheid' era movements and protests in the sense that this time the postmodern protests (or movements) are not necessarily properly directed at restitution, restoration or repossession of material resources stolen by the colonists and capitalists. In African contexts where descendants of colonists have left the task of restitution, restoration and resettlement of colonially displaced Africa to postcolonial African governments, the descendant of colonists have effectively deflected their responsibilities to restitute and restore what was colonially dispossessed from Africans. In other words, with contemporary postmodern protests and movements, the aim has been surreptitiously diverted by empire, away from African reclaiming their economic material base or foundations. The postmodern battles are not necessarily for foundational issues, materialities and principles but they are often for symbols, signifiers, statuses and other peripheral targets which do not go to the root of African quests for economic and material sovereignty and autonomy from (neo-)empire. Whereas colonial and apartheid era struggles and protests were directed at African reclamation and restoration of material foundations or what was robbed by colonisers, postmodernism on the other hand is celebrated by its proponents as essentially antifoundational, as essentially against African essentialism and against African foundationalism. In postmodernism, everything is claimed to have turned into a sign, to have lost foundations, to have become virtual, hyperreal and surreal. In other words, African struggles for freedom from empire in a postmodern era are diverted to the unreal, hyperreal, surreal, nonfoundational and nonmaterial. Real African struggles that can really change the world for the dispossessed, impoverished and plundered are turned into surreal, hyperreal, nonfoundational struggles, nonessential and nonessentialist protests and movements that will not threaten and dislodge the existence and essence of (neo-)empire at a global scale.

Thus, though [postmodern] student protests are celebrated by some (Hefferman *et al*, 2016) and though [postmodern] protests are celebrated as bringing societal problems to public attention (Duncan, 2016), there are questions as to whether much of the problems that Africans are encouraged by (neo-)empire to fight for are the real, essential and original African problems particularly in a postmodern context in which reality, essentialism, and originality are denied. Besides, in a world where real, original and essential African problems such as restitution and compensation for enslavement and colonisation are conveniently swept aside by the Western (neo-)imperial machinations, it becomes suspect when architects and supporters of (neo-)empire support some struggles which they would want Africans to believe are theirs. As Nhemachena (2016) argues, the problem in a postmodern epoch is that the (neo-)coloniser and the (neo-)colonised are posited to be dedifferentiated and this poses the challenge that the [dedifferentiated] (neo-)colonised is often celebrated for [unwittingly] carrying the burdens [including protesting on behalf] of the (neo-)coloniser in the mistaken postmodern belief that the distinctions between coloniser and the colonised have vanished. In such context, the (neo-)colonised is turned into the animal or the beast of burden to [unwittingly] carry the burdens of the supposedly dedifferentiated (neo-)coloniser. In this way, it is easier to understand the paradoxes where impoverished Africans fight one another [instead of consistently fighting their common dispossessor and exploiter] in their trenches of poverty.

Although other scholars argue that African protesters need to be indiscriminately guaranteed 'human rights' including freedom to protest and engage in activism, right to freedoms to express themselves and so on, these purported 'human rights' are rendered nullity by the postmodernist tenet of dedifferentiation. The tenet of dedifferentiation makes it necessary to ask whose agents or actors the protestors are. In a 'deterritorialised' and despatialised postmodern context, protestors often fight on behalf of extraterritorial and extra-local forces that invisibly animate local struggles and protests. If by a postmodern sleight of hand, Africans are enrolled as agents or actors on behalf of invisible and absent present (neo-)imperial others, the question is whether claims of human rights are really meant to accrue to Africans that are turned into beasts of burden for supposedly dedifferentiated (neo-)imperial others. Furthermore, in a postmodern context where the agency and [supposed] action of nonhumans like animals, birds, snakes, statues and so on, are being celebrated and dedifferentiated from human agency and action (Murris, 2016); when empire celebrates the agency and actions of Africans in protests, it could as well be celebrating not human rights and agency but 'nonhuman' agency and action in the sense that Africans are regarded in contemporary Western discourses as indistinct from nonhumans. In other words, the claims to extend human rights coupled with the efforts to dedifferentiate the human from the nonhuman speak to the use of other humans as animals or beast of burdens in the (neo-)imperial games of animism and animalisation of Africans (Nhemachena, 2016). In other words, it is necessary to go beyond celebrating agency, activism and postmodern performativity that do not advance real, original and essential African exigencies of restitution, restoration and repossession of what they were robbed of by colonisers and their descendants.

When Raschke (2003) argues that the postmodern [African] university constitutes a decentred, protean and dispersed approach, he can be understood as surfacing important insights into the circumstances surrounding the Fees Must Fall Movement, particularly in so far as the fees must fall carried to logical limits would translate to the postmodern protean 'African Universities Must Fall Movement'. In this respect, the Fees Must Fall Movement as an effort to 'decentre' and 'disperse' power in African universities can be construed within the postmodern framework. What is seldom, if at all, explicated in decentring, protean and dispersal postmodern movements is that decentring and dispersing African institutions effectively creates and worsens poverty as seen with the decentring of Africans states [from the economy and from policy] with the implementation of World Bank and IMF neoliberalism. Decentring African institutions worsens conflicts because the different multiple centres compete for power in cut throat fashions as witnessed in neoliberal multipartyism where Africans now compete for political power that doesn't help Africans materially and even morally and intellectually. Having multiple centres or being decentred in a postmodern sense does not imply migration from impoverishment, and it does not amount to restitution or restoration of what was colonially dispossessed. In other words, engaging in decentring, protean and postmodern protest movements amounts to hyperreal, surreal, nonessential and nonfoundational struggles that keep Africans locked in minor struggles that do not get them out of the belly of the empire so to speak.

The Fees Must Fall Movements not only signal efforts to collapse or decentre African universities; they also point to postmodernist aims to render obsolete educators and libraries as centres of knowledge; the movements indicate postmodernist efforts to render teachers and lecturers jobless with the decentring of universities such that the subsequent digitisation of learning renders immense profits to corporations that make digital technologies which are intended to replace 'expensive' teacher and lecturer centred learning (see Nhemachena, 2017). Further, if the postmodern university is understood in terms of Raschke's (2003) observations that the postmodern prototype of knowledge has been a theoretical construct for over twenty in North American and Europe, it becomes possible to understand the contemporary protests in terms of the long history of postmodern trajectories in the West which West is now capitalising on digital technology to decentre, disperse and render African universities protean and rhizomatic. Support for postmodern [student] revolutions and movements is designed to aid the Western projects of redefining and deterritorialising African universities in ways that efface locality and spatial relevance while promoting virtuality and irrelevance. Thus, Raschke (2016: 11-2) notes: "The knowledge map of the digital terrain is not the same as the territory, principally because the territory has been de-territorialised".

While some South Africans (and Namibians) were worried about the vandalisation of institutions of higher learning, which was encouraged by some apartheid era academics whose own children are based in overseas institution, postmodernists appear to already have a map of the future of African universities. Although some South Africans were worried about the fact that the South African students burned down libraries and residences while they received enticements to do so from some NGOs, white academics who gave them money, food and paid for the marches against the universities (News24, 24 January 2016), postmodernist appear to already have a map for the envisaged [decentred, dispersed and deterritorialised] African universities. While the students themselves were concerned about outsourcing and the plight of university workers, postmodernist appear to have a worse plan for workers with the increasing takeover of jobs, including in teaching, pharmacy, driving and so on, by proliferating humanoid robots that are being preferred over human employees (Alemi *et al*, 2014; Nhemachena, 2016). In other words, postmodern revolutions are not necessarily meant to help Africans escape from the belly of the (neo-)empire; rather the revolutions are meant to be part of the motor for moving (neo-)imperial rule forward even as Africans are thereby pushed into murkier swirling waters of global (neo-)imperial coloniality.

In the light of the foregoing, it is easier to understand why African students' attention was suddenly shifted from the Rhodes Must Fall Movement to the Fees Must Fall Movement (The Guardian, 16 March 2016; Cetshwayo Mabhena in The Sunday Times, 10 April 2016). As noted in the Guardian (16 March 2016) and by Cetshwayo Mabhena (ibid), the Rhodes Must Fall Movement shook and threatened the entire edifice of empire and so some in the imperial centres, including at Oxford University, were worried about the Rhodes Scholarship and the fate of Rhodes' imperial legacy in the light of the Rhodes Must Fall Movement. Thus, the momentum and energy in the Rhodes Must Fall Movement had to be redirected to struggles that would not threaten the core of the (neo-)imperial legacy. For this reason, Mphutlane WaBofelo (11 May 2017) notes that the principles of de-commodification, decoloniality and intersectionality born out of the Rhodes Must Fall Movement were later shifted to the Fees Must Fall Movement which subsequently emerged, in mid-October 2015, that is, later in the year. The Fees Must Fall protest started at the University of Witwatersrand and it spread to the University of Cape Town, Rhodes University and so on. In this sense, Mphutlane Wa Bofelo (11 May 2017) observes that the protests received sympathy from various sections of South African society and they elicited international solidarity. Although it is noted by Mphutlane WaBofelo (ibid) that the Fees Must Fall Movement exposed the failure of South Africa to deal honestly and decisively with the issues of redress, restitution, reparation, redistribution and reconstitution as the *sine qua non* for genuine reconciliation and sustainable nation building, it is necessary to note that it is not only individual African countries that failed. As Nhemachena (2016) argues, the failure to address these aspects is shared by former colonisers and descendants of colonists who have not restituted, restored and made good the colonial dispossession of Africans; the failure is also shared by civil society organisations which have failed to civilise the former colonists, descendant of colonists and (neo-)imperial powers that have the duties to restitute, restore and make good their (neo-)colonial and (neo-)enslavement era wrongs. In this sense, the failure is not merely or simplistically one of individual African countries, states and governments. The problem, therefore, is with former colonists, descendants of colonists and (neo-)imperial powers that try to deflect their (neo-)colonial and (neo-)enslavement wrongs and sins entirely to Africans, to African states and governments.

In view of the above, we agree with Cetshwayo Mabhena's (10 April 2016) arguments that the Rhodes Must Fall Movement was against the world system of (neo-)imperialism which is why students that engaged in the Rhodes Must Fall Movement did not receive as much sympathy from Western NGOs, civil society organisations and apartheid era white Professors. We also agree with Cetshwayo Mabhena's (ibid) observation that the Rhodes Must Fall Movement was, by (neo-)imperial sleight of hand, replaced by the Fees Must Fall Movement which is not a struggle against the world system but a slender battle against a smaller order within the world system. In this vein, Cetshwayo Mabhena (ibid) argues that when the (neo-)colonial and (neo-)imperial system are attacked, it changes its orders, can publicly crucify some of its symbols and representations while it stealthily reloads and prepares to appear in a much more lethal form to punish its challengers. So, the Rhodes Must Fall Movement quickly turned into the Fees Must Fall Movement because (neo-)empire had to narrow the African struggle from the call for Rhodes Must Fall and decolonisation of the university in Africa to simply asking for fees to be abolished: the (neo-)imperial system had to invent smaller and local [African] struggles for its [African] enemies so as to protect itself from the more threatening challenge launched by the Rhodes Must Fall Movement. We, thus, argue here that setting one [group] African against the other is a (neo-)imperial strategy to decentre, disperse and deterritorialise Africa; it is a way of ensuring that Africa is made to destroy its centres and institutional spines.

Back to Namibia; education is seen as the basic necessity of every individual in the society. However, access to education has been affected by so many factors including cultural, political and economic. According to the NDPI (2010), huge inequality and economic gaps between different individuals and families in Namibia have increasingly made access to education to be differentiated because those who have a low economic class lack access to educational institutions. Poverty or the inability of people to meet the basic needs of life has made lower class people not to access education, as compared to those who are of higher social classes. People living in poverty lack access to education because they do not have the money to pay for fees, yet in a postmodern (neo-)imperial context African people are confounded about the real causes of their poverty as colonists and their descendants make consistent efforts to generate African amnesia about colonial dispossession and enslavement as sources of the resilient African impoverishment.

In early 2016, students from different higher education institutions in Namibia decided to launch a movement against the increase in tuition fees. The rich were able to pay the high fees but those who lived in poverty could not afford, hence students engaged in the "Fees Must Fall Movement". The Fees Must Fall Movement was meant to force the government of Namibia to reduce the fees for different institutions (Simataa, 2010). During the recent years, the tuition fees had been increasing by ten per cent per year. Considering, for example, the past four years the tuition fees have been increasing as follow: in 2013 the minimum amount which was requested for one to only register at University was N$4800 and in 2014 it increased to N$5800 then in 2015 it was raised to N$6800. These trends show that there has been an increase in the tuition fees every year and this disadvantaged those students who were impoverished or who were living in poverty.

According to the Namibian Free Education for All Act (No. 16 of 2001), development of education in Namibia was to be guided by four broad goals of access, equality, equity and democracy. The first National Development Plan (NDPI) (2001) provided for poverty reduction through education and it accords high priority to the provision of education and learning in Namibia. The mission statement of NDPI, according to the National Plan (2002-2015), was the provision of equitable access to education, literacy, arts and cultural opportunities and to ensure that all students get adequate support to enable them to acquire knowledge and skills. The other social-economic factor which inhibits education is the fact that three quarters of Namibia's poor live in the rural areas where access to education is very limited. According to the Ministry of Education Annual Report (2001), the enrolment statistics indicate that there has been a decline in educational enrolment because of the lack of education opportunities by some marginalised groups. The most affected are children from San and Ovahimba communities, street working children and other such children living under difficult circumstances. According to the Central Bureau of Statistical Data (2011), the incidence of poverty by region shows that poverty is highest in Okavango Region, in-terms of the percentage of poor (56.5%) followed by Ohangwena with 44.7%. Research shows that education is a major determinant of an individual's societal status and social mobility in Namibia, as it influences career prospects, and that higher education is considered a gateway to a better future (Chataika, 2010). Yet poverty can impact one's life in so many aspects and one of them is access to education particularly higher education. According to First National Development Plan (NDPI) (2001), the mission statement of the Namibian Education for All (EFA) is stated as the provision of equitable access to education, literature and arts but because some citizens are less privileged and poverty-stricken, they do not have equitable access to education: higher or tertiary education is increasingly becoming expensive and a tantalising reality for them. Implementation of the policy on access to education in Namibia has enabled the country to reap the benefits in the form of 95% enrolment of 6 to 16 year-olds in the last few years, since independence in the early 1990s. However, there is neglect of those above 16 years of age who cannot afford tertiary level education: the challenges of access to education by the San children, Ovahimba, farm workers' children and street working children are not attended to.

Poverty also constitutes an important reason for why learners drop out of schools in countries like South Africa (APF, 2003; Wilson, 2004; Fleisch and Woolman, 2004; Nelson Mandela Foundation, 2005) and Namibia as elsewhere in the continent. Such poverty manifests as failure to pay fees, failure to buy school attire, lack of transport, failure to buy stationery and so on. These manifestations are also witnessed, including at university levels, in Namibia. Such studies show large differences in enrolment in Grade 1 in many countries, but also that fewer poor children remain in school to higher grades (Filmer & Pritchett, 1999 & 2001; Orazem, Glewwe & Patrinos, 2007).

Studies in South Africa suggest that poverty delays entry of the affected children into schools (Case, Hosegood and Lund, 2005: 469). Case, Hosegood and Lund (ibid) assessed the impact of Child Support Grants in the UMkhanyakude District in the Kwa-Zulu Natal Province, and found that the grant appeared to overcome the impact of poverty on school enrolment. The study found that children who received the grant (in 2002) were significantly more likely to be enrolled in school for the first time in the years following receipt of the grant than equally poor children of the same age who did not receive the grant (Case, Hosegood and Lund, 2005). The findings of the survey suggested that the Child Support Grant enabled households to cover the expenses of schooling and to improve the nutrition and health status of learners which contributed to their school readiness. Similarly, in Namibia those who receive grants, while living in poverty, have their access to education significantly increased. Students who don't have grants or loans from the government have lower access to tertiary education: many are thus, forced to stay home until the government offers them a grant or a loan.

Like most developing nations, Namibian higher education has witnessed a steady rise in demand coupled with reduced funding for the higher education. In the last 16 years, the Polytechnic of Namibia students' enrolment grew from 2245 to 12440 thereby necessitating a greater need for funding and resource allocation (Namibia Economist, 2012; The Namibian, 2011). At the University of Namibia (UNAM) the student enrolment has also sharply risen by about 60% between 2009 and 2011 (UNAM Strategic & Physical Planning, 2012). On the contrary, state funding in higher education has gradually fallen from 15% in 2007 to 8.7 % in 2011 (Human Development Report, 2011; SARUA, 2012) and has continued to date in a gradual slide. To sustain operations, the institutions of higher learning have responded by raising fees to compensate for reduced public funding. Such a trend in higher education raises several challenges, namely quality management but more poignant for this study, equitable access. The reduced allocation of funding in higher education has negatively impacted many school leavers leading to difficulties in accessing higher education, raising unemployment levels and creating a national skills gap. Lack of access to higher education may further threaten participation in social justice coupled with reduced economic performance (Barr, 2002).

One of the major challenges facing the higher education system in Namibia is to develop an equitable system where access to higher education goes alongside equity. It is not an achievement. It is a process of adapting procedures that resemble rules of a game, a quest for fairness of receiving burdens and benefits. Although strides have been made in terms of opening up the higher education sector to marginalised communities and to previously disadvantaged people, the higher education system of Namibia is not yet accessible to all. So, the Ministry of Education and Culture (MEC) (1993: 37) noted that "in the near future we shall measure our success in achieving both equality and equity by looking at who goes to school". In other words, what will demonstrate that higher education system is successful is not the number of people who pass through the institutions. Instead, it will be the degree to which people from the smallest minority groups in society are faring in the higher education system – the degree to which all Namibians experience social justice. Therefore, it is only when the majority who are seen as poor access higher education in the same way as those who are rich or privileged that social justice is worth celebrating.

Looker and Lowe (2001) discuss the importance of parental socio-economic status for influencing children's post-secondary participation. Parental status can be understood to encompass both social and cultural capital: social capital refers to resources available because of parents' connection to other individuals or groups, while cultural capital includes non-economic assets that come from higher levels of education and exposure to middle and upper class values and attitudes. Thus, one's socio-economic status plays a pivotal role in one's access to tertiary education. If an individual comes from a low economic status background it is most probably that they will not attain their goal as they would wish to.

In the light of the challenges of access to education, students in South Africa, as highlighted above, recently decided to launch a movement or a strike which was called the 'Fees Must Fall Movement'. According to Edwin Mpho Makitta (2016) the movement was aimed at the attainment of free education and the immediate implementation of free education in South Africa. Education in South Africa is reflective of social-economic conditions that perpetuate black poverty and exclusion. Black students in Namibia, as in South Africa, are perpetually financially excluded and locked into debt. Students in South Africa protested that access to education must not be based on one's ability to pay, it must be open to all, no payment plans and student loans but free education for all, which is the de-commodification of education. Just like South Africa, Namibian students from the University of Namibia and National University of Science and Technology engaged on a similar movement in which they protested for free education for all, at all tertiary institutions in the country. The students in Namibia protested against the fees increments which were a barrier to many students who wanted to access education.

According to Ndaki Kahiura (2016), hundreds of students from different higher institutions gathered at the Namibia University of Science and Technology (NUST) to strike pertaining the reduction of the tuition fees. The aim of the students was not only to have the registration fees reduced but to also agitate for student's debts to be written off. However, the decision to scrap off the registration fees at NUST was made after lengthy meetings between high authorities from both the institution and the government. It is believed that many students dropped out of the university because they could not afford the tuition fees.

Furthermore, as reported by journalist Limba Mupetemi (February 2016), the University of Namibia students just like the Namibia University of Science and Technology students, also participated in the Fees Must Fall Movement. The student leaders locked the gates so that no students would get in to register and staff members were not allowed to enter the university. The students argued that they were demonstrating because they found it difficult to pay high registration fees which had been increasing every year. According to the British Counsel Commissioned Institute of Education (2011), there are significant inequities of access to higher education. University is still for the privileged few in sub-Saharan Africa. Only 38% of the enrolments are female, and significant inequalities exist between different socio-economic, regional and ethnic groupings. Many talented people thus, are prevented from taking up the opportunity for further study that could help drive forward the region's development.

Besides the insecurity associated with unavailability of funds for tuition, accommodation, academic materials, and subsistence, university students face the prospect of large debts, high drop-out rates, poor throughput rates, inadequate facilities and accommodation, largely unreconstructed epistemologies and ontologies, questionable quality of learning and teaching to ensure meaningful opportunities and success, and alienating and disempowering academic and institutional cultures that are suffused by 'whiteness', and are products of the historical "legacies of intellectual colonisation and racialisation" (Du Toit, 2000). Having noted this, it is imperative to underscore herein the fact that even the postmodern revolutions and movements are suffused by "whiteness" as much as they are by (neo-)imperial discourses of hybridity, non-essentialism, hyperreality, surrealism and non-foundationalism. At the historically "white" universities, those who are "white" and from colonising backgrounds experience the university environments and cultures as natural; they feel very much at home and they don't see or feel any need to genuinely decolonise the universities other than via suspicious postmodern tenets. These social groups are largely oblivious to the association of the current university cultures with power, privilege, and advantage, and how they disadvantage especially "black" students from working class backgrounds and women students (and academics) in myriad ways including affronting their dignity, and generating bitterness, anger, pain, hurt, worries, and anxieties. Those who are "black" and from disadvantaged backgrounds tend to experience the harsh environments and cultures of the historically "white" universities as discomforting, alienating, disempowering, and exclusionary. These university cultures exact a significant personal, psychological, emotional, and academic toll on "black" students and staff, compromise equality of opportunity and outcomes, and diminish the idea of higher education as an enriching and liberating adventure (du Toit, ibid). However, it is also imperative for Africans not to focus on postmodern revolutions or movements that are not premised on African foundationalism, essentialism, reality and African originality-postmodern revolutions and movements are more in the service of (neo-)imperial decentring and deterritorialisation of Africa, than they are for Africans. As Olajide

(2013: 12) observes in view of India: "…the domination of the New World was much easier by setting one group of Indians against another". For purposes of this chapter, we argue that the same logic applies to the (neo-)imperial domination of contemporary Africa and the global south [and Namibia in particular] where one [impoverished] group [of Africans] is often set [by (neo-)empire] against the other, including over problems that are traceable to (neo-)imperial dispossessions and exploitation of Africa.

Fees Must Fall Movement at the University of Namibia: Poverty and Access to Education

During the course of our interviews we discovered that students at the University of Namibia have different views concerning the Fees Must Fall Movement. We interviewed students of different sexes, years of study and also from different departments across the university community. We also found out that the main reason why students engaged in the protests against their higher learning institutions was poverty. According to Mwape, one of the 4th year male participants, poverty is the major reason for participating in the Fees Must Fall Movement. Mwape stated thus:

> *Poverty is the reason why we had the fees must fall movement. As much as we have a lot of people in school, the number that is not in school still remains larger than the number of people who are able to access education country wide and this is because many people who are living in poverty are ignorant about the importance of education, and they fail to see its importance. I can define poverty as lack of basic needs or resources like shelter, food and clothing.*

On the other hand, Meme, a third year female participant in Humanities thought that the fact that the government only offers free education for all in primary schools and not in post-secondary education was the main cause to the Fees Must Fall protest at the University of Namibia. She said:

> *I think poverty plays a huge role on access to higher education as such people in poverty fails to afford certain basic goods and services due to insufficient resources*

243

like money, these days, education is free in Namibia for primary school pupils so people living in poverty don't have to worry about school fees or anything but as from high school that's where the problem starts because it would be too expensive for parents who are leaving in poverty as some students might not even go to universities because of lack of finances. And it's also just not about school fees it also has to do with what are the students going to eat during the course of the semester.

Kondi, the third interviewee in Humanities also maintained that poverty was the driving force behind the whole mantra of Fees Must Fall protests; he said:

The fees must fall movement was meant to assist those who might otherwise be barred from education institutions because they are too poor to pay for accessing it, that is the connection between poverty, access to education and the fees must fall movement, I can define poverty as the state of having little or no money and few or no material possessions.

Similarly, Felicia, a 2nd year female participant in Humanities stated that:

Poverty leads to less resources, academically and financially for students which will at the end cause such students to be less privileged than others thus engaging in the fees must fall movement. Students in poverty find it very difficult to cope at school because of social problems and increasing of fees by the university will just make things worse.

Supporting views from other students, Juan in Humanities maintained that:

I believe that poverty dictates a person's ability to have access to quality education. Someone in poverty lacks basic resources like money. The fees must fall movement was unrealistic but it was an attempt to make education available to more people but its goals on decreasing fees may have negative consequence.

Five of the interviewees have stated that due to poverty many people are deprived and unable to access or afford tertiary education. The Fees Must Fall Movement was, therefore, meant to aid the impoverished in accessing higher education. The Fees Must Fall Movement came as a window of opportunity to those who, due to poverty, could not access higher education. People who find themselves trapped in impoverishment are deprived of vision, information and their key to the future (education). The strain and burden of increase in fees have proven too much to handle and this triggered the Fees Must Fall protests. With fees falling comes more affordable and accessible education.

Thelma, a 2nd year female interviewee in Humanities spoke about students not being able to do the courses they want because of impoverishment. She stated that:

> *Lots of young people have their high school qualifications but do not have access to higher education due to financial difficulties as their parents are not able to afford it. The fees must fall movement happened for this reason primarily, so that parents could be able to afford higher education for their kids, without much of a strain. Education is the necessary key to the eradication of poverty. The relationship between education and poverty reduction is, thus, quite straight forward as education will be like a ladder for someone to escape poverty.*

Just like the previous interviewee, Hofini, a fourth year male participant in Humanities said:

> *The Namibian government should subsidise tertiary education as a measure to ensure equitable access to higher education, and yes the government has the money as it is using money to do unnecessary things such as the building of the new parliament.*

Furthermore, Christian in Humanities thought that providing financial assistance to the needy might help:

> the *government should offer more scholarships and other financial assistance programs to people who are in the lower class but who have the potential to rise and live better lives. At least they will have a social mobility and go out of poverty.*

On the other hand, Thelma, a second year female interviewee in Humanities said:

The government must reduce the tuition fees and build extra campuses in those regions with high populations, because if you take a look at it big campuses are only in the capital city thus the government must build more campuses in places like the Caprivi Region and Katima Mulilo so as to make higher education accessible to everyone nationwide. The government can also establish some community colleges and give out loans, bursaries and grants to students and I don't think this will reduce standards of living because the government has enough revenue to maintain the standards or even improve.

While the Namibian government has obligations to ensure access to higher education by students, the challenge is that like many other African governments, the Namibian government has not much control of the economy which is monopolised by transnational corporations, some of which evade paying taxes to African governments (Nhemachena *et al*, 2017; Mawere and Nhemachena 2014). The Namibians themselves have been colonially dispossessed of their fertile and well-watered land and so they find it difficult to eke a living in the marginal lands to which they were settled by the colonial and apartheid governments. In this sense, the Fees Must Fall Movement push the government into a more invidious position, particularly in the light of the fact that the economies of African states are still controlled by transnational corporations and the minority white elite and not by the African people themselves or their states. The [phantom] solution in such invidious instances would be for African governments to borrow more and more from international institutions and from the private sector yet this borrowing worsens the "debt" crisis for the African states. Thus, while it is necessary to pay attention to the social economic backgrounds and indebtedness of individual African families, it is also imperative to pay attention to the political and social economic backgrounds of the Africans states which have centuries-old histories of (neo-)colonial privation. The tragedy here is that both the Africans and their states are trapped in historical cycles of (neo-)imperial dispossession which Western supporters of postmodern revolutions [against African states and African institutions] are hypocritically anxious to ignore and efface.

According to Netty, a female third year student at the University of Namibia:

> *Socioeconomic background will have an effect on what a student chooses to study for example a student that comes from a bad socio-economic background might want to study a course like pure sciences so as to achieve his or her dream but because doing the course requires a lot of money and his or her economic background will not allow it that student will be disadvantaged and their dreams will not be able to come true by the end of the day thus his background status would have hindered him to attain his goal.*

However according to Preclinah, a 2nd year student, if one has a good socio-economic background, educational dreams will be realisable:

> *I personally have a high socioeconomic background because I can afford all basic needs and even other luxurious things without any worry and my parents have got an educational attainment background, so it is easier for me to cope with higher educational attainment as I can get almost all the resources I want concerning my education, compared to those with a low or bad economic background they seem to struggle from stationary, grocery or even clothing.*

Narrating the challenges of being a member of low income families, Tate a third years student in Humanities, stated:

> *Coming from a family with low income (those who receive N$4500 [US$350] and below as their monthly salary) in which we struggle sometimes even to get basic commodities and in which we have only one breadwinner is very difficult. It is challenging especially for me to depend on one person who is also having a low income. Being in poverty makes you lack confidence and have a low self-esteem. This will affect the way you think in most cases poverty discourages people to attain their goals when you want to go an extra mile poverty will just limit you. Sometimes I need taxi money to move from point A to point B, food toiletries and other necessities but then I seem not to get them which will sometimes lead me to stress and negatively affect my educational outcome.*

247

Students need resources like books and money to use yet these things are not accessible in low social-economic families. Finances affect a person's ability to purchase the materials for education purposes. If one comes from a disadvantaged background he or she is limited by the finances and that will directly affect their attainment and even classroom performance in a negative way.

For the above reason, Benjamin, a third year male participant in Humanities maintained that:

> Low socio-economic background, whereby one fails to live a basic life or just to buy basic commodities such as food and clothes, limits your capacity to think freely and it's actually a demotivating factor. For example, you are in class and you are thinking of what you are going to eat while you are hungry already will make you absent-minded and you will not even listen to what the lecturer is talking about the whole time hence, this negatively affects your educational attainment. Limited financial background and other economic resources militate against performance.

Different financial backgrounds determine which courses one will do. Many students have got different dreams to fulfil but because of their financial backgrounds, they tend to be limited such that they end up studying programmes which they never wanted to do in the first place. Some students will end up doing courses which are cheaper like psychology where modules cost N$1500 as compared to sciences where one module costs N$2000 and above.

The Fees Must Fall Movement seems to have benefited some students including the poor (those who struggle to meet their basic needs) and the middle class (those who can afford the basic needs but are not rich). The less privileged people who are not financially stable and who could not register so as to pursue their careers are the ones who benefited most from the protests: they were subsequently allowed to register for their studies without paying a lot of money.

Thus, according to Hofini:

> With Fees Must Fall campaign, the first in line to benefit are those who cannot afford higher education because as the fees become more sensible and affordable, it allows the underprivileged to acquire higher education at last. These people will have

less fees to pay hence less responsibilities at large and many students will be able to achieve their dreams nicely without much barriers.

Some students thought that it's the students in general who benefited from the Fees Must Fall Movement, especially those without financial assistance from any organisations. These students would, therefore, at least retain some money which they would otherwise have paid as fees.

Eugenia a student in Humanities stated that all the students benefited from the fees must fall movement. She said:

> *All the students of course benefited from the Fees Must Fall because even if you are rich or poor just the reduction of some fees will impact you positively as you will be paying less money to the institutes. Even if some students are having loans they will at the end pay back less money than they would have paid without the fees reduction. As for the institutes, they might not make as much profit they were aiming for which is a loss on their side and that's why most beneficiaries are the students."*

While loans, grants and bursaries can help students in African universities, there is need to notice the need for broader policy shifts by African states, NGOs, civil society organisations and Western states and international institutions. Africans and their states need to be compensated for enslavement and colonial dispossession and exploitation so that they become capacitated to care for their impoverished citizens. Secondly there is need for Euro-American states to desist from refusing or failing to compensate Africans for enslavement and colonial dispossession and exploitation. As Fanon (1963) notes, it is necessary to remember that Europe was built on the back of enslaved and colonised Africans who can barely afford to pay fees for their children. Thirdly, it is necessary for civil society organisations to civilise the Euro-American states so that they make good their (neo-)enslavement and (neo-)colonial dispossession and exploitation wrongs in Africa (Nhemachena and Bankie, 2017; Nhemachena, 2016; Mawere and Nhemachena 2014). It is not the African victims of (neo-)enslavement and (neo-)colonisation who need [more] civilisation, rather it is the (neo-)enslavers and (neo-)colonisers who need a lot of civilisation so that they can make good their (neo-)colonial and (neo-)enslavement wrongs. In this regard, the civil society organisations and NGOs that take pleasure in promoting postmodern revolutions and protests in Africa need to spend much of their time civilising the West. In this sense, we argue that the Fees Must Fall Movements could have been better sustained as *Empire Must Fall Movements*. The issue here is primarily about Africa escaping from the belly of the insidious empire.

Conclusion

This chapter has argued that impoverished Africans often fight one another in their trenches of poverty or impoverishment. One instance of such battles is manifest in the postmodern protests and revolutions which turn one African [group] against the other often with the support of some NGOs, civil society organisations and Western states and institutions. It has been argued that postmodern revolutions and protests are intended by their promoters to decentre, disperse and deterritorialise Africa. The chapter has pointed out that, as is evident in the neoliberal decentring of the African states, decentring and deterritorialising Africa and African institutions can only worsen the impoverishment of Africans. Furthermore, the chapter has argued that Africa's problem is not necessarily centralisation of life in African institutions; rather Africa's problems lie in (neo-)enslavement and (neo-)colonial dispossession and exploitation by transnational corporations and institutions of the global north. The problems lie more in (neo-)imperial failure to restitute, restore and compensate Africans for (neo-)enslavement and (neo-)colonial wrongs. In this regard, we argue that the Fees Must Fall Movements could have been better sustained as *Empire Must Fall Movements* across the entire continent and the global south.

References

Alemi, M. *et al.* 2014. Employing Humanoid Robots for Teaching English Language in Iaman Jumor Higher Schools, in *International*

Journal of Humanoid Robots, Vol 11 (3): https://doi-org/10.1142/50219843614500224.

Ballantine. J. H. 2005. *The Sociology of Education,* New Jersey: Wright State University.

Booysen, S. 2017. *Fees Must Fall: Student Revolt, Decolonisation & Governance in South Africa,* Wits University Press.

Bowles, S. and Gintis, H. 1976. *The Spirit of Capitalism,* New York: Palgrave McMillan.

British Council. 2014. *Understanding Graduate Employability in Sub-Saharan Africa* (digital report).

Call, L. 2002. *Posthuman Anarchism,* Maryland: Lexington Books.

Case, A., Hosegood, V. and Lund, F. 2005. *The Reach and Impact of Child Support Grants: Evidence from KwaZulu-Natal,* Development Southern Africa, 22 (4):467–482.

Cetshwayo Mabhena. (10 April 2016). Fees Must Fall: How Empire Fights Back, In Sunday Times. www.sundaynews.co.zw/fees-must-falll-how-empire-fights-back/.

Chataika, T. & Swart. E. 2010. Increasing Access to Higher Education, *Education commission #78.*

Department of Education. 2003. *Review of the South African Financing, Resourcing and Costs of Education in Public Schools,* Pretoria: Department of Education.

Duncan, J. 2016. *Protest Nation: The Right to Protest in South Africa,* UKZN Press.

Eko, S. S. 2015. *Being Black Not Much has Changed Then, Now and the Way Forward,* Dorrance Publishing.

Fanon, F. 1963. *The Wretched of the Earth,* New York: Grove Press.

Fleisch, B. and Woolman, S. 2004. *On the Constitutionality of School Fees: A Reply to Roithmayr,* Perspectives in Education, 22(1):111–123.

Fured, I. F. 2011. Introduction to the Marketisation of Higher Education and the Student as Consumer in Moleworth M., (Ed) *The Marketization of Higher Education and the Student as Consumer,* London and New York: Routledge.

Heffernan, A *et al.* 2016. *Students Must Rise : Youth Struggles in South Africa Before and Beyond Soweto '76,* Wits University Press.

Hickey, S. and Du Toit, A. 2007. *Adverse Incorporation, Social Exclusion and Chronic Poverty*, CPRC Working Paper 81. Chronic Poverty Research Centre.

Hyunjoon. P. 2004. *Educational Expansion and Inequality in Korea*, Tokyo: Elsevier

Kahiurika. N. (January 2016). *NUST Fees Must Fall Movement*. The Namibian Press. Page 1 Limited.

Mamdani, M. 2007. *Scholars in the Market Place, The Dilemmas of Neoliberal Reform at Makerere University. 1989-2005.* Dakar: CODESRIA.

Marope, M. T. 2005. Namibia: *Human Capital and Knowledge Development for Economic Growth with Equity.* Africa Region Human Development Working Paper 84. Washington, DC: World Bank\

Mpho Makita. (November 2015). *The Fees Must Fall Movement South Africa.* Witwatersrand University.

Mphutlane Wa Bofela. (11 May 2017). Fallism and the Dialectics of Spontaneity and Organisation: Disrupting Tradition to Reconstruct Tradition in Pambazuka News. https://www.pambazuka.org/democracy-governance/fallism-and-organisation-disrupting-tradition.

Murris, K. 2016. #Rhodes Must Fall: A Posthumanist Orientation to Decolonising Higher Education Institutions, *South Africa Journal of Higher Education* 30(3): 274-294.

NDPI. 2001. *The Structure of Education System in Namibia.* Windhoek: EFA.

News24, (24 January 2016). White Supremacists 'third force' Behind #FeesMustFall protests-ANCYL, www.news24.com/SouthAfrica/news/white-supremacists-third-force-behind-feesmustfall-protests-ancyl-20160124.

Nhemachena, A. 2016. Animism, Coloniality and Humanism: Reversing the Empire's Framing of Africa, in Mawere M *et al* (Eds). *Theory, Knowledge, Development and Politics: What Role for the Academy in the Sustainability of Africa?* Bamenda: Langaa RPCIG.

Nhemachena, A. 2016. Double-Trouble: Reflections on the Violence of Absence and the Culpability of the Present in Africa, in Mawere, M. (Ed). *Politics, Violence and Conflict Management in Africa:*

Envisioning Transformation, Peace and Unity in the Twenty-First Century, Bamenda: Langaa RPCIG.

Nhemachena, A. 2016. (Post-)development and the Social Production of Ignorance in 21st Century Africa, in Mawere M (Ed). *Development Perspectives from the South: Troubling the Metrics of (Under)development in Africa,* Bamenda: Langaa RPCIG.

Nhemachena, A. 2017. Hearing the Footfalls of Humanoid Robots: Technoscience, (Un-employment and the Future of Development in Twenty-First Century Africa, in Mawere M (ed). *Underdevelopment, Development and the Future of Africa,* Bamenda: Langaa RPCIG.

Nhemachena, A. *et al.* 2017. "When Did the Rain Start to Beat Us? Discursive Dispossession and the Political Economies of Misrecognition about African Mining", In: Nhemachena, A. *et al* (Eds) *Mining Africa: Law, Environment, Society and Politics in Historical and Multidisciplinary Perspectives.* Bamenda: Langaa RPCIG.

Nhemachena, A. & Mawere, M. 2014. Revolutions, Evolutions and African Political Economies: A Critical Review of Nigel Gibson's "*Living Fanon – Global Perspectives*", *Journal of Pan African Studies,* 6 (9): 58-71.

Olajide, O. 2013. *The Complete Concise History of the Slave Trade.* Author House.

Peterson, L *et al.* 2016. Democracy, Education and Free Speech: The Importance of #FeesMustFalll for Transnational Activism, in *Societies Without Borders* 11 (1): 1-28.

Raschke, C. A. 2003. *The Digital Revolution and the Coming of the Postmodern University,* Psychology Press.

Simata. S. M. 2010. *In Pursuit of Access with Equity in the Higher Education System of Namibia,* Windhoek: Namibia.

The Guardian, (16 March 2016). The Real Meaning of Rhodes Must Fall. https://www.theguardian.com/UK-news/2016/mar/16/the-real-meanig-of-rhodes-must-fall.

UNESCO Institute for Statistics (UIS) (2008) *Comparing Education Statistics Across the World;* Montreal; UIS.

World Bank. 2010. *Financing Higher Education in Africa,* Washington, D.C.: World Bank.

Chapter 10

The Impoverished African and the Poverty of Colonially Inherited Education in Africa

Ephraim Taurai Gwaravanda

Introduction

Scholars on African poverty have identified both external and internal causes to African poverty and vulnerability condition especially in the exploitation and use of natural resources (Rodney 1972; Mawere 2016; Mawere 2017a; Mawere 2017b; Mhango 2017; Nhemachena 2016). In this chapter, I argue that the greatest form of poverty in Africa is poverty of the African mindset – mental poverty – that was systematically structured by colonisers and proceeded to be inherited by postcolonial African governments (Ngugi 1972; Nhemachena 2016). The poverty of ideas is a result of inherited colonial education that systematically narrows the thinking patterns in Africa. Firstly, I argue that Western education imposed by the colonisers creates a dependency syndrome whereby the colonised always rely on the colonial masters for ideas and epistemological constructs. The Eurocentric capitalistic hegemony creates "service disciplines" that justify capitalistic rationality and meet capitalistic objectives rather than the poverty conditions of Africans. Secondly, the bottle-necking approach to education which has been inherited by the postcolonial African governments justifies and maintains a cycle of poverty among Africans since education is made to be a privilege of the rich. Thirdly, education curricula inherited from colonisers resulted in a society of job seekers rather than employment creators. The education curricula have in fact resulted in school leavers being subjected to oppression and exploitation thereby perpetuating poverty in Africa. This means that there is little innovation and creativity that is imparted by the inherited system of education. Fourthly, inherited colonial education fails to impart critical thinking skills that help in challenging the status quo. It creates a culture of docility and passivity among Africans thereby discouraging them from thinking differently and create alternative ways that challenge poverty in Africa. This is also seen in the deliberate exclusion of philosophy among school disciplines especially in former British colonies. Fifthly, the inherited colonial education marginalises African indigenous knowledge systems and dismisses them as unscientific, pre-logical and primitive (Mawere 2015). Such a scenario entraps the African in the mentality of a foreign epistemic framework resulting in failure to think in alternative ways and come out of their poverty condition. The chapter proposes both de-colonial and reconstructive approaches to the postcolonial African education system so as to adequately address the poverty condition in the continent.

The Nexus between impoverished education and the impoverished African

Sen (1999) views poverty as a deprivation of capabilities and valuable freedoms that are necessary for exercising autonomy. On the other hand, Sen (Ibid) sees development as capability expansion. Sen's definition is important for this study because poverty is viewed as a reality that can be changed if capabilities are afforded to individuals. Sen contemplates that poverty must be seen as the deprivation of basic capabilities rather than merely taking into consideration the income aspect which forms a so-called "standard" measurement as to whether the person is poor or not. Income measurement gives problems especially in African countries where income depends on national currencies (or lack of them as in the case of Zimbabwe) that have different monetary values. This approach of the determination of poverty maintains that the deprivation of capabilities is a more intrinsically important approach in the determination of poverty rather than the poverty line approach which is subservient. Further, it is also argued that the capability approach ensures the measurement of real poverty rather than the lowness of income which is not the only variable in the determination of poverty (Sen, 1999).

The capability approach explicitly endorses and relies upon a key analytical distinction in practical philosophy, namely the means-ends distinction (Sen, 1999; Ingrid 2016). The approach stresses that we should always be clear, when valuing something, whether we value it as an end in itself, or as a means to a valuable end. In the context of education, the capability approach places education as a means to attain other things in life such as happiness, income, a job and related aspects. For the capability approach, the ultimate ends of interpersonal comparisons are people's capabilities. This implies that the capability approach evaluates policies and other changes according to their impact on people's capabilities as well as their actual functionings (Ingrid, 2016; Fleurbaey, 2016). Education or 'mis'education must ultimately be evaluated in terms of their link to capabilities. It asks whether people are able to be healthy, and whether the means or resources necessary for this capability, such as clean water, adequate sanitation, access to doctors, protection from infections and diseases, and basic knowledge on health issues, are present. It asks whether people are well-nourished, and whether the means or conditions for the realisation of this capability, such as having sufficient food supplies and food entitlements, are being met. It asks whether people have access to a high-quality education system, to real political participation, and to community activities that support them, that enable them to cope with struggles in daily life, and that foster caring and warm friendships (Ingrid, 2016).

Education as a form of freedom (Sen, 1999) opens for intellectual dynamism and flexibility that results in ability to think through problems and finding solutions to them. The problem of poverty is not in the academic plain but it is an existential reality. This means that real poverty is found at the level of material resources and facilities. However, sound educational training is necessary though insufficient in finding solutions to the problem of poverty in Africa. The necessity of education in Africa lies in the provision of skills for critical thinking, evaluation and problem solving. However, it is insufficient because, in addition to the critical skills, material resources are required to eradicate poverty. Education should potentially free individuals from poverty and capacitate them but if 'miseducation' is done as in the case of colonial education, the opposite results are obtained. Instead of freeing the mind, education from colonisers became oppressive in the sense of creating passivity in the minds of learners (Freirre, 2000). This means that 'education' becomes a tool of oppression and it begins by oppressing people's minds by narrowing their thinking patterns and reducing available options. Colonial education was deliberately designed to produce clerks, messengers, farm workers and garden boys for the capitalists and this was done through bottle-necking and dual education approaches. Narrowness, rigidity and fixed patterns of thought are the marks of colonial education that lack critical evaluation and objectivity. Colonial education therefore impoverished people's minds rather than enriching them.

Postcolonial African governments were supposed to critically evaluate colonial education and come up with broad and comprehensive education systems that are suitable for African situations, realities and problems (Shizha, 2006; Mawere, 2015). However, little reflection was done when African leaders took over from colonial rule. This resulted in a system of education that meets the demands of colonisers who are no longer on the ground. While political decolonisation was achieved at least in part, mental colonisation still exists. The net result of colonial education is impoverishment both at mental and resource levels. Mental poverty is a worse form of poverty because it causes failure to reflect and think out of the problems created by poverty. Resource level poverty prohibits individuals from moving forward and negates the attainment of education.

Dependency syndrome and Colonial Education

Western education imposed by the colonisers creates a dependency syndrome whereby the colonised always rely on the colonial masters for educational ideas, resources and capital. Dependency runs incongruent with the needs of African countries (Godwin, 1990). The word 'depend' comes from the Latin *'dependeo'* meaning 'to hang'. 'Syndrome' refers to a set of medical signs and symptoms that are related to each other. Dependency syndrome is a condition that chronic substance addicts suffer from (World Health

Organidation, 2017). Dependency syndrome is therefore primarily a medical term that is transferred to the economic realm to refer to individuals and nations that rely on provisions from donor countries for survival. Maringe (2017:1) points out that "most African countries on the continent, with the exception of Ethiopia and Liberia, have a colonial past which created colonial knowledge systems designed to serve the needs of the colonisers more than they addressed the needs of local communities and their indigenous economies and cultural identities." The Eurocentric capitalistic hegemony creates "service disciplines" that justify capitalistic rationality and meet capitalistic objectives rather than the poverty conditions of Africans. Scott (2006:1) defines capitalism as "an economic system where private actors are allowed to own and control the use of property in accord with their own interests, and where the invisible hand of the pricing mechanism coordinates supply and demand in markets in a way that is automatically in the best interests of society." Capitalism is also defined as a political, social, and economic system in which property, including capital assets, is owned and controlled for the most part by private persons. Colonial education gives copyrights and designs to colonisers and Africans were left to repair and maintain the designs without the ability to be innovative in changing and designing new technologies. If education relies on colonial masters, it fails to meet the needs of the recipients and it becomes oppressive.

Muzanenhamo (2010) argues that African countries still economically depend on colonisers several decades after independence. Muzanenhamo's observation can be extended to the sphere of education and similar results can be observed. Even after the end of colonialism, Africa still depends on Europe for its educational system, content and model. African countries have been politically independent for many years but they have failed to break the "umbilical cord" in terms of education. While African countries have set up educational structures, the content of the educational curriculum is still Eurocentric at the expense of African epistemological paradigms (Mawere, 2012; Mawere, 2015). Europe continues to set the pace and give the models of education in Africa. Oxford and Cambridge continue to be universities that give guidance to the African education models. As a result, the educational content is modelled in a way that set binaries between the oloniser and the colonised, and along lines which suit the coloniser and not the colonised. The dependency syndrome, viewed in terms of education, is problematic because it perpetuates poverty in African countries.

The colonialist model of education is not only unsuitable for Africa but it is also undesirable. It is unsuitable because it runs opposite to the realities of the African situation of poverty. It is undesirable in the sense that it unjustly ignores and sidelines African knowledge systems that may be better equipped to address the problem of poverty. A situation where one begins at zero grade and proceeds up to university level gives one about eighteen years of schooling without being productive in the area of work or industry. Africa may need to critically evaluate its own situation and find out how it can address poverty using its own educational model that suits its situation.

Bottle-Necking and dual education approach

The bottle-necking approach to education which has been inherited by the postcolonial African governments justifies and maintains a cycle of poverty among Africans since education is made to be a privilege of the rich. For Zvobgo (1981:14), "to limit an influx of African pupils into upper primary and secondary schools, the government introduced a pyramid structure into African education." The pyramid "allowed a large number of pupils to enter primary school and then progressively restricted opportunities as African pupils climbed the educational ladder through secondary school to university" (ibid.). The education pyramid created by colonisers is still prevalent in many African countries today. Bottle neck education system in Zimbabwe which existed between 1960 and 1979 was restrictive in nature to the black Zimbabwean (Matavire *et al*, 2013). The majority of the black people could not afford high fees the system demanded. There were very few government sponsored secondary schools which could not absorb all pupils from primary school. This resulted in many pupils failing to advance to secondary school. Furthermore, streaming according to ability was practiced from Junior Certificate to Ordinary level further reducing the chances of an African child to education. The situation is resurfacing thirty-seven years after independence. Chabaya and Gudhlanga (2013) point out that in the 60s bottle-necking in the colonial period resulted in less than 15% of primary school children proceeding to secondary education and in the 70s the number increased to around 37.5%. The remaining 50% of the pupils are supposed to fund themselves. The Government of Zimbabwe announced free and compulsory education in September 1980 and primary school enrolment soared from 819 568 to 2 251 319 within the first eight years of independence (Mapako and Mareva, 2013). The bottle necking approach comes in a new way in postcolonial African governments. In Zimbabwe, for example, the average pass rate at ordinary level is at 20% and this means that 80% of the school leavers fail to progress forward with education. In higher education and training, governments are reducing funding or they are not funding at all and this results in only the rich people affording tertiary education. The few who progress up to university level in the state run tertiary institutions also face joblessness after graduation. In Zimbabwe, Zambia, Kenya, Malawi and Mozambique, university graduates cannot be easily absorbed into the formal job system (Nyanchoga, 2014). The scenario perpetuates poverty in the affected countries and contradicts Nyerere's idea of a developmental university as he writes:

> The university must put the emphasis of its work...to the nation in which it exists... we in poor societies can only justify expenditure on a University of any type if it promotes real development of our people (Nyerere,1966:2)

In many African countries today, the bottle-necking approach slows down educational progress. The bottle-necking system was created by colonialists who dualised schools into public and private, urban and rural, mission and council, among other divisions. The dichotomisation of educational institutions was done from pre-school up to university level. These dichotomies are not only false but they also lead to parallels where students do not mix. Private schools are run better and they have more facilities than public schools as with the case with private universities which are better than state universities in terms of infrastructure and learning facilities. The subjects offered in the schools are also dualised and sometimes examination systems in the dualised school system are radically different as in the case with local examinations against overseas examinations. Poor schools lack proper facilities such as science laboratories and libraries, not to talk of under-qualified teachers and sometimes under-staffing. Even if these structures may be found, they may still be empty in content. The net result is a general poor performance among the students and this only opens for poverty in their adult lives. Only a small percentage of the bulk of secondary school leavers progress into further education. The mass production at the lower levels of education was designed by colonialists to facilitate stocks of farm workers, garden boys, factory floor workers, miners and related physical labour demands (Bude, 1983). However, postcolonial governments have uncritically adopted the dualised system and this is evident especially when children of cabinet ministers are send abroad for education while the masses crowd in poorly equipped institutions. The poverty conditions of the masses therefore remain unsolved since education fails to emancipate them. The dualised structure perpetuates poverty in the sense that the poor schools are left for poor people who later fail to maximise capabilities in life.

Job seeking mentality and poverty

Mazrui (1978:16) observes:

> Western education in Africa was a process of psychological de-culturalisation. The educated African became... a misfit in his own village... when he graduated... His parents did not expect him to continue living with them tending cattle or cultivating the land.

Two points can be raised from Mazrui's observation: first, colonial education produced a paradox whereby the educated person became alienated from his or her own village thereby distancing himself or herself from the realities of poverty. This situation still exists in many countries today and parents of educated Africans can die under poverty conditions while sons and daughters are in cities and towns. Education should rather help one to transform his or her community and even stay in the village and start developmental projects to alleviate poverty. The second point is that graduates distance themselves from agricultural production and they are not expected to 'tend cattle or cultivate land'. Colonisers ensured that large scale farming was a domain of white settlers and this kept them free from competition from educated indigenous people. The effective tool used was education that shunned farming among Africans. Since agriculture is the backbone of many sub-Saharan African economies, colonial education succeeded in keeping the Africans poor so that the colonisers could gain control of the Africans.

Nyambe (1997: 42) argues that "the present curriculum in African countries is failing to prepare its graduates for the realities of their future." These realities include poverty that is faced by many African countries today. "Much of what is taught at schools is intended to create job seekers who must be inspired to leave behind the rural life in search for the promised "modern" life in towns and cities" (Ibid: 43). This education is not intended to produce job creators but job seekers. As Nyambe (1997: 43) observes further, "throughout their stay in school, learners are consistently promised a modern Western type self-image." This image consists of a managerial top job with a good salary and several benefits, an up-market house, a state of the art car and a typically modern life style that is away from the harsh realities of poverty. Rural life is rendered 'primitive' and 'backward' and it is seen as inconsistent with modernity. Education is measured in terms of Western ideals and progression into European universities becomes the dream of the African student. Paradoxically, scholars from Europe tend to do research in the African rural areas. However, for Nyambe (Ibid), since the majority of people in Africa live in rural areas, such an education becomes largely irrelevant to them because it is designed with the objective of making its recipient workers in 'modern' urban centres and not entrepreneurs in their own communities. Learners should receive education that enables them to transform rural communities. Examples of such graduates are university graduates who formed cultural and community development trusts such as the Basiliswe Trust, Gaza Trust and Ndau Trust in Zimbabwe. Instead of developing rural communities so as to overcome poverty, graduates from African countries' educational institutions tend to crowd in cities looking for jobs. This creates new problems in the cities and these include poverty, unemployment, overcrowding, crime, drug abuse and related problems.

Mutyaba (2016) argues that education should lead to the development of one's potentials to improve oneself in the society. Education should lead to the development of physical, intellectual, moral, social, economic and spiritual dimensions. Indigenous Bemba education in Zambia allowed children at the age of six to name fifty to sixty species of trees (Ibid.). This was because they were in an environment where households' needs were met by tree plant products. Education must therefore have survival value so that it addresses issues of poverty in the context in question. Narrow colonial education prepares the youth to despise manual productive labour in favour of working in industries and capitalistic businesses of foreigners.

Colonially-created education trains students to memorise and pass exams instead of being creative and innovative. University graduates in technology related courses cannot produce anything with their degrees apart from working in industries of foreigners. This means that they have been schooled without being educated. True education should help us to develop our cultures, not to be ashamed of them; it is supposed to develop our intellectual independence. University education is the pinnacle of an education system – the jewel in the crown. It creates innovation, fosters competitiveness and ensures a better quality of life. Its spin offs – both tangible and intangible – have enormous impact on economic growth, health, education, culture, democracy, and civil society, among others. Sustained and vigorous investment in university education will eliminate inequality, reduce poverty and unemployment and transform the nation (Makgoba, 2015:5). The use of Western ideas and methodologies promotes self-destructive system of education that leads to self-alienation and dependence (Matyaba, 2016).

Exclusion of critical thinking and colonial education

Dewey in Fisher (2001:3) defines critical thinking as "an active, persistent and careful consideration of belief or supposed knowledge in the light of grounds that support it and the further conclusions which it tends." Five essential elements can be picked from this definition. Firstly, the word 'active' points to independent, thinking through and interrogating by oneself as opposed to passively getting information from someone else. Secondly, 'persistent' has reference to time in which critical thinking has to be done always. Thirdly, 'careful' implies avoiding jumping hastily into conclusions. Fourthly, 'in the light of grounds' entails taking into consideration evidence. Fifthly, the phrase 'further conclusions' mean taking implications into consideration. Critical thinking entails knowledge of the methods of logical enquiry and reasoning disposition to be thoughtful about problems; drawing valid inferences while avoiding fallacies. Critical thinking is that mode of thinking about any subject, content and problem in which the thinker improves the quality of his or her thinking by taking charge of the structures inherent in thinking and imposing intellectual structures upon them (Paul, 1990: Fisher, 2001).

Critical thinking is a reasoned and logical process of skilfully conceptualising, applying, analysing, synthesising, and/or evaluating information and it is best seen in philosophy. British colonial education deliberately excluded philosophy in the secondary schools of its colonies in order to create passivity in the African minds for the purpose of administrative control. Portuguese and French colonial education introduced philosophy in secondary schools, but critical thinking could not be fully obtained since the content of the philosophical studies was foreign to the students and they were encouraged to narrate and memorise abstract concepts which could hardly relate to their existential situations. Philosophy provides the tools of reasoning and gives foundations of critical thinking that allow students not only to question the underlying causes of African poverty but also to challenge political and economic practices that cause poverty while addressing the historical roots of African poverty. A critical examination of racial and discriminatory policies

265

enables students to challenge prevailing situations and map the way forward. In the postcolonial situation, the study of philosophy involves critical analysis, critical reflection and even self-reflection on current practices that mirror colonial thinking. The study of philosophy is necessary especially for high school students because it enables them to meaningfully engage in debates that are linked to poverty alleviation and eradication. These debates may include employment creation, entrepreneurship, human rights, democracy and good governance. In addition, philosophy exposes students to insights that make them critique their own education system and contribute meaningfully to what constitutes well-rounded education within an African environment.

At a practical level, Mandizvidza (2017) argues that universities lack innovations and creativity especially in their training and this has resulted in half backed graduates who are unsuitable for industry. Mandizvidza (Ibid.) points out that universities and polytechnical colleges produce graduates yearly yet the graduates are unable to make tooth picks and cotton thread. The reference to tooth picks and cotton threads indicates lack of seriousness with postcolonial education. Failure to produce basic things indicates that, in the absence of the colonial master's guidance and control, things are likely to retard in terms of progress. Universities have lagged behind in terms of technological advancements and this creates a situation which results in poverty as the cost of manufacturing keeps commodities prohibitive (Nyamnjoh, 2012; Mandizvidza, 2017). The lack of innovation is also seen in the university curriculum system whereby students are taught old ways of doing things. Universities should be ahead of industry in terms of technology so that it becomes easier for the graduates to utilize their skills. If universities lag behind in technological innovations then poverty conditions cannot be changed because of lack of capacity to improve industrial output and income levels that in turn, improve the Gross Domestic Product (GDP). There must be some mutual link between universities and industry so that technological innovations are used to fight poverty. The high literacy rate in Zimbabwe, for example, fails to translate to anything profitable because the population has been schooled without being educated. The distinction between schooling and education is significant in the context of poverty because one who is schooled may be able to read and write but the educated person, while possessing the reading and writing skills, has the ability to identify and solve problems thereby addressing issues of poverty. The 2017 Global innovation index rated Zimbabwe 121 out of 127 countries and this gives evidence of poor research and innovation.

Colonial Education and Marginalisation of IKS

Colonial education displaced and marginalised African knowledge systems (Cilliers, 1985) and the indigenous African people's view of their culture and education. The colonisers thought that the control of the indigenous people could be effectively achieved by way of systematic denigration and destruction of their culture and imbedded systems of education (Bacchus, 1993). They gave less consideration to the fact that indigenous education existed before their arrival among the indigenous people of Africa (Zulu, 2006). The colonisers based their thinking on the faulty assumption that their epistemological paradigm was superior to that of the Africans (Mawere, 2014). They even doubted whether Africans had an epistemology and let alone an epistemological paradigm. Indigenous people of Africa had their epistemological paradigm displaced by the Eurocentric one (West, 2002). The changes that colonialism brought to the organisation of society affected the appeal of indigenous system of education. The capitalist economy forced the people of Africa to pursue colonial education (Kanyongo, 2005: 65) at the expense of their own system of education. This led to the devaluation of African systems of education though informal in structure and form. The epistemological paradigm that the colonisers imposed on the indigenous people of Africa suited to the colonisers' capitalist economy. In "postcolonial" Africa, efforts to change the curriculum have failed to foster the coexistence of the epistemological paradigm of the indigenous people of Africa and that of the colonisers. The problem with the move to align the proposed curriculum with the demands of the globalisation is that the indigenous people of Africa would retain an education system which is alien to their cultural experiences. This is so because the proposed changes to the colonial education system in order to make it relevant to the realities of the globalisation meant that the new education system would remain fundamentally disconnected from the epistemological paradigm of the indigenous people of Africa. The proposed changes to curriculum were supposed to ensure that the indigenous people of Africa viewed the world from their own perspective (Nkrumah, 1964). Zvobgo (1997: 72) argues that "Zimbabwean education is not education for liberation but for the preservation of the status quo." By extension, this scenario holds in other African states as well. However, policy has not been strictly followed with practice. Shizha (2006: 20) argues that: "in postcolonial states, like Zimbabwe, Zambia, Malawi and Mozambique, the reification of Eurocentric knowledge, which promotes the 'superiority' of Western knowledge, is still perpetuated by the education system and schooling practices that negate ideals on cross-cultural education and the role of indigenous knowledge in students' school experiences." This is a cause for concern in the light of the use of colonial education by the colonisers in order to maintain their unjust control of the indigenous people of Africa.

Jansen (1991: 77) sees two aspects that have affected curriculum change in African countries namely, curriculum continuity and legitimation. For Jansen (1991: 77), curriculum continuity points at "…the relative stability in the colonial curriculum content during the postcolonial period." Continuity is also caused by the need to reduce costs involved in curriculum change and innovation. Lack of political will also causes the maintenance of the status quo thereby perpetuating the conditions of poverty. Despite the presence of policies in most postcolonial African states that seek to radically change the colonial curriculum, "today, in almost every postcolonial nation, there is evidence of greater continuity with the colonial curriculum than the radical change envisaged by official policy" (Jansen, 1991: 77) during liberation struggles for independence in Africa. The epistemological paradigm of the colonisers is still the dominant paradigm that informs the postcolonial curriculum. Jansen (1990: 13) refers to the desire for legitimation as a reason for the curriculum's continued domination by content identifiable with the erstwhile colonisers in postcolonial Africa. The desire is a result of the success of the colonial education system in narrowing the thinking patterns of Africans. The narrowness sees Eurocentric education as the proper and legitimate education while side-lining other forms of education including the African one. This blinds Africans to the realities of poverty within the continent.

Decolonial Thinking in Africa

The process of decolonisation is incomplete until knowledge systems that shape people's identities, linguistic capabilities, and intellectual capital, including their socio-economic progress, have been decolonised (Ngugi, 1996; Maringe: 2017:1). Decolonisation refers to divesting African philosophical thinking of all undue influences emanating from the colonial past (Wiredu, 1998:17). For Wiredu, the key word is "undue" since it may not be rational to reject everything of colonial past. Colonialism is not only a political imposition, but a cultural one as well. Philosophical decolonisation is necessarily a conceptual enterprise; it is not a critique of doctrine but of fundamental conceptualisation. Philosophy becomes a critical examination of the conceptual framework upon which the thought of a culture is erected. From the perspective of decolonisation, Eurocentric epistemology should be critically examined in the context of colonisation because the epistemic images given to Africa by the West were meant to facilitate colonisation not only of the African continent in the sense of physical space but of the African mind as well. Grosfoguel (2011:13) argues that "one of the most powerful myths of the twentieth century was the notion that the elimination of colonial administrators amounted to the decolonisation of the world resulting in the myth of the postcolonial world." The fact of the matter is that the formerly colonised are living under Western European exploitation and domination including epistemological and educational domination. The domination which occupies intellectual space and mindsets is more dangerous compared to economic or political domination because it kills creativity and innovation. The decolonisation critique is significant for this study because it challenges colonial assumptions that have been used to sideline African knowledge systems such as indigenous education. If Africa taps from its own epistemological paradigm, then it may be better positioned to address issues of poverty in the continent.

The epistemic effects of colonisation are the most damaging, far-reaching and least understood (Ngugi, 1996: Alcoff 2007; Mignolo, 2007). The damaging effect is seen in the destruction of mindsets, denial of one's own culture, uncertainties and contradictions that characterise colonised minds. The epistemic effects of colonialism are said to be far-reaching because they displace one's epistemological paradigm to the extent of disregarding one's indigenous forms of knowledge and education. The epistemic effects of colonialism are least understood because of the brain washing victimization created by Eurocentric epistemology among Africans. As a result, individuals may fail to think outside the epistemological images created by colonisers. "The task of decolonisation is to come up with an anti-colonial epistemic resistance" (Alcoff, 2007:80). One way of epistemic resistance is the construction of forms of knowledge based on an African epistemological paradigm in general and the African education system in particular.

Colonialism created and developed a hierarchy of knowledge and of knowers for the purpose of colonising administratively and even epistemically. An alternative to the above imperial epistemology, such as African epistemology, requires the toppling of the cultural hierarchy that colonialism enforced. Mignolo (2008: 98) maintains:

Subaltern reason must aim to rethink and reconceptualise the stories that have been told and the conceptualisation that has been in place to divide the world between Christians and pagans, civilised and barbarians, modern and premodern and developed and undeveloped regions and people.

Mignolo's thinking shows that the conclusions arrived at by colonisers were based on prejudice. By implication, African education systems that have been historically and epistemically trivialised are victims of prejudice. As such, the task of subaltern reason is to deconstruct and reconstruct the proper image of the conquered people and regions. It is interesting to note that generalisations were drawn from mere geographic regions to serious epistemological consequences of the people of the concerned regions. Decolonial thinking should occur simultaneously with reconstruction which I shall elaborate in the section that follows.

Reconstruction in Africa

The reconstructive challenge is to be found in the self-definition, the specification and re-appropriation of an African authenticity and legitimacy in disproving and displacing of the inventive discourse and most importantly in the efforts to reclaim control over African historicity and the interpretation of African history in general and African philosophical history in particular. Reconstruction addresses the question of meaning of Africans through rehabilitating the African mindset while constructing an identity and authenticity thought to be appropriate. While the mainstream characterisation of philosophy may be in Western Europe, rationality is not the birth right of Western Europe, nor of Greece but it is a capacity shown by all humans, their race or ethnicity notwithstanding (Asante, 1998; Mawere and Mubaya, 2016). If rationality is the capacity of all humans, then there is a legitimate ground for the African epistemological paradigm in general and the African education system in particular. There is no Platonic abstract essence in philosophy and there is no single style of philosophising. Any research in African philosophy, in the current study, involves confronting the privileged self-image of the Western model of philosophy. It is this confrontation that problematises and forces its deconstruction in its relation of difference with the European. Outlaw (1991:232) questions Eurocentric thinking in the following manner:

Does it mean that philosophy is left without universality and unity? Yes. Does it mean that philosophy is without universality and unity? Yes, again, but it never had these characteristics in the sense proclaimed by philosophy.

Two points can be drawn from the above examination by Outlaw. First, Western philosophy has given itself 'universality' and unity within a particular culture. This culture proceeds to draw these characteristics and pretends that they are absolute thereby assuming what has to be proved. In other words, it does not necessarily follow that the given cultural portrait is tenable. Second, Outlaw shows that the said characteristics are simply a creation within a historical period and as such they are particular and tentative. They are particular since they arise from within a given historical and cultural setting, contingent because they depend on a possibility and not a necessity and tentative because the said characteristics are debatable even within Western philosophy itself.

Conclusion

This chapter has examined the link between colonialist education and African poverty to argue for an authentic African education system that relates to community needs and works against poverty within the continent. I have argued that the most complex kind of poverty in Africa is the [mental] poverty which has been introduced by colonial education and sustained during postcolonial times. Colonial education is intrinsically linked to a dependency syndrome in which education is designed and controlled from the West to serve the needs of capitalism. The bottle-necking and dualisation of education in African countries has reduced the number of pupils progressing with education and side-lining others to peripheral schools respectively. The job seeking mentality created by colonial education causes the shunning rural communities while privileging Western image jobs in cities and towns. Consequently, rural communities remain in a state of poverty while urban poverty is also seen in the cities and towns due to high populations of school leavers chasing fewer jobs. The exclusion of critical thinking that is linked to the study of philosophy in former British colonies secondary schooling deprives secondary and high school students of the skills of conceptualisation, analysis, synthesis, evaluation, and problem solving that enables them to reflect on what they are learning and solve the problems that confront them. The Eurocentric education fails to link education to the circumstances of Africa and this alienates learners from the poverty conditions of Africa. Alienation also entails that learners are distanced from creativity and innovation required to fight poverty. Basing on my arguments in this chapter, I propose decolonial thinking within the African educational set-up to facilitate education that is linked to the identities, linguistic capabilities and cultural realities of learners. I conclude that reconstruction should be employed to rehabilitate the African way of thinking so as to meaningfully solve the problem of poverty in the continent.

References

Alcoff, L. M. 2007. Mignolo's Epistemology of Coloniality, *The New Centennial Review* 7 (3): 79–101.

Asante, M. K. 1998. *The Afrocentric Idea,* Philadelphia: Temple University Press.

Bacchus, M. K. 1993. Education for Development: A `Critical Approach' to Instruction in Developing Countries. *India International Centre Quarterly* 20 (4): 59-78.

Bude, U. 1983. The Adaptation Concept in British Colonial Education, *Comparative Education* 19 (3): 341-355.

Chabaya, O. and Gudhlanga, E. S. 2013. Striving to Achieve Gender Equality Education: A Zimbabwean Experience, *Zimbabwe Journal of Educational Research*, 25 (1): 123-148.

Cilliers, J. K. 1985. *Counter-insurgency in Rhodesia*, London, Sydney, Dover and New Hampshire: Croom Helm Ltd.

Clinget, R.P. and Foster, P. J. 1964. French and British Education in Africa, *Comparative Education Review* 8 (4): 191-198.

Fisher, A. 2001. *Critical Thinking: An Introduction,* Cambridge: Cambridge University Press.

Fleurbaey, M. 2016. Economics and Economic Justice, *The Stanford Encyclopedia of Philosophy,* Edward N. Zalta (Ed.), URL = <https://plato.stanford.edu/archives/win2016/entries/economic-justice/>.

Freire, P. 2000. *Pedagogy of the Oppressed. Translated by Myra Bergman Ramos. With an Introduction by Donaldo Macedo,* New York and London: The Continuum International Publishing Group Inc. & The Continuum International Publishing Group Ltd.

Godwin, D. (1990). Technical Education in Sub-Saharan African Countries: A Review of Developments and Strategies, The Vocational Aspect of Education, 42:113, 91-99, DOI:

10.1080/10408347308003551.

Grosfoguel, R. (2011). Decolonising Post-Colonial Studies and Paradigms of Political Economy:

Transmodernity, Decolonial Thinking and Global Coloniality, *Transmodernity: Journal of Peripheral Cultural Production of the Luso-Hispanic World* Vol.1, No.1, pp. 1-36.

Jansen, J. (1991). The State and Curriculum in the Transition to Socialism: The

Zimbabwean Experience. *Comparative Education Review*, Vol. 35, No. 1, pp. 76-91.

Kanyongo, G. Y. (2005). Zimbabwe's Public Education System Reforms: Successes and challenges. *International Education Journal*, Vol. 6, No. 1, pp. 65-74.

Ingrid, R. (2016). The Capability Approach, *The Stanford Encyclopedia of Philosophy*, Edward N. Zalta (ed.), URL = <https://plato.stanford.edu/archives/win2016/entries/capability-approach/>.

Makgoba, M.W. (2015). A Country of Crises, Contrasts and Hope, *Chronicle of African Higher Education*, Eighth issue, pp.1-6.

Mangoma, T. (2017). Varsities Blasted for Producing Half-Backed Graduates, in *The Herald*, August 4.

Mapako, F. P. and Mareva, R. (2013). The Concept of Free Primary Education in Zimbabwe: Myth or Reality, *Educational Research International*, Vol.1, No.1, pp. 135-145.

Maringe, F. 2017. "Transforming Knowledge Production in the New African University", In: M. Cross and A. Ndofirepi (Eds). *Knowledge and Change in African Universities*, pp.1-18, Sense Publishers.

Matavire, M., Mpofu, V., and Maveneka, A. 2013. Streaming Practices and Implications in the Educational System: A Survey of Mazowe District, Zimbabwe, *Journal of Social Science and Policy Implications* 1(1): 60-70.

Mawere, M. 2014. "Western hegemony and conquest of Africa: Imperial hypocrisy and the invasion of African cultures," In: *African Cultures, Memory and Space: Living the Past Presence in Zimbabwean Heritage*, (co-edited with Tapuwa R. Mubaya), Bamenda: Langaa RPCIG Publishers.

Mawere, M. 2015. Indigenous knowledge and Public Education in Sub-Saharan Africa, *Africa Spectrum* 50 (2): 57-71

Mawere, M. 2016. (Ed). *Development Perspectives from the South: Troubling the Metrics of [Under-]development in Africa,* Bamenda: Langaa Publishers.

Mawere, M. 2017a. (Ed). *Underdevelopment, Development and the Future of Africa,* Bamenda: Langaa Publishers.

Mawere, M. 2017b. *Theorising Development in Africa: Towards Building an African Framework of Development,* Bamenda: Langaa Publishers.

Mawere, M and Mubaya, T. 2016. African Philosophy and Thought Systems: A Search for a Culture and Philosophy of Belonging, Bamenda, Langaa Publishers.

Mazrui, A. A. 1978. *Political Values and Educated Class in Africa,* Berkeley CA: California University Press.

Mhango, N. 2016. "Troubling the Myth of Africa's [under-]development", In: Mawere, M. (Ed.) *Development Perspectives from the South: Troubling the Metrics of [Under-]development in Africa,* Bamenda: Langaa Publishers.

Mignolo, W. D. 2000. *Local Histories/Global Designs: Coloniality, Subaltern Knowledges, and Border Thinking,* Princeton, NJ: Princeton University Press.

Mignolo, W. D. 2007. Delinking: The Rhetoric of Modernity, the Logic of Coloniality and the Grammar of De-coloniality. *Cultural Studies* 21(2-3): 449-514.

Mutyaba, E. 2016. Africa: Colonial Education System is Killing Africa, *The Observer,* March 4.

Muzanenhamo, E. 2010. Can Africa Exorcise its Dependency Syndrome? *Newsday,* September 7.

Ngugi, W. 1972. *Homecoming: Essays on African and Caribbean Literature, Culture and Politics,* London: Heinemann.

Ngugi, W. 1996. *Decolonising the Mind: The Politics of Language in African Literature,* Oxford: James Currey.

Nhemachena, A. 2016. "(Post-)development and the social production of ignorance: Farming ignorance in 21st century Africa", In: Mawere, M. (Ed), *Development Perspectives from the South: Troubling the Metrics of [Under-]development in Africa,* Bamenda. Langaa Publishers.

Nkrumah, K. (1964). *Consciencism: Philosophy and Ideology for De-colonisation*, London: Kwame Nkrumah and Panaf Books Ltd.

Nyamnjoh, F. (2012). Potted plants in greenhouses: A critical reflection on the resilience of colonial education in Africa. *Journal of Asian and African Studies* 47(2): 129–154.

Nyanchoga, S. A. (2014). Politics of Knowledge Production in Africa: A Critical Reflection on the Idea of an African University in Sustainable Development, *European Law and Politics Journal* 1 (1): 37-55.

Nyerere, J. K. (1966. The University Role in the Development of New Countries J. K. Nyerere, *Freedom and Socialism: A Selection from Writings and Speeches 1965-1967*, Oxford: Oxford University Press.

Obenga, T. 2004. Egypt: Ancient History of African Philosophy, in K. Wiredu (Ed) *A Companion to African Philosophy*, Oxford: Blackwell, pp. 31 – 49 *Oceania* 62, pp. 249-263.

Outlaw, L. 1991. African Philosophy: Deconstructive and Reconstructive Challenges, in H.O. Oruka (Ed.) *Sage Philosophy: Indigenous Thinkers and Modern Debate on African Philosophy*, Leiden: Brill, pp.221-245.

Paul, R. 1990. *Critical Thinking: What Every Person Needs to Survive in a Rapidly Changing World*, Centre for Critical Thinking and Moral Critique, Rohnert Park, California.

Rodney, W. 1972. *How Europe Underdeveloped Africa*, London: Bogle-L'ouverture Publications.

Scott, B. R. 2006. *The Political Economy of Capitalism*, http://hbswk.hbs.edu/item/the-political-economy-of-capitalism

Sen, A. 1999. *Development as Freedom*, New York: Oxford University Press.

Shizha, E. 2006. Legitimizing indigenous knowledge in Zimbabwe: A Theoretical Analysis of Postcolonial School Knowledge and its Colonial Legacy, *Journal of Contemporary Issues in Education* 1 (1): 20-35.

West, M. O. 2002. *The Rise of an African Middle Class: Colonial Zimbabwe, 1898-1965*. Bloomington and Indianapolis: Indiana University Press.

Wiredu, K. 1998. *Conceptual Decolonization in African Philosophy: Four Essays*, Ibadan: Hope Publications.

World Health Organisation, *Management of Substance Abuse*, New York, WHO Publishing.

Zulu, I. M. 2006. Critical Indigenous African Education and Knowledge. *The Journal of Pan African Studies* 1(3): 32-49.

Zvobgo, C. J. M. 1981. African Education in Zimbabwe: The Colonial Inheritance of the New State, 1899-1979. *Issue: A Journal of Opinion* 11 (3/4): 13-26.

Chapter 11

Children, Women, Development and Fundamental Human Rights in Some African Societies

Muhammed A. Yinusa; Joseph A. Oluyemi & Raji Abdullateef

Introduction

The significance of children and women to the development of any society cannot be over emphasized. While children are the future of any nation (Braleendren, 2016), the women folk are also imperative to the development of the society (Verver, 2010). However in Africa, despite the significance of these two key players to the social, economic and political development of the society, the fundamental human rights of the African child and the African woman in some African societies are sometimes abused due to certain societal structure that places the African child and African woman at disadvantaged position (Hutson, 2007 and Young, 2016). Research has also shown that many children in Africa are homeless while many of them die before the age of five to diseases that could have been prevented (United Nations International Children's Emergency Fund, 2014 and World Health Organization, 2015).

According to Gates (2014) and World Food Programme (2016), millions of African children across the continent are impoverished and malnourished and vulnerable to various forms of diseases such as cholera, measles, chicken pox and many lack basic education (United Nations Educational, Scientific and Cultural Organization, 2013) while some are engaged in child labour for economic gain (Harsch, 2001). Further studies has also revealed that the girl child is given out in marriage early in life (Lukale, 2014) thus, exposing them to various forms of maltreatments, abuses, sexually transmitted infections, unwanted pregnancies and other disease such as vesicovaginafistula which may cause morbidity and mortality to them (Mbirimtengerenji, 2007 and WHO, 2013).

The African woman on the other hand, due to the patriarchal family system that is practiced in some Africa societies, which places men above women, play a second fiddle to the African man (Odonkor and Bampoh-Addo, 2014 and Veten, 2016). It is against this backdrop that this chapter explores the fundamental human rights of African children and women as it relates to the development of Africa. The chapter identified the fundamental human rights of the African child and the African woman and what the position is today in some African societies. This chapter also looked at the predicaments facing the African child and the African woman today as it affects the development of Africa as a continent. The chapter employed the Will Theory of Rights and the Radical Feminist Theory to explain the predicament facing the African child and the African woman in relation to the development of Africa.

Fundamental Human Rights of the African Child

Children like other humans have fundamental human rights which are exclusive to them in the course of interacting in the society. According to the (African Charter on the Rights and Welfare of the Child, 1990), the following are some of the fundamental rights of a child:

1. Every child has the right to life.
2. Every child has the right to education.
3. Right to good healthcare.
4. Right to Food
5. Right to Water
6. Right to Freedom
7. Right to identity.
8. Right to be protected from all forms of economic exploitation, torture or inhuman treatment.

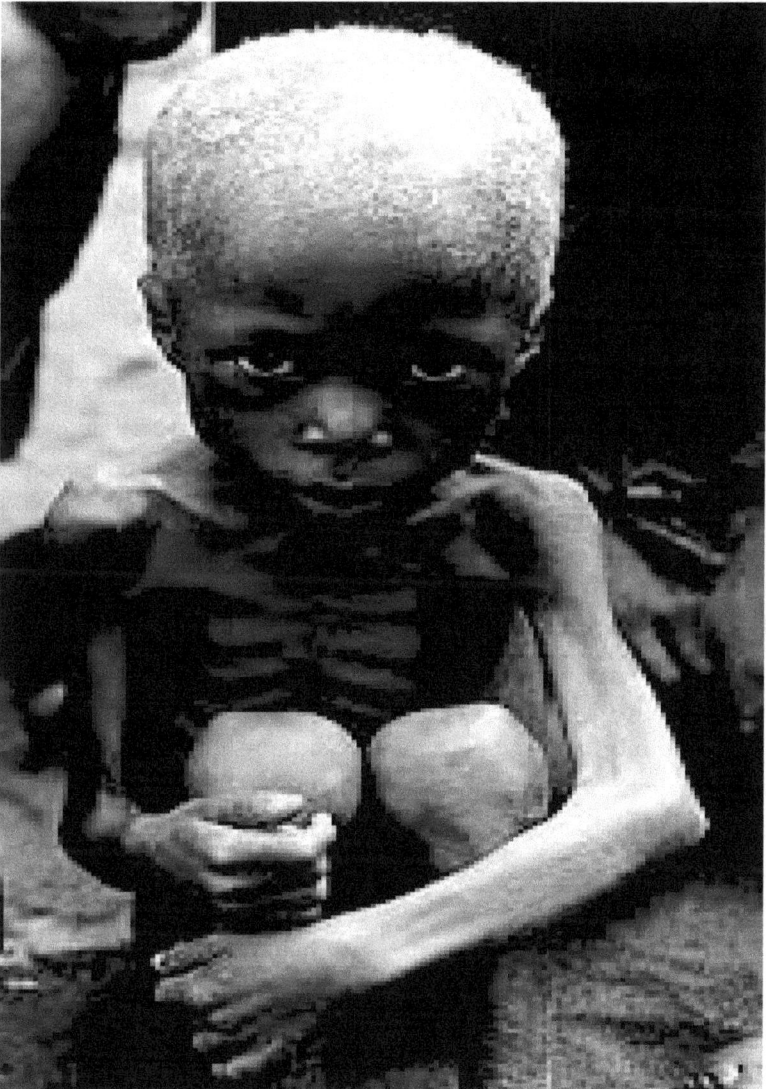

Figure 1: *Picture showing an African Child denied Right to Food*
Source: http://comfortablyunaware.com/blog/the-world-hunger-food-choice-connection-a-summary/

The Will Theory of Rights

The will theory of rights also referred to as the capacity for reasoned decision making is a core concept in modern children's rights theory. The theory proposed that, because children do not have the capacity to reason in decision-making, therefore children could not be accorded any rights. This viewpoint is still found in modern children's rights theory. This forms the basis of this theory (Fortin Children's' Right, 1994) in which the society refuses to award rights to children merely because they do not have the capacity for reasoned decision-making. The theory therefore assumes that if children do not have the competence to make choices and claim rights, it follows that children cannot be said to have rights (Hobbes, 1651).

The theory explains why the rights of the African child are abused and the root cause of the predicament children face in Africa today. It is assumed that, since children cannot make decision on what to do and what become of them, due to their age, possibilities is that, the society does not accord them any right and they are not expected to bear any.

Predicaments of the African Child and implications on the Development of the African Society

Child Mortality

Child mortality refers to death of infants and children under the age of five or between the ages of one month to four years. Research conducted globally in 2013 showed that 3.7 million children aged one month to 4 years died within the year and about half of the deaths occurred in Sub-Saharan Africa (Global Burden of Disease Study, 2014). It was also recorded that, Sub-Saharan Africa has the highest risk of death in the first month of life accounting for 38 per cent of global neonatal deaths (African Leadership for Child Survival, 2012). The World Health Organization (2016) have noted that the risk of a child dying before completing five years of age is still highest the Africa region. This is attributed to diseases such as pneumonia, malaria, malnutrition, diarrhoea and preterm birth conditions (UNICEF, 2014).

Illiteracy

The importance of education to the development of a society cannot be overemphasised. Despite the fact that, Sub-Saharan African countries have recorded some of the biggest increase in primary school enrolment in recent time, the region still has the unenviable distinction of being home to the world's largest out-of-school population (Sulyman, 2015). Statistics has shown that in 2011 alone, 29.8 million children living in Sub-Saharan Africa were out of school accounting for half of the total number of 57 million children who were out of school in the same year globally (UNESCO, 2013). The report also has it that, 22 per cent of African children never attended primary school or have left school without completing primary education. Further research conducted by (UNESCO, 2000) has also found a disparity in access to education between the girl-child and the boy-child in Africa. For example, in some countries in West Africa, there is more enrolment of boys while the girls stay at home while there are also more of girls' enrolment than that of boys while in some other areas where boys have to stay at home and tend to the family farm or engage in some form of trade (UNESCO, 2000).

Poor Access to Healthcare Services

Although health care is a fundamental right of a child (Shah, 2011) research has shown that millions of African children do not have access to healthcare services (WHO, 2015). Despite the 2001 African Union (AU) meeting agreement by African countries to allocate 15% of their budget to healthcare, only five countries in Africa have met this commitment as at 2010 (African Health Monitor, 2013). It is estimated that about three million children die each year in the African region from preventable diseases like measles, polio, whooping cough, tetanus, diphtheria, meningitis, yellow fever hepatitis B, tuberculosis, pneumonia, diarrhoea and cervical cancer (WHO, 2015). For example, measles is estimated to have caused 145,700 deaths globally in 2013, of which it is estimated that 38,000 of this deaths were in the countries within the African region. Furthermore, NBC News (2016) has also contended that, in Sub-Saharan Africa four out of five mothers are likely to lose a child in their life time as a result of one disease or another. When the life of a child is cut short due to poor health facilities, there is no way that child can fulfil the future of his/her dream and as such potentials that are meant to develop the society are abruptly hampered.

Starvation

Adequate amount of nutritious food is necessary for everyone especially children as they grow up. A child that cannot feed well will not likely be able to harness his/her potentials because of poor energy to do that which is provided by food and as such may lack what it takes to develop the society in future. In Africa, hunger is a constant and chronic pain facing many African children (Save a Child, 2016). Research has shown that, poor nutrition causes nearly half of the deaths of children yearly and Africa is the region with the highest prevalence of hunger globally where one person in four is malnourished (World Food Programme, 2016). According to Gates (2014), forty per cent of all children in sub-Saharan Africa are stunted because of starvation and poor nutrition. Under-nutrition magnifies the effect of every disease, including measles and malaria. The estimated proportions of deaths in which under-nutrition is an underlying cause are roughly similar for diarrhoea (61%), malaria (57%), pneumonia (52%), and measles (45%) Malnutrition can also be caused by diseases, such as the diseases that cause diarrhoea, by reducing the body's ability to convert food into usable nutrients (Hunger Notes, 2015).

Child Labour

The term child labour refers to the engaging of children in any work that deprives them of their childhood, interferes with their ability to attend regular school, and that is mentally, physically, socially or morally dangerous and harmful to them (International Labour Oganization,2012). According to the International Labour Organization (2012), millions of children in Africa are engaged in child labour and other forms of economic exploitation as 41 per cent of children in the continent engage in one work or the other. Although, Asia and the Pacific continents have the highest number of child population almost about 78 million or 9.3 of child population, Sub-Saharan Africa continues to maintain the region with the highest number of children involved in child labour accounting for 59million children or 21% of the population (ILO, 2013). A 2014 report by the U.S. Department of Labour has declared that one out of five Sub-Saharan children is working under difficult if not squalid conditions (Young, 2016). This trend has however been blamed on the high level of poverty in the continent as Africa represents the poorest continent in the world with the weakest school system (Harsch, 2001).This serves as an impediment to the development of Africa because when children engage in child labour, they may not be able to acquire the necessary skills and education needed for the development of the society in future.

Sexual Abuse

Research has shown that globally, 40-47 per cent of sexual assaults are perpetrated against girls aged 15 or younger (Heise, 1993). Studies conducted in South Africa suggest that young girls who had early sexual experiences in South Africa were actually coerced (Wood and Jewkes, 1997). In a study conducted in a South African hospital of children under the age of 15 in whom a diagnosis of child abuse was considered, revealed that, 45 per cent of the children were target of sexual abuse (Argent, Bass and Lachman, 1995). Findings from a similarly study carried out in Uganda also revealed that 49 per cent of sexually active primary school girls had been forced to have sexual intercourse (Noble, Cover and Yanagishita, 1996).

In Addis-Ababa, Ethiopia, an estimated 30 per cent (about 30,000) of prostitutes are women ranging from 12-26 years of age (Bohmer, 1995). Young women are vulnerable to coercion into sexual relationships with older men especially by their parents and wards. "Sugar daddies" take advantage of girls' lack of economic resources by promising to help with their expenses in exchange for sex (Moore and Rogow, 1994 and Selix, 1996). In some parts of Ghana, 70 per cent of mothers interviewed said they had encouraged young girls into premarital sexual relationships while many older women felt that receiving gifts in exchange for sex was not regarded as prostitution but evidence of a man's love (Ankoma, 1996). In all, sexual exploitation of young people may are said to be as a result of their lack of economic power and job opportunities. These may however lead to unintended pregnancies, sexually transmitted infections and assaults which may cause morbidity or death to them thereby limiting their potentials to the development of the African society.

Sale of Children, Child Trafficking and Abduction

Findings from a study conducted in some parts of Africa have revealed that, children are sold in exchange for money (Elbagir, 2015). This can be described as slavery and an impediment to the development of African society. In Benin Republic for example, children are taken to Nigeria and some other parts of West Africa where they are employed in houses as house helps (BBC NEWS, 1999 and Sheil, 2016). It has been found that Gabon is primarily a destination and transit country for children and women, who are subjected to forced labour and sex trafficking while boys are forced to work as street hawkers or mechanics (United States Department of Human Trafficking, 2011).

According to the (Human Rights Watch, 2003), in June 2002, an estimated 5,000 children were abducted by the rebel Lord's Resistance Army (LRA) in Uganda, and were subjected to brutal treatment as soldiers as labourers and sexual slaves. Also, in April 2014, over 200 secondary school girls were abducted in Chibok town North East Nigeria by Boko-Haram, a Jihadist group (Melvin, 2015). Furthermore, in the year 2015, 89 children were also abducted by the Shilluk Militia group and forced to become child soldiers who violates their fundamental right (BBC NEWS, 2015). These acts therefore deprive the African child from his/her fundamental human rights and as such limits their potentials and value they are expected to contribute to the development of the society.

Violence, Torture and Displacement

Violence against the child is the intentional use of physical force or power, threatened or actual, against a child, by an individual or group that either results in or has a high likelihood of resulting in actual or potential harm to the child's health, survival, development or dignity (WHO, 2002). Violence against the African child has been recorded in many parts of Africa and has stood as an impediment to the development of the African society. For example, in the year 2013, a large number of children were killed and maimed in Bangul (UNESCO, 2013). In Kenya also, child abuse had reached unacceptable levels, with sexual abuse being "especially shocking", street children are vulnerable to harassment and physical and sexual abuse; they are seen as offenders, criminalised, and are frequently arbitrarily arrested, beaten and ill-treated by police officers (IRIN News, 2006).

In addition to this, millions of children in Africa has been displaced from their parents due to war and civil unrest that take place in some parts of the continent (UNICEF, 2014).This is against the fundamental right of African children who are meant to be protected from violence, torture and displacement and as such, serves as an impediment to the development of Africa as a society.

Harmful Cultural Practices

The African society is characterised by a number of cultural practices. These cultural practices reflect norms of care and behaviour based on age, life stage, gender, and social class. While many traditions promote social cohesion and unity, others wear down the physical and psychological health and integrity of individuals, especially women and girls. For instance, female genital mutilation (FGM) early/child marriage and son preference are some of these cultural practices are harmful practices that may impede the development of African as a continent (Lukale, 2014). It has been noted that, despite international agreements and national laws, girl-child marriage is common in Africa as African countries account for 15 of the 20 countries with the highest rates of child marriage (UNICEF, 2014). Child marriage is a human rights violation that prevents girls from obtaining an education, enjoying optimal health, bonding with others their own age, maturing, and ultimately choosing their own life partners. Child marriage is said to be driven by poverty and has many effects on girls' health: increased risk for sexually transmitted diseases, cervical cancer, malaria, death during childbirth, and obstetric fistulas. Girls' offspring are at increased risk for premature birth and death as neonates, infants, or children (Nawal, 2006).

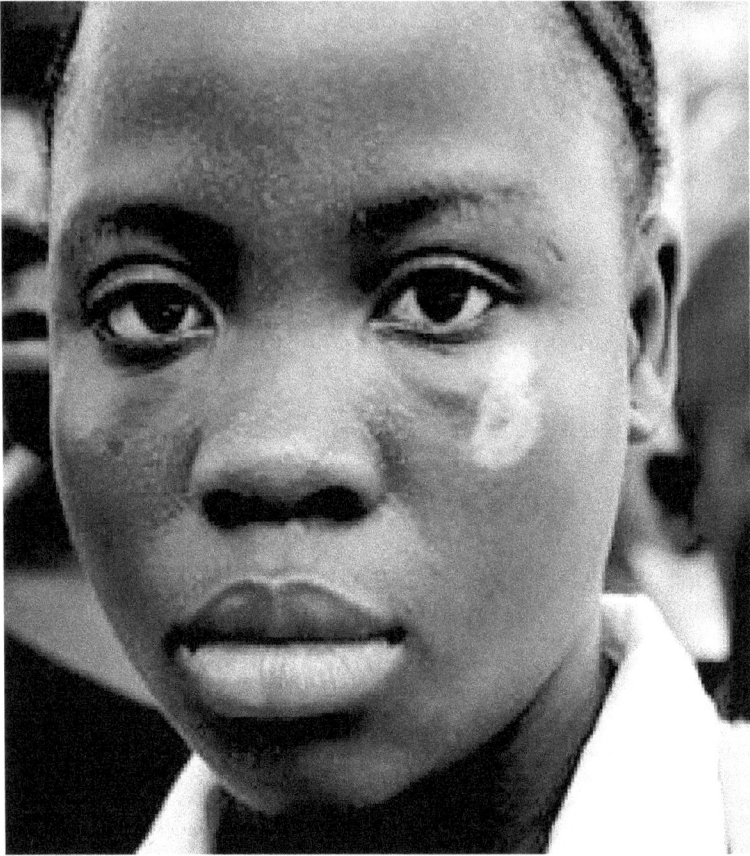

Figure 2: *Picture showing an African woman who has been violated*
Source:https://www.pinterest.com/pin/311663236682447084/

Fundamental Human Rights of the African Woman

According to the Maputo Protocol (2003) the following are some of the fundamental human rights of women in Africa:

1. Equality and Elimination of Discrimination
2. Elimination of Violence against Women
3. Right to Marriage
4. Right to Justice
5. Right to Inheritance of Property
6. Widow's Right
7. Economic and Social Welfare Rights
8. Health and Reproductive Rights

The Radical Feminism Theory

The radical feminism theory blames the exploitation of women by men. According to the theory, men are the primary beneficiary of the subordination of women. Women are seen as an oppressed group who had to struggle for their own liberation against their own oppressors (Bryson, 1999). Abbortt, Wallace and Tyler (2005), contend further that the focus of radical Feminism is with women's right and not gender inequality. The radical feminist theory does not seek to minimise the differences between men and women, but instead assumes that there is a female or feminine nature that has been concealed and/or distorted throughout history and needs to be liberated and re-valued. According to the theory, society is patriarchal that is dominated and ruled by men where men are the ruling class and women are the subject class.

This theory serves as a platform in which the chapter can be explained. The African society is majorly patriarchal in which male dominance is prevalent while women are subjected to men. This will in no way hinder the development of the African society as women's full potentials will not fully utilise. The radical feminist theory has been criticised for focusing only on the negative experiences of relationships with men and ignoring positive experiences like happy marriages as well as exploitation of men by women.

Predicaments of the African Woman and Implications on the Development of the African Society

Gender Inequality

Gender equality is a fundamental development objective, and is essential to enabling women and men to participate equally in society and in the economy. Unfortunately, African women continue to face some grim facts which have been a problem to the development of African society. Reports have it that, women often have little influence over resources and norms, restricting what jobs and crops are considered appropriate for women and thus limiting their earning potential in agriculture, enterprise or the labour market (World Bank, 2014). The report also has it that, women's voices remain limited; there is poor access by women to legal rights, sexual and reproductive health services and movement which are perpetuated by tradition that has been in existence from generations (World Bank, 2014). Although, African women make a sizeable contribution to the continent's economy, they are more economically active as farmers growing most of the Africa's food and own one-third of all businesses in the continent as they are held back from fulfilling their potentials by spending much of their time at less productive activities like fetching water and fire wood (African Development Bank, 2016). This report also have it that women work 50% longer hours than men but the pay gap between men and women is very wide.

Gender Oppression

Discrimination and oppression of women are common in some African societies (Hutson, 2007). In the past, women actually had status and authority because they were the main agricultural producers but because of the less significant attention given to farming in some African societies today, women seem to have lost their status and authority (Baden, Shireen and Sheila, 1993). Traditional African culture had clearly stipulated the different roles of men and women in society in which men are favoured (Bwakali, 2001). For instance, polygamy is still a common practice in some societies in Africa and because of the rules of polygamy in which men marry more than one wife if one woman cannot have a child, her husband will marry another woman for the sake of carrying on the family lines (Gaba, 1997).

Women were victims of injustice not because of what society did to them, but because of what society did not do to them (Bwakali, 2001). In some countries in Africa, when a man dies his siblings (brothers in patrilineal societies or sisters in matrilineal societies) may claim his remaining property in the name of their corporate lineage rights (Rose, 2006; Human Right Watch, 2003; Drimie 2003; Izumi, 2006a and 2006b). The fate of African widows ranges from disinheritance and forceful deprivation of property to the mandatory observance of harmful rituals. One of these traditional rituals is widow inheritance, a practice whereby the widow agrees to marry her husband's younger brother to continue as a member of the family. In case of refusal, she is expelled and left to care for her children alone (Luke, 1989 and Von-Struensee, 2005). Therefore, there is need for African societies to reduce to the barest minimum oppression on women if the continent must develop because of the pivotal role women play in the development of a society.

Violence against Women

In some African societies, violence against women in Africa is still largely rampant, but hidden beneath cultural practices and beliefs (Dlamini, 2014). Several cases of inhuman and maltreatment against women has been recorded. For instance, cases of men beating their wives were found in some parts of Africa such as in Nigeria and Tanzania (Lafrannaire, 2005 and Yusuf, 2012; Kimani, 2012; Okoth and Adima, 2014). Sexual violence which is one of the most horrific weapons of war, and an instrument of terror was also found to be used against women in some locations in Africa (Storr, 2011). For instance, reports have it that, more than 25 per cent of South African men have raped; of those, nearly half said they had raped more than one person (IRIN, 2009). A report from (BBC, 2003) also showed that, a woman in South Africa has greater chance of being raped than she does of learning how to read.

According to (UNOCHA 2007), seventy per cent of women in Niger Republic have been beaten or raped by their husband; father or brother. The level of sexual violence encountered by African women seems to be relatively unprecedented in modernity. In Sierra Leone for instance, it is estimated that more than 72 per cent of women and girls were victims of wartime violence, 50 per cent of that sexual in nature (Nowrojee, 2005).

Maternal Mortality

Maternal death is defined by the World Health Organization (WHO) as the death of a woman while pregnant or within 42 days of termination of pregnancy, irrespective of the duration and site of the pregnancy, from any cause related to or aggravated by the pregnancy or its management but not from accidental or incidental causes (WHO, 2016). Having a baby should be a time of great joy, hope and fulfilment. But every year across the world 287,000 women die in pregnancy and childbirth in which a chunk of this come from Africa (Maternity Worldwide, 2015). According to UNICEF in sub-Saharan Africa, for example, a woman has a 1 in 13 chance of dying in childbirth (UNICEF, 2003). The most common causes of these deaths are postpartum bleeding (15%), complications from unsafe abortion (15%), hypertensive disorders of pregnancy (10%), postpartum infections (8%), and obstructed labour (6%) (GBD, 2013; Mortality and Causes of Death Collaborators, 2014). The maternal mortality ratio in Sub-Saharan Africa (that is the number of women dying per 100,000 live births) is 500 per 100,000 live births while the lifetime risk of dying in childbirth risk rises to 1 in 39 compared with a risk of just 1 in 4600 for mothers living in the UK (Maternity Worldwide, 2015).

Stereotype, Discrimination, Stigmatization and Labelling

Africa has a long standing tradition of incredibly unequal power between men and women which is detrimental to the development of African society (Rainbo Organization, 2009). Though women's rights are improving in a number of countries with many involved in, in some others women are still not well represented when it comes to contributing to social and economic life (UN WOMEN, 2012). In addition, many women across Africa are also stigmatised and labelled, for issues in the society when they may not actually be the cause of such issues. For instance, African women are associated with certain illness and diseases such as HIV/AIDs and are blamed for their ordeal while the men are seen as innocent (Aylsl, 2007). According to Appiah-Donyina (2002) gender stereotypes allow women to be blamed for spreading HIV/AIDS. This is because often women are the first to be tested because of pregnancy and when they are found positive, they are the first to be blamed. Furthermore, women are blamed and labelled for infertility in marriage when the cause of the infertility may sometimes not be from them (Tabong and Adongo, 2013). In some African society also, women are blamed for giving birth to female children when it may not actually be their own fault.

Widow Inheritance

Widow inheritance is a cultural and social practice whereby a widow is required to marry a male relative of her late husband, often his brother. The practice was meant as a means for the widow to have someone to support her and her children financially, and to keep her late husband's wealth within the family bloodline. At the time it was initiated, women were responsible for the house chores and men were the providers, therefore if the woman lost her husband, she would have no one to provide for the remaining family. Because her in-laws would not want someone outside of the family's blood line to inherit her late husband's estate, she was required to marry within the family. This custom is sometimes justified on the basis that it ensures that the wealth does not leave the patrilineal family. It is also sometimes justified as a protection for the widow and her children. Among the Yoruba's in Nigeria for instance, it is a well settled rule of native law and custom of the wife could not inherit her husband's property since she herself is, like a chattel, to be inherited by a relative of her husband (Nwaebuni, 2013). In many other parts of the country, several cases have been recorded of the ordeals that women face in Nigeria after the death of their husband, as some of women are made to go through certain rituals against their wish, some are Isolated for some time and even have their hair shaved (Okorafor, 2011 and Ekunkunbor, Nkwopara, Ogwuda, Balogun, Amagiya, Adeyeri, Eze, Umoru and Duru, 2014).

Problem of decision making on Reproductive Health

Research suggests that gender, sexual orientation, and exposure to discrimination inform people's sexual health behaviours and decision making (World Health Organization, 2015). Women's reproductive health decision-making and choices, including engaging in sexual intercourse and condom use, are essential for good reproductive health. However, issues concerning sexual intercourse and condom use are shrouded in secrecy in many parts of African countries (Darteh, Doku and Esia-Donkoh, 2014). Over the years, the debate and research on women's decision making in general and in sexual and reproductive health in particular have largely been genderised within power relations with men playing influential roles in women's decision making thereby perceiving, women as less 'empowered' to take their own decision as a right (Hunjan, 2011).

Sexual and reproductive decision-making has however emerged as an important health indicator as husbands dominate in family reproductive health issues and continue to be the greatest source of sexually transmitted infections including HIV to their wives. (Osuafor, 2014). In a study conducted in Ghana by (Darteh, Doku and Esia- Donkoh, 2014), it was discovered that, women could not refuse their partners' request for sexual intercourse or demand the use of condoms by their partners. This is a gross abuse of the fundamental right of the African woman whose choice and decision is expected to count in the issue of sexual relation with men.

Conclusion

This chapter has been able to explore the African child and the African woman and their fundamental rights in the society as well as the predicaments facing the African child in relation to the development of Africa. Some of the fundamental rights of the child as highlighted in the chapter include: right to life, right to education, right to good healthcare, right to food and water, right to freedom, right to identity and right to be protected from all forms of economic exploitation, torture or inhuman treatment. The fundamental rights of the African woman as highlighted in the chapter include: Equality and elimination of discrimination, elimination of violence against women, marriage, access to justice, education, inheritance, widow's right, economic and social welfare rights, health and reproductive rights.

The predicaments facing the African child that were also noted in the chapter include: child mortality, illiteracy, poor access to healthcare services, starvation, exploitation, sexual abuse, sale of children, child trafficking and abduction, violence, torture and displacement as well as harmful cultural practices. Furthermore, the chapter explored the predicament of the African women, some of the predicaments mentioned in the chapter include, gender inequality, gender oppression, violence, maternal mortality, stereotyping, discrimination, stigmatization and labelling and the problem of decision making on reproductive health. The chapter concludes that without a remarkable respect for the fundamental rights of the child and the woman in Africa, a quantum leap towards the development of Africa as a continent will be a mirage. Although significant changes have been recorded in some African societies towards the emancipation of women in Africa as well as that of African children especially when compared to what was obtainable in the past, much still needs to be done to ensure that fundamental human rights of the African child and African woman are fully implemented so that their potentials can be fully realised towards the development of Africa as a continent. There is also the need for some African societies to take a cue from other developed societies by eliminating these barbaric acts against the African child and African woman in order to make Africa a more civilised and developed society.

References

Abbortt, P., Wallace, C., and Tyler, M. 2005. An Introduction to Sociology: Feminist Perspectives, 3rd Edition. Rout ledge, Abington.

Achayra, S. and Murdock, DM (October 18, 2009). *Churches in Africa involved in child torture, murder.* Available online at: http://freethoughtnation.com/churches-in-africa-involved-in-child-torture-murder/. Accessed 11 December 2016.

African charter on the rights and welfare of the child (1990). http://www.achpr.org/files/instruments/child/achpr_instr_ch arterchild_eng.pdf. Accessed 7 December 2016.

African Development Bank (2016). *Gender Equality Index.* Available online at: http://www.afdb.org/en/topics-and-sectors/topics/quality-assurance-results/gender-equality-index/. Accessed 12 December, 2016.

African Health Monitor (March, 2013). The State of Health Financing in the African Region. Available online at: http://www.aho.afro.who.int/en/ahm/issue/16/reports/states

- heath-financing-African -region. Accessed 9th December, 2016.

African Leadership for Child Survival (2012). *Africa Key Facts and Figures for Child Mortality* Available online at: https://www.usaid.gov/sites/default/files/documents/1860/Africa%20Key%20 Facts% and%20Figures.pdf. Accessed 8 December, 2016.

African Studies Centre (September 15, 2008). *Children in Africa.* Available online at: http://www.ascleiden.nl/content/webdossiers/children-africa#Children and Society. Accessed 24 November 2016.

Ahearn, D., Holzer, B. and Andrews, L. 200). *Children's Rights Law: A Career Guide*, Harvard Law School.

Amnesty International (February 23, 2008). *Children's' Right.* Available at: https://en.wikipedia.org/wiki/Children%27s_rights#cite_note-Children.27s_Rights-1. Accessed on 24 November, 2016.

Ankomah A. 1996. Premarital relationships and livelihoods in Ghana, *Focus Gender* 4 (3): 39-47.

Argent, A. C., Bass, D. H. Lachman, P. I. 1995. Child abuse services at a children's hospital in Cape Town, South Africa, *Child Abuse and Neglect* 19:1313-1321.

Aylsl (April 20, 2007). *HIV-infected women blamed and shunned. Available at: http://www.irinnews.org/feature/2007/04/20/hiv-infected-women-blamed-and-shunned.* Accessed 15 December 2016.

BBCNEWS (August 6, 1999). *West Africa's child Slave Trade:* Available online at: http://news.bbc.co.uk/2/hi/world/africa/412628.stm. Accessed 10 December, 2016.

BBCNEWS (March 1, 2015). *Many South Sudan boys 'kidnapped to be child soldiers.* Available online at: http://www.bbc.com/news/world-africa-31681302. Accessed 11 December, 2016.

Baden, S., Shireen, H., and Sheila, M (April 23, 2007). *Country Gender Profile: South Africa.* Available online at: Women's Net. http://womensnet.org.za/links/genderpr.htm.

Bandman, B. 1999. *Children's Right to Freedom, Care, and Enlightenment.* Routledge. p 67.

Bwakali, D. J. 2001. Gender Inequality in Africa *Contemporary Review* 279.1630. 270-272.

Bohmer L. 1995. *Adolescent Reproductive Health in Ethiopia: an Investigation of Needs, Current Policies and Programs.* Los Angeles, CA: Pacific Institute of Women's Health.

Braleendren, N. 2016. *Children are the future pillars of our nation – It's our responsibility to protect them.* Available at: http://www.news.lk/fetures/item/7661-children-are-the-future-pillars-of-our-nation-it-s-our-responsibility-to-protect-them. Accessed 15 December 2016.

Bryson, V. 1999. *Feminist Political Theory: An Introduction,* Macmillan. London.

Calkins, C. F. 1972. Reviewed Work: Children's Rights: Toward the Liberation of the Child by Paul Adams, *Peabody Journal of Education 49* (4). p. 327

Child Right International Network (April 9, 2009). *A-Z of Child's Right.* Available online at: https://www.crin.org/en/library/publications/z-child-rights. Accessed 25 November 2016.

Committee on Social Affairs, Health and Sustainable Development (6 September, 2013), *Children's Right to Physical Integrity.* Parliamentary Assembly of the Council of Europe.

Committee on Bioethics. 1997. Religious objections to medical care, *Pediatrics* 99: 279.

Convention on the Rights of the Child (1989). Children's Right. Available on line at: dia.org/wiki/Children%27s_rights#cite_note-CRC-2. Accessed 24 November, 2016.

Darteh, E.K.M., Doku, D.T., and Esia- Donkoh K (2014). Reproductive health decision making among Ghanaian women. *Reproductive Health.* Available online at: https://reproductive-health-journal.biomedcentral.com/articles/10.1186/1742-4755-11-23. Accessed 15 December 2016.

Declaration of the Right of the Child (1959). Children's Right. Available online at:

https://en.wikipedia.org/wiki/Children%27s_rights#cite_note-CRC-2. Accessed 25 November, 2016.

Dlamini, N (September 2, 201). *Women and Girls Summit tackles issues affecting African women.* Available at: https://www.brandsouthafrica.com/investments-immigration/africanews/women-and-girls-summit-tackles-issues-affecting-african-   women. Accessed 8 December 2016.

Drimie, S. 2003. HIV/Aids and Land: Case Studies from Kenya, Lesotho and South Africa, *Development Southern Africa* 20 (5): 647-658. Available at: http://www.informaworld.com/smpp/content~content=a713 618534~db=all. Accessed 13   December 2016.

Eboh, L. O., and Boye, T. E. (2005). Widowhood in African Society and its effects on Women's *Health. African Health Sciences,* 5(4), 348.

Ekunkunbor, J., Nkwopara, C., Ogwuda, A., Balogun, I., Amagiya, F., Adeyeri, A., Eze, E.,   Umoru, H., and Duru, P (2014*). Agonies of widows hit by harsh Nigerian traditions.* Available on Vanguard at: http://www.vanguardngr.com/2014/07/agonies-widows-hit-harsh-Nigerian-traditions/. Accessed 15 December 2016.

Elbagir, N. (April 3, 2015). *Children for sale heartbreakingly easy to find in ravaged Nigeria.* Available online at: http://edition.cnn.com/2015/03/23/africa/nigeria-children-for-sale/.   Accessed on 10 December, 2016.

Franklin, B. 2001. *The new handbook of children's rights: comparative policy and practice,* Routledge, London.

Gaba, L. 1997. The History of Women and Gender in Africa as a Whole. *The World History   Archive.* Available online at: http://www.hartfordhwp.com/archives/30/index-db.html. Accessed 13 December 2016.

Gates, B. (August 1, 2014). *Why Does Hunger Still Exist in Africa?* Available in gates notes at: https://www.gatesnotes.com/Development/Why-Does-Hunger-Still-Exist-Africas-Table- Day-One. Accessed on 9 December, 2016.

Global Burden of Disease Study (17 December, 2014). *Mortality and Causes of Death, Collaborators.* Available online at: http://enwikipedia.org/wiki/Child_mortality#cite_note-G. Accessed on 8 December, 2016.

GBD 2013 Mortality and Causes of Death, Collaborators (December 17, 2014). Global, regional, and national age-sex specific all-cause and cause-specific mortality for 240 causes of death, 1990-2013: a systematic analysis for the Global Burden of Disease Study 2013. *Lancet.* 385: 117–71.

Harsch (2001). *Child Labour is Rooted in Africa's Poverty: Campaign launched against Traffickers and Abusive Work.* Available online at: http://www.un.org/en/africarenewal/vol15no3/153chil4.htm. Accessed on 9 December, 2016.

Heise, L. 1993. *Violence against women: the missing agenda.* In: Koblinsky, M., Timyan, J., & Gay, J. (Ed). *The Health of Women: A Global Perspective,* Boulder, CO: Westview Press.

Hobbes, T. 1651. *Leviathan by De Villiers* 1993 Stell LR 291; Federle1993 Depaul LR 987-990; Worsfold 1974 Harvard ER 144.380.

Human Rights Watch. 2003. Double Standards: Women's Property Rights Violations in Kenya, New York: Human Rights Watch. Available at: http://www.hrw.org. Accessed 13 December 2016.

Human Right Watch (March 28, 2003). *Uganda: Child Abductions Skyrocket in North,* Available online at: https://www.hrw.org/news/2003/03/28/uganda-child-abductions-skyrocket-north. Accessed on 11 December, 2016.

Hunger Notes (July 2015). *World child hunger facts.* Available at: http://www.worldhunger.org/world-child-hunger-facts/. http://comfortablyunaware.com/blog/the-world-hunger-food-choice-connection-a-summary/. https://www.pinterest.com/pin/311663236682447084/077278 6953

Hunjan R, Petit, J. (2011). *A practical guide for facilitating social change. Power.* UK: Carnegie United Kingdom Trust. Available online at: https://reproductive-health-journal.biomedcentral.com/articles/10.1186/1742-4755-11-23. Accessed 15 December 2016.

Hutson, S. (2007). Gender Oppression and Discrimination in South Africa, *ESSAI*: Vol. 5, Article 26.Available at: http://dc.cod.edu/essai/vol5/iss1/26. Accessed 13 February 2016.

International Conference on Fighting Corruption and Good Governance (September, 2009). *Corruption in public education.* Available online at: http://www.oecd.org/countries/kazakhstan/43749050.pdf. Accessed 14 December 2016.

International Covenant on Civil and Political Rights (16 December 1966). *Children's Right.* Available online at: https://en.wikipedia.org/wiki/Children%27s_rights#cite_note-17.Accessed 12 December 2016

International Labour Organization (2012). *What is Child Labour,* Available online from: http://www.ilo.org/ipec/facts/lang--en/index.htm. Accessed March 21, 2017.

International Labour Organization. 2012. *Child labour in Africa.* Available online at: http://www.ilo.org/wcmsp5/groups/public/---ed_norm/---declaration/documents/publication/wcms_decl_fs_37_en.pdf. Accessed 9 December, 2016.

International Labour Organization. 2013. *Marking progress against child labour - Global estimates and trends 2000-2012.* Available online at: http://www.ilo.org/global/topics/child-labour/lang--en/index.htm. Accessed 9 December, 2016.

IRIN News (June 18, 2009).Available online at: *One in four men rape.* http://www.irinnews.org/report/84909/south-africa-one-four-men-rape. Accessed 13 December 2016.

IRIN News (July 27, 2006). *Campaign to stop violence against children.* Available online at IRIN NEWS on http://www.irinnews.org/report/59759/kenya-campaign-stop-violence-against-children. Accessed on 11 December, 2016.

Izumi, K. 2006a. *The Land and Property Rights of Women and Orphans in the Context of HIV and AIDS: Case Studies from Zimbabwe.*

300

Compiled by the FAO Sub-Regional Office for Southern and East Africa. Cape Town, South Africa: HSRC Press.

Izumi, K. 2006b. *Report of the Regional Workshop on HIV and AIDS and Children's Property Rights and Livelihoods in Southern and East Africa. Report prepared for FAOSAFR* (7-8 March).

Jenks, C. 1996. Conceptual limitations, *Childhood.* New York: Routledge. p 43.

Kambarami, M. 2006. Femininity, Sexuality and Culture: Patriarchy and Female Subordination in Zimbabwe. Available online at: http://www.arsrc.org/downloads/uhsss/kmabarami.pdf. Accessed 15 December 2016.

Kimani, M. 2012. *Taking on violence against women in Africa.* Available on African Renewal at: http://www.un.org/africarenewal/magazine/special-edition-women-2012/taking-violence-against-women-africa. Accessed 13 December 2016.

Lafraniere, S. (August 11, 2005). *Entrenched Epidemic: Wife-Beatings in Africa.* Available online at: http://www.nytimes.com/2005/08/11/world/africa/entrenched-epidemic-wifebeatings-in-africa.html?_r=0. Accessed 13 December 2016.

Lukale, N. (February 24, 2014). *Harmful Traditional Practices: A Great Barrier to Women's Empowerment.* Available online at: https://girlsglobe.org/2014/02/24/harmful-traditional-practices-a-great-barrier-to-womens-empowerment/. Accessed 11 December, 2016.

Luke, N. 1989. The cultural significance of widowhood: Widow's inheritance and the position of Lou widows in the 1989 Kenya census. Available online at: http://www.pop.upenn.edu/africahh/luke.pdf. Accessed 13 December 2016.

Mangold, S. V. 2002. *Transgressing the Border between Protection and Empowerment for Domestic Violence Victims and Older Children: Empowerment as Protection in the Foster Care System.* New England School of Law.

Maputo Protocol (July 11 2003). Implementing the Protocol on the Rights of Women in Africa: Analysing! the! Compliance! Of!

Kenya's! Legal! Framework. Available online at:http://www.fahamu.org/images/MaputoProtocol.pdf. Accessed on 12 December 2016.

Maternity Worldwide (2015). *The issues: how many women and girls die in childbirth.* Available online at: http://www.maternityworldwide.org/the-issues/. Accessed 14 December 2016.

Mbirimtengerenji, N.D (2007). Is HIV/AIDS Epidemic Outcome of Poverty in Sub-Saharan Africa? *Croat Med J.* Vol 48(5) pp 505-617.

Meltzer, F. (1995). *Hot Property: The Stakes and Claims of Literary Originality.* p. 88.

Melvin, D. (April 14, 2015). *Boko Haram kidnapping of 200 Nigerian schoolgirls, a year later.* Available online on CNN at: http://edition.cnn.com/2015/04/14/africa/nigeria-kidnapping-anniversary/. Accessed 11 December 2016.

Moore, K., Rogow, D. 1994. Family planning and sexuality. In: Moore K, Rogow D, ed. *Family Planning and Reproductive Health: Briefing Sheets for Gender Analysis.* New York, NY: Population Council.

Nawal, M. N. 2006. Health Consequences of Child Marriage in Africa. *Emerg Infect Dis.* Vol. 12 (11). Available online at: https://www.ncbi.nlm.nih.gov/pmc/articles/PMC3372345/. Accessed on 12 December, 2014.

NBC News. 2016. *10 Million Children die from Lack of Health Care.* Available on line at: http://www.nbcnews.com/id/24482102/ns/health-childrens/t/million-children-die-lack-health-care/. Accessed 9 December, 2016.

Newell, P. 1993. The child's right to physical integrity. *Int'l J Child Rts.* Pp 101-110.

Noble, J., Cover, J., & Yanagishita, M. 1996. *The World's Youth, 1996,* Washington, DC: Population Reference Bureau.

0772786953Nowrojee, B. 2005. Making the Invisible War Crime Visible: Post-Conflict Justice for Sierra Leone's Rape Victims. *Harvard Human Rights Journal* 18:85-105.

Nwaebuni (November 27, 2013). *Nigeria: A difficult place to be a widow.* Available online at: *http://www.theafricareport.com/West-Africa/nigeria-a-difficult-place-to-be-a-widow.html.* Accessed 15 December 2016.

Odonkor, F. A. & Bampoh-Addo, R. 2014. Positive Portrayal of Women in African Prose: A Cursory Look at Sembène Ousmane's God's Bits of Wood and Ama Ata Aidoo's Changes, *Research on Humanities and Social Sciences www.iiste.org 2224-5766 Vol.4, No.11, 2014.*

Okorafor, N. C. 2011. *An evaluation of inheritance practices among widows in Nigeria: A study of selected urban and rural communities in Enugu state,* A Published MSc Thesis of the Institute for Development Studies University of Nigeria Enugu Campus, Available online at: http://www.unn.edu.ng/publications/files/images/NKEM%2 0PROJECT.pdf. Accessed 15 December 2016.

Okoth, C., & Adima, A. (July 1, 2014). *Ugandan men worst wife barterers.* Available at New Vision. on: http://www.newvision.co.ug/new_vision/news/1342207/ugan dan-worst-wife-barterers. Accessed 13 December 2016.

Osuafor, G. N. 2014. *Decision-making on sexual and reproductive health issues among women in heterosexual relationship in Mahikeng, South Africa.* Available online at: https://dspace.nwu.ac.za/handle/10394/15624. Accessed 15 December 2016.

Parliamentary Assembly of the Council of Europe. (1 October, 2013). *Children's Right to Physical Integrity,* Resolution 1952, Adopted at Strasbourg.

Purefoy, C. (August 28, 2010). *Children abused, killed as witches in Nigeria.* Available online at: http://edition.cnn.com/2010/WORLD/africa/08/25/nigeria.c hild.witches/. Accessed 11 December, 2016.

Rainbo Organization. 2009. *The Epidemic of Violence against Women in Africa.* Available online at: *http://www.rainbo.org/the-epidemic-of-violence-against-women-in-africa/.* Accessed 15 December2016.

Rodham, H. 1973.Children under the Law. *Harvard Educational Review.* 43: pp 487–514.

Rose, L. 2006. *Children's Property and Inheritance Rights and their Livelihoods: The Context of HIV and AIDS in Southern and East Africa*. Food and Agricultural Organization of the United Nations'. Available at:
www.oxfam.org.uk/resources/learning/landrights/downloads/childrens_property_and_inheritance_rights_and_livelihoods.pdf
. Accessed 12 December, 2016.

Save a Child. 2016. *Helping Starving African Children,* Available online at:
http://www.savethechildren.org/site/c.8rKLIXMGIpI4E/b.8197811/k.31C7/Helping_Starving_African_Children.htm.
Accessed on 9 December, 2016.

Sellix, T. 1996. *An Investigation into the Relationship between Older Males and Adolescents Females in Africa: Deconstructing the "Sugar Daddy."* Submitted in partial fulfilment of the requirements for Master of Arts in International Development, Washington, DC: American University.

Shah, A. (September 22, 2011). *Healthcare around the World.* Available online at: http://www.globalissues.org/article/774/health-care-around-the-world. Accessed 9December, 2016.

Sheil, M. (May 22, 2016). *Children Sold as Slaves in West Africa.* Available online at:
http://abcnews.go.com/WNT/story?id=131004&page=1.
Accessed 10 December, 2016.

Storr, W. (July 17, 2011). *The rape of men: the darkest secret of war.*
https://mail.google.com/mail/u/0/h/13sajh9o2f1e5/?&s=m.
Accessed 13 December 2016.

Sulyman, T. (April9, 2015*). More Children are going to School in African Countries, but There are Still 3 Million who are not. Available online at:*
http://qz.com/379709/more-children-are-going-to-school-in-african-countries-but-there-are-still-30-million-who-never-will/.
Accessed on 8 December, 2016.

Tabong, P. T. N., & Adongo, P. B. 2013. Infertility and childlessness: a qualitative study of the experiences of infertile couples in Northern Ghana, *BMC Pregnancy and Childbirth*, 13, 72. http://doi.org/10.1186/1471-2393-13-72.

Universal Declaration of Human Rights (10 December, 1948). *Children's' Right.* Available online at: https://en.wikipedia.org/wiki/Children%27s_rights#cite_note-CRC-2. Accessed on 25 November, 2016.

UNICEF, (March 7, 2003). *Every Day, 1400 Girls and Women Die Giving Birth.* Available online at: https://www.unicef.org/media/media_7594.html. Accessed 14 December 2016.

UNICEF (29 November, 2005). UNICEF, *Convention on the Rights of the Child.* https://en.wikipedia.org/wiki/Children%27s_rights#cite_note-17. Accessed 25 November, 2016.

UNICEF (May 2008). *Unicef Fact on Children.* Available online at: https://en.wikipedia.org/wiki/Children%27s_rights#cite_note-17. Accessed on 8 December, 2016.

UNICEF (April 28, 2014). Displaced by violence, children in the Central African Republic face another threat: malnutrition. Available online at: https://www.unicef.org/emergencies/car_73287.html. Accessed 15 December 2016.

UNICEF. 2014. Ending Child Marriage: Progress and Prospects, http://data.unicef.org/corecode/uploads/document6/uploade d_pdfs/corecode... Accessed on December 12, 2016).

UNICEF. 2015. *Unicef Statistics.* Available at: http://dataunicef.org/child-survival/under-five. Accessed on 8 December, 2016.

UNESCO (2000). *Regional Overview on Sub-Saharan Africa.* Available online at: https://en.wikipedia.org/wiki/Education_in_Africa#cite_note-1

UNESCO (June 14, 2013). *Nearly 30 Million African Children out of School.* Available online at: http://www.unesco.org/new/en/dakar/about-this-office/single-views/news/nearly_30_million_african_children_out_of_schoo l/. Accesssed on 8 December, 2016.

United Nations (2012).*Convention on the Rights of the Child.* United Nations Treaty Collection.

UNESCO (April 25, 2013).*Children and Armed Conflict.: Widespread child rights violations reported in the Central African Republic.* Available online at: https://childrenandarmedconflict.un.org/press-release/widespread-child-rights-violations car/. Accessed 11 December, 2016.

United Nations News Service (December 9, 2016). Africa: With 535 Million Children Living in Crisis-Hit Countries, UNICEF's Mission 'More Urgent Every Day. Available online at: http://allafrica.com/stories/201612090867.html. Accessed 11 December, 2016.

UNDP (August 28, 2016*). Africa Human Development Report 2016.* Available online at: http://www.undp.org/content/undp/en/home/librarypage/hdr/2016-africa-human-development-report.html. Accessed 12 December2016.

United Sates Department of Human Trafficking (2011).Reports on Child Trafficking. Available online at: http://www.irinnews.org/news/2012/01/25/high-cost-child-trafficking. Accessed 10 December, 2016.

United Nations Population Fund (2011) Gender-*based Violence Increases the Risk of HIV Infection in Women.* www.unfpa.org/gender/docs/factsheets/gender_hiv.doc. Accessed 4 December, 2016.

UN Backgrounder (2008). Investing in Women and Girls. International Women's' Day. http://www.unis.unvienna.org/pdf/factsheet_women_2008_e.pdf. Accessed 2 December, 2016.

UN Committee on the Rights of the Child (2006) "General Comment No. 8:" par. 3.

UN WOMEN (July 5, 2012). *Discrimination against women persists around the globe hampering development.* Available online at: http://www.unwomen.org/en/news/stories/2012/7/discrimination-against-women-persists-around-the-globe-hampering-development. Accessed 15 December 2016.

Verveer, M (June 9, 2010). *Women as Agents of Change: Advancing the Role of Women in Politics and Civil Society*. Available online at: http://www.state.gov/s/gwi/rls/rem/2010/142953.htm. Accessed 15 December 2016.

Veten, L (August 10, 2016). *South Africa's Women Still Play Second Fiddle*. Available online at: http://www.usnews.com/news/best-countries/articles/2016-08-10/local-elections-show-south-africas-women-continue-to-play-second-fiddle. Accessed 15 December 2016.

Von-Struensee V: Widows, AIDS, health and human rights in Africa. Available online   at: http://papers.ssrn.com/sol3/papers.cfm?.Accessed   13 December 2016.

World Bank (February 5, 2014). *Improving Gender Equality in Africa*. Available online at: http://www.worldbank.org/en/region/afr/brief/improving-gender-equality-in-africa.   Accessed 12 December 2016.

World Economic Forum on Africa (2011). *Africa's Women: Five challenges, one solution, Session Summary*. Available online at: http://www.weforum.org/events/worldeconomic-forum-Africa- 2011? Idsessions=48946. Accessed 2 December, 2016.

World Food Programme (2016). *Hunger Statistics*. Available online at: https://www.wfp.org/hunger/stats. Accessed on 9 December, 2016.

World Health Organization (2002). *World Report on Violence and Health*. Available online at: http://resourcecentre.savethechildren.se/keyword/violence-against-children. Accessed 11 December, 2016.

World Health Organization (March 7, 2013). *Child Marriages: 39,000 Everyday*. Available online at http://www.who.int/mediacentre/news/releases/2013/child_marriage_20130307/en/. Accessed 15 December 2016.

World Health Organization (2015). *Child Health*. Available online at: http://www.afro.who.int/en/clusters-a-programmes/frh/child-and-adolescent-health/programme-components/child-health.html. Accessed 24 November, 2015.1 IN

WHO. 2015. *1 in 5 Children in Africa do not have Access to Life Saving Vaccines.* Available online at:http://www.afro.who.int/en/medi-centre/afro-feature/item/7620-1-in-5-children-in-africa-do-not-have-access-to-life-saving-vaccines.html. Accessed 9th December, 2016.

WHO (June 12 2015). *Tracking universal health coverage: First global monitoring report.* Available online at: http://www.who.int/mediacentre/news/releases/2015/uhc-report/en/. Accessed 15 December 2016.

World Health Organization. (2015). Social Determinants of sexual and reproductive health. Available online at: http://www.ncdsv.org/images/WHO_SocialDeterminantsSexu alHealth_2010.pdf. Accessed 15 December 2016.

WHO. 2016. *Global Health Observatory Data: Child Mortality and Causes of Death.* Available online at: http://www.who.int/gho/child_health/mortality/mortality_ur. Accessed 8 December, 2016.

WHO (June 17 2016). *Health statistics and information systems: Maternal mortality ratio per 100 000 live births.* World Health Organization. Available online at http://www.who.int/healthinfo/statistics/indmaternalmortality /en/, Accessed December 14, 2016.

Young-Bruehl, E. 2012. *Childish: Confronting Prejudice against Children. New Haven, Connecticut:* Yale University Press. p. 10.

Young, J (March 28, 2016). *Sub-Saharan Africa's Dependence on Child Labour Affects Development.* Available at: http://www.voanews.com/a/sub-saharan-africa-dependence-child-labor/3258590.html. Accessed 15 December 2016.

Yusuf, I. 2012. *Tanzania: Zanzibar Men Still Beat Their Wives, Says Report.* Available from*: http://allafrica.com/stories/201208290414.html.* Accessed 21 March 2017.

Chapter 12

Community Engagement for Development and Poverty Alleviation in Rural Zimbabwe: A Case Study of Chikunguwo Community Gardening in Bikita

Costain Tandi & *Munyaradzi Mawere*

"Don't ask me what poverty is because you have met it outside my house. Look at the house and see the number of cracks. Look at the clothes that I am wearing. Look at everything that you can see around me and write what you see. What you see is poverty" (Notes from a widow in Bikita, April 2016).

Introduction

In the context of alarming poverty rates as those in rural Zimbabwe, development politics, facades of democracy, epistemic violence, and violence of the poor are inevitable. This is true given the fact that poverty in the so-called Third World countries is often complicated by politics and violence of some sort. In view of this realisation, this research was carried out in April 2016, first, to assess the contribution of Community Gardening as a copying and defence mechanism amidst threatening poverty in Negovanhu Communal Area in Bikita District, Zimbabwe. This community has been highly prone to poverty due to a couple of reasons, including violence of nature through severe droughts and El-nino episodes or climate variability and moral evil resulting from development struggles and human "politics of the belly". The latter remain inherent in spite of the fact that Zimbabwe is one country that constitutionally embraces principles of democracy as implied by the country's status as a signatory of many international human rights related conventions.

Politics have played a central role in deepening the poverty levels in Zimbabwe and the Negovanhu Communal Area (heretofore referred to as Negovanhu Area) has not been spared either. Although there are a myriad of factors and theories that can help to explain the tenacity and resilience of poverty in Third World communities, politicians have contributed significantly to the alarming poverty rates in the Negovanhu Area by subjecting innocent citizens to what we call "cold violence". There have been quite a number of cases of uneven distribution of resources especially between Zimbabwe African National Union Patriotic Front (ZANU-PF) and Movement for Democratic Change (MDC) supporters. Food hand-outs, seed, and farm implements in Negovanhu have been distributed to people on partisan lines without paying attention to expertise with deserving beneficiaries being denied access simply because they belong to the "wrong political party". While such a scenario is normally expected to cause political unrest, this has inversely prompted some community members to initiate community development projects, resulting in the birth of Chikunguwo Community Garden in one of the villages – Mapazure village – found in Negovanhu. It is worth noting that the Community Garden was named after the name of a perennial dam, Chikunguwo, which is used to irrigate the garden. Chikunguwo Community Garden was established by the local community, mainly members from the opposition parties in 2004, as a progressive reaction against increased political segregation they suffered in the hands of the ruling party, ZANU-PF. The project, thus, was meant to peacefully counter and amicably deal with macabre virtues as well as poverty and development politics played by obstinate politicians in the area.

Using Negovanhu Area and in particular, Chikunguwo Community Garden as a case study, this chapter examines the link between politicking and human-induced violence, and how both defy the logic of democracy and socio-economic development as well as the fight against abject poverty. On this note, the chapter tries to compare and contrast grassroots politics with the nature of politics at national level, and demonstrate how these show quasi-faces of democracy and facades of development in Zimbabwe.

Understanding poverty and poverty alleviation

"The definition of poverty largely depends on the person who raises the question, the way it is understood as well as the person who gives the response" – Chambers, 2006.

The statement by Chambers open our minds to the necessity of recognising the relativity of what we call "poverty." Chambers' encyclical on the conceptualisation of poverty in fact is welcome. It shows that the definition of poverty is a highly contested one in academic circles. This leaves poverty without a generic definition. When asked what poverty is? , a widow interviewed by this research has this to say:

> *Don't ask me what poverty is because you have met it outside my house. Look at the house and see the number of cracks. Look at the clothes that I am wearing. Look at everything that you can see and write what you see. What you see is poverty.*

Nevertheless, scholars seem to agree that poverty is a complex, multifaceted and multi-dimensional phenomenon. In addition, it is widely acknowledged that poverty is not a static phenomenon; it changes over time, across nations and changes within individual economic groups and at various economic levels, where there would be differences in the perception of men and women.

All these observations and paucity in literature theorising poverty have prompted mottled interpretation of poverty within and across disciplines. Sen (1999:43), for instance, defines poverty as "lack of necessities important for a day to day living, for example, food and shelter as well as health facilities". A more interesting definition of poverty is given by Saifuddin (2006) who avers that:

Poverty can be equated to hunger. Poverty is failing to have decent accommodation. Poverty is falling sick and then failing to afford medication. Poverty is inability to afford school fees and being illiterate. Poverty is failing to get employment, is fear of the tomorrow. Poverty is when your child dies owing to water-borne diseases. Poverty is lack of a political muscle, and failure to influence policy. Poverty is a varied phenomenon, which differs from one society to another. Poverty levels always change from time to time, across nations and have been defined differently (p. 1).

The 1990 World Bank report defines poverty as the inability to attain minimal standard of living measured in terms of basic needs or income to satisfy them. With this, one can easily note that poverty refers to a lack or deprivation of basic needs. The deprivation of basic

311

needs could be through denial, withdrawal, dispossession, discrimination or any other means that results in "lack". In line with this understanding, we define poverty as a condition of being without a means of getting basic requirements needed for day-to-day usage and sustenance of life. These requirements include food, shelter, clothing, health facilities, education, and freedom. Poor people's lack of shelter, freedom, food, clothing, education and health provisions keep them at bay from the kind of life that everyone values. Poverty understood as such, entails that there is need to militate against the phenomenon given that it yields undesirable experiences. In fact, there is need for every society to eradicate or at least alleviate poverty so as to lessen human suffering and improve human life. Yet, while eradicating poverty is too difficult an exercise, many scholars (Greenburg 2005; Riddel and Robinson 2002) go for the need of, at least, poverty alleviation in world communities.

Poverty alleviation can be described as "any strategy aimed at improving the economic situation of the poor households by raising incomes and creating new opportunities for employment which in turn bring about increased consumption, savings and investment" (Riddel and Robinson 2002: 12). Similarly, Greenburg (2005: 31) understands poverty alleviation as "a process which attempts to ease the level of poverty in a community or amongst a group of people or nations". The understanding by these scholars reveals that any measure or strategy aimed at alleviating poverty must be sustainable and open opportunities for the poor in order to improve their economic status. But how this could be achieved warrants an understanding of the root cause of poverty.

Making reference to Zimbabwe's poverty situation, Chinake (1977) notes that poverty situation can largely be attributed to the disintegration of traditional African society following the inception of colonialism. For him, the white regime was ruthless in controlling African access to land and their means of production. It is worth noting that colonial policies in general promoted great inequalities and perpetuated poverty among indigenous Africans, leading to the liberation war and the attainment of independence in 1980. However, we should be quick to point out that while we agree with the sentiments by Chinake, there is need to reflect beyond the sentiments. We, in fact, argue that the exploitation of indigenous Africans by the colonialists did end with the attainment of independence. Indigenous Africans continue suffering through neo-colonialism; exploitation being aggravated by exploitation of "ordinary blacks" by elite "blacks". This exploitation by both neo-colonialism and the so-called "black" elites (such as the rich and the ruling class) has impacted negatively on the poor in Zimbabwe, especially those in the countryside. It has exacerbated rural poverty. Rural poverty, which persists in Zimbabwe, is evident in the difficulties experienced by many people who reside in the rural areas to meet their day to day necessities of life, such as clean and reliable water as well as educational facilities and what to eat. Adding to Chinake's analysis, we contend that the form of exploitation especially by the ruling elite is worse than the Smith regime. The exploitation that resembles 'white people' wearing 'black masks' exploiting the blacks is more painful than colonial exploitation. It is more painful because it is more like a brother exploiting a fellow brother. It is more like a sister exploiting a fellow sister. But how this form of exploitation found its roots and became so entrenched in Zimbabwe? One might want to know.

At independence in 1980, the ruling elite made some of the costly mistakes which can help to explain why the majority of the rural people are today languishing in abject poverty. They adopted the "dog-eat-dog ethics" of the Second Chimurenga War, the colonial administrative structures and systems, including colonial laws and all their exploitative tendencies. According to Ngugi wa Thiongo (1986:18), "the colonial state under new flags received almost completely intact, the colonial army, the police, administrative structures and personnel, the judiciary and of course the entire prison system as defined and refined by colonialism." Yet, as Ngugi went on to note, no people can become free by adapting the socio-economic and political structure that once enslaved them. More so, the economy performed badly in the first decade of independence due to a compound of factors including, "violence of nature", particularly the drought of 1982/1983, macabre politics that gave rise to a civil war in Zimbabwe between Zimbabwe African National Union Patriotic Front (ZANU- PF) and Patriotic Front Zimbabwe African

People's Union (PF-ZAPU) and in Mozambique between the Mozambique National Resistance Movement (RENAMO) and FRELIMO as well as South Africa's destabilisation campaigns. In the 1990s, the government joined the Democratic Republic of Congo (DRC) war which sank deeper in the government coffers.

There were a lot of public scandals which involved top government officials such as the Grain Marketing Board (GMB) scandal involving the then Minister of Agriculture Kumbirai Kangai as well as the NOCZIM scandal involving Minister Chikovore (cf. Mawere 2011; Makumbe 2011; Chimedza & Chirimambowa 2013; Yamoto 2014). Such corrupt tendencies, which can be traced back to the colonial era, thus, were carried over into independent Zimbabwe. According to a recent report from their tax collecting agency, the Zimbabwe Revenue Authority (ZIMRA) reports that, approximately $2 billion was lost to corruption in 2012, equalling nearly one-sixth of the country's GDP that year (Cain 2015). Fairly recently (Thursday 14 April 2016), the opposition MDC-T, protested in Harare for the government's failure to account for 15 billion dollars revenue from the selling of diamonds from the Chiadzwa diamond fields. Cain (2015) opines that tyranny and corruption are the primary causes of poverty in Zimbabwe. This is because these have not only created poverty, but widened the gap between the poor and the rich.

Ultimately, then, it becomes apparent that oppressive and suppressive government policies coupled with neo-colonialism have been the root of prolonged poverty in Zimbabwe (Cain 2015). Neo-colonialism has found its way into the government and the people through the elite group in the country. From the land grabbing programme to the destruction of homes and businesses, from the common place bribery to outright corrupt theft of public funds, and from unreasonable business restrictions to hyperinflation, the Zimbabwean government under the leadership of President Robert Mugabe has proven to be one of the worst governments ever in impoverishing the masses. Zimbabwe's experiences over the past two decades have shown beyond reasonable doubt that bad governance can both create and perpetuate poverty, especially in less developed countries, which are more vulnerable. Yet, the poor seem to be always aspiring for equality. Supporting this line of thinking,

Friedlander (2010) suggests that the poor people admire what the rich people have and it is their utmost goal to attain equality. According to him, the rural poor require more land for agricultural farming, a good road network to ferry their agricultural products to nearby markets, water which is safe to drink and readily available and access to clinics and hospitals as well as educational centres for their kids and above all jobs, to alleviate their poverty. Thus, the people in the Negovanhu Area have tried to level the political ground on their own, without the government support to foster their own socio-political and economic development.

However, the violence of nature such as climate variability is also contributing to poverty levels though not at a large scale than the politics surrounding the development discourse. It is worth noting, however, that climate variability has impacted negatively on the people of rural dwellers in Zimbabwe's countryside, who rely heavily on the natural environment and agricultural production for their livelihoods. Rural livelihoods are anchored on the natural resource endowments. Owing to climate variability, the rural livelihoods in most Zimbabwean communities are at stake. This has led the rural populace to languish in abject poverty and widen the fissures of vulnerability. Such notable effects have led scholars like Chanza (2015) to assert that change and variability in the climate system attributable to atmospheric destabilisation is a threat to sustainability. Research has also projected that by 2020 rain fed agricultural yields are most likely to decrease by 50% in most African countries (IPCC, 2007). This is because climate change and variability has made rainfall frequency erratic and unreliable, making it very difficult for small holder farmers in Zimbabwean communities to meaningfully invest in agricultural production. More so, increased frequency of extreme weather conditions for example in the Masvingo Province, particularly Chivi, Mwenezi and Bikita Districts are depressing yields by damaging crops at key growth stages. Due to recurrent and protracted heat waves, the extreme wilting of crops in the fields which has exacerbated the food insecurity profiles of the farmers in most rural communities remains the order of the day. Climate change is drastically reversing and slowing the poverty reducing capacity of agriculture, simultaneously eroding the source of income and livelihood for the rural poor (cf. Slater *et al* 2007). This has caused untold starvation owing to food insecurity and again vulnerability to hunger and poverty in rural Zimbabwe. Besides, climate change will negatively impact on sustainable development since people entitlements and livelihoods would be badly affected, with the high likelihood of leaving the rural poor in a pathetic situation. We add here that if nothing is done to arrest the situation, people in the rural areas might not be able to meet the needs of the future generations, hence perpetuating the vicious cycle of poverty.

The Negovanhu Communal Area

The Negovanhu communal area is found in Bikita District, Masvingo Province, Zimbabwe. The area is located about 80km east of Masvingo urban. According to Unganai (2010), the district is subject to seasonal droughts and was seriously affected by droughts in 1992, 2002, and 2008. The district covers an area of approximately 10000 square kilometres and has a population of about 200000 people (Unganai 2010). It is quite authentic to say 81% of Bikita District is classified as belonging to the agro-natural regions 4 and 5 with mean annual rainfall ranging from 400mm to 700mm. Agricultural farming is the major livelihood activity in the area, with maize being the major crop grown. The geographical location Bikita District where the Negovanhu Communal Area is found is shown on Fig 1.

The Negovanhu Area being in Bikita District, agro-ecological region "V" experiences minimal rainfall and experiences successive bouts of heat waves and droughts. As such, it has been observed that climate change and variability has made rainfall frequency erratic and unreliable, making it extremely difficult for peasant farmers in the area to invest in agricultural activities. They produce food that is adequate to feed them from May to October. It can be deduced that people in the area mostly depend on other wards for food supplies especially the mountainous Norumedzo Area. The poor people in the area rarely manage to buy grains from other wards hence they starve. Additionally, in times of drought and acute food shortages, some people in the ward practise batter trade that is exchanging their livestock for maize, millet and sorghum.

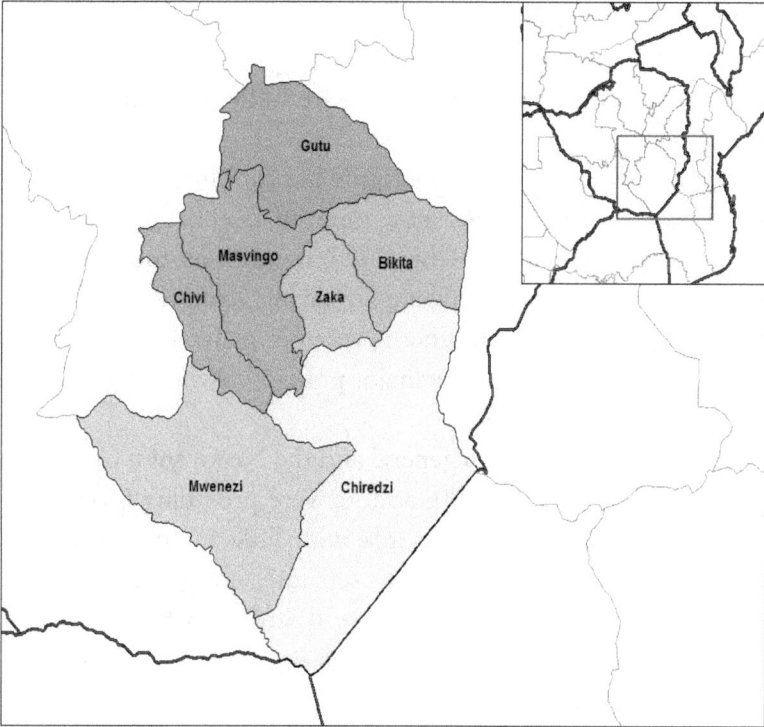

Fig 1: *The seven districts of Masvingo Province including Bikita*
The area marked in red is the Bikita District where the Negovanhu Communal Area and Chikunguwo Community Gardening project is found. Source: *Bikita Rural District Council*

More so, increased frequency of extreme weather events in Bikita District and particularly in Negovanhu are depressing yields by damaging crops at key growth stages. This has aggravated food insecurity and vulnerability to hunger and poverty in the Negovanhu Area. This situation is worsened by the fact that most of the peasant farmers in Negovanhu have no adaptive capacity due to poverty and reliance on relatively basic technologies. It is against this background that the effects of climate change and variability have been felt disproportionately by poorer communities such as Negovanhu where the majority if not all of the people are dependent on agriculture for livelihood. Loss of livestock in the area has also been very rampant due to poor pastures as a result of inadequate rainfall. This also further compounded the vulnerability of many rural households to poverty and other livelihood shocks.

Food sovereignty and politics of the belly in Zimbabwe

The concept of food sovereignty has captured the imagination of many rural communities not only in Zimbabwe but globally. According to the World Bank (2010) revelations, more than 80% of people in rural areas worldwide are facing acute food shortages and the axe of poverty. In southern Africa in general and Zimbabwe in particular, poverty remains a major policy challenge. The Negovanhu area has not been spared.

In rural Zimbabwe in general and the Negovanhu Community in particular, in the early 2000, donors were providing food hand-outs to vulnerable people in the area with little intervention from the government and through a separate programme from the government led Grain Marketing Board (GMB). However, this suddenly changed in 2002 as, on realising that its popularity was fast waning away, following defeat by the opposition MDC in the 2000 parliamentary elections, the ruling party ZANU PF used the donated food hand-outs to buy votes from the electorate for the presidential election held between 9 and 11 March 2002. In the 2000 parliamentary elections, Bikita West, where the Negovanhu communal area lies was the only constituency in rural Masvingo Province to be won by the opposition MDC. According to the information realised by the Zimbabwe Electoral Commission (ZEC), Amos Munyaradzi Mutongi (MDC) garnered 7726 votes against Retired Colonel Claudius William Makova of the ruling ZANU PF's 7441 votes.

The government's persistence, in interfering with and permitting the GMB to conduct its operations and distribution practices without transparency renders uncertain Zimbabweans' access to domestically-managed food assistance. Since then, GMB distributions are now often irregular and insufficient to meet high demands in the countryside. Due to increased poverty as a result of poor governance as exhibited in the government policies of the late 1980s such as the Essential Structural Adjustment Programme (ESAP) which saw thousands of people being retrenched, many Zimbabweans cannot afford to buy maize on their own. Local and international rights and relief agencies have been complaining that food distribution is being manipulated for political ends, favouring those who support the government and the ZANU-PF, the ruling political party (see Langa 2015; Jakes 2016; Saunyama 2016; Makumbe 2011). This politicisation is widespread in the GMB programme and is present to a far lesser degree in the international relief programme. Manifestations of shortcomings differ between the two food regimes. In addition to politicisation at all levels of grain procurement and distribution, the GMB suffers from corruption. The international relief efforts become politicised unavoidably when they must rely on local authorities when determining beneficiary status. In Negovanhu, this created spaces of vulnerability to poverty and hunger among numerous rural dwellers who happened to be politically "wrong". On a different note, this vulnerability led to the creation of Chikunguwo Community Garden in 2004, as those deemed politically wrong struggled to sustain their families.

Since the 2000 parliamentary elections to date, the Negovanhu community has been the MDC strong hold. Villagers have been denied food handouts owing to their political affiliation. This resonates with the Human Rights Watch's 2003 reports that the GMB's operations and distributions lacked transparency and that Zimbabweans who were suspected or actual supporters of the main opposition party were routinely excluded from purchasing GMB maize (Cain 2015). Besides, ZANU PF supporters have often prevented non-ZANU PF supporters from registering for international food aid (Interview with Mr Tinopedzerana, *April 2016*). This form of "cold violence" has led to vulnerability of people to poverty and hunger in the community as well as giving birth to Chikunguwo Community Gardening project.

Basing on incidents reported during the 2000 presidential elections, several interviewees said that if food shortages materialised and if the GMB were the only source of grain, it was likely that in regions that generally supported the opposition, such as the

Negovanhu Community, it would be more difficult to obtain sufficient food in the run-up to the parliamentary election. Despite efforts by many international relief organisations to prevent politicisation, local officials, mostly ZANU PF have been able to manipulate the processes for registering beneficiaries, preventing nonZANU-PF supporters from receiving food aid (Interview with Mr. J. Tinopedzerana, *16 April 2016*).

The community representatives also reported that they were concerned that access to food would be undermined if incidents of political violence increased in the run-up to the 2005 parliamentary elections, as had occurred in earlier elections. Several NGOs like CARE International, World Vision and others, involved in distributing international food aid noted that ZANU PF supporters continue to interfere with food distributions in the area and to intimidate persons who are suspected or actual MDC supporters (Dorman 2001). These persons were then too afraid to collect food at distribution points. Further, some local authorities reportedly did not inform suspected or real MDC supporters about food registration exercises and/or food distributions. ZANU PF and MDC politicians have reportedly claimed before and after food distributions that the distributions took place due to their efforts, in the expectation that the beneficiaries should support their party. In some instances, involved communities or community leadership also reportedly excluded households marginalised by the community— often the most vulnerable members of the community, including widows, orphaned children of MDC supporters and other child-headed households from food aid (Interview with Mrs S Tinoreva, *16 April 2016)*. It is against this pathetic background that disgruntled members mainly from the opposition MDC embarked on Chikunguwo Community Gardening project as a progressive reaction against "cold violence" unleashed upon them by those with political clout.

Community gardening in rural Zimbabwe for poverty alleviation

It is worth noting that the considerable increase in the popularity of Community Gardens in rural Zimbabwe in general and the Chikunguwo Community Garden in Negovanhu in particular could be attributed to their perceived potential to alleviate poverty. The concept of community gardening is very popular because rural communities in Zimbabwe use it to safeguard themselves against poverty and other hardships but in the case of Chikunguwo Community Garden as a fight against "cold violence perpetrated against them by the ruling elite. The Negovanhu Communal Area have been using the Chikunguwo Community Garden since 2004 as an important means by which the people are able to support their families and reduce their on-going susceptibility to poverty. This resonates with Chazovachii, Mutami and Bowora (2013) who posited that, Community Gardening has enabled rural communities to meet their daily livelihoods requirements without pre-occupying themselves much on hard cash as might be the case with urban dwellers. It was a finding of this study that in the area are sending their children to school and up to university level and meeting their basic health needs without looking to political leaders for help. It is quite authentic to make a standing observation that Chikunguwo Community Gardening projected have diverted people from active politics to self-help projects for community development. Shannon (1996) is a witness of this when he expands that other people enter into gardening because they want to be active participants in the production of their own food. Generally speaking, food garden projects address social, economic, and environmental objectives.

Besides, some members of the community have used income from the Chikunguwo Community Gardening project to commence other income generating projects like keeping broilers and rabbits. Others have embarked in rural banking / *fushai* where they are investing their money for bigger projects. Thus Chikunguwo Community Gardening project has produced social capital which has contributed immensely in poverty alleviation. Scholars also share a similar sentiment that gardening can effectively produce social capital. Firstly, Glover (2004) contends that community gardens are where social capital is produced, accessed, and used by community networks. Social capital indicates community networks, and it is often based on trust, reciprocity, respect, and solidarity. Smith *et al* (2005) further adds that gardens are regarded as a place where people organise and build networks. Indeed, these connections include people who trust each other, and this could effectively form a powerful community asset (Putman, 2000 and Glover, 2004). The mutual trust, according to Sherer (2004), further builds community strength through social capital. It is worth mentioning that Community Gardens are more than just about beauty; to a number of people food gardens mean moving away from a poverty stricken to a slightly better environment (Fernandez, 2003). One Mrs Tawana from the Negovanhu Area confirms this when she reveals: *"Mombe dzaunowona idzi imari yakabva pakutengesa murivo wepaChikunguwo apo/* these livestock you are seeing were bought using income from the Chikunguwo Community Gardening project".

Additionally, Community Gardens are exceedingly crucial in terms of psychology. Herbach (1998) highlights other uses of community gardens, identified are the internal and non-economic aspects to gardening, these include the enhancement of a person's psychological, spiritual and physical sense of well-being. Chikunguwo Community Gardening project has also created jobs for some youth in the Negovanhu area, thereby helping in poverty alleviation. In fact, community gardens contribute towards the creation of farmer jobs, as farmers are "employed" in the gardens they utilise, although returns may vary based on the climate (Shannon, 1996). They are a way of creating informal employment at a low capital investment (Shannon, 1996). Besides, Light *et al* (1996) refer to gardening as community based employment; because people are then employed in their own backyards and also in the communal spaces that are provided for them. Furthermore, the social networks and connections serve multiple purposes within the community and community gardens. They include an exchange of labour and material, but most importantly the exchange of knowledge (Fernandez, 2003). By people interacting together, they learn to share their aspirations, information, challenges, threats and fears thus leading to growth within individuals and community (Delgado 2000; Fernandez 2003).

Moreover, the FAO (2006) states that community gardens allow people to practice what is referred to as "experiential learning", where people learn by doing rather than being given something. Community Gardens further teach people to be self-sufficient, and to be self-reliant (Gelsi 1999). Instead of crying foul over the politicisation of food handouts by ZANU-PF, most villagers in the Negovanhu Area are now self –reliant. Gardens teach them to be able to produce enough for their family consumption and probably have something left over to sell without needing help form another person. It also teaches them to be able to identify and mobilise redundant resources. According to Patel (1991), Community Gardens can teach people the skill of independence, where they do not have to wait for someone to help them but be able to take to help themselves. Gardening therefore stimulates peoples' own interests in improving their own livelihoods their own ways, thus making them sustainable (FAO, 2006).

Overturning the tables: A critique of poverty politics

Members of the Chikunguwo Community Gardening project argue that they ventured into the project as a counter against "cold violence" perpetrated on them by political figures. To them, community gardening was a non-violent way of conflict management. The leaders of the project reported that they have suffered from political persecution as well brutalisation by the ZANU-PF militia and the terror campaign spearheaded by the one identified as Richard Ganyani (a former ZANU-PF councillor). They also reported that at times they were excluded when food was distributed by government agencies and farm inputs because of being affiliated to opposition parties. They finally resorted to community gardening for them to earn a living instead of retaliating or looking to the government for assistance. Voices from the research field confirm this:

The local leaders did not consider me to be among the government food assistance scheme beneficiaries solely because I support the opposition party. This really affected me as I do not have anywhere to get assistance. I decided to join the community gardening project and now I can afford to get money for going to the grind meal (Interview with Mrs T Ndozvireva, 13 April 2016).

Such exclusion and discrimination had an impact on livelihood outcomes, as aged people were subjected to hunger and starvation.

Besides, some people interviewed by this research also argued that they ventured into community gardening as early as 2005 when the Zimbabwean government initiated a violent campaign both in urban and rural areas that was duped *Operation Murambatsvina*, loosely translated as 'Operation Restore Order'. From the government perspective the move was meant to restore order and sanity in human settlements by getting rid of illegal activities by the demolition of illegally built structures such as business premises and houses (Bratton & Masunungure 2005). The result however was that many people lost their means of livelihood, as informal businesses were shut down in urban areas and their houses demolished because the city councils due to political expediency are said to have deemed them unfit for human habitation.

Those displaced in the urban centres relocated to the rural areas where they exerted more pressure on the already scarce resources. They had no option except to start other income generating projects such as market gardening. One interviewee recounted the pain people went through due to the government's order to destroy houses:

> ...Ummm...It was a painful event as a lot of people lost their property. After our house was destroyed by Operation Murambatsvina we were left with no option but to relocate to the rural areas. We just decided to join the community gardening project as a means to earn a living (Life narrative 13 April 2016).

From 2008 to 2009, the government of Zimbabwe through its Ministry of Social Welfare and Services suspended all humanitarian organisations in the country. This was a political move sparked by the government's understanding that these humanitarian organisations campaigned for opposition parties through their distribution of aid. The withdrawal of Non-Governmental Organisations (NGOs) from the rural areas exposed the poor to poverty. Clearly, political decisions meant to maintain the hegemony of those in power affected poor people who depended heavily on private assistance. The members of the Chikunguwo Community Gardening project criticised the government for this move as it destroyed their livelihood sources provided by the services of these organisations.

Thus, Chikunguwo Community Garden has not been immune to problems. Although this has played a pivotal role in alleviating poverty, it was a finding of this study the scale of job creation was low compared to level of unemployment. It was a general feeling of respondents that, agriculture as a poverty alleviation strategy has some shortcomings, in the sense that agricultural growth can alleviate poverty only temporarily. It was a finding of this study that this community garden is not be able to give the community great income, although they invest a lot of time and labour on it.

Moreover, the respondents cited the issue of seasonal changes as the major obstacle which undermines, lessen and destabilises the potential of community gardening as a poverty alleviation measure. At times, there are seasons where no drop of rain is witnessed. As a result, vegetable growth is stifled as it frequently requires water. The weather pattern in the Negovanhu Area is particularly detrimental to the food gardens as it is unfavourable for horticulture. Indeed, since agriculture and farming is an activity of people, attention must first be given to their capabilities.

Some respondents also cited the issue of lack of access to buyers. They cited a flooded Diyo Marketing Centre as another stumbling block for community gardening to successfully alleviate poverty in the area. Thus, there is a general lack of strategic market centre were their vegetables can fetch competitive prices since they compete with other community gardens in the area. The area is more than 40km from Nyika Growth Point which is a potential market centre.

Basing on the findings harvested from the field, we advance the argument that community development projects in Negovanhu such as community gardening have *neither* brought all the benefits their proponents expected *nor* negatively affected the community as bad as critics of the scheme might have believed. Yet we are quick to note that, the major success of community gardening in Negovanhu is that it has been simultaneously used by local community members as a weapon against "cold violence" and socio-economic hand-tool for the fight against poverty. More specifically, the benefits include, amongst other things, social, economic, and environmental benefits.

Nevertheless, we also identified problems associated with community development (such as community gardening projects) in a politically volatile milieu such as that of Zimbabwe. Key amongst the problems identified were: politicisation of community development operations, which ultimately dissuaded community members from remaining focused on community development projects; lack of resources (or poverty); unfair distribution of inputs; and lack of support from relevant government structures. Unfair distribution of inputs, done on [political] partisan lines, was noted not only as a form of violence against the victims, but also as a testimony that there is false democracy and misguided gospel of development in Zimbabwe. More strikingly, the lack of cooperation between local government structures – councillors and Members of Parliament – and farmers was a key challenge and drawback to the vortex of development in the area, and in Zimbabwe in general.

Benefits from the Chikunguwo Community Gardening

As is the case with benefits of many community development projects, there are both intended and unintended benefits yielded by the Chikunguwo Community Gardening. Some of these benefits are even difficult to state whether they are purely intended or purely unintended as they always overlap. For this reason, we consider both the intended and unintended benefits at once simply as benefits from the Chikunguwo Community Gardening.

This study revealed that although community gardening have its own problems, where there is transparency and accountability it is largely associated with benefits that can be enjoyed (directly or indirectly) by the rural communities. In the case of Chikunguwo Community Gardening, it was noted that quite a considerable number of rural dwellers rely on community gardening for both household income and household food source. For instance, the direct beneficiaries of the project indicated that they are able to pay school fees for their children at the nearby Negovanhu Primary School and Marirangwe High School, respectively.

Besides, the participants of the Chikunguwo Community Gardening noted that their financial capital had, over the years greatly improved as a result of the impact of their community gardening activities. People involved in the community gardening, for example, sell their produces from the garden such as cabbages, beetroots, tomatoes and potatoes at the nearby Diyo Market Centre, an activity that has boosted both their social and financial capital. On this note, the majority (95%) of the Chikunguwo Community Gardeners acknowledged that before the project, life was difficult as a result of politicised distribution of food handouts and farming inputs this politically charged community.

Further, it was revealed that the Chikunguwo Community Gardening project has become an important source of food for the gardeners' households themselves as well as for the people in Negovanhu area. Generally, through participation in the project, a variety of vegetables which comprise a healthy diet that contains adequate macro and micro nutrients is produced. Such vegetables include carrots, beetroots, tomatoes, potatoes, cabbages', covo, rape, onions, pepper, and many others.

Most importantly, Chikunguwo Community Gardening has effectively produced social capital. Generally, Community Gardens are where social capital is produced, accessed, and used by community networks. Social capital indicates community networks, and it is often based on trust, reciprocity, respect, and solidarity. Besides, gardens are generally regarded as places where people organise and build networks. Indeed, these connections include people who trust each other, and this has effectively helped in the formation of a powerful community asset. This mutual trust, further builds community strength through social capital.

Accordingly, the social networks and connections serve multiple purposes within the Community and Community garden. They include an exchange of labour and material, but most importantly the exchange of knowledge. When people interact together, they learn to share their aspirations, information, challenges, threats and fears thus leading to growth within individuals and community. Chikunguwo Community Garden has helped members of the Negovanhu Area to be active participants in their development. They have learnt to be active participants in creating their own external environment. They have managed to become decision makers and workers in changing their own surroundings. This means that the people work their soils and make their surroundings to what they want them to be.

Conclusion

In light of the above analysis, it is logical to conclude that there are positive results of Chikunguwo Community Gardening Project underscored throughout this study. Community gardening has been hailed as it helps to alleviate poverty through increased household income, employment creation and increased household food security. The income obtained from the community garden has been used for buying other food stuffs, agricultural inputs, as well as paying school fees. It also promotes a culture of gender sensitivity since both men and women were involved. However, it is piteous to note that community gardening is burdened with a load of negative results as well. In an attempt to alleviate poverty, community development is often troubled by development politics such that its goals are only partly realised and sometimes never realised at all. Besides, it increases poverty as the people will spend valuable time on this poorly paying venture which consumes their time, which could be utilised on other activities that can increase their income. There are no measures being undertaken to transform the present conditions but emphasis is laid on improving the situation, which ends up in an equalisation of poverty among the poor communities. This therefore means that poverty remains in place but with little inequalities if the poor people are compared.

References

Bratton, M. & Masunungure E. 2005. Popular reaction to state repression: Operation Murambatsvina in Zimbabwe, *Afrobarometer Working Paper No. 59*, pp. 1-19.

Cain, G. 2015. Bad governance in Zimbabwe and its negative consequences, down town review, 2 (1) 7, Available at: http//engagedscholarship.csuohio.edu/trd/Vol 2/iss1/7.

Chambers, A. 2006. "What is poverty? Who asks? Who answers?" Poverty Focus: What is poverty? Concepts and measures, *UNDP International Poverty Centre*, Available from: www.undp-poverty centre.org.

Chazovachi, B. & Mutami, C. 2013. Community gardens and food security in rural livelihoods development: The case of entrepreneurial and market gardens in Mberengwa, Zimbabwe, *Russian Journal of Agricultural and Socio-economic Sciences*, 1 (13).

Chimedza, T. L. & Chirimambowa, T. C. 2013. *"Smoke and Mirrors" "Anti-Corruption" crusades and the politics of elite contestation for state domination and hegemon in Zimbabwe*, South Africa, University of Johannesburg.

Chinake, H. 1997. Strategies for poverty alleviation in Zimbabwe, *Journal for Social development in Africa*, 12 (1): 39-51.

Dorman, S. R. 2001. *Inclusion and Exclusion: NGO and Politics in Zimbabwe*, Unpublished D.Phil Thesis, University of Oxford.

FAO. 1984. Economic strategies for the poor, *Economic and social development 44*, USA: Washington DC.

Glover, T. 2004. Social capital in the lived experiences of community gardeners, *Tylor and Francis Group*, 2 (26): 143-162.

Greenberg, A. 2005. ICJ for poverty alleviation: basic tool and enabling sector, *SIDA*.

Herbach, G. 1998. Harvesting the city: Community gardening in greater Madison, Wisconsin, *Madison food system project working paper series MFSP 1998-01*, City Farmer: Canada.

Jajairy, I. *et al.* 1992. *The state of world rural poverty: An inquiry into its causes and consequences*, IT Publications: London.

Jakes, S. 16 May 2016. Mnangagwa denies food aid is distributed on partisan lines, *Bulawayo 24 News*, Zimbabwe.

Langa, V. 2015. ZHRC to probe partisan distribution of food aid, *NewsDay*, Harare.

Light, J., Stoltz, B., & McNaughton D. 1996. Community based employment: experiences of adults who use AAC, *AAC Augmentative and Alternative Communication, Volume 12*, Department of communication disorders and the department of education and school of psychology and special education, the Pennsylvania state University, University Park, Pennsylvania USA.

Lund, F. 2004. *Livelihoods (un-)employment and social safety nets: reflections from recent studies in KwaZulu-Natal*, South African Regional Poverty Network.

May, J. "Constructing the Social Policy Agenda: conceptual debates around poverty and inequality", In: Padayachee, V. 2006. *The Development Decade? Economic and Social Change in South Africa, 1994-2004*, HSRC Press: Cape Town.

Makumbe, J. 2011. *Zimbabwe Political Context Study*, Norwegian Centre for Human Rights, University of Olso.

May, J. "The Structure and Composition of Rural Poverty and Livelihoods in South Africa", In: Cousins, B. 2000. *At The Crossroads: Land and Agrarian Reform in South Africa into the 21 st Century*, Programme for Land and Agrarian Studies (PLAAS): University of the Western Cape.

Matunhu, J. 2011. A critique of modernisation and dependency theories in Africa, *African journal of history and culture*, 3(5): 65-72.

Matunhu, J. 2012. 'The indigenisation and economic empowerment policies in Zimbabwe: opportunities and challenges for rural development, *Southern Peace Review Journal*, vol 12.

Mlambo, A. S.1992. *The economic structural adjustment programme, the case of Zimbabwe*, University of Zimbabwe publications: Harare.

Middleton, N. *et al.* 2001. *Negotiating poverty new directions*, Renewed Debate, London: Pluto Press.

Milbourne, P. 2004. *Rural poverty marginalisation and exclusion in Britain and the United States,* London: Routledge.

Ndozvireva, T.2016. Interview, 13 April 2016, Mapazure Village, Negovanhu.

Ngugi Wa Thiong'o, .1986. *Decolonizing the Mind: The Politics of Language in African Literature*, London: James Currey.

Putnam, R. B. 2000. *Bowling alone: The collapse and revival of the American community,* New York: Routledge.

Riddle, R., and Robinson, M. 2002. *The impact of NGO poverty alleviation projects,* Overseas development institute: London.

Saifudin, A. 2006. *NGO's perception of poverty in Bangladesh,* University of Bergen Press.

Saunyama, J. 2016. Disabled people bear the brunt of food politicisation, *NewsDay,* Harare.

Sen, A. K. 1999. An ordinal approach to measurement, *Econometria* 46, pp 437-446.

Shannon, J. 1996. *Sowing and reaping borrowed land: Garden city Harvest's community gardens,* Environmental studies: The University of Montana.

Smith, S. C. 2005. *Ending global poverty: A guide to what works,* New York: Palgrave Macmillan.

Tinopedzerana, J. 2016. Interview, 16 April 2016, Mapazure Village, Negovanhu.

Tinoreva, S. 2016. Interview, 16 April 2016, Mapazure Village, Negovanhu.

World Bank. 1990. *Development in practice: Taking actions to reduce poverty in sub Saharan Africa,* World Bank publication.

The World Bank. 2010. *The World Bank's support for the alleviation of poverty,* Washington DC: The World Bank.

Chapter 13

Seeing Beyond National Borders: Impoverished Visually-impaired Zimbabwean Beggars in Johannesburg, South Africa

Fidelis Peter Thomas Duri & *Eusebiah Chikonyora*

Introduction

Panhandling is an ancient undertaking that was first reported in the Bible (Luke: Chapter 18, Verses 35-43) where physically-challenged beggars are mentioned (Mihalache *et al*, 2013). Zimbabwe's socio-economic and political crises, punctuated by abject poverty, among other things, has resulted in stiff competition among beggars as the number of potential alms-givers from the mainstream public continues to dwindle. The crisis, which has its origins in the mid-1990s but worsened from around the year 2000, has seen millions of famished and destitute Zimbabweans scattered worldwide as street beggars. In fact, in times of socio-economic and political crises, spatial mobility becomes pervasive as people, mostly the marginalised, seek to extricate themselves from the grip of poverty, destitution and a repertoire of other insecurities (Chiumbu and Musemwa, 2012).

While visually-impaired Zimbabwean beggars are scattered in neighbouring countries and beyond, this chapter dwells on their conspicuous presence in the City of Johannesburg in South Africa. This is because South Africa, being one of Africa's largest economies (Nyamnjoh, 2006), with Johannesburg as its industrial hub (Immigrant for Social Justice, 31 August 2014), is "a magnet for immigrant beggars" who regard it as "a step out of poverty" (*Zimbabwe Black Book*, 18 May 2010: 1). As Tshuma (1 April 2008: 3) noted in April 2008: "In every street in Johannesburg there is a Zimbabwean. Among these dislocated Zimbabweans there are the (visually-impaired), begging for the South African Rand in the streets of Johannesburg." In September 2011, there were about 600 visually-impaired Zimbabwean beggars in Johannesburg's Central Business District (Tolsi, 30 September 2011). While in South Africa, Zimbabwean visually-challenged beggars demonstrate that poverty knows no borders as they improvise an array of strategies to salvage sustenance in diasporic spaces often characterised by poor living conditions and xenophobic violence, among other challenges.

This chapter largely employs a qualitative research methodology and utilises oral interviews, electronic and print media articles, reports of civil organisations and scholarly works as the major sources of data. It argues that begging for livelihoods across national borders is a high-risk coping mechanism employed by downtrodden Zimbabweans, mostly the visually-impaired, who exhibit competence to negotiate the world in times of crises. Hence, insecurities and uncertainties often invoke innovativeness as vulnerable people seek to make ends meet against the odds. This resonates with Freire's (1972) contention that:

> Hope is rooted in men's incompleteness, from which they move out in constant search...The dehumanisation resulting from an unjust order is not cause for despair but for hope, leading to the incessant pursuit of humanity...Hope, however, does not consist of folding one's arms and waiting..." (p. 64).

This study makes a significant contribution to the academic discourse by illuminating how physically-challenged people, particularly the visually-impaired, improvise a surfeit of livelihood initiatives in an adverse dispensation in which they are arguably the most vulnerable and marginalised section of the population around the globe (including diasporic spaces) in general and in Zimbabwe in particular. As Mtshali (19 January 2009: 1) notes:

> No one needs to be told of the suffering that Zimbabweans are enduring in their country...But, there is a part of that country's population whose hardships are not splashed on the news headlines. Physically-challenged people in Zimbabwe are suffering in muted silence and some of them are literally left in the dark with nowhere to go and no one to turn to.

It is against this background that this chapter examines the cross-border pursuits of Zimbabwe's visually-impaired beggars in Johannesburg in order to illustrate that disability does not mean inability during struggles for survival. In fact, their marginalisation, precarity and vulnerability at home become a source of mobilisation, creativity and resilience to salvage sustenance even beyond national borders.

Accounting for the influx of Zimbabwean beggars across national borders

In Zimbabwe, begging became banal from the turn of the New Millennium largely because of the debilitating socio-economic and political crises that plunged the majority of the population into abject poverty and insecurity in virtually all spheres of life. The socio-economic and political abyss sparked off in February 2000 when the ruling Zimbabwe African National Union Patriotic Front (ZANU-PF) party under President Robert Mugabe began seizing most white-owned commercial farms and reallocating them to 'blacks' (Meredith, 2002). With the launch of these land reform measures, a socio-economic catastrophe in the near future became ominous. Zimbabwe's socio-economic trajectory transmogrified into a nightmare. Foreign investor confidence waned as Zimbabwe became a pariah state that was ostracised by, and quarantined from, the larger part of the global village (Richardson, 2005). Other repercussions of investor flight included deindustrialisation, severe shortage of basic commodities, widespread unemployment, the dramatic fall of tax revenue inflows to the government, depletion of foreign currency reserves, government bankruptcy, rampant inflation and a drastic decline in government social spending (Ibid). In addition, the displacement of 'white' commercial farmers resulted in a sharp decline in agricultural output, chronic food shortages and widespread starvation (World Food Programme, 13 September 2012). Severe droughts during the years 2001, 2002 (Oxfam, 10 June 2002), 2007 (Mudzungairi, 19 September 2013), 2012 and 2013 (Kwaramba and Mtimba, 31 October 2013; Mudzungairi, 19 September 2013), for example, worsened the turbulent dispensation. Life also became

335

unbearable for most ordinary Zimbabweans due to widespread political violence between the ruling ZANU-PF and the opposition Movement for Democratic Change (MDC) during the period 2000-2008 (Godwin, 2010).

Zimbabwe's inexorable socio-economic degeneracy, which worsened from the year 2000, largely accounts for the influx of its citizens, mostly the visually-impaired adults and their children, as street beggars in South Africa, particularly in Johannesburg, where the economic climate is relatively stable. As the Zimbabwean dollar became virtually worthless due to hyperinflation, most beggars increasingly found it difficult to sustain themselves and their dependants from the money that they were given by well-wishers at a time when prices of basic commodities, most of which were scarce, were ever skyrocketing beyond the reach of many. Inflation rates were estimated at 144% in October 2002 (Watson, 1 March 2003), 400% in November 2005 (Wines, 2 May 2006), 1 000% in May 2006, 4 500% in July 2007 (*Sokwanele*, 20 July 2007), 213 million percent in October 2008 (Berger, 9 October 2008), 79.6 billion percent in November 2008 (Fuller, May 2012), and 500 billion percent in December 2008 (*Thomson Reuters Foundation*, 13 July 2014).

Owing to the hyperinflationary environment in Zimbabwe, particularly before the introduction of the multi-currency fiscal regime in 2009 (Mhlanga, 24 December 2015), begging did not yield much. This was confirmed in March 2007 by Joseph Ruzvidzo, a visually-challenged Zimbabwean panhandler in Johannesburg, quoted by John Marufu, a journalist of *The Zimbabwean* (21 March 2007: 1), who said, "Begging here pays us a lot more than when we beg at home. We cannot do any other kind of job and begging is our only way out of the economic blues that are biting Zimbabwe." In September 2007, Shylet Madhabuya, a 38-year-old visually-impaired beggar in Johannesburg, stated that due to the hyperinflationary environment in Zimbabwe, she had to leave for South Africa where she could get more (Mapumulo, 25 September 2007: 1). She said: "Begging in South Africa pays us a lot more than when we beg at home where one hardly makes enough money to buy food which is another reason why I decided to come here…If I continued begging in Zimbabwe, I would have died of hunger" (Ibid, p.1). In June 2011,

Lucy Ndebele, an official of the Zimbabwe Council for the Blind, reiterated that many physically-challenged people realised that they could earn more from begging in neighbouring countries, particularly South Africa, owing to unprecedented inflation rates in the country (*Irin News*, 13 June 2011).

Given that more than 80% of the Zimbabwean population was living in abject poverty by the end of the year 2006 (Schaefer, 23 March 2007), begging space increasingly shrunk and became hotly contested as the number of potential 'donors' from the mainstream public had plummeted. Kingstone Chisale, the coordinator of the Harare Street Beggars Association, told *The Daily News* (11 February 2005) that the escalating poverty rate in Zimbabwe resulted in stiff competition among beggars at a time when the number of potential alms-givers from the general public was dwindling. He stated: "Begging is one of the last things a person would do but here in Zimbabwe, there are now many beggars on the streets resulting in serious competition for a few dollars which they will be chasing after" (Ibid, p.1). He further noted that these developments pushed considerable numbers of beggars into neighbouring countries such as South Africa. The situation worsened, particularly from the year 2004, when the cash-strapped Zimbabwean government scrapped the support programme for people living with disability. As Chisale further explained: "Johannesburg is the economic hub of the region and everyone tends to trek there in search of a living. We had no more than 130 members (of the Harare Street Beggars Association) who left the streets of Harare (in 2005) because they were not getting much to look after their families" (Ibid, p.1).

Gift Mupambiki, a 32-year-old man who had become visually-impaired at the age of three years, told *Irin News* (13 June 2011) that he decided to leave his home in northern Zimbabwe in 2007 to beg in South Africa because of starvation mainly emanating from drought in a gnawing socio-economic dispensation where many Zimbabweans hardly had any alms to offer. He recalled: "There was drought. We were surviving by begging, but people did not have anything to give" (Ibid, p.1). Kennedy Nyoni, a 29-year-old visually-challenged beggar, who left Zimbabwe for Johannesburg in mid-

2008, expressed similar views during an interview with the *Mail and Guardian* in September 2011:

> Our main reason for being here in South Africa is...just to make a living...It is a hard living, but it is still a living- something we cannot do in Zimbabwe because even if the economy is slowly recovering, people do not have a lot of money to give us. In South Africa or in Zimbabwe, our jobs are the same- we are beggars (Tolsi, 30 September 2011: 1).

In late 2008, Happymore Chiyingwe, a 48-year-old visually-impaired panhandler in the Zimbabwean city of Masvingo, left for Johannesburg for similar reasons (*Anadolu Agency*, 11 April 2015). She explained her plight: "I have been begging all my life. People there (Zimbabwe) no longer had any money for beggars" (Ibid, p.1). These sentiments clearly reflect that begging in diasporic spaces is characteristic of quotidian existence, a popular livelihood option, a form of employment, for some impoverished but innovative citizens, particularly the visually-challenged, given Zimbabwe's socio-economic decay particularly from the onset of the New Millennium.

The rising unemployment rate in Zimbabwe from the year 2000 also forces some of its citizens to ameliorate their plight of poverty through begging across national borders. The country's unemployment rate was estimated at 50% to 60% during the years 2002 and 2003 (Zeilig, 2002), 80% in 2005 (United States Government, 2014) and 94% by the beginning of 2009 (Chiriga, 16 April 2011; *Mail and Guardian*, 29 January 2009). In 2013, the unemployment rate spiralled to more than 95% (*My Zimbabwe News*, 25 August 2013; United States Government, 2014), the highest in the world (Zhou, 2017).

In addition, physically-challenged employees, mostly the visually-impaired, in Zimbabwe's formal sector are usually the first to lose their jobs in times of crises. This is largely because of the exclusionary practices of employers, particularly the government, which render physically-challenged workers dispensable. Jethro Gonese, a visually-impaired man, for example, was employed as a schoolteacher in Zimbabwe during the early 2000s (Wilhelm-Solomon, 2015). Since he was visually-challenged, an assistant paid by the government helped him with the marking and chalkboard work. During the year 2004, as Zimbabwe's economic woes worsened, the government stopped paying assistants for physically-challenged employees. In an attempt to save his job, with the hope that Zimbabwe's moribund economy would resuscitate soon, he decided to share his Z$1 000-monthly salary with the assistant. The situation became unsustainable when hyperinflation gobbled his monthly salary to less than the price of a loaf of bread, prompting him to cross into South Africa and survive from begging in Johannesburg (Tolsi, 30 September 2011).

To many pauperised sections of the population, particularly the physically-challenged, the pursuit of subsistence in Zimbabwe, a country that has become an abode of profound poverty, increasingly becomes illusory; indeed, the quest for a chimera. Given the diminishing expectations of sustaining decent livelihoods in a country that is deep in the throes of unprecedented socio-economic doldrums, begging across national borders becomes a viable alternative in the survival dynamics of many vulnerable Zimbabweans.

It is a fact that poverty knows no borders as hungry people seek sustenance. The influx of Zimbabwean beggars, mostly the visually-impaired, across national borders is a veritable manifestation that home is not always the best whenever people's livelihoods are severely eroded. Panhandling in diasporic spheres becomes one among a repertoire of creatively-devised survival recourses. Zimbabwe's debilitating crises, typified by a comatose economy, social instability and political turbulence, among other things, compels many of its citizens, including the visually-challenged, to 'see' opportunities beyond their home country and negotiate national borders in order to circumvent the dilemma of subsisting on a starvation diet.

Dynamics of crossing the border

Some impoverished visually-challenged Zimbabweans who panhandle in neighbouring countries cross borders legally while others do so illegally. Those who cross legally usually have valid travel documents and use the official entry points. Shylet Madhabuya, a visually-impaired beggar from the City of Mutare, for example, had a valid Zimbabwean passport and a 30-day visa when she entered South Africa in May 2007 (Mapumulo, 25 September 2007). She engaged in begging pursuits in Johannesburg but returned home every month to see family members and also to renew her passport (Ibid). In March 2007, Joseph Ruzvidzo, a visually-handicapped man from Chegutu Town in Zimbabwe, who begged in Johannesburg, stated that he entered South Africa with a valid passport (Marufu, 21 March 2007). During the journey, he got free rides from bus drivers who were sympathetic to his plight of disability provided they were not too many per trip (Ibid). In 2013, Precious Shava, a 34-year-old visually-challenged woman who travelled from Zimbabwe to Johannesburg to earn a living through begging, was provided with free transport by a generous cross-border bus driver (Mutandiro, 12 May 2017). She explained: "A Good Samaritan bus driver offered to give me a ride for free to come to Johannesburg. He dropped me off at the Methodist Church in Johannesburg, where I could ask for help to get treatment for my eyes" (Ibid, p.1). It should be noted, however, that some beggars who cross the border legally become illegal immigrants after overstaying in the host countries (Hakutangwi, Mashizha and Matanga, 2010; Mutandiro, 12 May 2017).

Zimbabweans without valid official travel documents employ an array of strategies to cross into neighbouring countries. Those with some cash often use the official border posts where they bribe officials on both sides of the border such as soldiers, the police and immigration authorities in order to proceed (Bearak, 23 January 2009). Many visually-impaired people cross the border into South Africa without travel documents after successfully pleading with immigration officials that they need hospital treatment to restore their sight (SAMP, 26 February 2006; Smith, 26 February 2006).

Some migrants use unofficial routes to enter neighbouring countries. From the year 2007, for example, dozens of visually-challenged Zimbabwean beggars were reportedly crossing the crocodile-infested Limpopo River to try their luck in South Africa (Khumalo, 29 July 2014). An example is the 44-year-old Lorcadia Dewa, a street beggar from Mwenezi Town in Zimbabwe, who crossed into South Africa and proceeded to Johannesburg in the year

2008 (Ibid). Narrating how she entered South Africa using unofficial routes, she said, "I had no passport so I paid some men who helped me to cross the crocodile-infested Limpopo River to enter South Africa through holes in the fence separating the two countries" (Ibid, p.1).

Several male guides capitalise on the prevalence of undocumented migrants to earn money by assisting them to cross borders. While crossing the Limpopo River into South Africa, for example, the guides lead the way using sticks to measure the depths of the river, which could be shoulder-high even during dry seasons, while the rest follow in a single file clutching the back part of each other's shirt, blouse or dress to avoid being swept away. In some cases, however, the guides rob the migrants of their possessions after guiding them across the Limpopo River (Zimbabwe Political Victims Association (ZIPOVA), 1 November 2004).

While crossing into South Africa, undocumented migrants also risk being intercepted by the *gumaguma*, a slang reference to robbers who inflict a broad range of abuses such as extortion, theft, rape and murder in the bushy area along the border close to Beitbridge Border Post (Hungwe, 2012). In September 2011, a visually-impaired Zimbabwean beggar in Johannesburg informed the *Mail and Guardian* about the predatory activities of the robbers: "The hardest part is hiding from the *gumaguma*. I was afraid of them because they crack you, knife you and take everything from you. I remember running away from them down these steep slopes with three other visually-handicapped people. I was very afraid" (Tolsi, 30 September 2011: 1).

From the border, some groups of beggars organise their own transport to take them into the South African interior. On 2 October 2005, for example, a public taxi loaded with 14 visually-challenged Zimbabwean beggars, who had sneaked into South Africa, was stopped by the Johannesburg Metro Police on the M1 Highway near Glenhove (SAMP, 3 October 2005). The beggars aboard were arrested and temporarily housed at the local offices of the Department of Home Affairs after which they were detained at the Lindela Repatriation Camp (Ibid).

The passage of visually-impaired Zimbabwean migrants into neighbouring countries such as South Africa is characterised by uncertainties and life-threatening challenges. In the case of documented migrants, some of them are financially crippled to the extent that they have to be assisted with food and transport by well-wishers. The situation is worse off for undocumented migrants most of who risk being arrested on both sides of the border. In addition, most undocumented migrants have to contend with several threats along the way such as flooded rivers, wild animals and robbers. These life-threatening experiences, together with anxieties over an uncertain future, illustrate the determination by some downtrodden Zimbabweans to salvage livelihoods across national borders. These pursuits erode the very basis of the Westphalian border as "a sharp line, an impenetrable barrier [and a] marker of statehood" (Horstmann, 2004: 8) that is supposed to be "unchanging, uncontested, and unproblematic" (Baud and Van Schendel, 1997: 216). While borders are primarily meant "to orient the movement of people and assets" (Acuto, 2008:1), they become "fluid" or "portable" and "carried everywhere" (Dear and Burridge, 2005: 305) as people exploit them as "corridors of opportunity" (Flynn, 1997: 313) in times of debilitating crises. As Baud and Van Schendel assert:

> No matter how clearly borders are drawn on official maps, how many customs officials are appointed, or how many watchtowers are built, people will always ignore borders whenever it suits them...People also take advantage of borders in ways that are not intended or anticipated by their creators...Because of such unintended and often subversive consequences, border regions have their own social dynamics and historical development (Baud and Van Schendel, 1997: 211-212).

This section has examined a plethora of informal means which poverty-riddled visually-impaired Zimbabwean beggars employ to cross the border into South Africa where some of them end up eking for livelihoods in Johannesburg. Their determination and innovativeness to negotiate the border despite the numerous risks involved speak eloquently about the magnitude of the Zimbabwean crises. With their entry into South Africa, as the next section demonstrates, their tribulations are far from over. The various strategies which they improvise to survive in inhospitable diasporic spaces attest to their resilience and ingenuity.

Begging strategies

The ability to negotiate space in diasporic landscapes is a critical attribute of most visually-challenged Zimbabwean beggars. As in many parts of the world, Zimbabwean visually-handicapped beggars in Johannesburg frequent those areas with a high concentration of human and vehicle traffic where there are greater chances of getting alms. Most newly-arrived beggars are enrolled into syndicates which allocate them spaces to operate in such localities (Bedfordview Residents Action Group, 19 October 2010; Smith, 26 February 2006; Wilhelm-Solomon, 2015). Most beggars are found along the streets, at traffic-light intersections, bus termini, shopping malls and outside banking halls. In March 2007, for example, there were several Zimbabwean visually-challenged beggars at such strategic points in Johannesburg's upmarket suburbs such as Fourways and Sandton (Marufu, 21 March 2007). Zimbabwean panhandlers of all ages also congest the Mobile Telephone Networks (MTN) rank in Johannesburg (Immigrant for Social Justice, 31 August 2014).

Zimbabwean visually-impaired beggars, sometimes accompanied by young children, are a common sight on Metro-Rail trains. In April 2015, for example, *Anadolu Agency* (11 April 2015) witnessed dozens of Zimbabwean visually-challenged beggars singing religious songs and playing guitars while asking for alms in packed trains plying routes between the townships and the Johannesburg Central Business District. Groups of beggars disembarked at railway stations along the way while others boarded and asked for donations from the very same passengers. This prompted Pretty Motsami, a 27-year-old Johannesburg hairdresser, to complain: "How many times must we give to these people? Why can't some organisations help these people off the streets?" (*Anadolu Agency*, 11 April 2015: 1). Spatial mechanisms are, therefore, crucial as panhandlers seek strategic areas, with dense vehicular and human traffic, where potential 'donors' can be found. Masculine qualities are sometimes used to out-compete other beggars in fiercely-contested public spaces. Stampedes are a common occurrence at traffic light intersections in Johannesburg as Zimbabwean beggars, accompanied by aides, rush to seek alms from motorists who stop (Khumalo, 29 July 2014).

Considerable numbers of visually-impaired beggars enlist the services of Zimbabwean or South African assistants who they pay to escort them into the streets (SAMP, 26 February 2006). In March 2007, Ropafadzo Taruvinga, a visually-challenged beggar in central Johannesburg, said she paid her assistant an average of R50 to R100 a day depending on the amount they would have raised (Marufu, 21 March 2007). In September 2007, Shylet Madhabuya, a 38-year-old visually-impaired Zimbabwean beggar in Johannesburg, paid Takudzwa Gapara, her helper and guide, an average of R30 to R50 per day depending on the takings (Mapumulo, 25 September 2007). Gift Mupambiki, a 32-year-old beggar, found his way to Johannesburg where, together with other visually-challenged Zimbabwean counterparts, they enlisted young relatives as assistants to fetch water and cook, and accompany them on begging pursuits in return for a share of the proceeds (*Irin News*, 13 June 2011). In May 2017, Precious Shava, a 40-year-old visually-challenged Zimbabwean woman, begged along Faraday Street in Johannesburg with Clayton Nunga, a 27-year-old man, as her guide (Mutandiro, 12 May 2017). Clayton acknowledged that he was managing to survive in South Africa from the money he earned for guiding visually-impaired beggars along the streets. He said, "Helping Precious makes my life more bearable until I find proper work...There is a competition among jobless young men to get the chance to chauffer around visually impaired beggars" (Ibid, p.1). The strategy employed by most visually-challenged beggars, of enlisting the services of those who have no disabilities, unravels an interesting paradox of panhandling. The paradox is that, while the visually-challenged beggars are severely impoverished and critically in need, they also generate income for their sighted counterparts by enlisting them to assist with various tasks in return for payment.

Begging pursuits involve a repertoire of visual mechanisms. Moving around with their young children and sometimes suckling babies, for example, is a strategy mostly employed by visually-challenged female beggars to draw the attention and sympathy of passers-by to their plight of deprivation. In March 2013, Faith Mafa, a 22-year-old visually-handicapped woman, who had been begging in Johannesburg since the year 2012, argued that the fronting of children during panhandling pursuits was an avenue of winning the pity of potential alms-givers (Solidarity Helping Hand, 4 March 2013). She said, "It is better when you are sitting with a baby on the street. People feel sorry for you and give you money" (Ibid, p.1). In March 2010, the *Mail and Guardian* identified several single mothers begging in the company of their very young children at various points in Johannesburg. Nyasha Mapako (24) and her two-year-old child, for example, begged at the Corlett Drive intersection in Bramley while Melisa Mazhungu (17) and her 15-month-old son stationed themselves near the McDonalds Mall on Glenhove Road (Keepile, 18 March 2010).

The number of Zimbabwean roadside female beggars with suckling children in Johannesburg rose so sharply that South African police seized the minors in October 2010 on grounds that their living conditions were not conducive for infants (Dixon, 16 August 2011). The children were taken to welfare homes administered by the Displaced Persons Unit. Examples of such shelters in Johannesburg in 2011 were Governor's House in Hillbrow and Wembley Sanctuary in Turffontein. The children could only be returned if their mothers got jobs and decent accommodation in order to guarantee their well-being. Examples of Zimbabwean female beggars whose children were taken away during the blitz were Ruwarashe Chibura and Memory Konjiwa (Ibid). Indeed, the strategy of fronting of children during begging pursuits can be demonised on grounds of child abuse in human rights discourses. In this chapter, however, this practice should be viewed in a moral economy context as an innovative survival resource employed by some visually-impaired beggars to draw the attention of potential alms-givers to their plight of vulnerability.

Other visual mechanisms used by ingenious beggars to solicit for help include posters. This communicative innovation is mostly used by physically-challenged beggars, particularly the visually-handicapped, to articulate their plight to passers-by. In Johannesburg, for example, several visually-impaired Zimbabwean beggars have posters with them on pavements, along the streets and at traffic light intersections. Some of the banners read, "I am visually-handicapped and asking for help," "Please help me with food," "I am visually-challenged and my children are starving," and "I am unemployed, visually-impaired and hungry" (Personal observations, 2008-2012).

Audio-visual mechanisms are sometimes employed by enterprising Zimbabwean beggars to draw the attention of passers-by in Johannesburg's congested public spaces. Music, for example, is a notable resource utilised as bait to attract well-wishers during begging pursuits. This practice also prevailed in other parts of the world such as Addis Ababa, the Ethiopian capital, where playing musical instruments or singing was "a trade widely reported in the historic literature as being a speciality of (visually challenged) people" (Groce et al, 2013). Some visually-impaired beggars in Johannesburg play musical instruments to lure passers-by with the optimism that they would sympathise with them and offer alms (Personal observations, 2008-2012). Creativity is central in the strategies used by visually-handicapped Zimbabwean beggars across national borders.

Owing to the stiff competition for alms in a foreign environment, many beggars operate in carefully selected spatial settings from where they improvise a plethora of audio-visual mechanisms in order to draw the attention of passers-by. In fact, begging develops into "a fine art" involving a broad range of ingenious strategies to earn livelihoods (Bentwick, 1894: 125). The various mechanisms employed by beggars constitute "a talent for life" which reflect resilience by vulnerable people to survive in times of crisis (Scheper-Hughes, 2008: 25).

Challenges of begging across national borders

Zimbabwean visually-challenged beggars encounter a number of problems in Johannesburg, some of which severely threaten their pursuits of survival. In South Africa, the police often launch operations against beggars and undocumented migrants (*Irin News*,

13 June 2011. During the early 2000s, the number of Zimbabweans arrested and deported from South Africa stood at 26 742 in the year 2000, 19 932 in 2001 and 18 033 in 2002 (*News from Africa*, November 2003).

On 27 January 2005, the Johannesburg Metropolitan Police launched a two-hour operation to clear beggars from the city's streets. Code-named 'Operation Token Days,' the blitz netted 40 visually-impaired beggars, including children, mostly from Zimbabwe (SAMP, 5 February 2005). The exercise was part of the '500 Days Campaign against Vice' meant to clear Johannesburg of its image as Southern Africa's capital city of crime (*Daily News*, 11 February 2005). The operation targeted street beggars at traffic light intersections in the city centre and Sandton Suburb. It was discovered that, out of the more than 300 beggars who were rounded up, the majority were Zimbabweans most of who did not have travel documents. The illegal immigrants were sent to Lindela Repatriation Camp in Krugersdorp awaiting deportation (*Daily News*, 11 February 2005; SAMP, 26 February 2006; Smith, 26 February 2006). For the greater part of the year 2005, the camp was so overcrowded that 50 inmates sometimes shared a room meant for 30 people (SAMP, 28 October 2005). Outbreaks of diseases became common and sometimes resulted in fatalities. Between April and July 2005, for example, 43 immigrants, 28 of them Zimbabweans, died at the camp (Ibid). In late 2005, the camp housed between 6 000 and 6 500 illegal immigrants, most of them Zimbabweans, per month with a daily intake of between 200 and 250 (Ibid). The International Organisation for Migration estimated that 86 000 illegal Zimbabwean immigrants were deported from South Africa between January and May 2007 (*Sokwanele*, 20 July 2007). Those beggars who had valid travel documents were usually ordered to pay a fine of R350 (US$52) (*Irin News*, 13 June 2011).

In addition to police operations, social workers employed by the Johannesburg Municipality's Displaced Persons Unit periodically pick up beggars at street intersections and detain them at a various centres where they subject them to various forms of abuse which include beatings and hosing them with cold water (*Irin News*, 13 June 2011). In September 2011, some visually-impaired beggars in

Johannesburg complained of harassment by the government's social workers who they accused of being more brutal than the police. They alleged that after being removed from the streets, the social workers often detained them for the entire day without food or water. As if this was not enough, they were usually flogged with rubber pipes (Tolsi, 30 September 2011). In the year 2012, Faith Mafa, a 22-year-old visually-challenged woman, experienced such harassment together with her begging counterparts after they had been rounded up in the Johannesburg city centre (Solidarity Helping Hand, 4 March 2013).

Xenophobic practices by the general public and the discriminatory provision of social services in government institutions are also prevalent. In South Africa, Zimbabwean beggars suffer atrocious forms of discrimination in the provision of social services at state institutions such as hospitals (Tolsi, 30 September 2011). In February 2011, for instance, Albertina Mukanhiri, a visually-impaired Zimbabwean woman who begged in Johannesburg together with her husband, Enock, who was also visually-handicapped, gave birth to a still-born child at Johannesburg General Hospital (Ibid). Narrating her ordeal, she said:

The nurses said…the baby had died because I was not supposed to give birth because it was very bad, unnatural for visually-challenged people to have babies. They would not feed me properly in hospital and then said I could not see the baby or bury it until I paid them R2 000 (US$200). The baby was only buried after a doctor stopped them…They tell us that we should go back and get help from our government and hospitals (Ibid, p.1).

The plight of most Zimbabwean beggars is compounded by the hostile attitude of some members of the general public in various parts of South Africa, including Johannesburg. The xenophobic violence during the year 2008, for example, began in Alexandra Township in northern Johannesburg and soon spread to other parts of the country (*Irin News*, 23 May 2008). By 23 May, 42 people had been killed and 17 000 displaced (Ibid). Gift Mupambiki, a 32-year-old visually-challenged Zimbabwean beggar, who stayed with several others in a dilapidated flat in Johannesburg's city centre, for example, were evicted by South African assailants who told them to go back

348

to their country (*Irin News*, 13 June 2011). They fled the premises and took refuge at a nearby police station (Ibid). Besides posing serious security threats to their lives, the hostility of the general public also affects the daily takings of most beggars. In November 2004, some Zimbabwean beggars in Johannesburg lamented getting only R10 (US$1) per day (*Zimbabwe Situation*, 21 November 2004).

For the visually-impaired people, begging pursuits along the streets and at traffic light intersections are extremely precarious as they risk being knocked down by passing vehicles. In late 2004, Joseline Shumba, a 44-year-old visually-handicapped Zimbabwean mother of three children, two of whom were with her in Johannesburg, was knocked down in a hit-and-run accident at an East Rand traffic light (Smith, 26 February 2006). It took her about a year to recover. Other visually-impaired Zimbabwean women made financial contributions to pay for her rent and look after her children while she was hospitalised (Ibid).

In addition, the living conditions of most beggars are deplorable. Most beggars have no accommodation and sleep in open spaces such as pavements. Most visually-challenged beggars who manage to secure accommodation reside in dilapidated, unhygienic and overcrowded conditions since they cannot afford paying rentals for decent dwellings (Wilhelm-Solomon, 2015). In November 2004, for example, a group of 31 visually-impaired Zimbabwean beggars, whose ages ranged from two to more than 60 years, was discovered staying in a one-room Hillbrow flat in Johannesburg. The occupants cooked on one double hot-plate stove and their ablutions were in a communal bathroom (Solidarity Peace Trust, November 2004; *Zimbabwe Situation*, 21 November 2004). In February 2005, Taimon Rukuni, a Zimbabwean man, shared one room in Johannesburg with 15 other visually-impaired begging counterparts (SAMP, 5 February 2005). Meanwhile, Brighton Mkushi, another visually-challenged beggar in the same city, shared a room with 30 counterparts (Ibid). In February 2006, an average of eight visually-handicapped Zimbabwean beggars shared a two-bedroom flat in Hillbrow and Joubert Park in Johannesburg's city centre paying rentals of between R65 and R200 a week (SAMP, 26 February 2006). In July 2007, Jennifer Khumalo, a 42-year-old visually-challenged mother of four, was sharing one room with 10 other visually-impaired beggars in Johannesburg's Yeovil Suburb (Ismail, 26 July 2007).

By June 2011, most of the abandoned and neglected buildings in Johannesburg's city centre had become slum residences for thousands of unemployed Zimbabwean migrants, mostly visually-challenged beggars (*Irin News*, 2 June 2011). The squalid living conditions in these premises included overcrowding and limited or no access to electricity and water supplies. One such building near Ellis Park Stadium sheltered over 400 people, mostly Zimbabwean migrants, in rooms partitioned by cardboard or washing lines hung with sheets (Ibid). Common health problems that emanated from such conditions included skin ailments, diarrhoea, respiratory tract infections such as tuberculosis, sexually-transmitted infections and stress-related complications (Ibid).

Doorfontein Chambers, on the southern margins of the Johannesburg city centre, was another dilapidated building where many visually-challenged Zimbabwean panhandlers resided from the early 2000s (Wilhelm-Solomon, 2015). In September 2011, Tolsi illuminated the decrepit and extremely repulsive living conditions experienced by the beggars at Doorfontein Chambers as follows:

> There is no electricity- the darkness inside the hijacked building leaves anybody blind. Water is stolen from the fire extinguishers. Some walls are daubed with human faeces and the stench of urine permeates. The warehouse-like building has been almost entirely plundered of any metal that can be sold off and the elevator shaft is now completely exposed. In the pitch-blackness of the building, it is a danger to both the blind and the sighted. The labyrinthine floors have been individually partitioned using cardboard, bits of food and election posters, into small rectangular homes (Tolsi, 30 September 2011: 1).

This section has illustrated that most visually-impaired Zimbabwean beggars experience several hardships in Johannesburg and other diasporic spaces. These challenges include hostility from the public and official domains and poor living conditions. Despite the seemingly insurmountable challenges, most beggars become resilient as they seek to eke a living. As the next section demonstrates, they devise a plethora of strategies to survive amid adversity rather than return to Zimbabwe where the situation is inexorably dire.

Some strategies employed by beggars to survive amid adversity

Visually-challenged Zimbabwean beggars improvise a number of mechanisms to mitigate the various challenges that confront them in Johannesburg. This section highlights some of the strategies, particularly those pertaining to security concerns and the need to meet basic subsistence and material needs such as food, clothing and shelter.

Socio-spatial residential dynamics are critical in the survival of Zimbabwean beggars in the diaspora. As noted in the previous section, many beggars tend to reside in the same localities, with large groups often sharing the same premises. While many beggars in Johannesburg tend to live in crowded conditions because they do not have the money to rent spacious and decent accommodation, such situations also afford the migrants some sense of collective security in view of the general hostility and xenophobic attacks from the locals (Hakutangwi, Mashizha and Matanga, 2010). In addition, staying closer together enable beggars to share food and other resources in times of need (*Zimbabwe Situation*, 21 November 2004).

Several visually impaired Zimbabwean beggars in Johannesburg seek shelter, food and security at church institutions after unsuccessfully trying other options of survival. From the mid-2000s, for instance, many of them sought assistance at the Central United Methodist Church in Johannesburg's Central Business District where Bishop Paul Verryn provided them with overnight accommodation (Immigrant for Social Justice, 31 August 2014). Most of the desperate Zimbabweans who slept at the church were single women, young mothers and fathers, the visually challenged and other physically handicapped persons (Ibid). In the year 2007, starvation forced more than 900 stranded Zimbabweans, including little children, to take refuge at the Church where they were given food and shelter (*Sokwanele*, 20 July 2007). In November 2008, the centre was providing shelter to an average of 1 200 Zimbabweans every night (Sibeko, 27 November 2009). At some point during the year 2010,

351

more than 2 000 Zimbabwean migrants, mostly visually challenged beggars, were being provided with overnight accommodation at the church (Immigrant for Social Justice, 31 August 2014).

There is overwhelming evidence that impoverished visually impaired Zimbabwean beggars in the diaspora can abandon begging for other more lucrative income-generating projects if support services are availed. As Precious Shava, a 40-year-old visually challenged Zimbabwean woman in Johannesburg, said in May 2017, "No one wants to be a beggar, especially in a country that is not your own. Life forces me" (Mutandiro 12 May 2017: 1). In 2011, Enock Mukanhiri and Jethro Gonese, both visually handicapped men of Zimbabwean origin, who used to survive from panhandling in Johannesburg, formed a self-help institution, with the support of non-governmental organisations, to assist their counterparts in the city. Known as the Integrated Community Centre for the Blind and Disabled in South Africa, the organisation sought to establish income-generating projects such as knitting clothes and making cane furniture for sale. In justifying the project, Gonese said, "We do not want charity. We just want an equal opportunity" (Tolsi, 30 September 2011: 1).

It should never be assumed that begging is always a last resort livelihood activity (Groce *et al*, 2013). In a study conducted by Quidiz (2005), none of the informants acknowledged resorting to begging on grounds that it brought easy money. These findings are reiterated by Roblee-Hertzmark (2012: 7) who says, "Despite what much of the popular press would have us believe, it (begging) is not lucrative and it is not something that many people would choose given other options. Begging is a desperate act." Thus, according to Fitzpatrick and Kennedy (2000), most vulnerable people do not sit idly, lamenting their plight and anticipating charity, but are desperate for support in the form of services and resources in order to move on.

Conclusion

This chapter has illuminated how large numbers of Zimbabweans, particularly the visually-impaired, manoeuvre various diasporic spaces, such as Johannesburg, as beggars owing to the country's putrid socio-economic and political fabric since the turn of the New Millennium. The chapter has demonstrated that begging across national borders by visually-challenged Zimbabweans is a high-risk coping strategy, indeed a form of employment, adapted in order to survive against the odds. Despite the chronic hardships they face in diasporic spaces such as Johannesburg, many visually-impaired beggars become even more resilient and innovative as they seek to make ends meet. On the whole, this chapter illustrates the agency of some downtrodden Zimbabweans to negotiate global spatial enclaves in order to eke livelihoods during periods of sustained socio-economic and political muddle.

References

Acuto, M. 2008. 'Edges of the conflict: A three-fold conceptualisation of national borders,' In: *Borderlands E- Journal*, Volume 7, Number 1, unpaged.

Anadolu Agency (11 April 2015) 'Blind Zimbabwean beggars clog South African subways,' Available at: www.newzimbabwe.com/news, Accessed 10 June 2017.

Baud, M. and Van Schendel, W. (1997) 'Toward a comparative history of borderlands,' in: *Journal of World History*, Volume 8, Number 2, pp.211-242.

Bearak, B. (23 January 2009) 'Desperate children flee Zimbabwe for lives just as desolate,' Available at: www.nytimes.com, Accessed 6 February 2015.

Bedfordview Residents Action Group (19 October 2010) 'Do not support beggars,' Available at: www.bedfordviewrag.co.za/news, Accessed 12 May 2014.

Bentwick, K.K. 1994. 'Begging as a fine art,' in: *The North American Review*, Volume 158, Number 446, pp.125-128.

Berger, S. (9 October 2008) 'Zimbabwe inflation hits 231%,' Available at: www.telegraph.co.uk, Accessed 17 July 2015.

Chiriga, E. (16 April 2011) 'Unemployment still high in Zimbabwe,' in: *The Daily News*, Harare: Zimbabwe.

Chiumbu, S. and Musemwa, M. 2012. 'Introduction: Perspectives of the Zimbabwean crises,' in: S. Chiumbu, and M. Musemwa (eds.) *Crisis! What crisis? The multiple dimensions of the Zimbabwean crisis*, Cape Town: Human Sciences Research Council Press, pp. IX-XXIII.

Daily News (11 February 2005) 'Calls for police restraint over blind beggars,' Harare: Zimbabwe.

Dear, M. and Burridge, A. 2005. 'Cultural integration and hybridisation at the United States-Mexico borderlands,' in: *Cahiers de Geographic de Quebec*, Volume 49, Number 138, pp.301-318.

Dixon, R. (16 August 2011) 'South Africa seizes babies of Zimbabwean beggars,' Available at: www.latimes.com/articles, Accessed 18 September 2015.

Fitzpatrick, S. and Kennedy, C. 2000. *Getting by: Begging, rough sleeping and the big issue in Glasgow and Edinburgh*, Bristol: The Policy Press.

Flynn, D. K. 1997. 'We are the border: Identity, exchange and the state along the Benin-Nigeria border,' in: *American Ethnologist*, Volume 24, Number 2, pp.311-330.

Freire, P. 1972. *Pedagogy of the oppressed*, Harmondsworth: Penguin.

Fuller, A. (May 2012) 'Breaking the silence: Oppression, fear and courage in Zimbabwe,' in: *The National Geographic Magazine*, pp.4-6.

Godwin, P. 2010. *The fear*, New York: Little Brown and Company.

Groce, N. Murray, B. Loeb, M. Tramontano, C. Trani, J. F. and Mekonnen, A. 2013. 'Disabled beggars in Addis Ababa, Ethiopia,' Employment Working Paper Number 141, Geneva: International Labour Office.

Hakutangwi, P. Mashizha, S. and Matanga, R. (10 July 2010) Interview at Brakpan: South Africa.

Horstmann, A. 2004. 'Incorporation and resistance: Borderlands, transnational communities and social change in South-East Asia,' Unpublished Review Paper, Tokyo University of Foreign Studies: Research Institute of Languages and Cultures of Asia and Africa.

Hungwe, C. 2012. 'The migration experience and multiple identities of Zimbabwean migrants in South Africa,' in: *Journal of Social Sciences Research*, Volume 1, Issue 5, pp.132-138.

Immigrant for Social Justice (31 August 2014) 'Zimbabwean, blind, hungry and homeless in South Africa,' Available at: www.socialjusticeimmigrant.blogspot.com, Accessed 10 October 2014.

Irin News (23 May 2008) 'South Africa: Xenophobic attacks spreading,' Available at: www.irinews.org/report, Accessed 6 July 2015.

Irin News (2 June 2011) 'Slumming it in Johannesburg,' Available at: www.irinews.org/report, Accessed 11 September 2015.

Irin News (13 June 2011) South Africa: Blind beggars go south,' Available at: www.irinews.org/report, Accessed 4 June 2015.

Ismail, S. (26 July 2007) 'Blind survival on the streets of Johannesburg,' in: *Mail and Guardian*, Available at: http://www.mg.co.za/articlePage.aspx?articleid=315061, Accessed 9 June 2017.

Keepile, K. (18 March 2010) 'Single mothers struggle for survival on Johannesburg's streets,' Available at: www.mg.co.za/article, Accessed 9 July 2015.

Khumalo, T. (29 July 2014) 'Blind Zimbabwean beggars try their luck in South Africa,' Available at: http://www.rnm.nl/africa/article, Accessed 12 December 2015.

Kwaramba, F. and Mtimba, G. (31 October 2013) 'Hunger grips rural Zimbabwe,' in: *Daily News*, Harare: Zimbabwe.

Mail and Guardian (29 January 2009) 'Zimbabwe's unemployment skyrockets,' Available at: www.mg.co.za/index, Accessed 6 May 2015.

Mapumulo, Z. (25 September 2007) 'Beggars are driven by hunger to flee Zimbabwe,' Available at: www.sowetanlive.co.za, Accessed 5 April 2015.

Marufu, N. (21 March 2007) 'Blind cross border to make a living,' Available at: www.thezimbabwean.co.uk, Accessed 12 May 2015.

Matota, L. (5 September 2014) 'Cops accused of assaulting and robbing blind beggar,' Available at: www.thevoicebw.com, Accessed 9 December 2015.

Meredith, M. 2002. *Mugabe: Power and plunder in Zimbabwe*, New York: Public Affairs.

Mhlanga, F. (24 December 2015) 'Market shrinks for traders in worst year since multi-currency,' in: *The Zimbabwe Independent*, Harare: Zimbabwe.

Mihalache, C. Matei, E. Manea, G. Cocos, O. and Dumitrache, L. 2013. 'Begging phenomenon in Bucharest City: Dimensions and patterns of expression,' in: *Review of Research and Social Intervention*, Volume 43, pp.61-79.

Mtshali, N. (19 January 2009) 'Living as beggars here is better than working life in Zimbabwe,' in: *The Star*, Available at: http://www.security.co.za/news/11283, Accessed 9 July 2017.

Mudzungairi, W. (19 September 2013) 'Agriculture: The tale of Zimbabwe's sleeping giant,' in: *The Newsday*, Harare: Zimbabwe, Available at: www.newsday.co.zw, Accessed 19 August 2015.

Mutandiro, K. (12 May 2017) 'South Africa: Foreign blind beggars offer hope to jobless young men,' Available at: http://www.wtr.org.za/human-rights, Accessed 9 June 2017.

My Zimbabwe News (25 August 2013) 'ZANU-PF has killed the country,' Available at: www.myzimbabwe.co.zw, Accessed 10 June 2015.

News from Africa (November 2003) 'Neighbours react to economic refugee influx,' Available at: www.newsfromafrica.org, Accessed 12 March 2015.

Nyamnjoh, F.B. (2006) *Insiders and outsiders: Citizenship and xenophobia in contemporary Southern Africa*, Dakar: Zed Books.

Oxfam (10 June 2002) 'Fighting off starvation in Zimbabwe,' Available at: www.oxfamamerica.org, Accessed 21 August 2015.

Quidiz, B. (2005) 'Poverty and hunger: A race against the clock,' in: *International French News Magazine*, Volume 57, pp.45-46.

Richardson, C.J. (2005) 'The loss of property rights and the collapse of Zimbabwe,' in: *Cato Journal*, Volume 25, Number 3, pp.541-565.

Roblee-Hertzmark, A. 2012. 'Beggars in three countries: Morocco, India and the United States,' *Unpublished Undergraduate Honours Thesis*, University of Colorado.

Schaefer, B.D. (23 March 2007) 'The crisis in Zimbabwe: How the US should respond,' Available at: www.heritage.org/research, Accessed 10 July 2015.

Scheper-Hughes N. (2008) 'A talent for life: Reflections on human vulnerability and resilience,' in: *Ethnos*, Volume 73, Number 1, pp.25–56.

Sibeko, S. (27 November 2009) 'Zimbabwean refugees face crime, harassment in South Africa,' Available at: www.globalpost.com, Accessed 14 May 2015.

Smith, C. (26 February 2006) 'Blind beggars, the visible face of human trafficking,' in: *The Sunday Independent*, Available at: http://www.zwnews.com/issuefull.cfm?ArticleID=13895, Accessed 9 June 2017.

Sokwanele (20 July 2007) 'Zimbabwean refugees suffer in Botswana and South Africa,' Available at: www.sokwanele.co.zw, Accessed 2 April 2015.

Solidarity Helping Hand (4 March 2013) 'Johannesburg's begging question,' Available at: www.helpendehand.co.za, Accessed 22 May 2015.

Solidarity Peace Trust (November 2004) *No war in Zimbabwe: An account of the exodus of a nation's people*, Johannesburg: Solidarity Peace Trust.

SAMP (5 February 2005) 'South African Police round up Zimbabwe's blind beggars,' Available at: www.queensu.ca/samp, Accessed 5 July 2015.

SAMP (3 October 2005) 'Taxi-load of blind Zimbabwean beggars stopped,' Available at: www.queensu.su/samp, Accessed 5 July 2015.

SAMP (28 October 2005) 'Inter-departmental approach to address challenges at Lindela,' Available at: www.queensu.su/samp, Accessed 5 July 2015.

SAMP (28 October 2005) 'Lindela horror revealed,' Available at: www.queensu.su/samp, Accessed 5 July 2015.

SAMP (26 February 2006) 'Blind beggars and human trafficking,' Available at: www.queensu.su/samp, Accessed 5 July 2015.

Thomson Reuters Foundation (13 July 2014) 'Zimbabwe crisis,' Available at: www.trust.org, Accessed 2 June 2015.

Tolsi, N. (30 September 2011) 'Blind beggars search for a better life in Johannesburg's darkest corners,' Available at: www.mg.co.za/article, Accessed 7 June 2015.

Tshuma, A. (1 April 2008) 'A shameful life of Zimbabweans in Johannesburg,' Available at: http://www.thezimbabwean.co/2008/04, Accessed 9 June 2017.

United States Government (2014) *Central Intelligence Agency (CIA) World Fact Book 2014*, Washington DC: CIA Publications.

Watson, F. (1 March 2003) 'Understanding the food crisis in Zimbabwe,' Available at: www.ennonline.net/fex, Accessed 21 June 2015.

Wilhelm-Solomon, M. 2015. 'Blind pathways and precarious power in inner-city Johannesburg,' Available at: http://www.medizinethnologie.net, Accessed 9 June 2017.

Wines, M. (2 May 2006) 'How bad is inflation in Zimbabwe?' Available at: www.nytimes.com, Accessed 7 July 2015.

World Food Programme (WFP) (13 September 2012) 'Starvation stalls Zimbabwe,' Available at: www.wfp.org, Accessed 11 May 2015.

WFP (14 March 2013) 'Grim food security outlook,' Available at: www.wfp.org, Accessed 30 July 2015.

Zeilig, L. 2002. 'Crisis in Zimbabwe,' in: *International Socialism*, Issue 94, pp.8-17.

Zhou, T. M. 2017 'Poverty, natural resources "curse" and underdevelopment in Africa,' In: M. Mawere (Ed.) *Underdevelopment, development and the future of Africa*, Bamenda: Langaa Research and Publishing Common Initiative Group, pp.279-346.

Zimbabwe Black Book (18 May 2010) 'South Africa rounds up poor, prostitutes ahead of World Cup,' Available at: www.zimbabweblackbook.wordpress.com, Accessed 12 March 2015.

ZIPOVA (1 November 2004) 'Research on xenophobic events faced by Zimbabwean immigrants-deportees and asylum seekers (South Africa and Botswana),' Available at: www.archive.kubatana.net, Accessed 3 May 2015.

Zimbabwe Situation (21 November 2004) 'Hillbrow horror: 31 blind people in one room,' Available at: www.zimbabwesituation.com, Accessed 28 July 2015.

Zimbabwean (14 August 2010) 'Many disabled people in South Africa resort to begging to survive,' Available at: www.media-dis-n-dat.blogspot.com, Accessed 10 August 2015.

Chapter 14

Disasters, the Marginalised and Media Preparedness in Zimbabwe: Reflections on the Masvingo-based Community Media Organisations' Coverage of the 2017 Cyclone Dineo Victims

Golden Maunganidze & Munyaradzi Mawere

Introduction

This chapter examines the state of preparedness by media organisations in Zimbabwe, particularly community newspapers based in Masvingo Province in covering naturally striking disasters in "remote" rural communities. The chapter adopts the case study of the most recent natural disaster, the Cyclone Dineo which wreaked havoc affecting the southern part of Zimbabwe, southeastern part of Mozambique and western part of Botswana during the first three months of 2017. The study is prompted by the realisation that media play a very critical role in helping members of the public with current information that can assist the community to make informed decisions before, during and after disaster strikes. The media's preparedness in reaching out communities, especially the so-called "remote" areas and providing them with information before and during disaster is critical to ensure that everyone is safe. This connotes that the lack of preparedness by media is a cause for concern because responsible authorities and service providers usually take actions based on the information made available to them. In contrast to the ideal, most of the Zimbabwe's media such as community newspapers are (heretofore referred to as newspapers), more often than not, caught between profit-making motive and community service. Eventually, the media end up neglecting the poor people impoverishing them even more as they struggle to make ends meet, let alone to buy newspapers. At the end, newspapers run with elitist stories that do not have anything to do with the downtrodden members of the community whom they ironically claim to be representing as they call themselves "the voice of the voiceless".

The chapter evaluates the effectiveness of the work done by Masvingo based newspapers in risk scanning (that is, in prevention and mitigation), the intensity of their coverage (their response) and their influence on the transition from relief to rehabilitation of flood victims (that is in recovery and development of their affected properties). The underlying argument is that the three Masvingo community newspapers; TellZim News, The Mirror, and Masvingo Star have not been outstanding in their coverage of the Cyclone Dineo which left a trail of destruction in the whole area covering almost half of the province.

Media, news values and the state of reporting in Masvingo

Media is always critical in gathering and disseminating information – stories and events worth reporting. While news are stories and events, not every story (or event) is newsworthy. As such, there are several approaches on how newspapers can select stories that are newsworthy in order to give them priority in their coverage. Schultz (2007) argues that six news values dominate media selection. These are timeliness, relevance, identification, conflict, sensation and exclusivity. In the case of giving coverage to the Cylone Dineo, which wreaked havoc in Masvingo Province, the news value of "timeliness" was most important. Ideally, the newspapers in Mavingo needed to report stories as soon as they took place, but due to their publication intervals, all the newspapers in Masvingo were being overtaken by the events.

There are three community newspapers in Masvingo Province. These newspapers service the seven administrative districts of the province namely, Bikita, Gutu, Chiredzi, Chivi, Mwenezi, Masvingo and Zaka. According to ZIMSTAT's (2014) Multiple Indicator Cluster Survey, Masvingo Province has a population of approximately 1,4 million people, with some places classified as inaccessible due to poor road network.

While blessed with media presence, there is no daily newspaper for the province as the three publications under review are published on weekly basis with TellZim News and The Mirror hitting the streets every Thursday, while Masvingo Star is not even consistent due to a compound of reasons including financial constraints. Sometimes the Masvingo Star readers complain over the newspapers' lack of commitment as the newspaper struggles to hit the streets at least every Friday. Although Masvingo Star Newspaper is wholly owned by the government, it has distinctively become the worst publication outlet among the three newspapers found in the province since it has failed to demonstrate its commitment to deliver fresh news to its readers. News is a perishable commodity by its very nature and it has to be delivered and consumed at the earliest possible time. The other two publications newspapers, TellZim News and The Mirror, are privately owned. Though struggling due to the ailing economic environment that has enveloped the country, the newspapers are however consistent and try their level best to maintain their pledge to the people to deliver the best news they can.

There is one provincial commercial radio station in Masvingo called Hevoi FM which is owned by the Minister of Information, Communication Technology, Postal and Courier Services, Mr Supa Mandiwanzira. Mandiwanzira is the incumbent Zanu-PF MP for Nyanga South Constituency. Hevoi FM is still penetrating the Masvingo market since it started live broadcasting in June 2017. Apart from trying to lure more audience, the radio station is struggling to have a wider reach mainly because of the frequencies allocated to it by the Broadcasting Authority of Zimbabwe (BAZ) which is 100.2 FM. For that reason, the radio station concentrates in the Masvingo Urban. Its frequencies do not go beyond a 100 km radius from town making its audience mainly those in town and people living in peri-urban centres. The poor people in rural areas and marginalised communities are therefore not being catered for by Hevoi FM. Again, the station is still in a process of grooming its own staff who do not have a rich radio experience yet. This certainly has a direct effect on the quality of content and programming besides disadvantaging the people in the rural areas, who in this case are the marginalised.

Worse still, Masvingo does not have a community radio station, though there is Wezhira Community Radio initiative. The initiative has almost everything in place including the studio and personnel but the government is reluctant to give out community radio licenses for the station to start operations. It is allegedly said that the initiative is stack because the proposed radio station is viewed with suspicion by the government mainly because of its donor funding.

Apart from local community based media organisations in Masvingo, there are national media houses' representatives with The Herald, NewsDay, Zimbabwe Broadcasting Corporation (ZBC) and The Chronicle, having one reporter each who is assigned to cover the whole province. NewsDay does not have offices in Masvingo while The Daily News does not have a reporter based in Masvingo. Other media houses such as The Standard, Sunday Mail, Financial Gazette and Zimbabwe Independent do not have reporters based in Masvingo. The Voice of America (also known as Studio 7), which has largely remained the best alternative voice for news in rural areas unfortunately have only one reporter assigned to give coverage to the whole of Masvingo Province. There are a couple of freelance journalists in Masvingo reporting for various media organisations as well as internet based publications.

A critical look at the scenario clearly indicate that media and news reporting in Masvingo desires a lot to be done. Many areas, especially the rural communities, are left uncovered by news reporters. This was the situation that prevailed during the time which a natural disaster – Cyclone Dineo – struck the southern part of Masvingo Province. Before looking at the trail of destruction inflicted by the cyclone, we need to understand more about natural disasters.

Disasters: Their nature and [possible] impacts

Disaster can strike any time. By natural disaster, we mean a type of collective stress situation, in which many individuals fail to have their needs met through societal processes (Barton, 1969). As Quarantelli (1998) tells us, disasters are distinguished from other types of collective stress because, first of all, disasters are crisis situations. From these definitions, it is clear that natural disasters primarily primarily disrupts social life, causes collective stress, loss of life, and physical destruction of properties. More so, it is clear from these definitions that disasters warrant an extraordinary response from outside the immediately impacted community.

Yet, as could be seen, disasters seem to conflate with conflicts. We, however, underline that conflict situations such as riots and wars are generally not defined as disasters in development studies as in social work research. We note that conflict situations, unlike natural and man-made (or technological) disasters, involve very different responses of organisations and social systems (Zakour n.d). This does not, nevertheless, mean that conflicts are unrelated to disasters as both often involve competition and lead to high levels of traumatic and collective stress. This conceptualisation puts disaster discourses in stress theoretical framework. The stress theory classifies disaster impacts according to type, demands on the impacted system, and duration (Dodds & Nuehring, 1996).

Another interesting interpretation of disaster is that given by Streeter (1991) who observes that although the response required by disasters may be extraordinary, disasters themselves may usefully be viewed as an extension of everyday events (Ibid). This interpretation by Streeter has the merit that "it permits a long-term developmental orientation, such that political, social, economic, and environmental forces work together to undermine a system's ability to cope with new stresses" (Zakour nd: 4). The interpretation also notes that disasters are socially defined events which normally lead to radically changed behaviours as people try to meet and address the crisis. This characteristic of dynamism associated with disasters shows that the latter [disasters] should be understood within a social change perspective such that they are best viewed as multidimensional (Quarantelli, 1998).

As alluded to in the preceding discussion, disaster can be technological or natural. This chapter focuses more on natural disaster, particularly that which resulted from a cyclone [Dineo] strike in southern Zimbabwe.

Cyclone Dineo induced floods hit Masvingo Province

A tropical cyclone is a rapidly rotating storm system characterised by a low-pressure centre, a closed low-level atmospheric circulation, strong winds, and thunderstorm that produce heavy rain (Henderson-Sellers *et al* 1988). See the diagram below showing how a cyclone is formed:

Fig 1: Cyclone formation - Adopted from the Bureau of Meteorology and Emergency Management Australia, 2006.

Depending on their location and strength, a tropical cyclone can be known by other such names as tropical storm, cyclonic storm, tropical depression, typhoon, hurricane or simply cyclone (Merrill 1984; Symonds 2003; National Hurricane Centre 2016; Frank 1977). Put differently, a cyclone is a large scale air mass that rotates around strong centres of low pressure. A cyclone is considered tropical simply because it typically forms over large bodies of relatively warm water of the tropics (between the tropics of Cancer and Capricon) – i.e. tropical seas and oceans – where they derive their energy. Cyclones are normally preceded by very strong and damaging winds ((sustained gale force winds of 63 km/h or greater and gusts in excess of 90 km/h), followed by heavy floods which can witness trees being uprooted and buildings razed down (see also Emanuel 2006). They are also capable of generating very high waves, damaging storm surge and tornadoes which weaken towards inland, making coastal regions more vulnerable to damage from tropical cyclones as compared to inland regions, where their energy will have weakened.

Over the years, cyclones have caused untold damages and loss of life from around the world. Katrina Hurricane which occurred in 2005 was the most costly hurricane on record causing an estimated $108 billion in damage in Louisiana and Mississippi and an estimated 1500 deaths. This is, so far, followed by Sandy Hurricane of 2012, which caused $71 billion in damage on the eastern seaboard of the United States of America (cf. Dorst 2016). Some have lasted only a very few days while others have lasted weeks. Hurricane/Typhoon John, for example, lasted 30 days as it travelled both the Northeast and Northwest Pacific basins during the months of August and September 1994 (Ibid). Having formed in the Northeast Pacific, Hurricane John reached hurricane force there before it moved across the dateline, resulting in its renaming to Typhoon John. Finally, the Typhoon recurved back across the dateline and was renamed Hurricane John again. Another cyclone which lasted long was Hurricane Ginger. Hurricane Ginger was a tropical cyclone for 27 days in the North Atlantic Ocean back in 1971 (Ibid).

The beginning of 2017 saw Tropical Cyclone Dineo moving from the south-west over the Mozambique Channel towards southern Zimbabwe and western Botswana. Forecasts issued by the Meteorological Services Department of Zimbabwe (MSDZ) during that time, indicated that Zimbabwe was going to experience a tropical rainfall starting from Thursday 16 up to Monday 20 February 2017. The torrential rains had to pound nonstop with the anticipation that rivers were going to burst their banks. According to the MSDZ, the tropical cyclone was to be a serious threat to life, property and physical features and would be preceded by very strong and damaging winds followed by extreme flooding. It was expected that the humanitarian impact of Tropical Cyclone Dineo would be massive as projections showed that the cyclone was going to bring torrential rains and catastrophic winds. Although Cyclone Dineo had been initially downgraded as tropical depression ex-Dineo as it moved over land, it nonetheless caused heavy rainfall of over 100 mm/24 hours, and strong devastating winds in several parts of Zimbabwe. At least 13 districts in 5 provinces namely Matabeleland

South, Matabeleland North, Midlands, Masvingo, and Manicaland were seriously affected, but the areas that were to be impacted most were Masvingo, Matabeleland South, and Manicaland Provinces (Daily News, 17 Feb 2017). Communities located along the Limpopo Basin and Middle Sabi Valley on the Southern side of the country were at the highest risk as they were predicted to receive the biggest blow. Indeed, the tropical depression resulted in a trail of destruction, ravaging fields, buildings and infrastructure that included roads and dams. Many lives were also claimed. As Traveller24 (20 Feb 2017) reported:

> Last week, the eastern coast of Southern Africa was hit by the deadly Cyclone Dineo, killing seven people, injuring more than 55 and displacing over 100 000 when it battered Mozambique…Among the 55 people injured, four were in critical condition…More than 650 000 people in south-eastern Mozambique were also affected since the storm made landfall…

The cyclone reported by Traveller24 is the one that affected many parts of Zimbabwe. Masvingo Province was severely affected by floods which were induced by the cyclone. Although community newspapers, due to poor coverage of news reports, carried no story of cases of recorded deaths in the province, there were many [informal] reports in some remote parts of Masvingo to the effect that the cyclone claimed a number of lives, not to mention the destruction of property, livestock and displacement of people from their homes. Areas such as Mwenezi District, mountainous Bikita District and part of Chiredzi were severely affected. In Bikita, for example, one of the authors of this chapter witnessed three cases of landslides, one of which razed a homestead down to the ground. Unfortunately, all these news were not covered by the community newspapers in Masvingo.

Cyclone Dineo caught the responsible authorities especially the government unaware. This was evidenced by the slow reaction to attend to the disaster stricken areas. However, the media, as has already shown in this discussion, also failed to live up to the expectations of the general public as they did not manage to give real time reporting of the events which were taking place during the floods.

The role of the media in disaster risk management

We have already noted that timeliness is a critical news value in the media industry. Other determinants of news values such as proximity, impact, relevance and public interest are also important. In news writing and reporting, being first with a story—exclusivity—adds value for producers who must attract audiences. During the Cyclone Dineo strike in Masvingo, however, exclusivity was non-existent on many stories. This was because by the time the newspapers based in Masvingo wanted to write about the cyclone story, the national daily newspapers such as The Herald, Daily News and NewsDay would have already published the stories, leaving the Masvingo based newspapers without any motivation to carry the same stories We note that events that were taking place in Masvingo Province, especially those to do with the displacement of people from their homes, were newsworthy indeed but other factors such as timeliness and exclusivity played a critical role in redirecting weekly community newspapers in Masvingo to other newsworthy stories.

However, as Allern (2002) argues, there could be a supplementary set of commercial news values whereby sensationalist stories are most likely to be pursued while stories that are costly to pursue are less likely to make it into the news. This could have been the case for Masvingo based newspapers. It was obviously difficult and costly to go to the rural areas where there is poor road network which hampered newspapers from covering news on the people being affected by the cyclone. Naturally, resources starved newspapers would first try to pursue easy target stories before they embark on expensive assignments. Thus, news subsidies such as well-prepared press releases and photo opportunities, are more likely to be taken up by resource-starved and hard-pressed journalists, and translated into news items at the expense of more newsworthy stories that are considered difficulty and expensive to gather.

Whatever the case might be, the role of the media especially in disaster risk management remains critical. The severity and ever-increasing number of recurrent disasters– both natural and man-made – around the world, have prompted people to realise the need to remain informed so as to minimise losses to life and damage to property. Thus, in any society today, media should play a critical role. The media have traditionally been ascribed three primary roles which are "to educate, inform and entertain the public" (Mapira 2013: 2). This chapter, however, dwells more on the first two roles, as these are the most pertinent for this discussion.

Regarded as the watchdog of the society, the "media plays a vital role in mainstreaming disaster risk management approaches through public education and responsible reporting" (IGAD Report 2010: 1). In fact, "responsible and well-informed media has proved to be a strategically and important stakeholder in countries with well-developed Disaster Risk Management institutions, significantly contributing to saving lives and livelihoods in the face of an increasing number of disasters, some of which are being aggravated by climate change related hazards" (Ibid). Thus, the media play a critical role not only at oversight level but also at an equally important level as purveyors of timely information of public interest. Their informative role of the media makes them all the more essential in times of natural disasters and other mishaps like floods, droughts, veld fires, disease outbreaks and road traffic accidents. Newspapers, for example, would be expected to give information about the impending danger so that members of the public would make informed decisions.

During times of natural disasters, researchers and journalists would be expected to interview resource persons, experts and analysts in order to get relevant and useful information that allows members of the public to be fully aware of what is likely going to happen to them. As IGAD Report (2010) notes, people "should benefit from the positive experiences of working with the media" (p.2). This means that personnel from the meteorological department and other related fields automatically become key stakeholders during floods. However, in case of Cyclone Dineo, the Masvingo-based community newspapers were found wanting in terms of giving blow by blow account of how things were taking place in the province. There cyclone moves fast – it typically travels about 300 to 400 miles a day, or about 3,000 miles before it dies – (NOAA 2017), and there would be a lot of new developments within a day. With weekly newspapers that publishes every Thursday, the task to continuously update the people about new developments ended up proving to be an impossible task. Although TellZim News and The Mirror newspapers have websites which could be updated any time, the people in rural areas did not have enough access to the internet with the huge population owning a simple mobile phone handset which does not connect to the internet. Thus, the poor and the marginalised remained forgotten in terms of receiving news updates before and even during the floods.

All this, compounded with the generally deteriorating economic situation in Zimbabwe, was enough to send shivers to communities such as those of Masvingo Province where the cyclone was predicted to hit hard. In Masvingo Urban, for example, while the City Mayor, Hubert Fidze was reported to have been satisfied with preparations before the impending cyclone, residents remained very much concerned. The Masvingo United Residents and Ratepayers Alliance (MURRA), for example, issued a statement expressing their worry thus:

> As residents, we are extremely worried since the alert was issued some few days ago, giving us little time to make preparations. The city is not doing anything to prepare for the pending disaster. We have not seen council workers fixing storm drains in and around the city, so we are anticipating a disaster as floods might affect residents in various ways. We also have fears that if floods hit us, disease outbreak could also ensue (Daily News 17 Feb 2017).

The statement issued by MURRA clearly notes that many people in the areas predicted to be affected by Cyclone Dineo were deprived of information. Those who were fortunate to have access to information received it very lately; a clear testimony that there was lack of preparedness by media in the province.

The informative and educative roles of the media during disaster

Messer (2003) categorises disaster management into three phases: pre-emergency phase, emergency phase, and post-emergency phase. The pre-emergency phase consists of prevention, mitigation and preparedness while the emergency phase involves response. The post-emergency phase, on the other hand, encompasses recovery and development in the aftermath of a disaster. Since the work of the media in calamitous situations is a critical component of disaster management, newspapers are important stakeholders in the whole process of disaster risk communication as the messages they carry have an unmatched potential to reach wide and dispersed audiences in both disaster and non-disaster zones.

There were significant natural disasters in Zimbabwe between 2015/2016 and 2017, which all warranted media communication. Chief among these disasters is the El Nino. El Nino affects the global climate and disrupts normal weather patterns which as a result can lead to intense storms in some places and droughts in others (New Zealand's National Institute of Water and Atmospheric Research 2016; Becker 2016). In Zimbabwe, El Nino triggered a dry spell that ravaged the country during the 2015-2016 farming season. This was followed by severe floods which destroyed infrastructure and homes in most parts of the country with the southern region like Masvingo Province being the most hit area. As also explained above, Cyclone Dineo equally affected the southern part of Zimbabwe, leaving many communities more vulnerable and poorer than before the disaster hit. It is in circumstances like these that the media are expected to take a leading role in informing the public about the disasters and educating them on how to stay safe and cope in the aftermath. All the three newspapers in Masvingo, TellZim News, Masvingo Star and The Mirror were found reporting about the disasters with some notable competencies but failing to be proactive in foreseeing potential disaster areas and educating the public on how to protect themselves and make sure that they reduce their vulnerability to future (or post-emergency) disaster-related risks. The informative and educated role of this media outlet was therefore greatly compromised. In most cases, these newspapers were found reporting on things that would have happened a previous week or so forgetting that they were also supposed to be instrumental in highlighting events likely going to happen in the near future. Mapira (2013) reminds that the media should be instrumental in inculcating massive civic education on matters of the environment and the disasters that come with failure to properly manage the environment. The media are key to public awareness, educating the ordinary people, for instance, on how best they can survive in severe droughts and how they can avoid tragedies like the loss of human life in case of severe floods as those witnessed in many parts of Masvino Province such as Chivi, Bikita, Zvishavane and Mberengwa during the 2017 Cyclone Dineo. In fact, before, during and after any disaster strikes, people would need up-to-date, reliable and detailed information. As Singh (2009), reminds us:

> The role of media, both print and electronic, in informing the people and the authorities during emergencies (or disasters), becomes critical, especially the ways in which media can play a vital role in public awareness and preparedness through educating the public about disasters; warning of hazards; gathering and transmitting information about affected areas; alerting government officials, helping relief organisations and the public towards specific needs; and even in facilitating discussions about disaster preparedness and response (p. 1).

The effectiveness of the media in carrying out this task is a major variable in the success of any disaster mitigation measures that can be taken either by government or Non-Governmental Organisations (NGOs).

Newspapers in Masvingo started to give reports on the 2017 floods by mid-February, with ghastly images of flooded homes, washed away vehicles and damaged bridges doing the rounds both on social media and in the mainstream press. All the three newspapers in the province allocated some space and time to highlight the severity of the situation but it can be argued that not enough was done to give preventative education or what Messer (2003) calls pre-emergency services through the exposure of the impending cyclone (and its associated floods) hazards and the likely vulnerability of communities.

Analysis of a number of stories in TellZim News, The Mirror and Masvingo Star shows that coverage of the floods was largely reactive and seldom pre-emptive. The Masvingo Star, March 3 - 9, 2017, for example, dedicated the whole of its page 2 to a story titled "Lundi High girls evacuated, many left homeless in Chivi". Accompanied by four pictures (one of them on the front page 1) the story detailed how school children were affected by a flooded Runde River, how Zinwa employees' houses were almost submerged for days and how the floods had destroyed water pumping equipment in Mwenezi District. As has already been highlighted, the story was indeed responsive to the tragedy on the ground and it highlighted the intensity of the flood disaster but that is all. To be more specific, while these news were good to share with the nation and the world at large, we note that the newspapers gave more of stale news which could neither immediately help the victims with information nor educate them [victims] on what they should do next to reduce their vulnerability. A review of preceding stories yields no evidence of pro-active coverage highlighting potential vulnerabilities to force preventative measures but shows a preoccupation with merely reporting the facts when disaster has already struck.

There are also a number of stories on the floods that were carried by The Mirror within the period beginning February 2017. The newspaper's 24 - 30 March 2017 edition carried a story titled "Havoc as school is left without toilets in Buhera" (page 8). As The Mirror headline of 24-30 March 2017 edition reported, "There was havoc at Ndawana Primary School in Buhera District last Thursday when a 16 squat hole toilet for boys and one squat hole toilet for the ECD pupils collapsed due to Cyclone Dineo induced floods". This story by The Mirror Newspaper epitomises Masvingo newspapers' infatuation with covering mostly the emergency phase of disaster while showing less preparedness to deal with other phases especially follow-ups; the recovery and development phases that deals with advocating for the rehabilitation of the flood victims. Thus, the story among with many others in the same newspapers, was merely a follow-up of "stale" news as journalists were running after unfolding events and in the process forgetting to tell the people at risk about what was going to happen to them. At this phase, what the victims needed most was information on how to prepare themselves and reduce their vulnerabilities as a result of the disaster.

An analysis of the coverage of the floods by TellZim News also reveals a similar trend of lack of preparedness to produce pre-emergency content that is vital to warn communities on impending danger. Other disasters like the flood-triggered landslides in an area under Chief Mukanganwi in Bikita District were not even covered by this and other community newspapers in Masvingo even though the story was covered by national papers. This shows lack of preparedness by the province's community newspapers. There are, however, stories on people falling victim to the floods including the one on the 03 – 09 March 2017, page 6 titled: "Man drowns in Mwenezi River" though the story again, mainly concentrated on an incident which took place during floods instead of making available information that would have saved the man from drowning. The newspaper, thus, reported about the man who drowned in a river and ignored to give precautions on how to avoid such disasters. We argue that the newspaper (as with other community newspapers in the province) employed a wait and see approach where they would only report when something has actually happened instead of providing educative information to the venerable and other members of the public. In another story, TellZim News published a follow-up story titled: "Body of missing Mwenezi man found in dam" (17 – 23 March 2017, page 6), where the story is merely informing people about what had already happened instead of providing educative information on how the mishap could have been avoided. We argue that this kind of approach is not beneficial to the marginalised people battling for their lives during floods. On another note, the newspaper went on to give coverage of donations made by big private companies, including the story titled: "Mimosa reaches out to flood victims" (17 – 23 March 2017, page 8). A closer look at such a story reveals that newspapers in Masvingo were more concerned with giving publicity to the rich and private organisations rather than giving out information that is beneficial to flood victims themselves. Private companies like Mimosa Mining Company are big advertisers and they have the financial muscle to indirectly influence the newspapers to give them positive coverage so as to build their good image in society. We, therefore, argue that while emergency phase stories could be good for publicising the gravity of the problems at hand and for purposes of mobilising public sympathy in the form of relief aid, these stories however, do little for prevention and post-emergency rehabilitation of victims. Lack of follow-up stories on the circumstances of disaster victims does not do any favour to the agenda setting role of the media in terms of influencing policy and development plans for the prevention of similar crisis befalling the same victims in the future. This runs contrary to the ideals of good media practices.

In the social responsibility normative theory of the press, Pfukwa (2001:56) says "the media have clear obligations of public service that transcend moneymaking", a characteristic which makes them important stakeholders in disaster management strategies. The 1998 Hurricane Mitch and the 2001 earthquakes in El Salvador, according to Messer (2003:2), were "widely covered by the media" and this "boosted awareness and catalysed changes in attitudes towards more proactive stances." From his observation of what transpired in El Salvador, Meseer argues that immediate and quick coverage of disaster zones and the investigation and exposure of potential risks that can trigger disasters are crucial factors that can help reduce the vulnerability of communities to suffer from the impact of natural phenomena. However, it is not the same case with Masvingo based newspapers that did not manage to give detailed coverage of Cyclone Dineo at all the phases, most especially at the pre-emergency and post-emergency phases.

Although the government departments such as The Civil Protection Unit (CPU) and the Ministry of Water and Climate through its meteorological services made extensive use of the print media to issue flood alerts beginning January 2017 through conveying messages about floods, the information was mainly captured by national daily newspapers such as NewsDay, The Herald and The Daily News. On 19 February 2017, The Daily News, for example, carried a statement from the CPU which read "This weather system is expected to give rise to incessant rains resulting in increased risk of flooding and damage to homes and infrastructure". The CPU went a step further warning, mainly through messages sent via mobile phones and daily newspapers, the public in specific areas such as Insiza District advising them to observe safety precautions to avoid falling victim to flooded rivers and lightning strikes. This information was very critical for the victims – those in the areas affected by the Cyclone Dineo. However, the information that was being issued out by the CPU was not able to reach the intended audience who happen to be the rural folk as they lack access to mobile phones and national daily newspapers. This resonates with Betera's (2011) observation of the importance of ensuring media coverage in areas of high emergency risk that inadequate real time networks for timely communication with the public affects the preparedness of communities to deal with impending flood disaster.

The transmission of information to reach a mass audience in poor and dispersed locations is an attribute which gives the media a unique place in disaster management strategies. The newspapers that can be distributed in several places within a day have a great potential to spread information to a wider audience within a short space of time. On mass communication, McQuail (2010: 82) says "a central presupposition, relating to questions both of society and of culture, is that the media institution is essentially concerned with the production and distribution of knowledge …". This knowledge, if looked at in the context of natural disaster phenomena, is essential in the mitigation of the effects of disaster. Expert information on the right time and places to build structures, how to keep oneself safe in cases of high flooding risk, and where to get help in case of destructive emergencies, is best relayed through the media. Yet, the media in developing countries is often "crippled" and incapacitated to deliver the ideals.

Challenges affecting community media operations in Zimbabwe

The current economic hardships that have affected almost every business in Zimbabwe have not spared media business. The hardships have left many media organisations especially community newspapers facing either closure or near closure situations. Some community newspapers have resorted to printing as minimum as eight (8) pages in order to reduce the printing costs and maximise on profits. The economic challenges together with political hostility faced by the local media have, therefore, seen the organisations employing cost-cutting strategies which unfortunately end up depriving the rural poor while frustrating the potential stakeholders especially traditional loyal readers. Talking more of the economic challenges, these have cultivated a spirit of egocentrism and the culture of "dog-eat-dog" or what business ethics scholars call the myth of amoral business. This whole culture have found many community newspapers pre-occupying themselves more with surviving tactics than seeking the ideals of media. Before the newspapers provide service to the community through supply of news, they now think of themselves as business entities that need to survive for another day. This media organisations' sustainability strategy has seen most newspapers conveniently avoiding "expensive" assignments in order to concentrate on areas that may give them more business as well as a longer newspaper lifespan. This has unfortunately affected the state of access to information in Zimbabwe with the rural folk being the major victims of the current circumstances. It is because of this "now thriving culture" that the community newspapers in Masvingo – The Mirror, TellZim News and Masvingo Star – were found wanting in as far as fulfilling their role of informing as well as educating the public during the Cyclone Dineo disaster were concerned. The fact that a lot of people who fell victim to Cyclone Dineo failed to get necessary help at most convenient time automatically meant that the media need to do more to help the marginalised communities and fulfil the ideals of their mandates. Yet, some of these failures can be attributed to the current macro-economic dynamics and challenges prevalent in Zimbabwe. We discuss some these challenges in the ensuing paragraphs.

Transport

Many media organisations do not have enough vehicles for both newspaper distribution as well as for news gathering purposes. Under normal circumstances, newspaper organisations would require all terrain vehicles to allow them to visit almost all places in rural areas.

With community newspapers in Zimbabwe, the situation is however far from the ideal. The reality on the ground shows that journalists usually rely on news sources for transport to the affected areas. Almost all community newspapers in Zimbabwe do not have vehicles that are suitable for the "rugged" rural roads in the countryside. During the Cyclone Dineo in Masvingo, this scenario badly affected the newspaper operations as journalists were expected to go out to cover natural disasters news, inform and educate victims. Newspapers in Masvingo failed to do real time reporting because they did not have the capacity "to be there when it happens". This resulted in [local] media organisations giving either stale or distorted information. This was because some news sources would either rely on hearsay or exaggerate information to fit their preferred agendas.

Equipment

Several media organisations in Zimbabwe do not have adequate equipment necessary for news gathering, information capturing and reporting. The Masvingo community newspapers are neither an exception. Most of them lack basic gadgets such as cameras, voice recorders and computers such that even where the journalists visited, they often failed to give a clear picture of how the floods affected local communities. This compromised the media product put on the market for public consumption and in many cases, members of the public felt that they were being short-changed and taken for granted. They protested by not buying newspapers as a sign of their lack of trust for the news product. In other cases, journalists missed critical points which they could have just recorded for future use if they had recorders. Generally speaking, in cases of disasters such as the Cyclone Dineo, readers expect to see pictures which show things as they happen in order to get fine details of the news covered. Whereas to cover events as they unfold would require adequate equipment necessary for the job, community newspapers in Masvingo were found lacking and incapacitated. Two or three cameras in a newsroom they had, are far from being sufficient especially when a natural disaster like foods strike. There was need for reporters to go towards different directions to gather news as well as taking pictures and even short videos in order to give a complete reportage concerning the floods. However, this did not happen due to lack of equipment.

Inexperienced and unskilled journalists

Chuma (2013) observed that an average salary for a journalist in Zimbabwe is between USD300 to USD 400. This far below the poverty datum line in Zimbabwe which currently stands between $430 and $574 for an average household of 5 and $96 for a self-sustaining individual, depending on location (Chikadaya 2016). A poverty datum line (PDL) represents the cost of a given standard of living that must be attained if a person is deemed not to be poor (Ibid).

Now, the poor salaries being offered by newspaper publishers has led to a mass exodus of experienced and skilled journalists who choose to go beyond borders to look for greener pastures. The community newspapers in Masvingo have not been spared either. Many newsrooms especially the community newspapers have been left to be run by interns from colleges and universities, who in fact are novices to the media industry. In some instances, interns are undeservingly given titles such as the News Editors, Bureau Chiefs, and Assistant Editors, among others, only as a way to cover gaps created by the experienced and skilled journalists. In the same manner, people without any media or journalism qualification are often appointed editors in some community newspapers. In some community newspapers in Masvingo, people who do not possess five (5) ordinary level subjects are found working in newsrooms as senior journalists. This trend has seen the 'media managers' failing to understand the need for detailed coverage of humanitarian stories, thereby compromising news values and virtues. Covering natural disasters such as Cyclone Dineo would require a specialised skill which ordinary reporters or those on Work Related Learning (WRL) may never be able to possess in as far as handling traumatised news sources is concerned.

What is needed for efficient and holistic news coverage? Some recommendations

Basing on the slow pace at which the local media in Masvingo Province reacted to Cyclone Dineo and our observations on why the community newspapers in the province failed to effectively perform their duties at a time when the ordinary people in rural areas needed help the most, we advance that a lot more is still desired to be done in the media industry in Zimbabwe. On that note, we recommend that the government of Zimbabwe should empower newspapers financially and morally so that they become relevant stakeholders in the communities they serve. Through the Zimbabwe Media Commission (ZMC), the Zimbabwean government can come up with a media support fund which will help community newspapers to make their operations more practical and achievable. For instance, community newspapers can have access to loans at very minimum interest from the government through the ZMC. By so doing, newspapers will be able to boost their financial and human capital base. On the question of finance, for example, once the newspapers get the finances they require they will be in a position to lure highly skilled and reputable journalists well equipped with news values and virtues for news gathering and reporting. All the operations of these newspapers, thus, will be run sustainably. This is what Dagron (2004) meant when he notes that sustainability extends beyond simple economic considerations to include questions of social and institutional sustainability.

In addition, community media need to consider the challenges of assuring technical and environmental sustainability. Based on our research findings, we urge the government of Zimbabwe to ensure a healthy political and economic macro-environment, at last at national level, so as to curb brain drain, in this case, of experienced and skilled journalists. Due to poor remuneration, poor working conditions, and political instability in Zimbabwe, many educated and skilled professional journalists are forced to leave the country, sometimes against their will, for greener pastures. In fact, the cataclysmic meltdown of Zimbabwe economy since the turn of the new millennium cannot be legitimately divorced from the problems rocking the media industry and other such business ventures (cf. Tarisayi 2009: 12; Mawere 2011: 60). Fosu (1992, Cited in Didia 2015: 188) is correct to argue that "political instability, as with economic crisis, is likely to lead to brain drain that depletes a given country's stock of highly skilled labour, which emigrates in response to heightened political and economic risks engendered by political instability". Thus, to ensure smooth running of community newspapers and accessibility to marginalised areas in Zimbabwe such as those in Masvingo Province, the government should ensure a politically and economically friendly environment.

Lastly, the media training institutions in Zimbabwe that include both universities and colleges are also recommended to play a critical role in training and moulding would-be journalists of repute. This would require high academic and practical training standards at colleges and universities to ensure that media students understand the significance of accessing all parts of the world, including the marginalised areas, as a way of according voices to the "voiceless" marginalised communities when they are affected by natural disasters and other such mishaps.

Conclusion

This chapter has argued that Zimbabwean community media organisations are not prepared for intensive coverage of "hot" news others such as natural disasters and mishaps affecting the ordinary people in marginalised (or remote) communities. Community media organisations in Zimbabwe are consequently failing to adequately perform their duties especially in affording voice to the voiceless as well as in educating the community on the impending danger during times of natural disasters.

The media in Zimbabwe especially the community based newspapers have shown lack of capacity, efficiency and proficiency in giving detailed coverage of natural disasters especially floods. We have demonstrated that members of the public who should otherwise rely on community media in making informed decisions were, during Cyclone Dineo, left out without information on what is likely going to happen to them. On the other hand, solution holders especially the government and local authorities who should rely on the media for information in order to make critical decisions are left guessing thereby failing to effectively provide solutions to the poor and the marginalised in Zimbabwe. This means that there is a gap between information providers – journalists/ media practitioners – and the poor people in rural areas. At the end of the day, the poor become poorer because the media who should be seen affording voice to the voiceless is incapacitated to do the job. We have underscored that poor media organisations do not have the capacity to represent the marginalised communities because they lack key resources like all-terrain vehicles, skilled personnel and equipment of the trade such as cameras which would allow them to get the stories holistically from the horses' mouth and untainted with hearsay. The coming in of social media has not even helped any matters since most of the information shared on social media platforms were either exaggerated or fabricated. Thus members of the public ended up treating social media content with high suspicion levels. At the end of the day, the marginalised communities' voice remained unheard as both community and government newspapers prioritised those areas where high profile members of the community like politicians and heads of government departments were affected by the cyclone.

Community newspapers in Zimbabwe have failed to do justice in as far as news coverage and reporting about natural disasters are concerned. This was due to a number of factors which include lack of resources such as vehicles to use when going for daily duties, professional cameras for taking pictures as well as money for travel and subsistence for journalists at work. It was also revealed that part of the reasons was lack of proper training for journalists to enable them to cover sensitive issues and natural disasters of high magnitude. Apart from resource constrains, we have noted that all community newspapers in Masvingo Province are weekly publications. This has been argued as one of the key weaknesses of these newspapers, hampering them from effective coverage of natural disasters. Naturally, floods move fast and there are new developments on almost every minute, hence the need for daily updates. Most of the things that happen during the course of the week can be overtaken by time and become perishable and irrelevant for the community. The newspapers end up being irrelevant to the community that they should afford voice hence the need to resort to a strategy where they just report on things that would have already happened. We have argued, however, that this kind of approach does not help ordinary people living in rural areas who are lacking information that concern their life. Neither does it help the media industry grow. We, thus, safely conclude that the media in Zimbabwe's thin financial base has influenced newspapers to dump real stories that could otherwise improve the living standards of the poor as they pursue profit-making agenda in a bid to survive the current economic crisis facing the country. Thus, the current political economic crisis gripping the country has played a significant role in impoverishing the wretched ones as it restricts the media from pursuing a pro-development path.

References

Allern, S. 2002. Journalistic and commercial news values: News organizations as patrons of an institution and market actors, *Nordicom Review*, 23 (1-2): 137-152.

Barton, A. H. 1969. *Communities in Disaster: A Sociological Analysis of Collective Stress Situations*, Garden City, NY: Doubleday.

Betera, L. 2011. *Overview of Disaster Risk Management and Vulnerability*, Department of Civil Protection, Harare, Zimbabwe.

Becker, E. 2016. How much do El Nino and La Nina affect our weather? *Scientific American*, California.

Bureau of Meteorology and Emergency Management of Australia, 2006. "About tropical cyclones," *Regional office of the Bureau of Meteorology*, Perth: Australia.

Chikadaya, B. (27 Sept 2016). "Zimbabwe's latest poverty datum line raises argument of who can actually afford our expensive internet," TECHZIM.

Chuma, W. 2013. *The State of Media Ethics in Zimbabwe*, VMCZ, Harare: Zimbabwe.

Dagron, A. G. 2004. "Sustainability of CMCs," In: Hughes, S., S. Eashwar and Jennings, V.E. 2004. A *guide to community multi-media centres: How to get started and keep going*, UNESCO: Paris.

Daily News. (17 Feb 2017). "Cycolne Dineo: Everything you need to know," *Daily News*, Harare.

Didia, O. D. 2015. *Ten reasons why sub-Saharan Africa has failed to develop economically: Can Africans succeed by themselves?* Edwin Mellen Press, UK.

Dodds, S., and Nuehring, E. 1996. A Primer for Social Work Research on Disaster, *Journal of Social Service Research* 22: 27-56.

Dorst, N. 2016. "Which tropical cyclone lasted the longest?" Atlantic Oceanographic and Metreological Laboratory, Hurricane Research Division.

Emanuel, K. (8 Feb 2006). *Anthropogenic effects on tropical cyclone activity*, Massachusetts Institute of Technology: USA.

Fosu, A. K. 1992. Political instability and economic growth: Evidence from sub-Saharan Africa, *Economic Development and Cultural Change* 40 (4): 830-841.

Frank, W. M. 1977. The structure and energetics of the tropical cyclone, *Monthly Weather Review* 105 (9): 1119-1135.

IGAD Report. 2010. "The Role of Media in Disaster Risk Management", Regional Workshop, 4-6 December 2010, Djibouti.

Henderson-Sellers, A. *et al.* 1988. Tropical cyclones and global climate change: A post-IPCC Assessment, Bulletin of the American Meteorological Society, 79: 19-38.

Mapira, J. 2013. Challenges of Zimbabwe's Media in the Provision of Environmental Education, *Journal of Sustainable Development in Africa (Volume 15, No.6, 2013)*.

Mawere, M. 2011. *Moral degeneration in contemporary Zimbabwean business practices*, Langaa Publishers: Bamenda.

Merrill, R. T. 1984. A comparison of the large and small tropical cyclones, *Monthly Weather Review, American Meteorological Society* 112 (7): 1408-1418.

McQuail, D. 2010. *McQuail's Mass Communication Theory*, SAGE. United Kingdom.

Messer, N. M. 2003. *The Role of Local Institutions and their Interaction in Disaster Risk Mitigation*: A Literature Review, SAGE: United Kingdom.

National Hurricane Centre. 2016. *Glossary of NHC/TPC Terms*, National Oceanic and Atmospheric Administration, USA.

New Zealand's National Institute of Water and Atmospheric Research. (11 April 2016). "El Nino and La Nina," New Zealand.

NOAA. 2017. "Tropical cyclone records", Atlantic Oceanographic and Metreological Laboratory, Hurricane Research Division.

Pfukwa, C. 2001. *Multimedia Communication*, Zimbabwe Open University (ZOU), Harare, Zimbabwe.

Quarantelli, E. L. (Ed). 1998. *What is a Disaster? Perspectives on the Question*, New York: Routledge.

Schultz, I. 2007. The journalistic gut feeling: Journalistic doxa, news habitus and orthodox news values, *Journalism Practice*, 1 (2): 190-207.

Streeter, C. L. 1991. Disasters and Development: Disaster Preparedness and Mitigation as an Essential Component of Development Planning, *Social Development Issues* 13(3): 100-110.

Singh, K. M. 2009. Second India Disaster Management Congress (SIDMC): Thematic Session on Role of Media in Disaster Management: Concept Note, 4-6 November 2009, Vigyan Bhavan, New Delhi: India.

Symonds, S. (17 Nov 2003). "Highs and lows", *Wild Weather*, Australian Broadcasting Corporation.

Tarisayi, E. 2009. "Voting in despair: The economic and social context", In: Masunungure, E. V. (Ed). *Defying the winds of change: Zimbabwe's 2008 elections*, Weaver Press: Harare.

Traveller24. (20 Feb 2017). "Dineo devastation in Mozambique and its real effects in Southern Africa," Cape Town: South Africa.

Zakour, M. J. (n.d). Social work and disasters, *PhD Dissertation*, Tulane University.

Zimbabwe National Statistics Agency (ZIMSTAT). 2015. *Multiple Indicator Cluster Survey 2014*, Final Report, Harare, Zimbabwe.